APPLIED QUALITATIVE RESEARCH DESIGN

Applied Qualitative Research Design

A TOTAL QUALITY FRAMEWORK APPROACH

Margaret R. Roller
Paul J. Lavrakas

THE GUILFORD PRESS
New York   London

© 2015 The Guilford Press
A Division of Guilford Publications, Inc.
370 Seventh Avenue, Suite 1200, New York, NY 10001
www.guilford.com

Printed in the United States of America

This book is printed on acid-free paper.

Last digit is print number: 9   8   7   6   5   4   3   2   1

Library of Congress Cataloging-in-Publication Data is available from
the publisher.

ISBN 978-1-4625-1575-2 (paperback)
ISBN 978-1-4625-1908-8 (hardcover)

Preface

Qualitative research embraces the complexities of human thought and behavior. The qualitative researcher acknowledges, accepts, and welcomes the challenges created by the fact that what people say, what they do, and how they think are not the products of any one thing, but rather the results of a mosaic of influences that contributes to individuals' life events. It is this complexity in qualitative research that invites a range of perspectives in the research community—with some researchers who may be unsure how to conceptualize and operationalize the complexity of human realities and are thereby tempted to skirt the issue by applying only a highly structured (near-quantitative) approach to qualitative research; and many other researchers who are comfortable in thinking deeply about the complexity of qualitative research and may be embroiled in ongoing and strongly worded rhetoric concerning the appropriateness of various theoretical underpinnings, philosophical paradigms, and related research design issues.

Yet we believe that all qualitative researchers share two important areas of interest: (1) a mutual respect for the intricacies associated with the life of human beings and (2) a desire to incorporate quality features into their research designs to maximize the ultimate usefulness of their research outcomes. These two shared interests present qualitative researchers with a unique challenge. On the one hand, qualitative researchers want to maintain some level of flexibility and innovation in their research designs so they can better discover the subtle connections (influences) that bring meaning to some aspect of a person's life; on the other hand, qualitative researchers strive to develop well-thought-out research designs that produce credible data along with the ability to conduct complete and accurate analyses. It is this challenge—maintaining innovation while fostering quality outcomes—that served as the impetus for this book.

If qualitative research is to provide something of value to the consumers of the research, then it must be done well. The need for flexibility and innovation in qualitative research designs does not justify an "anything goes" or sloppy approach. Like all forms of social research, qualitative methods benefit from an adherence to certain quality standards that are aimed at maximizing the researcher's and the consumer's confidence in research results. The idea of applying quality criteria to qualitative research is not a new concept, and indeed others before us have advocated variations of a "quality" approach at some stage in the research design. However, in our view, what has been missing is a comprehensive "quality strategy" in qualitative research that is (a) paradigm neutral, (b) flexible (i.e., does not adhere to a defined research method), and (c) applicable to all phases of the research process.

Our book, which is a product of an intensive and rewarding 3-year collaboration, presents an applied approach to qualitative research design that is grounded in a quality framework that can help researchers judge the efficacy of their qualitative research designs and incorporate design features that maximize the credibility of the data they gather, the accuracy of the analyses they conduct, and the usefulness of the outcomes from various qualitative research methods. Our Total Quality Framework (TQF) provides a comprehensive perspective for creating, managing, and interpreting quality research studies and evaluating the likelihood that they will provide information that is valid and useful for the purposes for which a study is intended.

There are four interrelated TQF components: *Credibility* (completeness and accuracy associated with data gathering), *Analyzability* (completeness and accuracy related to the processing and verification of data), *Transparency* (completeness of the final documents and the degree to which the consumer of the research is able to fully evaluate the study and its transferability to other contexts), and *Usefulness* (ability to do something of value with the research outcomes). The TQF may not be suitable for planning and evaluating every qualitative research study (e.g., critical theory research, which is not necessarily bound by conventional research protocol but rather is highly collaborative and used at times to incite activism among marginalized groups); however, we believe that it provides a very useful tool for most students as well as research scholars and practitioners to apply in designing, conducting, and interpreting their research so that their qualitative studies are more likely to (a) gather high-quality data, (b) lead to more robust and valid interpretations of the data, and (c) ultimately generate more highly useful outcomes. As we try to convey throughout the book, it is not our view that applying the TQF will yield a dichotomous (i.e., a thumbs-up vs. thumbs-down) judgment that a qualitative study is accurate or not accurate, useful or not useful. Rather, we believe that the TQF can help consumers of a given research study gain a greater sense of confidence that may range from "not at all confident" to "extremely confident" about the study's validity and usefulness.

Unlike other texts that relegate discussions of validity and quality issues to one or two chapters, quality concerns such as construct validity, interresearcher reliability, researcher bias, nonresponse, and verification strategies are discussed in great detail throughout this entire book. Furthermore, as an applied approach, our book is full of real-life examples—taken from education, psychology, health care, sociology, communications, marketing, and other disciplines, as well as from our own respective experiences conducting myriad qualitative research studies throughout our careers (which collectively exceed 80 years)—that illustrate effective uses of particular methods and demonstrate TQF best practices (e.g., related to mitigating interviewer bias, gaining cooperation from participants, developing an interview/discussion/observation guide, the suitability of specific moderator techniques, and use of observation grids in ethnography or visual displays in content analysis).

The core of this book revolves around five basic qualitative research methods: in-depth interviews (IDIs), focus group discussions, ethnography, qualitative content analysis, and multi-method research (specifically, case study and narrative research). Each chapter begins with a discussion of the method's fundamentals (what the method is and how it is used), followed by a critical look at the strengths and limitations of the method (as well as the most popular modes within that method) *from a TQF perspective*. It is this in-depth understanding of the method that, we believe, helps prepare the reader to consider the application of the TQF to that method by way of the lengthy elaboration we provide for the remainder of each chapter.

Each chapter presents unique concepts not found in many other texts. For example, in Chapter 3 (on IDIs), among many other topics, we provide a lengthy discussion of the strengths and limitations of the email IDI mode; discuss the appropriate number of IDIs to conduct (in any mode), stating that the point of "saturation" is not a good-enough measure by which to determine the appropriate number of IDIs and, instead, we pose 10 questions that the researcher should ask and satisfactorily answer at the fieldwork stage; and highlight the unstructured IDI from a feminist research orientation. In Chapter 4 (on focus groups), we describe and weigh the pros and cons of asynchronous online (or "bulletin board") group discussions, the role of enabling and projective techniques (especially in the face-to-face mode), and the effect of group dynamics and interaction on the quality of the data gathered. In Chapter 5, we present our definition of ethnography, describe the strengths and limitations of online and "mobile ethnography," and provide a schematic depicting our five distinct categories of observer roles. In Chapter 6 (on content analysis), we make the distinction between "primary" and "secondary" qualitative content analysis, outline the two broad phases (data generation and data analysis) and the eight steps in the qualitative content analysis process, illustrate an example of a codebook and coding form, and discuss the particular advantages and disadvantages associated with the utilization of computer-assisted qualitative data analysis software. Chapter 7 discusses multi-method research with specific attention to two case-centered approaches: case study and narrative research. This chapter includes an overview of the major typologies in case study and narrative research, presents a new internal–external classification scheme for case studies along with an explanation of what we mean by the "unit of analysis" and the "variables of analysis," and presents a six-step process to conducting case study and narrative research.

This book is intended for graduate-level students who have some basic familiarity with qualitative research, as well as for scholars and practitioners in the academic, government, not-for-profit, and commercial sectors. And, as addressed in Chapter 8, this book not only serves as a guide to developing, conducting, analyzing, and reporting quality research, but can also assist in the writing, review, and evaluation of research proposals as well as other research reports, such as conference papers and manuscripts for journals and books.

Our book is well suited to a straight-through reading—for example, spending approximately 2 weeks of a 13-week college semester on Chapters 1 and 2, 2 weeks on each of the method chapters, and the final week on Chapter 8 (proposal writing and other applications of the TQF)—or to being read selectively. If this book is read selectively, we strongly encourage the reader to first study Chapter 2 before reading any of the other individual chapters (i.e., Chapters 3–8).

To assist the reader as well as the college instructor, many pedagogical aids have been incorporated in this book. For example, each method chapter begins with a chapter preview, includes figures and tables throughout that highlight important content (e.g., the application of a method to vulnerable or hard-to-reach population segments), and ends with (a) a chapter summary, (b) exercise and discussion topics, (c) suggested further reading and Web resources, and (d) a case study that demonstrates the utilization of many of the TQF standards discussed within the chapter. The book also includes an extensive glossary of terms.

Acknowledgments

This book has been a long time in the making. The seed of the idea—that is, the idea of applying quality standards to qualitative research—began nearly 40 years ago when the first author, fresh out of graduate school, went looking for qualitative training in the real world that would supplement the thorough but one-sided quantitative orientation she had received while working on her graduate psychology degree. It is in this quest that she came to learn and appreciate qualitative research for what it is and what it could be. And, although the second author did not realize it explicitly at the time, he left graduate school 38 years ago with a "discomfort" about what he perceived to be the lack of a comprehensive framework for thinking carefully about the likely reliability and validity of any type of research, be it qualitative or quantitative.

This book could never have been written if it had not been for the countless opportunities we were given to nurture and grow the "seed." In particular, the first author would like to thank Clyde Rich for his invaluable guidance in the early years that taught her how to adapt her academic knowledge to conducting research in the real world. She would also like to thank Evert Gummesson (Stockholm University), Colleen Porter (University of Florida), Pete DePaulo (qualitative research consultant), and Naomi Henderson (RIVA Training Institute) for taking the time to review and comment on a white paper written several years ago that served as a precursor to the current book. And the second author would like to thank Emil Posavac, Marilyn Brewer, Frank Slaymaker, John Edwards, and Bob Boruch for the inspired instruction they provided during his graduate school years, which set him on what has been a career-long path of trying to improve the methods by which social research is carried out.

We want to thank the reviewers who took the time to read and provide thoughtful comments on an early manuscript of this book: Mary I. Dereshiwsky, Ed Leadership, Northern Arizona University; Gerald Kosicki, Communications, Ohio State University; and, Kimberley Ducey, Sociology, University of Winnipeg. Their suggestions allowed us to make important changes to the final manuscript.

Also, we are very grateful for the encouragement and advice we received from our editor, C. Deborah Laughton, who, throughout the process, gave us tireless support and guidance. We also want to thank Editorial Assistant Mary Beth Anderson, as well as Anna Nelson, Senior Production Editor, and Margaret Ryan, copy editor, and others at The Guilford Press who responded quickly and knowledgeably to our questions. Their dedication and patience have contributed immeasurably to the pleasure of creating this book.

And, finally, we want to thank our respective spouses—Jim and Barbara—for their unfailing love and support as we pursued this long, gratifying adventure.

Brief Contents

Extended Contents

Six	Qualitative Content Analysis	230

CHAPTER ONE

Making Sense of the Human Experience with Qualitative Research

1.1   INTRODUCTION

Human beings engage in some form of "qualitative research" all of the time. This is because there is not a context in which humans engage that does not require some process of taking in (i e, gathering) information from the environment and developing that information into an interpretive nugget that can then be used to make sense of and react to particular situations. Humans do this so routinely that they are rarely aware of the information-gathering stages they process, or even their constant and natural proclivities to do so. Although some human beings may be more successful at processing contextual information than others, humans generally do not consciously think about the quality of the information they take in and the quality of the decision-making processes they apply to that information as they go through their daily lives.

As a formal method of inquiry, qualitative research—with its emphasis on the individual and the role that context and relationships play in forming thoughts and behaviors—is at the core of what it means to conduct research with human subjects (or with artifacts from humans, e.g., in content analysis). Qualitative research assumes that the answer to any single research question or objective lies within a host of related questions or issues pertaining to deeply seeded aspects of humanity. A qualitative inquiry into breast cancer treatment, for example, might begin by asking "How do women cope with breast cancer treatment?", from which the researcher considers any number of relevant personal issues around "coping" and then addresses further and deeper questions, such as "What is the quality of life among women undergoing breast cancer treatment?", "How do various aspects of this quality of life compare to life before their cancer treatment, before

1

breast surgery, and before breast cancer diagnosis?", "What words do women use to describe their life experiences and what is the relevance (personal meaning) of these word choices?", "Which people in these women's lives have the most impact on their ability to cope?", and "How strong is their motivation to continue treatment and what is the biggest contributor to this motivation?"

Qualitative research is about making connections. It is about understanding that good research involving human beings cannot be anything but complex, and that delving beyond the obvious or the expedient is a necessary tactic in order to understand how one facet of something adds meaning to some other facet, both of which lead the researcher to insights on this complexity. A purpose of qualitative research, then, is to "celebrate the moment"—the in-depth interview, the group discussion, the observation, the particular document content, the case in a single point in time, or the life story—and the intricacies revealed from that moment. Qualitative research celebrates the fact that the complexities and intricacies—the connections—revealed at any one moment may or may not exist in another moment in time, reflecting the ever-changing reality of being human. Qualitative research embraces this reality and, in so doing, savors the nuances inherent in what people say, what they do, and how they think. Identifying, connecting, and finding meaning in these often vague, fleeting qualities of human reality comprise what it means to conduct a qualitative research study.

The Complexities of Human Realities and the Paradigm Debates

As the channel by which researchers explore the depths of human realities, qualitative research has gained prominent status that is accelerating over time as quantitatively trained mentors in academia are increasingly asked by their graduate students to assist in forming qualitative research designs in their dissertations, and as the volume of published works in qualitative research continues to grow by leaps and bounds (cf. Charmaz, 2008; Lincoln, Lynham, & Guba, 2011; Silverman, 2013). Even psychology, a discipline that has traditionally dismissed qualitative research as "subjective" and "unscientific," has come of age with slow but continued growth in the field of qualitative psychology (cf. Brinkmann & Kvale, 2008; Marecek, 2003; Wertz, 2014); evidence of which can be found in the 2014 launch of the *Qualitative Psychology* journal by the American Psychological Association. These advances in qualitative research have given rise to a vibrant array of scholars and practitioners who harbor varying, and sometimes contentious, perspectives on how to approach qualitative research. These differing perspectives are best exemplified by the paradigm debates that have raged, and continue to rage, among qualitative researchers. The focus of these debates is on the underlying belief or orientation—that is, the paradigm[1]—the researcher brings to any given qualitative study. In particular, these discussions center on the philosophical constructs related to the nature of reality (ontology) and that of knowledge (epistemology). It is the researchers' sometimes divergent views on the presence and scope of a "true" reality—for example, whether it is the **postpositivism** view that there is a single objective reality that can be found in a controlled scientific method, or the **constructivism–interpretivism** paradigm that emphasizes the idea of multiple realities that exist in the context of social interactions and subjective meanings—as well as the source of this knowledge—for example, the highly dominant role of the researcher in **critical theory** that interpolates the researcher's own values into the research process—that have fueled an ongoing dialogue concerning paradigms within the qualitative research field. (See Lincoln et al., 2011, for a thorough and up-to-date discussion of the paradigm controversies.)

And yet, regardless of the philosophical or theoretical paradigms that may guide researchers in their qualitative inquiries, all qualitative researchers face the same challenge of making sense of the convoluted and intricate world of human beings. In this way, qualitative researchers are united in the fundamental and common goal of unraveling the human experience. Qualitative researchers have debated and will continue to agonize over the various paradigms and scientific philosophies of ontology and epistemology that they espouse and bring to their research efforts; but these perspectives all share a mutual respect for the nuances of what it means to conduct qualitative research. On this, we believe, the qualitative research community can agree.

The Focus on Quality in Qualitative Research Design

The nuances and complexities of the human experience present unique challenges to qualitative researchers who strive to develop research designs that result in rich, contextual data while incorporating quality measures that maximize the ultimate usefulness of their research. Because of these challenges, research design considerations associated with trustworthiness, reliability, and validity are frequently examined and discussed among qualitative researchers. In addition to Lincoln and Guba (1985), whose seminal work on criteria for evaluating qualitative research is discussed in Chapter 2, many qualitative researchers routinely focus their attention on the importance of methodically rigorous data collection practices and in-the-field as well as post hoc verification checks (Creswell, 2013; Marshall & Rossman, 2011; Morse, Barrett, Mayan, Olson, & Spiers, 2002); systematic procedures and analytic rigor (Atkinson & Delamont, 2006; Berg & Lune, 2012); and issues related to reliability and validity (Brinkmann & Kvale, 2015; Merriam, 2009; Polkinghorne, 2007; Riessman, 2008; Seale & Silverman, 1997), including procedures that are "essential to the process of ruling out validity threats and increasing the credibility of [research] conclusions" (Maxwell, 2013, p. 125; see also, Yin, 2011).

These quality issues and the challenges that all qualitative researchers face in designing their qualitative studies are the reasons we have chosen to write this book—a book about bringing greater rigor to qualitative research without stifling or squelching the creative approaches and interpretations that skilled qualitative researchers properly embrace, practice, and celebrate.

1.2 UNIQUE ATTRIBUTES ASSOCIATED WITH QUALITATIVE RESEARCH

Researchers conduct qualitative research because they acknowledge the human condition and want to learn more, and think differently, about a research issue than what can be gleaned from most numerical quantitative studies. The unique nature and purpose of qualitative inquiry bring with it a distinctive set of attributes, all of which impact the design of qualitative research one way or the other. In our view, there are 10 unique attributes of qualitative research, as described in the following:

1. **Absence of absolute "truth."** With all the emphasis on reality and the human condition, it might be expected that qualitative research is in the business of garnering "the truth" from the participants who provide data. Yet there are many factors that conspire to maintain this purported solitary truth as an illusion. Although it might be said that an absolute truth is elusive in all forms of research, the interactive, personal, and interpretive approach in qualitative inquiry extinguishes the notion that the outcomes represent an absolute truth. Instead of truth, per se, the qualitative researcher strives to collect information from which some level of useful knowledge can be gained. The researcher does not acquire this information and knowledge in a vacuum but rather in a context and, often, in a situation where the researcher is highly involved (interactive) with the research participant(s). In this way, qualitative data are a product of various situational factors that provide information and ultimately knowledge—but not unconditional truth.

Of course, all knowledge is conditional as well. The knowledge gained rests heavily on the researcher's interpretation of the data and the meaning given to the outcomes in answer to the research question. We provide many examples in this book of how to mitigate incomplete and misguided interpretations of the data; however, in the end, total elimination of these biases is highly unlikely, if not impossible, because some portion of data interpretation—the gaining of knowledge from the data—remains a function of the researcher's own subjectivity. This is why qualitative researchers do not talk about the "truth" of their findings but rather about "the relative plausibility of an interpretation when compared with other specific and potentially plausible alternative interpretations" (Mishler, 1986, p. 112). And it is for these reasons that the verification process in analysis and transparency of the final research document is a critical element in rigorous qualitative research design.

2. **Importance of context.** A relevant factor in supporting the elusiveness of truth is the central and significant role context plays in qualitative research. Whether it be the physical environment or the mode by which an in-depth interview (IDI), group discussion, or observation is conducted; the juxtaposition of words and substance in a content analysis; the broader environment of a case

study; or manner in which a narrator tells a story, the outcomes in qualitative research—that is, the data and the researcher's interpretation of the data—hinge greatly on the contexts from which the data are obtained. Context is discussed in this book with respect to each of the qualitative methods and from various perspectives; for example, not just the location of a face-to-face group discussion but also the context that is created by way of the heterogeneity or homogeneity of a group's participants.

3. **Importance of meaning.** Although a goal of all research is to draw meaning from the data that ultimately proves useful to the end users, qualitative research is unique in the dimensionality of this effort. Qualitative researchers derive meaning from the data by way of multiple sources. Within any one research event (e.g., an IDI, group discussion, or observation), researchers evaluate any number of variables to make sense of the data. These variables include the context (as mentioned above); the language and, especially in narrative research, social linguistics[2]; the impact of the participant–researcher relationship (discussed below); the potential for participant bias (e.g., the withholding or falsification of information); and the potential for researcher bias (e.g., the failure to record relevant data because they express views contrary to the interviewer's personal values).

Looking across research events (i.e., looking at all IDIs, focus groups, observations, documents, or cases conducted for a particular study), the researcher considers the breadth or scope of the research (e.g., the sample and the potential for biased outcomes because some individuals in the sample may have declined to participate in the study); the depth of the research (e.g., sufficient investigation of the issues across all research events); and the verification of the data (e.g., the examination of outliers or deviant cases in the data).

4. **Researcher as the data-gathering instrument.** Along with the emphases on context, meaning, and the potential for researcher subjectivity, qualitative research is distinguished by the fact that it places the researcher at the center of the data-gathering phase, and indeed the researcher ultimately is the "instrument" by which information is collected. The researcher may be guided by written outlines of what to consider in an IDI, focus group, observation, or content analysis, but these are only accessories to be used by the principal data collection tool: the researcher or others on the research team. This researcher-as-instrument reality poses both strengths and limitations to the qualitative approach. On the one hand, the closeness of the data gatherer to the research participants and subject matter provides the opportunity for developing an in-depth understanding that can prove beneficial to a thorough analysis and interpretation of the outcomes; on the other hand, this intimacy heightens concerns regarding the data gatherer's ability to collect (and interpret) data in an unbiased manner. These issues are discussed extensively throughout this book, and design considerations to address these concerns—such as the use of reflexive journals to account for possible fieldworker biases—are proposed.

5. **Participant–researcher relationship.** Closely associated with the idea that the researcher is the tool by which data are gathered is the important function of the participant–researcher relationship in qualitative research and its possible impact on research outcomes. This relationship is at the core of IDIs, group discussions, participant observation, and narrative research, wherein participants and researchers share the "research space" in which certain conventions for communicating (knowingly or not) may be formed that in turn shape the reality the researcher is capturing in the data. For instance, depending on an interviewer's ability to build rapport with an interviewee, the IDI participant may be inclined to respond to interview questions in a socially desirable or normative manner; for example, a mother may exaggerate the extent to which she buys healthy foods for her children. This social component that is embedded in the participant–researcher relationship drives the "power dynamics" (Kvale, 2006) of the research environment in which both parties—participant and researcher—strive to control what is said and not said (e.g., the interviewer generally controls the questions that are asked, but the interviewee may elect to withhold information). This book discusses this power struggle, its implications for the integrity of research data, and the strategies that can be utilized in the research design to mitigate its effects.

6. **Skill set required of the researcher.** Qualitative research requires a unique set of skills from the researcher, skills that go beyond the usual qualities of organization, attention to detail, and analytical abilities that are necessary for all researchers. These skills are discussed throughout this book in conjunction with each of the qualitative methods and approaches. For example, techniques to build rapport with participants and active listening skills are particularly important for IDI interviewers and group discussion moderators, and focus group moderators also need to be adept at managing group dynamics. One of the many critical skills necessary for an ethnographer is his/her sensibility in relation to the observation environment, the observed, and the observer's potential influence on the outcomes. A researcher conducting a content analysis needs to be both systematic as well as perceptive, and the skills required of the case-centered (i.e., case study and narrative) researcher are not unlike that of a detective—for example, noticing the details and sequence of events, open-mindedness, and patience—who is searching for clues to help create a "picture" of the case or complete the narrative.

In addition to method-specific skills, qualitative researchers need a special class of analytical skills that can meet the demand of the "messy analysis" (see Point 9) of qualitative inquiry, where context, social interaction, and numerous other interconnected variables contribute to the realities that researchers "take away" from the field.

7. **Flexibility of the research design.** A defining characteristic of qualitative research is the flexibility built into the research design to modify or adapt it, as needed, during fieldwork to more accurately measure the research issue or phenomenon under study. This flexibility extends from making in-the-field determinations of the questions to ask or direction to take when investigating a case, to abandoning the prescribed research design altogether, based on unanticipated

revelations during the data collection phase. For instance, a focus group moderator works from a discussion guide (outline) containing issues and potential questions aimed at addressing the research objectives, but it may not be until the moderator is actually in the discussion with a particular group of people that he/she understands which areas to pursue more than others and the specific follow-up (probing) questions that will be necessary. Likewise, an observer has little control over the activities of the observed—and, indeed, the goal of the observer (even for participant–observers) is to be as unobtrusive and flexible as possible in order to capture the reality of the observed events without impacting them.

There may also be occasions when the researcher elects to alter or abandon the research design altogether. This might happen, for example, when a case researcher determines early in the fieldwork process that the underlying research questions that the case study was designed to address are actually misguided based on the evidence, at which point the researcher may decide to substitute one or more cases from those selected earlier or redesign the study based on a new set of objectives.

8. **Types of issues or questions effectively addressed by qualitative research.** Qualitative research is uniquely suited to address research issues or questions that might be difficult, if not impossible, to investigate under more structured, less flexible quantitative research designs. As discussed throughout this book, qualitative inquiry effectively tackles sensitive or personal issues such as domestic violence, pregnancy among teenagers, drug addiction, and sexual dysfunction; multifaceted, intricate topics such as personal life histories and corporate reorganization; nebulous questions such as "Is the current school leadership as effective as it could be?", and contextual issues such as in-the-moment decision making, for example, in-store observations of shopping patterns.

Similarly, qualitative research is useful at gaining in-depth, meaningful information from hard-to-reach, underserved, or hidden populations, such as children, same-sex partners; subcultures such as motorcycle bikers; mentally ill persons; deviant groups such as heavy drug users and convicted murderers; victims of domestic violence; individuals afflicted with an uncommon physical condition such as acromegaly (a condition of excess growth hormone); and minority segments of corporate employees. Although qualitative inquiry is just as appropriate in the investigation of the "average" consumer, corporate employee, senior citizen, educator, community volunteer, cancer patient, and the like, it is the ability to obtain insight from the less obvious, smaller niche segments of the population that gives special distinction to the qualitative approach.

9. **Messy analysis and the inductive approach.** Without a doubt, qualitative research analysis can be, and often is, "messy." The analysis of qualitative data does not follow a straight line, where Point *A* leads to Point *B*, but rather is a multilayered, involved process that continually builds upon itself until a meaningful and verifiable interpretation is achieved. The messiness of the interconnections, inconsistencies, and sometimes seemingly illogical input reaped in qualitative research demands that researchers embrace the tangles of their data from many

sources. There is no single source of analysis in qualitative research because any one research event consists of multiple variables that need consideration in the analysis phase. The analyzable data from an IDI, for example, are more than just what was said in the interview; they also include a variety of other considerations, such as the context in which certain information was revealed and the interviewee–interviewer relationship. This is why, although computer-assisted qualitative data analysis software can help to capture words and sentiment, it is the researcher and his/her ability to find meaning in context, not technology, that is the instrumental component of the data analysis process and has the greatest impact on research outcomes.

A large contributor to the "messiness" of the analytical process is the **inductive approach** as well as the verification processes used in qualitative analysis. Qualitative researchers analyze the outcomes from their fieldwork from the inside out, organizing and deriving meaning from the data by way of the data (and ancillary variables) themselves. It is the data that inform the qualitative analyst in the development of codes and categories, and it is the data that determine the connections that are made (or not made) between various points of information, as well as the meaningfulness of these connections in conjunction with the research issue or phenomenon. However, once the connections are made and meaningfulness established, the analyst's job is not over. From identifying relevant patterns in the data and drawing meaningful interpretations of the outcomes, the qualitative analyst is now faced with substantiating these insights through a verification process that might include peer debriefings and review, an analysis of deviant cases, and/or a triangulation exercise that considers the data on the research issue generated from other methods, other contexts, or other researchers.

So, qualitative analysis is difficult. And because it is messy and difficult, the reader will find that throughout our book we challenge qualitative researchers to take the high road in self-evaluation by proactively identifying and readily disclosing the limitations of their research, and by being explicit about plausible alternative interpretations of their findings.

10. **Unique capabilities of online and mobile qualitative research.** Online and mobile technology offer unique enhancements to qualitative research designs. In many instances, these technologies have shifted the balance of power from the researcher to the online or mobile participant, who is given greater control of the research process by way of increased flexibility, convenience, and varied ways to respond in greater detail and depth to the researcher's inquiries. For example, a participant in an email IDI study can thoughtfully reflect on a researcher's question before answering and can delay response until the participant is at a location where he/she can take the time to write a thoughtful reply. The opportunity to select the time and place for participation empowers online and mobile participants beyond that afforded participants of conventional, more restrictive modes that dictate a specific interview schedule or date and place for a group discussion or observation.

Online and mobile technologies have also ushered in a richer, deeper qualitative research experience. Not only do participants have the chance to write more thoughtful responses to interview questions compared to more time-limiting modes (e.g., telephone and face-to-face), but online and mobile participants can also enrich their text responses by attaching files, images (photographs, graphics), links to websites, as well as add a voice response via VoIP (Voice over Internet Protocol) or the mobile phone device. This possibility for multimedia communication can be particularly effective, for example, when capturing in-the-moment experiences or observations via the participant's smartphone, which may include a text message describing the event, photographs of the event, a short video of the event, and a voice message to the researcher elaborating on specific aspects of the event.

1.3 THE TOTAL QUALITY FRAMEWORK AND THE REASON FOR THIS BOOK

The distinctive attributes and underlying complexities in qualitative research necessitate a quality approach to qualitative research design. This approach, not unlike that which can be applied to quantitative research, requires qualitative researchers to build certain principles into their research studies by way of incorporating and practicing fundamental research standards.

We believe all research that is aimed at understanding how people think and behave requires a principled approach to research design that is likely to maximize data quality and to instill users' confidence in the research outcomes. *And yet, a qualitative research book devoted to quality standards has been missing.* Although books in the marketplace today discuss and embrace quality-design issues (e.g., Berg & Lune, 2012; Creswell, 2013; Marshall & Rossman, 2011; Maxwell, 2013), their primary focus is on such topics as the types of qualitative research, the theoretical underpinnings and particular models, logistical or how-to considerations, analysis, and reporting. These books are not dedicated solely to the discussion of quality criteria, nor do they provide the researcher with an applied approach to creating qualitative research designs within a principle-based framework. In contrast, our book was inspired by the need for a balanced discussion of qualitative research design within the context of a quality framework.

To that end, our **Total Quality Framework** (TQF) provides a basis by which researchers can develop critical thinking skills necessary to the execution of high-caliber qualitative research designs. This framework, which is discussed in detail in Chapter 2, is in no way intended to prescribe a formula or specific procedure by which qualitative researchers should conduct qualitative inquiry. Rather, the TQF provides researchers with a flexible way to focus on quality issues, examine the sources of variability and possible bias in their qualitative methods, and incorporate features into their designs that try to mitigate these effects and maximize quality outcomes. *Integral to the TQF is the idea that all qualitative research must be Credible, Analyzable, Transparent, and Useful.* These four components are fundamental to the TQF and its ability to help researchers identify the strengths and limitations of their qualitative methods while also guiding them in the qualitative research design process. The four fundamental TQF components are briefly described:

1. **Credibility** or trustworthiness of the outcomes. A design goal of qualitative research is to minimize researcher bias and researcher-created variability and provide results that are reasonably known to be an accurate account of reality at any one moment in time within the particular parameters and limitations of the qualitative method. The two primary elements of Credibility are *Scope* (e.g., coverage of the target population) and *Data Gathering* (e.g., question–answer validity and interinterviewer and interobserver reliability).

2. **Analyzability** or completeness and accuracy of the analysis and interpretations. A qualitative research design that maximizes Credibility will also contribute to maximizing the researcher's ability to provide a meaningful, accurate analysis. There are two aspects associated with the Analyzability component: *Processing* of the data (i.e., audio/video transcriptions and code development) and *Verification* of the data (e.g., by way of peer debriefings, a reflexive journal, triangulation).

3. **Transparency** or complete disclosure of the design, fieldwork, and analysis processes in the final document. This component includes the specific aspects of these processes that impacted the outcomes and interpretations of the data. By way of "thick description," qualitative researchers should reveal rich details of all phases of the research to enable the user or reader of the research report(s) to apply or transfer the design features to other contexts (i.e., enable transferability).

4. **Usefulness** or the ability to do something with the outcomes. The Usefulness component is a function of the other three components—Credibility, Analyzability, and Transparency—and is the ultimate goal of the research. A useful qualitative research design takes the researcher to the next step, advances the state of knowledge by way of new insights and hypotheses, and/or enables the transferability of the research to other contexts.

The primary goal of this book is to bring an applied approach to qualitative research design grounded in a quality framework by which education, social science, health care, communication, and marketing researchers can judge the efficacy of their qualitative research designs and build in design features that optimize the usefulness of the various qualitative research methods. By holding the quality of qualitative research design up to a deeper level of scrutiny than has heretofore been applied in these fields, we believe this book will significantly elevate the discussion of qualitative research and enable students, faculty, and practitioners to design and interpret qualitative research studies based on the quality standards that are the hallmark of the TQF.

Because qualitative researchers are a diverse group representing a wide assortment of research interests, this book takes a broad, multidisciplinary approach to explain or illustrate qualitative research concepts and constructs, utilizing examples from the fields of education; psychology; anthropology; sociology; nursing, public health, and medicine; communication; information management; business, including consumer and business-to-business research; geography and environmental science; and program evaluation.

A distinctive feature of this book is its combined focus on quality standards and qualitative research in its own right. Although many of the terms we use to discuss design principles may be more familiar in the context of quantitative research—words such as "bias," "error," "measurement," "validity," and "reliability"—the reader will find only one direct discussion in this book comparing qualitative and quantitative approaches, and that is in Chapter 6, to simply distinguish the qualitative content analysis method from its quantitative counterpart. We believe that qualitative–quantitative comparisons serve only to distract researchers from the more important goals of (1) learning about qualitative methods of inquiry; (2) determining how to identify research issues or objectives that are best examined by one or more qualitative methods; and (3) using quality criteria to maximize the credibility, analyzability, transparency, and ultimate usefulness of their qualitative research designs.

1.4   OVERALL ORGANIZATION OF THE BOOK AND ITS CHAPTERS

This book is intended to inform graduate students and faculty, as well as research practitioners, about the strengths, limitations, and uses of the primary methods in qualitative research. Based on this understanding, the book enables readers to apply the TQF in their research designs within each method to produce high-quality research outcomes. To this end, the bulk of this book is oriented around the primary typologies of qualitative inquiry: interviewing, observation, content analysis, and multi-method research. These broad classes of qualitative research encompass what we believe are the five most important (i.e., utilized and discussed) qualitative methods across the education, social, health, communication, and marketing sciences: (1) IDIs and (2) group discussions (the interview method, the focus of Chapters 3 and 4, respectively); (3) ethnography (observation method, Chapter 5); (4) content analysis (Chapter 6); and (5) case study and narrative research (multiple methods, Chapter 7).

Our discussions of these methods are bookended by (a) a complete explanation and rationale of the TQF, its four components, and the application of the framework to the five methods (Chapter 2); and (b) an applied discussion concerning proposal development, specifically, how to best incorporate the TQF in proposals written by graduate students working toward their theses and dissertations; proposals written by researchers in the academic, government, not-for-profit, and commercial sectors responding to clients' requests for proposal (RFPs); as well as proposals written for grant applications (Chapter 8). Chapter 8 also discusses the value of using the TQF in reviewing and evaluating qualitative research proposals as well as other reports, such as conference papers and manuscripts for journals and books.

Each of the five methods chapters (Chapters 3–7) are divided into three main sections. The first of these sections is an introduction that generally covers the fundamental aspects of the method as well as the appropriate uses, necessary researcher skills, and an overview of the strengths and limitations of the method. The second section in each of these chapters is devoted to an important facet specific to the method, such as the various modes appropriate for the method or, in the case of content analysis, the use of computer software. And, in each chapter, the third section focuses on the TQF, specifically how and why to apply TQF principles to the research design for that method. Each chapter ends with a case study to illustrate the concepts discussed in the chapter, as well as providing discussion topics, exercises, and recommendations for additional reading to further readers' thinking and understanding.

The following summary provides the highlights of each methods chapter, which may be particularly helpful to readers who want to read the chapters in an order other than that in which they appear.

Chapter 3. Interview Method: In-Depth Interviews

In addition to the basic IDI formats, appropriate uses, interviewer skills, and strengths/limitations of the IDI method, Chapter 3 examines four modes that can be used to conduct IDIs: face-to-face, telephone, online, and mobile. The primary strengths and limitations of these modes, from a TQF perspective, are discussed. In applying the TQF to the IDI method, Chapter 3 considers, among other matters, sampling design issues such as the appropriate number of interview completions, and it presents 10 questions the researcher needs to ask in order to review the quality of the interview completions at the field stage and assess the adequacy of the number of IDIs. The TQF section in Chapter 3 also discusses quality-control issues related to gaining cooperation from interviewees, the interview guide, interviewer bias and inconsistency, and the interviewee's willingness/ability to provide information.

Chapter 4. Interview Method:
Focus Group Discussions

Similar to Chapter 3, Chapter 4 discusses basic design considerations in the focus group discussion method as well as appropriate uses, moderator skills, strengths/limitations of the method, and three key modes by which qualitative discussions are conducted—face-to-face, telephone, and online—with a special mention of social media and online communities. In applying the TQF, Chapter 4 considers the quality issues related to the four TQF components and includes method-specific aspects such as the importance of the various steps in the recruitment process (e.g., advance notice, location, incentives) toward gaining cooperation from discussion participants, the appropriate role of enabling and projective techniques in the discussion content, and the moderator's ability to build rapport and keep control of the group dynamics.

Chapter 5. Observation Method: Ethnography

Ethnography is fraught with controversy and contradictory points of view among researchers. Is ethnography a discipline (field of study) or a set of methods? Are researchers conducting an "ethnography" or "observational research"? What are the observer roles and what terminology is used to describe these roles? Is covert observation ever acceptable and, if so, under what circumstances? All of these issues, and more, are discussed in Chapter 5, where we present our definition of ethnography (which combines a traditional and contemporary perspective with an emphasis on the observation method) as well as a clear classification of observer roles, and we note the special value of ethnography to study special and otherwise hard-to-reach populations. Chapter 5 also examines ethical considerations in ethnography related to covert observation, institutional review boards, and informed consent, as well as the quality implications of conducting ethnographic research in online contexts and in the mobile (smartphone) mode ("mobile ethnography"). Like the other methods chapters, Chapter 5 describes how to apply the TQF in an ethnographic study, including the appropriate number of observations, and how to mitigate possible observer effects (i.e., potential observer bias and inconsistency).

Chapter 6. Qualitative Content Analysis

Content analysis is a research method conducted by both qualitative and quantitative researchers. Chapter 6 considers the history of qualitative content analysis and gives a definition, based on six essential elements of the qualitative content analysis method. This definition describes qualitative content analysis as a systematic reduction in the data analyzed in its context to identify themes and extract meaningful interpretations. It is on the basis of this definition that Chapter 6 then examines the qualitative researcher's considerations prior to conducting a qualitative content analysis—including the key research objectives, relevant constructs, and the role of a deductive approach in combination with an otherwise inductive strategy—and the eight basic steps in the qualitative content analysis method process. Chapter 6 discusses the appropriate uses of content analysis—including in the realm of online social media and the differentiation between primary and secondary qualitative content analysis—as well as the required skills, strengths/limitations of the qualitative content analysis method, and the particular advantages and disadvantages associated with the utilization of computer-assisted qualitative data analysis software. The TQF section in Chapter 6 considers the special attention researchers need to pay to the primarily text-based data sources in content analysis and the quality standards required to achieve credible, analyzable, transparent, and ultimately useful outcomes.

Chapter 7. Multiple Methods in Case-Centered Approaches: Case Study and Narrative Research

In Chapter 7 we discuss multiple methods by focusing on two popular forms of case-centered research in qualitative inquiry: case study and narrative research.

The core characteristic for both case study and narrative research is the leading role played by the case itself and the use of various (multiple) methods based on the particular research situation. Chapter 7 examines the complexity of case-centered research as well as the range of definitions and perspectives specific to case study and narrative research. This chapter considers the typologies of case study and narrative research, while introducing an internal–external classification scheme. The chapter then goes on to discuss the respective uses, necessary researcher skills, strengths/limitations, and ethical considerations in these case-centered approaches. This chapter also describes six basic steps in conducting case study or narrative research.

The TQF section in Chapter 7 discusses a number of quality design considerations that are unique to case-centered research. The various demands on the researcher in using multiple methods is one such consideration, including the development of quality data-gathering tools across all methods as well as the ability to utilize and absorb the complexity of the collected data from more than one data source. Other TQF considerations in case-centered research pertain to the heightened importance of participant cooperation and compliance, and the special attention narrative researchers need to give to the (relatively intimate) interviewer–narrator relationship as well as the style or format of narrative transcriptions (which may impact the researcher's interpretation of the data). Because case-centered research generally relies on the methods discussed in Chapters 3–6, the reader is encouraged to read these chapters prior to reading Chapter 7.

1.5   GLOSSARY

Throughout this book we have **boldfaced** terms that the reader will find defined in the Glossary beginning on page 349. In most instances, these terms are **boldfaced** when they are actively discussed in the book, which may or may not be when the term first appears in the book.

NOTES

1. Paradigms as they relate to the focus of this book are discussed more fully in Chapter 2.

2. Riessman (2008) describes the application of "social linguistics" in narrative research as "a discrete unit or discourse, an extended answer by a research participant to a single question, topically centered and temporally organized" (p. 5).

CHAPTER TWO

The Total Quality Framework

CHAPTER PREVIEW

There is little agreement among qualitative researchers about how "quality" in a research study should be defined and evaluated. This chapter begins with a brief summary of research paradigms and the work of others who have put forth strategies or criteria aimed at maximizing the quality in qualitative research. We then present our Total Quality Framework (TQF), which provides a comprehensive roadmap for conceptualizing, implementing, and interpreting a high-quality qualitative research study. The TQF comprises four major interrelated components (*Credibility, Analyzability, Transparency,* and *Usefulness*), and the chapter provides a comprehensive overview of each. This chapter also explains the many ways the TQF can be of value beyond planning and conducting a particular qualitative research study. Reading this chapter is central to gaining the most value from the other chapters in this book.

2.1 INTRODUCTION

The field of qualitative research has paid considerable attention in the past half century to the issue of research "quality." Despite these efforts, there remains a lack of agreement among qualitative researchers about how quality should be defined and how it should be evaluated (cf. Lincoln & Guba, 1985, 1986; Lincoln, 1995; Morse et al., 2002; Reynolds et al., 2011; Rolfe, 2006; Schwandt, Lincoln, & Guba, 2007; Seale & Silverman, 1997; Stake & Schwandt, 2006). Some who seem to question whether quality can be defined and evaluated appear to hold the view that each qualitative research study is so singularly unique in terms of how the data are created and how sense is made of these data that striving to assess quality is a wasted effort that never leads to a satisfying outcome about which agreement can be reached. Taken to an extreme, this view would seem to suggest that findings from one qualitative study cannot lend insights to any other qualitative study, either in terms of method or substance. It also would suggest that validity—by which we mean "the correctness or credibility of a description, conclusion, explanation, interpretation, or other sort of account" (Maxwell, 2013, p. 122)—is solely in the eye of the beholder and that convincing someone else that a qualitative study has generated valid and actionable findings is more an effort of subjective persuasion than an effort of applying dispassionate logic to whether the methods that were used to gather and analyze the data led to "valid enough" conclusions for the purpose(s) to which they were meant to serve.

Controversy also exists between whether determinations of quality should be based on some objective assessment of the methods that were used to generate and analyze the data in a qualitative study or rather on post hoc judgments made by those who consume the findings. Arguments are made by some that the quality of a qualitative research study is determined solely by the methods and processing that the researchers have used to conduct their studies. Others argue that quality is determined essentially by how consumers of the study judge it (see Morse et al., 2002; Reynolds et al., 2011).

It is within this context of disharmony and controversy that we bring forth our Total Quality Framework (TQF). Although the TQF may not be suitable for planning and evaluating every qualitative research study,[1] we do believe that it provides a very useful tool for qualitative researchers to apply in designing, conducting, and interpreting their research so that the studies are more likely to (a) gather high-quality data, (b) lead to more robust and valid interpretations of the data, and (c) ultimately generate highly useful outcomes. The bulk of this chapter is devoted to an explication of how qualitative researchers should apply the TQF to accomplish all these goals.

We also believe that the TQF provides a guide for anyone who is consuming the findings and recommendations from a qualitative research study. In believing this, we think of the TQF as a tool for any consumer of a qualitative research study to help form a sense of confidence about the likely accuracy and usefulness of the study's findings. It is not our intention that applying the TQF will yield a dichotomous (i.e., a thumbs-up vs. thumbs-down) judgment that a qualitative study is accurate or not accurate, useful or not useful. Rather, we believe that the TQF will help the consumers of a given research study to form a sense of confidence that may range from "not at all confident" to "extremely confident" about the study's validity and usefulness. In this way, the TQF empowers the users of the research to make their own decisions about how much importance should be placed on a qualitative study's findings.

For example, a CEO of a pharmaceutical company whose research department commissioned a series of focus groups as part of their investigation of consumers' reactions to a new drug product concept has two basic strategies that she can use to decide what importance to assign the findings in making her decision to proceed with further product development, postpone product development in order to rethink the concept, or kill the product idea altogether. First, she can take the conclusions drawn from the group discussions at face value and factor them into her decision process with complete confidence that they are accurate and therefore useful—her research department commissioned the study, so the study must be accurate, right? Or the CEO could deploy a second strategy either on her own or with the help of an independent consultant. This alternative approach would be to evaluate the likely accuracy of the findings of the focus groups and, rather than decide to unconditionally accept or reject the findings, decide how confident she should be about the results. That judgment about confidence would then determine how important a role the focus group outcomes would play in influencing her decision about the further development of the new drug product. It may be that the CEO decides that she can be very confident in the study findings and allows those findings to play an important role in whatever decision she makes on how to proceed with product development. Or it may be that the CEO decides that she is not at all confident about the findings and therefore the study ends up playing little or no role in her decision regarding the further development of the new drug product.

The judgments that are made by sponsoring clients and users of the research concerning the soundness of qualitative research studies do not need to be based solely on an intuitive "gut sense." Instead, these judgments of clients and users could be based on applying a series of criteria that build confidence in the research outcomes and help them to make relevant decisions. As we go on to explain in this chapter and demonstrate throughout the book, we believe the TQF provides an excellent basis upon which to formulate a judgment as to how confident one can (and should) be about the findings of a particular qualitative research study.

In sum, we strongly believe that the TQF is a better way to plan, implement, interpret, and evaluate qualitative research. It is a comprehensive and interrelated way of thinking (i.e., a *framework*) that addresses the major threats that can undermine the accuracy and value of a qualitative research study. It does not lead anyone to a given conclusion that a particular study is or is not worthy of the purposes to which someone might put its findings. Rather, it provides a structure that empowers anyone interested in applying it to formulate their own conclusions about the likely accuracy and therefore usefulness of a qualitative research study. It is valuable to qualitative researchers who are planning a study, who are conducting a study, or who are interpreting a study. And, it is valuable to any and every consumer of the study.

2.2   PARADIGMS AND FRAMEWORKS

Paradigms

A good deal has been written about paradigms in qualitative research as they relate to assessing quality (Greene, 1994; Lather, 2004; Lincoln & Guba, 1985; Morrow, 2005; Patton, 1978; Ponterotto, 2013; Rolfe, 2006). And in our view, much of what has been written on this topic muddles the waters because of (1) the frequent failure to precisely define what is meant by the umbrella term **paradigm**, as it applies to qualitative research, and (2) the failure of some to consistently adhere to the explicit or implicit definition of the paradigm that they appear to be using.

Furthermore, some scholars, such as Rolfe (2006), start from the premise that "any attempt to establish a consensus on quality criteria for qualitative research is unlikely to succeed for the simple reason that there is no unified body or theory [i.e., an accepted paradigm], methodology or method that can collectively be described as qualitative research; indeed, that the *very idea* of qualitative research is open to question" (p. 305, emphasis in original). Rolfe then opines that "if there is no unified qualitative research paradigm, then it makes little sense to attempt to establish a set of generic criteria for making quality judgments about qualitative research studies" (2006, p. 304). To us, this line of thinking confounds attention to methods and attention to theory, when each deserves to be considered separately. We readily acknowledge that the belief that there is no paradigm capable of encompassing all of qualitative research has merit in its own right, but in our view, that belief has nothing to do with how well the methods that are used to generate qualitative research data and findings are conceptualized, implemented, and evaluated.

Distinguishing Research Methods from Paradigm Orientation

The idea that qualitative research design—its procedures and various components—transcends or is otherwise separate from a discussion of paradigms is an idea shared by many scholars. As shown in Table 2.1, it is an idea espoused by Morse et al. (2002), who believe that the "core research procedures . . . built into each phase of the research strategies that can act as a self-correcting mechanism to ensure the quality of the project" (p. 14) are important issues that go beyond the debate about paradigms. Morse et al.'s position is supported by Patton (1999, 2002) when he stresses the need to focus on the "appropriateness of methods" rather than the "adherence to some absolute orthodoxy that declares one or the other approach to be inherently preferred" (1999, p. 1206). It is a position consistent with Miles and Huberman (1984), who stated that "it is important not to confuse the systematic use of tools with one's epistemological position" (p. 21). Ponterotto (2013) and Morrow (2005), when they talk about specific aspects of qualitative research design that transcend paradigm orientation—such as ethical considerations and researcher competencies (Ponterotto), and the subjective nature of qualitative research as well as the adequacy and interpretation of data (Morrow)—champion the same view. Furthermore, the distinctiveness of methodological issues in relation to concerns regarding philosophical paradigms is an idea supported by Guba and Lincoln (1994), who distinguish "questions of method" from "questions of paradigm" (p. 105); by Lincoln et al. (2011), who identify two kinds of rigor—the "application of method" and the "salience to one interpretation over another" (p. 120); as well as by the notion that validity and validation pertain throughout the research process regardless of approach (Creswell, 2013; Brinkmann & Kvale, 2015; Morse et al., 2002; Whittemore, Chase, & Mandle, 2001).

TABLE 2.1. **Examples of Other Authors Who Distinguish Research Methods from Paradigm Orientation**	
Author(s)	**Applicable reference**
Creswell (2013)	Recommends the use of validation strategies "regardless of type of qualitative research" (p. 250).
Guba & Lincoln (1994)	Distinguish "questions of method" from "questions of paradigm" (p. 105).
Brinkmann & Kvale (2015)	Discuss seven stages of validation that form a "continual process validation" throughout every research stage (p. 283).
Lincoln, Lynham, & Guba (2011)	Identify two types of rigor: the "application of method" and the "salience to one interpretation over another" (p. 120).
Miles & Huberman (1984)	Emphasize the importance of the "systematic use of tools" over an "epistemological position" (p. 21).
Morrow (2005)	Believes there are quality standards that transcend paradigm orientation, including "sufficiency of and immersion in the data, attention to subjectivity and reflexivity, adequacy of data, and issues related to interpretation and presentation" (p. 250).
Morse, Barrett, Mayan, Olson, & Spiers (2002)	State that "core research procedures" (p. 14) go beyond the paradigm debate and that "the concepts of reliability and validity as overarching constructs can be appropriately used in all scientific paradigms" (p. 19).
Patton (1999, 2002)	Stresses the need to focus on the "appropriateness of methods" rather than adhering to "some absolute orthodoxy" (1999, p. 1206).
Ponterotto (2013)	Outlines ethical considerations along with researcher competencies that "are intended to transcend the various research paradigms and qualitative inquiry approaches," such as postpositivism, constructivism–interpretivism, and critical theory (p. 29).
Whittemore, Chase, & Mandle (2001)	Formulate validity criteria into three components and emphasize that this validity composite is "essential to all scientific endeavors" (p. 533).

With our TQF, we focus on issues related to the methodological choices that qualitative researchers make (or fail to make) in their efforts to generate data that are fit for the purposes for which a study is intended. The TQF also focuses on issues related to the choices that qualitative researchers make (or fail to make) in their efforts to make sense of (i.e., analyze and interpret) the data that their studies generate. It does *not* focus on any theoretical paradigm that might guide qualitative researchers in deciding how to identify and formulate the questions they seek to answer with their research or how to make their findings useful.

Rather than addressing the question of "What is qualitative research 'good for'?", the TQF is directed at the basic question of "How is qualitative research conducted?" If, philosophically, the goodness of qualitative research is of ultimate concern, and if it is agreed that qualitative research can, in fact, serve worthwhile (i.e., "good") purposes, then logically it would serve those purposes only to the degree that it is done (i.e., "executed") well, regardless of the specific objectives that qualitative researchers are striving to address.

Summary

In sum, we firmly believe that the controversy over whether there is or is not an overarching paradigm that encompasses qualitative research, although important for consideration in its own right, is superfluous to the applied framework we are advocating. Our framework concerns the issue of "how well is it done." We believe that by embracing and applying the TQF perspective, qualitative research will be "done" better—regardless of which theoretical paradigm the researcher follows—than would have occurred had a TQF perspective not been applied in planning, executing, and interpreting a qualitative research study. In this way, we see these paradigmatic debates as separate from our focus on a *Total Quality Framework*, because we believe that our TQF stands apart from, and actually transcends, the issue of paradigms.

Frameworks

Many others before us have advanced strategies, criteria, or frameworks for thinking about and promoting the importance of "the quality" of qualitative research at some stage in the research design. There are those who focus on quality as it relates to specific aspects—such as various validation and verification strategies or "checklists" (Barbour, 2001; Creswell, 2013; Brinkmann & Kvale, 2015; Maxwell, 2013; Morse et al., 2002), validity related to researcher decision making (Koro-Ljungberg, 2010) and subjectivity (Bradbury-Jones, 2007), or the specific role of transparency in assessing the quality of outcomes (Miles, Huberman, & Saldaña, 2014). There are others who prescribe particular approaches in the research process—such as consensual qualitative research (Hill et al., 2005), the use of triangulation (Tobin & Begley, 2004), or an audit procedure (Akkerman, Admiraal, Brekelmans, & Oost, 2006). And there are still others who take a broader, more general view that emphasizes the importance of "paying attention to the qualitative rigor and model of trustworthiness from the moment of conceptualization of the research" (Thomas & Magilvy, 2011, p. 154; see also, Bergman & Coxon, 2005; Whittemore et al., 2001).

The strategies or ways of thinking about quality in qualitative research that are most relevant to our TQF are those that are (a) paradigm neutral, (b) flexible (i.e., do not adhere to a defined method), and (c) applicable to all phases of the research process. Among these, the work of Lincoln and Guba (e.g., 1981, 1985, 1986, and 1995) is the most noteworthy. Although they profess a paradigm orientation "of the constructionist camp, loosely defined" (Lincoln et al., 2011, p. 116), the quality criteria Lincoln and Guba set forth nearly 30 years ago is particularly pertinent to the TQF in that it advances the concept of trustworthiness as a major criterion for judging whether a qualitative research study is "rigorous." In their model, trustworthiness addresses the issue of "How can a [qualitative researcher] persuade [someone] that the findings of a [study] are worth paying attention to, worth taking account of?" (Lincoln & Guba, 1985, p. 290). That is, what are the criteria upon which such an assessment should be based? In this way, Lincoln and Guba espouse standards that are flexible (i.e., can be adapted depending on the research context) as well as relevant throughout the research process.

In answering, they put forth the criteria of credibility, transferability, dependability, and confirmability. For Lincoln and Guba (1985), *credibility* is the extent to which the findings of a qualitative research study are internally valid (i.e., accurate). Credibility, or the lack thereof, is established through (a) **prolonged engagement**, (b) **persistent observation**, (c) triangulation, (d) peer debriefings, (e) negative case analysis, (f) **referential adequacy**, and (g) member checks. *Transferability* refers to the extent to which other researchers or users of the research can determine the applicability of the research design and/or the study findings to other research contexts (e.g., other participants, places, and times). Transferability, or the lack thereof, is primarily established through thick description that is "necessary to enable someone interested in making a transfer to reach a conclusion about whether transfer can be contemplated as a possibility" (Lincoln & Guba, 1985, p. 316). Thick description and transferability are key elements of the TQF Transparency component (as discussed below). *Dependability* is the degree to which an independent "auditor" can look at the qualitative research process and determine its "acceptability" and, in so doing, create an audit trail of the process. To that end, the Transparency component of the TQF deals directly with the idea of providing the user of the research with an audit trail pertaining to all aspects of the research in the final research document. And, *confirmability* refers to utilizing the same dependability audit to examine the evidence in the data that purportedly supports the researcher's findings, interpretations, and recommendations.

2.3 WHAT IS THE TOTAL QUALITY FRAMEWORK?

As previously stated, the TQF is a comprehensive perspective for creating, managing, and interpreting quality research designs and evaluating the likelihood that a qualitative study will provide information that is valid and useful for the purposes for which the study is intended. This framework comprises four interrelated components—*Credibility, Analyzability, Transparency,* and *Usefulness* (see Figure 2.1 for a schematic of the interlocking layout of the TQF). Credibility concerns the completeness and accuracy of the data a qualitative research study gathers. The Analyzability component pertains to the completeness and accuracy of the analyses and interpretations of the data. Transparency has to do with the completeness and full disclosure of all aspects of the research in the documentation of the study. And the Usefulness component concerns the ultimate goal of all qualitative research, which is the ability to "do something" of value with the findings and recommendations from the study. Each of these components is discussed below and in more detail in Chapters 3–7, regarding the specific ways the TQF applies to each of the qualitative research methods covered in those chapters.

Credibility

The TQF Credibility component focuses on the data collection stage of a qualitative research study, addressing whether there are complete and accurate data about the constructs the researcher purports to be investigating in the study. It is made up of two elements: Scope and Data Gathering.

Scope

The **Scope** of a qualitative research study concerns how well that study ends up representing the population of humans and/or documents it is investigating. By "ends up" we mean to differentiate what the researchers initially planned would happen in terms of representing the population from what actually happened once data collection was completed. As occurs in most social and marketing research, the final sample of participants in a study rarely is a perfect match to the sample the researcher originally planned to gather data from or about, and many times the final sample is not even a close match. This discrepancy occurs for a variety of reasons, many of which are beyond the control of the researcher due to the finite and practical limitations of the funding and time available for the study.

The following is a set of TQF criteria that we recommend be considered in assessing how well the Scope of a qualitative research project was conceptualized, conducted, and achieved. This set includes:

- Defining the target population.
- Selecting the listing(s) for sampling the population.
- Choosing a sample design.
- Deciding how large a sample to use.
- Identifying strategies to use to gain access to and cooperation from the sample.

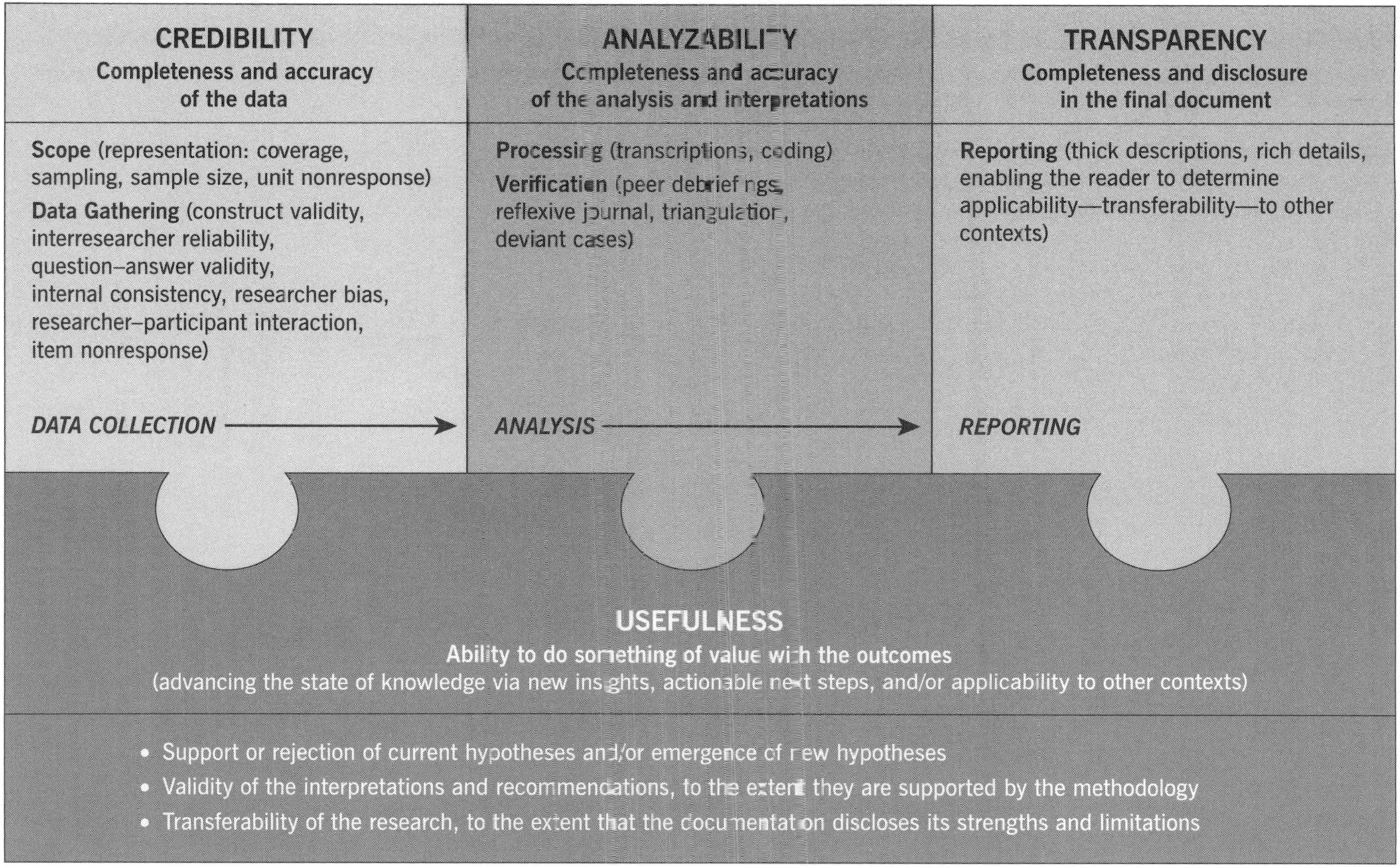

CREDIBILITY
Completeness and accuracy
of the data

Scope (representation: coverage, sampling, sample size, unit nonresponse)
Data Gathering (construct validity, interresearcher reliability, question–answer validity, internal consistency, researcher bias, researcher–participant interaction, item nonresponse)

DATA COLLECTION

ANALYZABILITY
Completeness and accuracy
of the analysis and interpretations

Processing (transcriptions, coding)
Verification (peer debriefings, reflexive journal, triangulation, deviant cases)

ANALYSIS

TRANSPARENCY
Completeness and disclosure
in the final document

Reporting (thick descriptions, rich details, enabling the reader to determine applicability—transferability—to other contexts)

REPORTING

USEFULNESS
Ability to do something of value with the outcomes
(advancing the state of knowledge via new insights, actionable next steps, and/or applicability to other contexts)

- Support or rejection of current hypotheses and/or emergence of new hypotheses
- Validity of the interpretations and recommendations, to the extent they are supported by the methodology
- Transferability of the research, to the extent that the documentation discloses its strengths and limitations

FIGURE 2.1. The Total Quality Framework schematic.

23

Defining the Target Population

When starting to plan a qualitative research study, explicit consideration should be given to precisely articulating the population of participants or objects (e.g., elements of content) that the study is investigating and for which the findings of the study are meant to apply. In some cases the **target population** is so small that the researcher may be able to (and want to) gather data from all members of the population. For example, in a content analysis of love letters between two prominent individuals in the 18th century, there may be only 43 such letters that were ever written. In this case the researcher may choose to **code** and analyze all the letters. Or a researcher conducting a narrative research study to understand the stories among homeless women who visit a particular community soup kitchen may learn that there are only five women who visit the soup kitchen on a daily basis. As a result, the researcher may elect to include all five in the study. Or in the case of conducting in-depth interviews (IDIs) of middle-level managers of a corporation, there may be only 11 positions in middle management, prompting the researcher's decision to conduct interviews with each of the 11 managers in those positions. In these examples, the entire target population can be easily and readily defined.

In many other cases, however, the population of interest is far too large to consider gathering data from all its members. For example, in a content analysis of all lead editorials written in major metropolitan daily newspapers in the United States during the years the country was involved in World War II, there are thousands of editorials in that target population. How the researcher chooses to sample those editorials that will be coded and analyzed is a later consideration (see p. 36), but at this stage in the research the researcher should clearly articulate that his target population is: "All lead editorials in major metropolitan American daily newspapers from December 7, 1941 through August 14, 1945." Identifying the target population in this example is a relatively easy task, yet it is more burdensome than in the previous examples with small population sizes because the researcher should also include a specific listing of all the newspapers that were considered to be "major metropolitan dailies" during this 45-month time period. Without including this exhaustive listing, the research study would fail to clearly define the target population.

Unfortunately, qualitative researchers who fail to be explicit about their target population definition jeopardize the quality of their studies. And, failure to clearly and explicitly define the target population from the start is an indication of a study that has likely not been planned rigorously—and certainly one not planned along the lines of the TQF.

Selecting the Listing(s) for Sampling the Population

The importance of precisely defining the target population is showcased by the next major consideration in applying the TQF: how the members of the population are identified by the researcher in order to sample them. Regardless of the size of the population to be studied—and even in studies that plan to gather data from all members of the population—the researcher should build a list of all the individuals in the target population. Not doing this typically leads to a lower-quality and less useful study.

As part of this step, the researcher must try not only to assemble a list (or lists) that covers (i.e., encompasses) the entire population, but must also work to understand the extent to which the list(s) may be incomplete and not include all members of the population. To the extent that the list(s) that the researcher assembles misses part of the target population, the data that are collected for the study may not be representative of the entire target population, and the researcher should later account for this lack of complete population coverage.

For example, in the case of the IDI study to be conducted with all middle-level managers of a corporation, it should be an easy task for the researcher to get permission from the CEO to obtain a complete and accurate listing of those 11 managers along with their contact information. But, in contrast, it would be considerably more burdensome, and no doubt less exact, to try to assemble a listing of all lead editorials during World War II printed in major metropolitan dailies in the United States. In this case it is not necessary for the researcher to physically assemble the entire listing of thousands of editorials from which to sample Instead, the researcher would treat a listing of these editorials as "existing in theory" and take a much more practical approach of drawing the sample of editorials to use in his/her content analysis, for example, by sampling newspapers and dates until the sample size of editorials that the researcher desired to code and analyze was met. (Of course, as discussed later, the researcher in this example has no guarantee that all of the sampled editorials will be found because of possible problems with the archives where the editorials are located.)

Ultimately, the TQF guides qualitative researchers to think carefully about how well the listing they use to represent their target population does, in fact, cover the entire population. To the extent the listing does not fully cover the population, the TQF recommends that the researcher should investigate how the missing part of the target population may differ from the part that is used to draw the sample. Following a TQF approach, the researcher should acknowledge any problems this omission is likely to cause and take these into consideration when conclusions are drawn and recommendations are made based on the study's findings.

Choosing a Sampling Design

Once the researcher has identified the list (or lists) that will be used to select the sample, a decision must be made about which sampling approach will be used. If the decision is to gather data from or about each member of the population on the list, then there is nothing more for the researcher to consider on this TQF matter. But for those studies where something less than the entire population on the listing will be chosen for study, additional TQF decisions need to be made about sampling.

Here, qualitative researchers may needlessly lessen the quality of their studies by not giving these decisions sufficient consideration. In fact, some qualitative researchers may think and act as though how they create a sample of the population is unimportant. Qualitative researchers may proceed in this manner because they mistakenly believe that systematic sampling is too hard to carry out (i.e., too complex, too expensive, and too time-consuming) and that it is "too quantitative" a concern. Yet in the vast majority of qualitative studies **systematic sampling** is neither complex, expensive, nor time-consuming, and should not only be a quantitative issue. Throughout the chapters of this book we give clear examples of how systematic sampling can and should be applied in qualitative research. And by using an organized approach for choosing which members of their target population (taken from the listing that has been assembled to represent that population) to study, as opposed to merely using a convenient and disorderly approach to sampling, qualitative researchers avoid a major threat to the credibility (related to representativeness) of the data they gather. That threat is the possibility that those from whom they gather data are not, in fact, representative of the population being studied.

Take, for example, a focus group researcher that has a list of men and women who completed a cardiopulmonary resuscitation (CPR) training class in the past year. The researcher can choose one of two basic approaches to selecting those who will be invited to participate in a group discussion. The often-used but misguided approach is to start at the top of the list and contact people, one after another, until the focus groups have been filled with ostensibly willing attendees. The rigorous and correct approach is to use an organized scheme to sample CPR class graduates from across the entire list. The second approach is preferred because it avoids the possible problem that the names on the list are ordered in a way that is not representative of the entire population of CPR graduates the researcher wants to study. There are many ways that systematic and representative samples can be drawn from lists, as explained throughout the book.

A final TQF issue related to choosing a sample applies to qualitative studies that utilize observations of naturally occurring human behavior to gather data, such as in ethnographic research. In these studies, sampling considerations need to be applied to the times and the locations during which the behaviors of interest will be observed. By systematically choosing which locations and which times to conduct the observations—among all possible locations and times in which the behaviors of interest will be taking place—the qualitative researcher is greatly raising the likelihood that the observations included in the study are a representative subset of all the possible behaviors of interest to the study.

Deciding How Large a Sample to Use

How large a sample to use is another decision that qualitative researchers need to make explicitly and carefully in order to increase the likelihood that their studies will generate credible data by well representing their population of interest. Unlike quantitative researchers who most often rely on statistical formulae to determine the sample sizes for their studies, qualitative researchers must rely on (a) past experience and knowledge of the subject matter; and (b) ongoing monitoring during the data-gathering period, which includes applying a set of decision rules, such as those listed on page 75 for IDI studies, to determine how many interviews are "enough." These decision rules consider (a) the complexity of the phenomena being studied, (b) the heterogeneity or homogeneity of the population being studied, (c) the level of analysis and interpretation that will be carried out, and (d) the finite resources available to support the study. These types of decision guidelines, along with past experience, should provide qualitative researchers with the considerations they need to be able to carefully judge the amount of data they need to gather to meet the needs of their studies. (Of note, if a researcher does not have sufficient past personal experience, a literature review, or speaking directly with other researchers who do have such experience, should serve well.)

As importantly, during the period when data are being gathered, researchers should also closely monitor the amount of variability in the data, compared to the variability that was expected, for the key measures of the study. Based on this monitoring, researchers are responsible for making a "Goldilocks decision" about whether the sample size they originally decided was needed is too large, too small, or just about right. In making a decision to cut back on the amount of data to be gathered, because there is less variability in what is being measured than anticipated, the researcher needs to make certain that those cases that originally were sampled, but would be dropped, are not systematically different from the cases from which data will be gathered. In making a decision to increase the size of the sample, because there is more variability in what is being measured than anticipated, the researcher needs to make certain that the cases added to the sample are chosen in a way that is representative of the entire population (e.g., using the same orderly approach that was used to create the initial sample). In all instances, from a TQF perspective, it is prudent for a researcher to error on the side of having more data than necessary, rather than less. Gathering too much data does no harm to the quality of the study's findings and interpretations (even though more resources were used than were necessary), but having too little data leaves the researcher in the untenable position of harming the quality of the study because the complexity of what was being studied will not be adequately represented in the available data. For example, case study research to investigate new public school policies related to the core science curriculum might include IDIs with school principals and science teachers, observations of science classes in session, and a review of students' test papers; however, as a complex subject matter, the research may be weakened by not including discussions with the students and their parents as well as by a failure to include all schools (or a representative sample of schools) in the research design.

Strategies That Will Be Used to Gain Access to and Cooperation from the Sample

Once a qualitative researcher has made all the decisions that are needed to carefully plan the sampling part of the study, TQF credibility decisions need to be made about how to gain access to and cooperation from those members of the population who were chosen for study. And this must be done in ethically justifiable ways.

In doing a company-sponsored IDI study of employees, for example, gaining access to the employees who have been sampled may be as simple as sending each of them a notification that their employer has authorized the researcher to contact him/her to request his/her participation in the research study. Or it may be as challenging as gaining permission from "gatekeepers" who have the right to deny access to the individuals the researcher wants to study; for example, parents of the children who will be studied, presidents of the professional organizations whose members will be studied, wardens of prisons whose inmates will be studied, etc. The challenge of gaining access from such gatekeepers is essentially finding successful strategies that (a) provide guarantees to the gatekeepers that no harm will come to the participants, (b) communicate the worthiness of the research study, and (c) offer some benefit to the gatekeeper or the organization.

Once access to the sampled participants has been granted, the researchers must use strategies to gain cooperation from those who have been chosen to be studied. Ideally a very large portion of those who have been sampled will agree to participate. From a TQF standpoint, if those who are chosen to be studied but from whom no data are gathered (e.g., because they were unable to be reached or refused to cooperate) differ in non-ignorable ways from those who do provide data, then bias may result, which can lower or even undermine the credibility of the qualitative study. If, for example, a disproportionately greater number of males, compared to females, who have been sampled from a list of college freshmen can never be contacted or refuse to participate, and if these sampled males would have provided data that are materially different from the data provided by the other freshmen on the list who did participate in the study, then the research findings will be biased because of the data missing from a major subgroup of the population.

To avoid these problems, qualitative researchers need to utilize strategies meant to overcome the reason(s) that causes some people who are sampled to not provide data. Such strategies include:

- Building rapport early with the participants, thereby gaining their trust.
- Assuring the participants of complete confidentiality.
- Explaining the nonmaterial benefits to be gained by participating (e.g., helping to raise the quality of life in the neighborhood).
- Explaining the material benefits, if any, to be gained by participating (e.g., the offer of a $50 Amazon gift card).

These and other strategies to gain cooperation are discussed throughout the chapters of this book. In any event, whichever strategies the researchers choose to deploy, ideally they will be tailored (at the individual level) to appeal to the particular types of participants in the sample in order to overcome reluctance or unequivocal refusal during the recruiting process.

The above discussion is applicable to qualitative research that involves gathering data from or about humans. In content analysis, data are gathered from inanimate elements of content that have been sampled for the study. As explained in Chapter 6, challenges nevertheless may be faced by qualitative researchers as they strive to gain access to the elements of content they want to code for their study (including being unable to find the sampled elements even if, for example, permission has been granted to access the archive in which they are stored). Furthermore, there may be problems with the legibility of sampled elements once access has been gained and in some cases this issue could cause bias in the resulting data.

All of these issues can impact the credibility of a qualitative study. It remains the responsibility of the researcher to think through what is the best solution from a TQF standpoint to minimize these potential threats and to acknowledge them when formulating the study's conclusions and recommendations and when reporting on the results of the study.

A final issue is related to any deception that may be used to help gain access to participants and elicit their cooperation for data collection. Although deceptive practices—such as not fully revealing the true purpose of the research—may be effective in gaining access and cooperation, the element of deception presents a very important ethical issue. We discuss the topic of deception on the part of qualitative researchers throughout the book and note here that decisions about its use are part of the TQF process that we advocate qualitative researchers use to enhance the scope of their research studies.

Summary of Scope-Related Issues and the TQF

As depicted in the Credibility segment of Figure 2.1, Scope-related issues include all those aspects of a research study that affect the extent to which the final sample from (or about) which data are gathered reflects the important characteristics of the target population that is being studied. There are many aspects that should be considered as opposed to being ignored as a researcher plans the coverage and representation of a qualitative research study. In identifying these aspects, as we have done above and as we do throughout Chapters 3–7, the TQF encourages researchers to seek the best possible solutions within the context of the resources available to conduct a given study. We believe it is preferable for a researcher to understand the myriad potential limitations of the study, and to acknowledge them, both in terms of doing so outright (i.e., disclosing them) and by taking them into consideration when interpretations are made and implications are drawn.

Data Gathering

The second aspect of the Credibility component in the TQF is **Data Gathering**, which some would call "construct validity," and what we regard as a concern about how well the data that are gathered actually represent what the researchers claim the study has measured. For example, if a study purports to measure alienation, then the Data Gathering component addresses the issue of how well the construct of alienation actually will be, or has been, measured.

As with Scope-related concerns, there are myriad issues related to Data Gathering that can affect the quality of the data a qualitative research study generates, which in turn impacts the study's credibility. By recognizing these issues and giving them explicit consideration from the TQF perspective, we believe that qualitative researchers are more likely to gather high-quality data in their studies.

The following is a set of TQF criteria that we recommend be considered in assessing how well the Data Gathering component of a qualitative research project was conceptualized and conducted. This set includes:

- Matching constructs[2] to the research objectives.
- Identifying the attributes to measure for each construct.
- Choosing the mode(s) of data collection.
- Operationalizing the constructs and attributes in the form of a data collection tool.
- Evaluating data collectors as sources of bias and inconsistency.
- Evaluating participants as sources of bias and inconsistency.

Matching Constructs to the Research Objectives

A TQF approach to qualitative research that strives to generate quality data requires that the researcher place a high priority on identifying the **constructs** that need to be measured in the study. These constructs should flow logically from the study's objectives. For example, if a study is trying to understand health care problems within lower-income groups, then choosing to gather data on constructs such as a family's health status and past history, heath care attitudes, health care access, and financial resources that can be devoted to health care would match the research objectives.

The decisions that a researcher makes at this stage of planning are crucial to the ultimate success or failure in gathering valid data for the needs of the qualitative study. Although it is inefficient (and adds what later may prove to be unnecessary costs) to gather data about more constructs than are needed to understand the phenomena being studied, it is better to gather data about "too many" constructs than "too few," if one is at all uncertain about how many constructs to include in the study. Among other factors, it is more expensive to gather data in a "remedial" or makeup round of data collection than gathering those same data the first time. Therefore, if a researcher is uncertain whether a particular construct should be investigated in the study, it is prudent to gather data about it the first time rather than regretting its omission if later it is found to be important to the study's objectives.

Qualitative researchers have many information sources they can seek out and consider when deciding upon the constructs that their study will measure. These sources include literature reviews of past studies that addressed similar topics, input from peers and experts (e.g., by asking them to review a draft research proposal or simply talking with them about the preliminary ideas for the new study), and for client-commissioned studies, of course, lengthy discussions with the client sponsor, who most likely has specific notions (from past internal research or otherwise) about the appropriate constructs associated with the research objectives.

Identifying the Attributes to Measure for Each Construct

After a qualitative researcher has identified the constructs that the research will investigate, decisions must be made about which attributes of a construct will be measured. For example, if health care history is a construct to measure, then the attributes of interest would likely include (a) all of the serious health conditions the person has experienced, (b) the age when each of these conditions was first experienced, (c) the treatments received for each condition, (d) the success of each treatment, (e) other instances of hospitalization not already noted, (f) the extent of each instance of hospitalization, (g) the outcome of each hospitalization, and (h) the types of doctors the person currently sees and has seen throughout his/her life at least for routine biannual checkups.

Not unlike making decisions about which constructs a study should measure, qualitative researchers face very important decisions in choosing the appropriate attributes of each construct to measure. The decisions that a researcher makes at this stage of planning a study are critical to the ultimate success or failure in gathering valid data to meet the needs of the study. As with deciding which constructs to gather data about, it is inefficient to gather data about more attributes than are needed to understand a given construct being studied, but it is better to gather data about too many attributes than too few. And, like the selection of constructs, the decision regarding which attributes to measure for each construct may be facilitated by consulting literature reviews of past studies that addressed similar topics, requesting advice from peers and experts, and discussing the issues and objectives with the sponsoring client.

Choosing the Mode of Data Collection

Another important TQF consideration is deciding upon the mode or modes that will be used to gather data for a qualitative research study. There are often several modes to choose from for a given qualitative research study, and they are listed here in the order in which they were first used by social and marketing science researchers: (a) in person (also called "face-to-face"), (b) traditional mail, (c) landline telephone, (d) email, (e) Internet from a desktop or laptop, and (f) mobile, including smartphones and tablets. Past research has documented that different modes can be associated with how people respond, which in turn can contribute to lower- or higher-quality data being gathered (Kreuter, Presser, & Tourangeau, 2008). For example, **social desirability** (i.e., the interviewee responding to the interviewer's questions in a way that paints him/herself in the best possible light) as a form of bias in a qualitative study may be less likely in a telephone IDI because it relieves some of the social pressure an interviewee may experience in a face-to-face IDI. And researchers such as Gibson (2010) have shown that this form of bias, when someone is revealing sensitive information, may be less likely in an online IDI (when a webcam is not utilized) compared to a face-to-face interview because there is no interviewer visibly present at the time the participant is responding to the questions being asked.

Because mode can affect data quality, the choices a researcher makes about which mode(s) to use for a particular qualitative study is not merely a choice of which mode is most convenient (e.g., the least expensive one or the one that requires the fewest logistics). Instead, when designing their qualitative studies, qualitative researchers should think as carefully about the mode of data collection as they do the other key TQF factors discussed in this chapter.

Operationalizing the Constructs and Attributes in the Form of a Data Collection Tool

After all the constructs and their attributes have been chosen for a qualitative research study, along with the mode, the researcher is ready to think about creating the data collection tool(s) that will be used to gather the research data. Examples of these tools are IDI guides, focus group discussion guides, content analysis coding forms, and ethnography observation grids. Not all qualitative research studies will use tools such as these, but for those studies that do, the creation of the data collection tool is a very important stage of the research preparation process. Depending on the particular objectives of a study, attention needs to be given to how the constructs and attributes will be measured in terms of both the substance (e.g., depth and breadth of the topical content covered) and form (e.g., wording, ordering) of the data collection tool.

Following a TQF approach for conducting qualitative research, a data collection tool requires that the tool be vetted in different ways, including having peers review it and provide feedback, and formal pilot-testing of the tool. Throughout the chapters of this book, pilot-testing is discussed as it applies to particular types of qualitative research. It is almost never the case that a tool that is used during data collection is the exact same tool the researcher first devised before pilot-testing. That is, improvements necessary to gaining higher-quality data are essentially always identified during the vetting process.

Evaluating Data Collectors as Sources of Bias and Inconsistency

In all qualitative research there is the potential for data quality to be raised or lowered because of the behavior and even the personal characteristics of the persons who are gathering the data. And, in fact, data collectors are not only gathering data, they are actively helping to create the data they gather. Some researchers may fail to recognize or think about the TQF implications of this reality in which both the member of the target population (e.g., IDI interviewee, focus group participant, element of content, member of a group being observed) who is providing data and the person (e.g., IDI interviewer, group discussion moderator, content analysis coder, ethnographic observer) who is seeking and capturing the data play central roles in its creation. In this way those doing the data collection can unintentionally or intentionally bias findings due to their own personal beliefs, expectations, and/or preferences about the study's outcomes. They also can bias the data they gather due to their personal attributes, including gender, age, race, ethnicity, education, etc. Furthermore, they may perform their data collection tasks in ways that are inconsistent (e.g., if they do not follow the same correct procedures during all the times they are engaged in data collection), which creates variability in the data they gather beyond the natural variability that is part and parcel of the phenomena being studied. These potentialities make it imperative that the researcher reflect upon and report all aspects of data gathering that may have impacted data quality and therefore the study's findings, conclusions, and recommendations.

Qualitative research outcomes will be no better than the quality of the data that are gathered—which, in turn, will be no better than the caliber of the data gatherers who carry out the work. To avoid or at least reduce problems in data gathering, it is critical that researchers pay close and careful attention to the capabilities of the people who are hired to collect the data, the depth of the training they receive, as well as the diligence of the monitoring that is carried out while data are being gathered. All of these issues are very important if the TQF Data Gathering component of Credibility is to produce high-quality data.

Evaluating Participants as Sources of Bias and Inconsistency

The TQF makes explicit that those individuals (including ones who are part of groups, as in the group discussion method and ethnography) who are being studied in qualitative research are also potential sources of bias and inconsistency in the resulting data. This may happen because participants are not always able to provide complete and accurate information about what is being asked and/or they may not be willing to do so. For example, if the interviewer in an IDI study does a poor job of developing rapport with an interviewee, the interviewee may not provide as complete information about what is being asked as when an interviewer spends more time developing better rapport with the participant. Or, if the interviewee in an IDI study does not fully trust the interviewer and researcher to keep the information completely confidential, the interviewee may actively censor part or all of what he/she tells the interviewer—leaving out details that may be very important to the research objectives but which the interviewee considers too private to disclose. Or, in a focus group study, a participant may want to impress one of the other participants by embellishing a comment in order to appear extremely knowledgeable, experienced, or important.

These are just a few examples of why the information a participant provides in a qualitative research study may be incomplete and/or inaccurate. From a TQF perspective, the prudent qualitative researcher anticipates these human proclivities and takes them into account as the data are being gathered (and later as the data are being analyzed). Throughout the book we address various approaches that researchers should consider implementing to try to reduce the damage that can be done to a qualitative study by participants who are unable and/or unwilling to provide complete and honest data.

Summary of Data Gathering Issues and the TQF

As depicted in the Credibility segment of Figure 2.1, Data Gathering–related issues include all those aspects of a research study that affect the quality of the data that are gathered from or about the members of the population being studied. As with Scope-related issues, there are many aspects related to Data Gathering that should be considered, as opposed to being ignored, as a researcher designs and implements a qualitative study. In identifying these aspects, as we have done above, the TQF approach to qualitative research encourages investigators to seek the best possible solutions within the context of the resources available to conduct a study. As we stated with respect to Scope, we believe it is preferable for a researcher to comprehend the many potential Data Gathering limitations of the study and to acknowledge them in the analysis process, as well as disclosing them in the final research documents.

Analyzability

As shown in Figure 2.1, the Analyzability component of the TQF is dependent on the Credibility component. The old adage GIGO (garbage in, garbage out) certainly applies to qualitative research. Without high-quality data to analyze, a qualitative research study is unlikely to yield valid and useful results. But having high-quality data is only a necessary condition, not a sufficient one, for a research study to attain high quality. That is, unless qualitative researchers also process and then analyze their data completely and accurately, they will not likely produce valid and useful findings. In the TQF, the Analyzability component comprises **Processing** and **Verification**.

Processing

Moving from Preliminary Data to Final Data

Once all the data for a qualitative study have been created and gathered, they are rarely ready to be analyzed without further analytic work of some nature being done. At this stage the researcher is working with what some call "**preliminary data**" from a collective **dataset** that most often must be processed in any number of ways before the analyses (i.e., the "sense making" in which the researcher will engage) can begin. There are several reasons why this processing may be necessary, including that the preliminary data (a) may be captured and stored in the wrong format for analytic purposes (e.g., the need to convert audio to text), (b) there may be errors in the dataset that need to be corrected (e.g., the moderator of an online discussion may incorrectly tag participants' responses), (c) there may be data that are missing (e.g., gaps in the audio recording of a focus group), and/or (d) some of the data may need to be subjected to other transformation processes that will enrich the researcher's ability to find meaning during the interpretation phase.

CHANGING THE FORMAT OF DATA. Take the example of data that might be created during a series of IDIs. Granted, in a small study with only a small number of brief IDIs, these data could simply be in the form of notes taken during the IDI by the interviewer, which may require the researcher to do little, if anything, to transform them into another format before going straight to making sense of them. However, in the vast majority of IDI studies, the output from the interviewing process—the lengthy back-and-forth question-and-answer conversation between the interviewer and interviewee—would be captured in an audio recording. It is these verbatim recordings that serve as the preliminary data in most IDI studies, as well as in the face-to-face group discussion method where audio and sometimes video recordings are made of the discussions. Before the researcher begins to analyze these recordings, a process of **transcription** typically needs to take place, which, at a minimum, would provide a verbatim transcript of each IDI or focus group. In ethnography, transcriptions need to be created from observers' field notes and observation grids in addition to any audio and/or video recordings that may have been made.

In creating transcriptions, however, the researcher needs to guard against errors that may enter the dataset due to mistakes made during the transcription process. A TQF approach to this transcription process would devote resources to monitoring the quality of the transcripts that are created. To this end, ideally the transcriptionist should be someone whose priorities are accuracy and thoroughness, as well as someone who is:

- Knowledgeable about the subject category.
- Trained and experienced in the specific research topic.
- Sensitive to how people speak in conversation (e.g., can detect a complete from an incomplete thought).
- Trained in how to account for portions of a recording that may be difficult to hear.
- Comfortable with the cultural and regional variations in the language(s) in which the participants and data collectors are speaking.
- Experienced in the group discussion method and pays particular attention to group interaction and dynamics.
- Trained in transcribing observers' field notes and observation grids. Ideally, the transcriber would be an observer.

A researcher can save money on transcription costs by not employing as high a caliber transcriptionist as is recommended by the TQF, but in doing so, the researcher may be jeopardizing the entire study by undermining the quality of the final data that are to be analyzed if lower-quality transcriptions are produced. Maintaining very high standards in the data collection phase does the researcher little good unless the transcribed data are also of very high quality, as those transcriptions become the data that will be analyzed.

Another example of changing the format of the preliminary data comes from a qualitative study that uses content analysis as its data collection method. In such a study, the individuals coding the sampled elements of content are creating the data that will be analyzed. In many content analysis studies that utilize human coders (i.e., without the assistance of computer software), the coding is done using a codebook and coding form (discussed in Chapter 6) that standardize and annotate the specific data elements for which coding decisions are made. For example, in a study of the political orientation of newspaper editorials, the coder may need to decide the extent to which the entire editorial section leans liberal or conservative and therefore will need to be well trained/instructed in how to make that coding decision. These data will need to be transferred into a format (e.g., a data display created in an Excel file) that the researcher will use to conduct the analyses. Errors can occur during this transfer process, against which the researcher must guard.

These examples illustrate the fact that it is commonplace in qualitative research for the preliminary data to need to be "massaged" into another format that is more usable for those who will be trying to make sense of what was learned in the study.

IDENTIFYING AND CORRECTING ERRORS IN THE PRELIMINARY DATA. It is essentially never the case that the original data, gathered and created in any type of research study (be it qualitative or quantitative in nature), are error free. People who gather data (e.g., interviewers, observers, coders) are fallible and may make mistakes for various reasons, such as fatigue, poor training, and inattention. The TQF approach alerts a researcher to recognize and act on the implications associated with the limitations of human participation in data collection.

To this end, a qualitative researcher should develop various techniques to check on the accuracy of the data that are initially gathered and decide if and how to remedy the errors that are found. The researcher, for example, might look for instances of internally inconsistent data elements from the same participant, when none should exist, or irrelevant data from a participant that should not have been gathered, or a moderator's incorrect tagging of content in an online discussion, or missing data from a participant when the data should be present (the TQF issue of missing data is discussed further below). Not every error that is found needs to be fixed, but a researcher using a TQF perspective will think carefully about the number and, particularly, the type of errors that are detected in this early stage of data processing. The researcher then has the responsibility to make an informed and justifiable decision about what, if anything, to correct in the dataset and how to correct it.

For example, the pattern of errors in a qualitative dataset may be infrequent and so small in nature that the researcher may be justified in deciding not to commit the resources needed to find all these errors and fix them (e.g., identifying and purging the occasional recording of observed events that are irrelevant to the research objective). In other cases, the decision may be made to correct the errors; however, the researcher should keep in mind that some errors may be fixable (e.g., retagging online discussion content with the appropriate tags), whereas others may not be amenable to correction (e.g., when the researcher is unable to resolve inconsistencies in the data). Even when such errors cannot be fixed, this stage of data processing nonetheless empowers the researcher with information to consider when sense is being made of the data, as well as what to disclose about data quality when later disseminating findings about the study.

DEALING WITH MISSING DATA IN THE PRELIMINARY DATASET. It may happen that after the data collection stage has been completed in a qualitative research study, the researcher finds that some of the information that was to be gathered from one or more participants is missing. For example, in a focus group study, the moderator may have forgotten to ask participants in one group discussion to address a particular construct of importance—for example, the feeling of isolation among newly diagnosed cancer patients. Or, in a content analysis, a coder may have failed to code an attribute in an element of the content that should have been coded.

In these cases, and following from a TQF perspective, the researcher has the responsibility to actively decide whether or not to go back and gather the missing data in instances where that is possible. Regardless of what decision the researcher makes about these potential problems that are discovered during the data processing stage, the TQF perspective specifies that the researcher should keep these issues in mind when the analyses and interpretations of the findings are conducted and when the findings and recommendations are disseminated.

OTHER DATA-PROCESSING TRANSFORMATIONS. One of the most intellectually creative aspects of what a qualitative researcher may do is to create something of value in the data that goes beyond what is provided in the preliminary dataset. In other words, the various elements of the preliminary data may be combinable in ways that provide research value exceeding the mere sum of their parts.

Take, for example, an IDI study of patients who have recently received treatment for prostate cancer at a university hospital. In this study, patients' satisfaction with the medical staff would be measured by asking several satisfaction-related questions about each staff member with whom the interviewee had close contact. Using interviewees' responses to each satisfaction question (including all the contextual cues that give meaning to the response) for each staff member, the researcher could create a kind of "qualitative satisfaction barometer" of staff members for each interviewee. From this, the researcher might create an "interviewee-specific qualitative satisfaction data element" associated with all physicians discussed in the IDI, all nurses, all technicians, and all administrative staff. In this way the original database that comprises what was directly gathered from the interviewees would be supplemented (and enriched) by the researcher's creation of new data elements before the formal analysis stage began. From a TQF perspective, whenever researchers create new data elements, they need to document what was done and provide rigorous justification for why this action was valid and useful.

SUMMARY OF PROCESSING ACTIVITIES RELATED TO PRELIMINARY DATA. As noted above, there are many TQF considerations that we advise qualitative researchers to explicitly and carefully consider when they are processing preliminary data to ensure that the data are ready to be analyzed. Taking a TQF approach to qualitative research does not require that all these approaches be used, but it does require that a qualitative researcher give explicit consideration to whether or not a particular data processing technique should be used. As part of this, the researcher should document and later disclose why the chosen data processing methods were used and why the ones not used were rejected.

The Analysis of Qualitative Data: Making Sense of the Final Dataset

Once the preliminary data have been thoroughly scrutinized and transformed, as necessary, into the final dataset, the researcher is ready to make sense of the information and draw relevant interpretations that further the research objective(s) and ultimately maximize the usefulness of the outcomes. The basic analytical steps that generally apply across the five qualitative research approaches discussed in this book are[3]:

- **Selecting the unit of analysis.** The **unit of analysis** is the basis by which codes will be developed that will then be used by the researcher to identify meaningful categories and themes. This unit might be a specific subject area discussed in an IDI or focus group, or activity observed within a certain timeframe, or a complete narrative.

- **Developing unique codes.** Code development requires careful scrutiny of the data (by way of the unit of analysis), with particular attention paid to the context of the thoughts conveyed. Each code should be explicit in its meaning (e.g., a code for some aspect of quality, such as "freshness," rather than just a code for "quality") and unique from the other codes. A codebook should be created that delineates the codes, their definitions, and includes examples of the decision-making processes used in coding. This codebook is particularly useful in content analysis (see Chapter 6) when the volume of text material may be especially large. Code development is usually iterative, with new codes added or existing codes altered as deemed appropriate, throughout the coding process.

- **Coding.** Coding the data should, from a TQF perspective, involve a preliminary step that allows the researcher to "test" the developed codes in terms of relevance and completeness. As in code development, particular attention needs to be paid to the context—at both the manifest and the latent levels—of the coded content (e.g., as discussed more fully in Chapter 6). A TQF approach to coding requires two or more coders who periodically recode each other's content in order to contrast and compare the consistency of coding (between each other or by way of the principal researcher) and resolve discrepancies if they exist. In this way, the researcher has achieved intercoder reliability.

- **Identifying categories.** The researcher looks at the coded dataset and derives meaningful categories of content. It is from these categories that the researcher can then look for themes or patterns across the data. A **category** is typically any group of codes that share an underlying construct. For example, data from a food-related study that is coded "fresh/freshness" and data coded as "organic" might be included in a category labeled "natural" or "health conscious." As in code development and coding, the identification of categories necessitates sensitivity to manifest and latent context of the content. In the group discussion method, this part of the process requires particular attention to group interactions and the influencing factors that may exist among participants' comments (e.g., an exchange between two people resulting in a change of attitude by one of them). A few researchers have discussed ways to analyze data from group discussions taking into account the interactive, dynamic environment (see p. 117).

- **Identifying themes or patterns.** By looking at the coding overall as well as the categories identified from the coding, the researcher can identify **themes** or patterns in the data that reveal the essence of the outcomes. This identification process is made easier by way of visual displays, such as Excel worksheets, or visual maps such as Schilling's (2006) "concept map," created in PowerPoint. The identification of themes and patterns may be facilitated by the ability of **computer-assisted qualitative data analysis software (CAQDAS)** to organize, label, and visually represent categories. An example of this is a visual display shown on page 250.

- **Drawing interpretations and implications from the data.** The ability to draw meaningful interpretations and implications from the data requires incorporating the coded data—that have been categorized and by which themes and patterns have emerged—as well as any number of ancillary materials, such as reflexive journals, coders' coding forms with their notes and comments, supporting documents that online discussion participants may have shared, and the like.

Verification

In the last stage of processing qualitative data, when interpretations and implications are being drawn from the findings, a researcher that is using a TQF approach will enter into a formal stage of Verification. The researcher should actually consider the preliminary interpretations derived from the last stage of processing as the starting point from which to look outside the data and consider other sources. Not unlike the techniques proposed by Lincoln and Guba (1985), the primary means advocated by the TQF to verify the findings of a qualitative study include (a) engaging in peer debriefings, (b) creating reflexive journals, (c) utilizing triangulation, (d) identifying deviant cases, and, to a lesser degree, (e) engaging in member checking. Although not all of these techniques are appropriate for all qualitative methods (e.g., member checking is irrelevant in content analysis), the researcher is encouraged to utilize as many of these as applicable in order to effectively judge the preliminary interpretations of the data and provide a more enlightened perspective of the final outcomes.

As stated throughout this book, it is not a primary purpose of the Verification phase of the TQF Analyzability component to seek alternative data or information that *necessarily* agrees with the researcher's preliminary interpretations. Rather, the researcher is mostly looking for evidence that supports or contradicts early explanations of the findings to provide a rich, meaningful analysis. The verification techniques and results from the process should be fully accounted for and discussed in conjunction with the analysis in the final study documents.

Peer Debriefings

A **peer debriefing** is an effective technique for revealing possible biases and/or errors in the data gathering and analysis that may have introduced inaccuracies into the data or led to faulty/weak preliminary interpretations of the outcomes. This approach to verifying the researcher's findings and interpretations in a qualitative study relies on the use of at least one impartial peer who (a) has known expertise in the method and in the subject area the researcher has focused upon; (b) is known to be objective, rigorous, and willing to exhibit complete candor in providing feedback to the researcher; and (c) is knowledgeable about the TQF approach and is able to conduct the review considering TQF quality issues. This independent peer review and feedback should cover all aspects of the research, including the procedures deployed to gather and analyze the data as well as the validity of the researcher's interpretations and implications. Ideally this feedback is provided in both written and oral form so that the researcher has the necessary documentation on the review for insertion into the final report as well as the opportunity to consider and discuss the feedback with the peer.

Reflexive Journal

A **reflexive journal**, also called by some a "reflective" journal, is a written document that is kept by the researcher and possibly by others involved in conducting the research (e.g., coders during the coding process, interviewers during a series of IDIs, observers during an ethnography). The reflexive journal is an invaluable resource that the researcher can use to review and judge the quality of the data-gathering process as well as the soundness of his/her interpretations during the analysis phase. Making entries in a reflexive journal also provides the researcher with details about what actually happened during the study that may later be useful in defending the study (e.g., to his/her dissertation committee, journal editors, clients). For this reason, it is better to err in the direction of capturing too much detail in a reflexive journal than too little detail.

Figure 2.2 shows an example of a reflexive journal format, highlighting the kinds of questions or issues the researcher should reflect on throughout the research process. The format of the journal is meant to be flexible and is typically informal, often written in a stream-of-consciousness-like style to capture the researcher's personal thoughts during the field period (i.e., while interviewing, moderating, observing), and includes accounts of what went "right" and what went "wrong" in conducting the study, and how the researcher may have impacted the outcomes. Also included in the reflexive journal should be a record of the decisions the researcher made during the course of the study that were not anticipated or were modified from the original design of the research. Ideally, the researcher will update his/her reflexive journal on a daily basis or after each research event (i.e., each IDI, focus group, observation), or, at the very least, weekly.

Triangulation

Triangulation, or the use of multiple sources in qualitative research, is an important technique that enables the researcher to validate research findings. By contrasting and comparing the data with other sources, the researcher enriches the analyses with supporting and/or contradictory information that ultimately gives the researcher and users of the research a deeper understanding than relying on the study data alone. Three of the four different types of triangulation discussed by Lincoln and Guba (1985)—data sources, methods, and investigators—are mentioned most frequently in this book. *Data triangulation* involves comparing the research data to that from another data source—for example, the outcomes from an IDI study with teachers compared to interviews conducted with school principals. In *method triangulation*, the researcher considers the study data in conjunction with data obtained by way of a different method. Method triangulation is built into qualitative research approaches such as ethnography and case study research, where multiple methods are part and parcel of these research designs. *Investigator triangulation* is a process by which members of the research team independently conduct aspects of the data collection and/or analysis phases and compare their results—for example, the data from focus group discussions conducted by one moderator is compared to discussions in the same study conducted by another moderator, or intercoder verification is used to compare coding between coders.

Deviant Cases

The technique of using **deviant cases** to verify the findings and interpretations in qualitative research is referred to by some scholars (e.g., Creswell, 2013; Lincoln & Guba, 1985) as "negative case analysis." It is based on the view that by actively

EXAMPLE OF JOURNAL FORMAT

Study name/designation _____ Date _____

Location _____ Time _____

Participant or group name/designation _____

Broad Takeaways from the IDI, Group Discussion, or Observation

What do I think I "know" from this/these participant(s)?

How do I think I "know" it?

At what point in the IDI, discussion, or observation did I arrive at that knowledge?

Does this knowledge change or support my earlier assumptions or beliefs?

Will this knowledge change the course of the research, in terms of objectives, methods, line of inquiry; and, if so, how?

Specific Reflections on the IDI, Group Discussion, or Observation Experience

Assumptions
What assumptions did I make (what did I assume to be true) about the participant(s)?

What assumptions did I make about comments/responses to my questions?

How did these assumptions affect or shape the questions I asked, the interjections I made, my listening skills, and/or my behavior?

Values, beliefs, life story, social/economic status
How did my personal values, beliefs, life story, and/or social/economic status affect or shape the questions I asked, the interjections I made, my listening skills, and/or my behavior?

Emotional connection with the participant(s)
To what degree did my emotions or feelings for the participant(s) affect or shape the questions I asked, the interjections I made, my listening skills, and/or my behavior?

How will my emotions or feelings for the participant(s) affect the analytical process and my ability to draw valid interpretations from the data?

Physical environment and logistics
How did the physical setting/location of the research event alter how I related to the participant(s), and vice versa?

How did the physical setting/location impact data collection?

What were the logistical issues (e.g., in gaining access) that contributed to the "success" or weakness of the outcomes?

FIGURE 2.2. Reflexive journal.

seeking instances in the data that contradict or otherwise conflict with the prevailing evidence, the researcher has gone further in explaining the outcomes as well as contributed divergent ways to think about the data, leading to additional food for thought. By identifying and investigating these "outliers," the researcher may, for instance, pursue a new line of analysis. This is the case in the example given in Chapter 5 (see p. 218), where observations of mothers performing atypical behavior gave the observer a different point of view that led to exploring other factors that might explain a key observation (i.e., mothers placing infants back in the crib). In this way, deviant cases that cannot be explained by the study's findings compel the researcher to develop an understanding about why this is so and to better understand the limits of the research data and his/her final interpretations.

Deviant case analysis is especially of value when the researcher is conducting interim analyses as data are being gathered. As deviant cases are found in those interim analyses—ones that run contrary to the general pattern of interim findings—the researcher can use the lessons from these cases to possibly revise the analytic approach and even to refine the methods used to gather the data (cf. Pope, Ziebland, & Mays, 2000).

Member Checking

Member checking, or "member checks," is the technique used by some qualitative researchers to confirm the research findings and interpretations with some (or possibly all) of the actual study participants. Although Lincoln and Guba (1985) stated that member checks "is the most crucial technique for establishing credibility" (p. 314), we concur with other researchers (e.g., Kvale, 2006; Morse et al., 2002) that asking participants whether they agree with the researcher's findings may often be both unrealistic (e.g., it relies on participants' memory recall) and unproductive (e.g., a participant may insist that the researcher change his/her response because of a "change of heart" since the original interview). As a result of the latter, "investigators who want to be responsive to the particular concerns of their participants may be forced to restrain their results to a more descriptive level in order to address participants' individual concerns" (Morse et al., 2002, p. 16).

For these reasons we generally do not endorse the value of member checks. There is, however, a form of member checking that we fully endorse and believe is an essential technique in the verification process. This form utilizes a **question–answer validity** process, by which the IDI interviewer or focus group moderator engages in real-time paraphrasing of interviewees' or participants' comments to confirm or clarify the intended meaning. This is a critical skill of all interviewers and moderators who want to ensure that, *during the data-gathering phase*, they are correctly interpreting the comments that are being made. If, for example, a focus group moderator asks, "What is the customer service like at Walmart?" and a participant responds, "The customer service at my local Walmart is poor during the holiday season," the moderator might clarify this answer by asking, "The customer service at your local Walmart is poor *only* during the holiday season or is it poor all year long *including* the holiday season?"

A final comment about Analyzability is that by using multiple approaches to verifying analyses, a qualitative researcher develops more confidence in deciding what should be the study's findings and interpretations. Taking a multipronged approach to the verification of a researcher's interpretations of the data is highly consistent with a TQF approach to qualitative research.

Transparency

Within the TQF, the Transparency component (see Figure 2.1) concerns completeness and disclosure in the final documentation that researchers create about a qualitative research study. This component requires detailed attention not only to the findings and recommendations of the study, but to all aspects related to the Credibility and Analyzability components of the TQF. The principal means for accomplishing this requirement is for qualitative researchers to use thick description, including rich (i.e., abundant and thorough) details, which among other benefits, will allow a consumer of the study to better determine the applicability—that is, the **transferability**—of the study's methods, findings, and recommendations to other arenas.

Thick Description

A **thick description** that uses rich details of the phenomena being studied in qualitative research includes not only a factual description, but also a clear and detailed description of the context within which the phenomena were occurring. In theory, this thick description allows someone external to the research team (e.g., a reader of the final research report) to gain a more meaningful understanding of the phenomena the study has investigated. A good example can be found in ethnography where thick description pertains primarily to the detailed portrait of the cultural or social "scene" that the observer takes away from an observation site providing detailed accounts that are at the center of what it means to conduct ethnographic research (see Chapter 5, p. 219). Geertz (2003) talks about the "multiplicity of complex conceptual structures" (p. 150) in ethnographic research and, for this reason, declares that "ethnography *is* thick description" (p. 156, emphasis added).

Ponterotto's (2006) "working definition" of thick description includes the notion of what a qualitative researcher does when creating such a description and the impact it has on the users of the research. It reads in part:

> Thick description captures the thoughts and feelings of participants as well as the often complex web of relationships among them. Thick description leads to thick interpretation, which in turn leads to thick meaning of the research findings for the researchers and participants themselves, and for the report's intended readership. Thick meaning of findings leads readers to a sense of verisimilitude, wherein they can cognitively and emotively "place" themselves within the research context. (p. 543)

When written by a skilled qualitative researcher, a thick description not only helps the consumer of the research better understand the "essential elements" of the study (Ponterotto, 2006, p. 547), but also empowers the consumer to (a) decide whether he/she would have reached the same or similar interpretations from the study data as did the researcher, and (b) evaluate the transferability of the research to other contexts.

A qualitative researcher who adopts the TQF perspective will expend the necessary time and effort to include thick descriptions related to data collection and analysis as well as thick interpretations of the findings in the final documentation of the study. To this end, the final document should create an audit trail by way of including all relevant materials, such as reflexive journal(s), transcripts, field notes, and the codebook.

Usefulness

As shown in Figure 2.1, the final component of the TQF is Usefulness, by which we mean the extent to which the data collection methods, the findings, interpretations, and recommendations of a qualitative research study provide value not only to the researchers and their sponsors but also to other users of the research, such as researchers working in comparable fields or students investigating the research topic for the first time. Assessing the usefulness of a study answers the overarching question, "What can and should be done with the study now that it has been completed?" This may lead to a number of more specific questions that relate to usefulness. For example: Has the study confirmed or refuted important hypotheses? Has the study identified important knowledge gaps that future research should try to help close? Has the study offered recommendations for action that are worthy of further testing or worthy of actionable next steps? Has the study demonstrated the value of using new or refined methods for gathering qualitative data? Has the study demonstrated new or refined methods for analyzing qualitative data?

In a series of more than 10 unpublished (proprietary) studies conducted by the second author in the 1980s with several of his graduate journalism classes, content analysis and IDIs were used to assess the issue of whether or not the mix of content in various medium and large daily newspapers was "a good one." In each study, the content analysis helped document for the newspapers' executives the extent to which certain kinds of news were covered heavily or lightly and given higher or lower prominence by where stories were placed in the pages of the papers. The IDIs were conducted with all the editors of the newspapers and assessed the editors' descriptive estimates of the news mix in their respective papers, the prominence of placement for different types of news stories, and the editors' views of the "ideal" news mix for their communities. The findings across the various studies were quite similar and showed the newspapers' executives that their respective editors did not have a very accurate understanding of the actual news mix in their newspaper and that the actual news mix did not generally correspond with the editors' visions of what the ideal mix of news should be. These studies provided useful information to the newspaper executives because of the rigor with which the data were gathered and analyzed and because the publishers and other senior executives could then use the results with confidence to deliberate whether the findings should be acted upon. The usefulness of these studies would have reached even greater potential if the proprietary nature of the research had not disallowed its publication for dissemination to scholars.

For qualitative researchers who use a TQF approach, it is recommended that a specific section in the study's final written documentation be included on "Usefulness of the Study," in which the researchers articulate and justify their views on how the study should be interpreted, acted upon, or applied in other research contexts and in the "real world." Doing so will help consumers of the research consider the ways in which the researchers themselves think others should consider the study's output. Of course, the consumers of the study may not agree with what the researchers suggest about usefulness, but, from a TQF perspective, expecting researchers to add such a section will hold them more accountable to all who may come across their study. Although we agree that knowledge is "good," in and of itself, we also believe strongly that qualitative researchers who generate knowledge have a responsibility to also suggest how that knowledge can and should be applied.

2.4 APPLYING THE TOTAL QUALITY FRAMEWORK

As the chapters in this book document in detail, there are many important ways we believe the TQF should be applied. These include (a) when the researchers themselves are conceptualizing and planning their study, (b) throughout the time the study is being conducted, and (c) during a self-evaluation process in which all qualitative researchers should engage soon after their study is completed.

However, there are many additional ways to apply the TQF, as discussed in Chapter 8. These include when (a) writing a proposal; (b) doing a critical literature review; and (c) evaluating a proposal, journal article, chapter, or book manuscript. By embracing a TQF perspective, we believe that qualitative researchers will raise the quality and therefore the usefulness of the research they conduct, and that this improvement in quality does not necessarily require appreciably more funding to support the research. As importantly, we believe the use of the TQF will provide qualitative research a means by which to raise the prominence of its utility to society by providing a more important basis for decision makers to be able to place more confidence in applying its findings and recommendations.

2.5 CHAPTER SUMMARY

✓ The field of qualitative research has paid considerable attention in the past half century to the issue of research "quality." Despite these efforts, there remains a lack of agreement among qualitative researchers about how quality should be defined and how it should be evaluated.

✓ The TQF provides (1) a comprehensive approach to qualitative researchers for designing, conducting, and interpreting their studies so that the studies are more likely to (a) gather high-quality data, (b) lead to valid interpretations of the data, and (c) generate highly useful outcomes; and (2) a critical guide for anyone "consuming" the final documents of a qualitative research study to help them (a) evaluate the extent to which a study's findings and recommendations are worth considering when making decisions related to the research objective and (b) determine if and how the study can be applied (i.e., transferred) to another research context.

✓ The TQF has four major interrelated components: Credibility, Analyzability, Transparency, and Usefulness.

✓ *Credibility* comprises *Scope*, which addresses how well the participants and/or documents from which data were gathered accurately reflect the population the study is meant to represent, and *Data Gathering*, which addresses the extent to which the data that were gathered fully and accurately reflect the constructs the study purports to have studied.

✓ *Analyzability* comprises *Processing*, which addresses how accurately the study's preliminary data are transformed into the final dataset to be analyzed, and the accuracy of the sense making based on the analyses carried out with the final dataset. Analyzability also requires *Verification*, which addresses the approaches a qualitative researcher uses to rigorously evaluate the initial conclusions and recommendations before finalizing and disseminating them, including the use of peer debriefings, reflexive journals, triangulation, deviant cases, and member checking.

✓ *Transparency* encompasses the use of thick description, including rich (i.e., abundant and thorough) detail, to describe all aspects of a qualitative study so that others can readily and accurately understand what was done to gather the study's data, how the researcher made sense of the data, and whether aspects of the study might be transferred in order to conduct similar research in other contexts or situations (i.e., the transferability of the study).

✓ *Usefulness* is the ultimate goal of qualitative research and concerns the extent to which a study provides value to the sponsors of the research and to other users, including practitioners and researchers who are implementing and/or investigating the same or similar topics.

✓ In addition to guiding the conceptualization, implementation, and interpretation of a qualitative research study, the TQF can and should be applied by (1) consumers of research to help them decide upon the value and usefulness of the study's design elements and/or findings and recommendations to their own interests and needs; (2) those who write requests for proposals (RFPs) to help clearly structure the expectations conveyed; (3) those who respond to RFPs to help clearly structure and defend their comprehensive proposals; and (4) anyone writing, or anyone reviewing anything written about, a qualitative research study, including a thesis or dissertation proposal, thesis or dissertation, technical report, conference paper, journal article, etc.

SUGGESTED FURTHER READING

Armour, M., Rivaux, S. L., & Bell, H. (2009). Using context to build rigor: Application to two hermeneutic phenomenological studies. *Qualitative Social Work, 8*(1), 101–122.

This article provides examples of two studies oriented around a particular paradigm (hermeneutic phenomenology) that examine the relationship between rigor and context. Specifically, these examples look at how methods and procedures were adjusted, based on the individual research contexts, to enhance the overall rigor of the research.

Lather, P. (2004). Critical inquiry in qualitative research: Feminist and poststructural perspectives: Science "after truth." In K. DeMarrais & S. D. Lapan (Eds.), *Foundations for research: Methods of inquiry in education and the social sciences* (pp. 203–215). Mahwah, NJ: Erlbaum.

This book chapter presents a compelling assessment of the critical theory paradigm from a feminist research perspective. The author discusses the methodological issues as well as research design considerations in conducting a qualitative critical inquiry, including the highly interactive and flexible approach, and the focus on finding "meaning to broader structures of social power" (p. 209) associated with a critical theory orientation.

Lincoln, Y. S., Lynham, S. A., & Guba, E. G. (2011). Paradigmatic controversies, contradictions, and emerging confluences, revisited. In N. K. Denzin & Y. S. Lincoln (Eds.), *The Sage handbook of qualitative research* (pp. 97–128). Thousand Oaks, CA: Sage.

This chapter provides a thorough overview of the current thinking regarding the paradigm debates, including an updated table from an earlier Guba and Lincoln chapter (1994) detailing the basic paradigm beliefs and corresponding positions on various issues. This chapter is a very useful source for learning about the fundamental as well as nuanced aspects of paradigms in qualitative research, and as important, this chapter serves to bring the reader up-to-date on the evolution of Lincoln and Guba's own thinking since their seminal work in 1985 concerning research criteria.

Miles, M. B., Huberman, A. M., & Saldaña, J. (2014). *Qualitative data analysis: A methods sourcebook*. Thousand Oaks, CA: Sage.

This is an updated version of a classic text in qualitative research that continues to advocate for improved analytical procedures and greater transparency. As in earlier editions, this book emphasizes the important point that research documentation (i.e., the final report) typically says "very little on how conclusions were drawn" (p. 316).

Morse, J. M., Barrett, M., Mayan, M., Olson, K., & Spiers, J. (2002). Verification strategies for establishing reliability and validity in qualitative research. *International Journal of Qualitative Methods, 1*(2), 13–22.

These authors provide a good discussion of the constructs of reliability and validity, arguing for their appropriateness across all paradigms, as well as the use of verification strategies. Specifically, the authors advocate for the utilization of verification strategies to manage reliability and validity throughout the research process rather than as post-hoc analytical procedures.

Reynolds, J., Kizito, J., Ezumah, N., Mangesho, P., Allen, E., & Chandler, C. (2011). Quality assurance of qualitative research: A review of the discourse. *Health Research Policy and Systems, 9*(1), 43.

This article provides a good overview, by way of a meta-analysis, on how quality is defined and discussed in the qualitative research literature. The authors' analysis derived two common "narratives" associated with the treatment of quality among the studies examined: (1) quality as determined by indicators in the research outcomes and (2) quality built into the process itself.

NOTES

1. For example, a TQF approach would not be appropriate in critical theory research where researchers are often driven by their own values or belief systems to effect social change. This type of research is highly collaborative, with researchers becoming involved with the participants, encouraging interaction and the formation of networks, and, in some instances, promoting activism. Creswell (2013) discusses critical theory and other forms of research (e.g., feminist research and queer theory) that address marginalized social groups to challenge the status quo.

2. By "construct" we refer to the topics that are being studied and thus measured in qualitative research. In some cases these are narrow and very precise and in others quite broad, multifaceted, and may even be ambiguous.

3. The reader is referred to the individual chapters (Chapters 3–7) for more detailed discussions, including examples of the steps outlined here.

CHAPTER THREE

Interview Method
In-Depth Interviews

CHAPTER PREVIEW

In-depth interviewing (IDI) is central to qualitative research in that it provides what all qualitative inquiry seeks: that is, a deep understanding of what people are doing and thinking, and why. This chapter reviews the basic steps in planning, conducting, and interpreting an IDI study. It explains that IDIs can be structured, semistructured, or unstructured, but the chapter focuses mainly on the semistructured approach. IDIs are conducted via four modes (in person, telephone, email, and mobile), and the main strengths and limitations of each mode are discussed. The role of the interviewer is critical to the success of the IDI approach; for this reason, a discussion of the necessary interviewer skills is interwoven throughout the chapter. From the perspective of the Total Quality Framework (TQF), the chapter addresses many key aspects of the IDI method that should be considered to ensure the credibility, analyzability, transparency, and ultimate useful-ness (value) of the research. For instance, interviewers need the ability to build close, positive rapport with interviewees without biasing the data that are gathered or causing unwarranted inconsistency in the data. Other important topics, also discussed in Chapter 2, include (1) the importance of adequately pilot-testing the interviewing guide, (2) how to determine the "correct" number of interviews to complete, (3) having all interviewers keep a reflexive journal, and (4) the specific transcription and verification procedures that should be followed.

3.1 INTRODUCTION

Interviewing is central to most qualitative research designs. Either as the sole method of data collection or as a complementary component to ethnographic or multi-method research, the act of interviewing some segment of the population under study is essential. **In-depth interviews** (or "**IDIs**") hold a unique position within the cadre of qualitative research methods. An IDI approach goes to the heart of a principal objective of qualitative research; that is, to gain a rich, nuanced understanding of the "thinking" (i.e., motivation) that drives behavior and attitude formation or otherwise leads to other consequences of research interest.

The research IDI has been compared to interviewing styles employed outside of qualitative research—such as the interviews used in journalism, psychotherapy, and law enforcement—with the assertion that "there are not necessarily hard-and-fast distinctions between these interview forms" (Brinkmann & Kvale, 2015, p. 4). It is true that there are no "hard-and-fast" rules that distinguish qualitative research IDIs from the interviews conducted by journalists, psychologists, and criminal investigators. In every case, the IDI consists of an interviewer who enters into a one-on-one dialogue with an interviewee in order to discover some aspect of personal information about and from the interviewee. The interviewer is typically in control of the questions that are asked and, when the interviews are completed, the information is analyzed in order to create a story or narrative that conveys an understanding of some topic of interest. Whether it is an interview with a cancer survivor in a qualitative IDI study, the new city mayor for the local newspaper, a psychotherapist's request for more details related to the patient's mood disorder, or a police detective's interrogation of a crime suspect, the IDI approach is "the method by which the personal is made public" (Denzin, 2001, p. 28) to the researcher and the information is used to convey a story about a person or phenomenon.

The qualitative research IDI does, however, differ from these other forms of interviews in two important aspects: the goals of the interview and the interviewing strategy. Whereas the goal of the journalist is to gather the facts for a news story, and the psychologist's objective is to alleviate an individual's mental suffering, and the police detective interviews witnesses and suspects to eventually gain a confession, the qualitative researcher conducts IDIs to obtain intricate knowledge, from a small number of members in a target population, based on a well-thought-out research design constructed to maximize credible and analyzable outcomes. Research IDIs are ultimately utilized to make changes or improve the lives of the target population as well as other target groups in similar contexts. With divergent interviewing goals, it is no wonder that qualitative researchers employ interviewing strategies that are partially at odds with especially those of the journalist or detective. Unlike these other variations of the IDI, the interview approach in qualitative research is not inherently combative or confrontational and does not purposely create conflict to provoke the interviewee but rather centers on building a trusting relationship where all input is honored and candid revelations can thrive because it is understood that they will remain confidential unless the interviewee permits them to be disclosed.

The interviewer–interviewee relationship is the cornerstone of the research IDI, and the intense and individualistic nature of IDIs in qualitative research makes this one of the most personal of all qualitative research design methods. The length of an IDI can range from 30 minutes to an hour or more and can be conducted in various modes—face-to-face, telephone, online, or mobile device.

This chapter section (3.1) discusses the IDI method in greater detail, including the basic steps and formats of the IDI, appropriate uses of this approach, interviewer skills, and an overview of the strengths and limitations of the method.

Basic Steps in the IDI Method and Interviewing Formats

The basic steps of an IDI design have been discussed by others and are not elaborated here. It is useful, however, to mention the IDI process espoused by a few researchers as a way of reference for the reader. With the exception of Briggs (1986),[1] the various recommended IDI design schemes are fairly similar. Creswell (2013) outlines nine "steps for interviewing":

- Determining the research issues or questions to be addressed.
- Identifying the appropriate interviewees.
- Choosing the interview method and mode (e.g., face-to-face or telephone).
- Determining how the content of interviews will be recorded or otherwise "captured."
- Developing the interview guide.
- Conducting preliminary pilot interviews.
- Selecting an appropriate location in the case of face-to-face interviews.
- Obtaining consent forms from interviewees.
- Using good interviewing techniques.

Rubin and Rubin (2012) and Brinkmann and Kvale (2015) propose variations of a seven-stage IDI design process, with the latter suggesting a plan that begins with "thematizing" (i.e., clarifying the purpose), followed by "designing," "interviewing," "transcribing," "analyzing," "verifying," and "reporting."

The design of the interview itself can take three formats: *structured, semistructured*, and *unstructured*. The **structured IDI** is relatively formal and rigid, with the interviewer asking an explicit set of questions as written and in the prescribed order. It is this rigid, inflexible aspect of structured interviews that makes this format more comparable to standardized survey interviewing—wherein the researcher has complete control over question wording and sequence, which the interviewer then follows exactly as designed—than a traditional qualitative research interview. For instance, Rogers, Gilbert, and Cabrera (1997) conducted a study concerning automatic teller machines (ATMs) using a "script of questions" that were asked of all interviewees in the same manner and order. In this study, people who use ATMs were always asked, "What transactions do you use the ATM for?" and "Have you had any problems with using an ATM?" Although interviewees were permitted to give lengthy responses, the question–answer format, much like that of a survey interview, did not allow the interviewer to ask follow-up questions for clarification and further understanding.

In contrast, the flexibility inherent in semistructured and unstructured IDI designs encourages an exchange or dialogue (i.e., a real conversation) between the interviewer and interviewee that manifests the personal component that is a unique and important benefit to qualitative research. The **semistructured IDI** format is particularly conversational in nature, with the interviewer referring to an **interview guide** to ensure that the relevant issues are covered, but modifying the questions for each interview as warranted by the particular responses or circumstances of the interviewee. "Responsive interviewing" (Rubin & Rubin, 2012) is a variation of the semistructured format, with the centerpiece being the interviewer–interviewee relationship and the special rapport that is built between them, specifically the ability to form a common bond and "friendship" that "often outlasts the period of the research" (p. 36). In this way, the interviewer attempts to create a "partnership" with the interviewee and conducts an interview that is conversational and tailored to each interviewee based on his/her responses to interview questions.

The third IDI format, the **unstructured IDI,** places the control of the interview with the research participant, enabling this individual to tell his/her personal story concerning the subject matter without interference—beyond **active listening** (e.g., paraphrasing or nodding the head)—from the interviewer. The unstructured format is typically used in narrative and life story research where the emphasis is on allowing the participant to tell his/her story, unfettered by the interviewer's need to keep to a particular agenda. This format can be especially effective when addressing sensitive subject matter and with vulnerable segments of the population. The work of feminist researchers such as Hesse-Biber (2014) provides one example of how the unstructured IDI is used to reveal the inequities impacting women in today's society by allowing women to freely tell their stories (see Box 3.1).

The critical difference between the three IDI formats—structured, semistructured, and unstructured—is the power the interviewer exerts in the interview process, or, put another way, the degree of latitude or flexibility built into the interview process that allows the participant's "voice" to be heard. The predetermined course of the structured IDI makes this the most restrictive of all formats and puts the interviewer squarely in charge of what will and will not be covered in the interview. In contrast, the semistructured interview is a shared experience between the interviewer and interviewee that encourages a back-and-forth dialogue and enables the interviewer to react to the interviewee's comments by changing question wording, changing the order in which questions are asked, interjecting relevant probing questions for clarification, and/or changing the direction of the interview (if only briefly). The unstructured format is the most freewheeling of all, with the interviewer relinquishing control of the interview to the participant, who guides its pace and content. Our discussion of the IDI method in this chapter refers, both implicitly and explicitly, to the semistructured interview format, and the unstructured interview is covered more fully in our discussion of narrative research in Chapter 7.

> ### BOX 3.1. Unstructured In-Depth Interviewing:
> ### Feminist Research and the Unstructured IDI
>
> Feminist research is uniquely interested in the societal issues—inequities and injustices—primarily (but not always) pertaining to women and in giving women a vehicle by which they can express their lived experiences. In her 2014 edited volume, *Feminist Research Practice: A Primer*, Hesse-Biber discusses the feminist orientation to the IDI generally and the unstructured IDI specifically:
>
>> As a feminist interviewer, I am interested in uncovering the *subjugated knowledge* of the diversity of women's realities that often lie hidden and unarticulated. I am asking questions and exploring issues that are of particular concern to women's lives. I am interested in issues of social change and social justice for women. . . .
>>   Interviewing is a particularly valuable research method feminist researchers can use to gain insight into the world of their participants. [In unstructured interviews] I tend to "go with the flow" of the interview, seeing where it takes me . . . I have a *minimum of control* over how the participant should answer the questions. I am often taking the lead from my participants—going where they want to go, but keeping an overall topic in mind. [An IDI concerning a college woman's relationship to food and her body image] might begin with asking her a simple open-ended question such as: Can you tell me about what it's like to be a female at this particular college? (pp. 184–186, emphasis in original)

Appropriate Uses of the IDI Method

The IDI approach has been the research method of choice for various purposes across the social and health care sciences. Compared to group discussions (the other primary interviewing method; see Chapter 4), IDIs enable a thorough examination of a topic unencumbered by social pressure or influence from group members. This freedom to speak candidly has made individual interviews (i.e., IDIs) the preferred method for investigating complex, sensitive, and unexplored topics. Whether it is a study concerning the perceptions and behaviors associated with caring for a spouse with early-onset Alzheimer's disease, environmental hazards, contraception use among urban adolescents, the communication needs among cancer patients, the teaching of children with autism, consumer preference for one product brand over another, or the usability of a company's website, an IDI approach provides the researcher[2] with a distinct opportunity to try to unravel the experiences and thoughts of an individual that led to particular needs, motivations, and behavior.

   IDIs can be particularly effective when the subject matter is sensitive and/or the target population is not easily accessible. This is why, for example, the IDI method is well suited for health and health-care-related issues, such as the attitudes and ways of coping among cancer survivors, patients, and their caregivers.[3] The IDI method is the preferred approach over group discussions (see Chapter 4) for these types of studies, given that (a) people are often more likely to participate in a one-on-one study due to the delicate nature of the research topic (e.g., asking about patients' experiences with cancer treatment); (b) the particular sensitivity required of the researcher with hard-to-reach and/or vulnerable populations (e.g., people who are physically and emotional affected by their cancer treatment); and (c) the need for a "safe" context or environment that fosters a meaningful conversation about the interviewees' personal experiences related to the disease. For these reasons, researchers in the medical field have successfully used the qualitative IDI method to examine not only patients' responses to cancer and its treatments but to a variety of other physical and mental health issues.[4]

The IDI method is also highly relevant to, and widely used in, the social sciences. Researchers in the following, and other social science disciplines, benefit greatly from the one-on-one approach of the IDI research method:

- Education (e.g., to explore school leadership, policy reforms, teaching practices, or minority student issues).

- Psychology (e.g., to understand coping strategies among women who have survived childhood sexual abuse, the emotional effects following a natural disaster, and age-related memory function).

- Communication (e.g., to investigate attitudes toward negative political advertising on television, the impact of magazine content on consumer behavior, online communication networks, and audience perceptions of information bias).

- Social work (e.g., to understand the barriers in disclosing domestic violence, the educational needs within a child welfare program, and the effect of cultural programs on parental well-being).

- Marketing (e.g., to examine shopping preferences among consumers, the corporate financial services needs among executives, the viability of new product lines, the usability of a newly designed retail website, and the effectiveness of communication strategies).

Interviewer Skills

Regardless of interview format, the skills of the interviewer are among the most important components of the IDI method. A quality interviewer demonstrates skills that minimize unintended variation in the data associated with potential interviewer and participant[5] biases, and thereby maximize the validity and the reliability of outcomes. As highlighted in Box 3.2, these skills include techniques for (a) building rapport with interview participants; (b) actively listening to interviewees by showing a sincere interest in their responses and asking appropriate follow-up questions; (c) staying focused on the research objectives while allowing for flexibility in the interview content; (d) maintaining a heightened sensitivity to verbal cues (e.g., a hesitation in response in a face-to-face or telephone IDI) and to nonverbal cues (e.g., a facial expression in a face-to-face IDI) that add meaning to the data; and (e) obtaining accurate and complete records of the interview (i.e., from note taking and/or recording devices). These and other interviewer skills

```
┌─────────────────────────────────────────────────────────┐
│                                                         │
│          BOX 3.2.   Interviewer Skills                  │
│                                                         │
├─────────────────────────────────────────────────────────┤
│                                                         │
│   An IDI interviewer needs techniques to . . .          │
│                                                         │
│      •  Build rapport.                                  │
│      •  Actively listen.                                │
│      •  Stay focused on objectives.                     │
│      •  Maintain sensitivity to verbal and nonverbal    │
│         cues.                                           │
│      •  Obtain accurate and complete interview records. │
│                                                         │
└─────────────────────────────────────────────────────────┘
```

are essential to a quality IDI study and are discussed more fully in chapter Section 3.3 pertaining to the TQF.

Overview of the Strengths and Limitations of the IDI Method

Strengths

The potential advantages or strengths of the IDI method reside in three key areas: (1) the interviewer–interviewee relationship, (2) the interview itself, and (3) the analytical component of the process. The relative closeness of the interviewer–interviewee relationship that is developed in the IDI method potentially increases the credibility of the data by reducing response biases (e.g., distortion in the outcomes due to responses that are considered socially acceptable, such as "I attend church weekly," **acquiescence** [i.e., tendency to agree], and **satisficing** [i.e., providing an easy "don't know" answer to avoid the extra cognitive burden to carefully think through what is being asked]) and nonresponse, while also increasing question–answer validity (i.e., the interviewee's correct interpretation of the interviewer's question).

An additional strength of the IDI method is the flexibility of the interview format, which allows the interviewer to tailor the order in which questions are asked, modify the question wording as appropriate, ask follow-up questions to clarify interviewees' responses, and use indirect questions (e.g., the use of projective techniques[6]) to stimulate subconscious opinions or recall. It should be noted, however, that "flexibility" does not mean a willy-nilly approach to interviewing, and, indeed, the interviewer should employ the quality measures outlined in Section 3.3 (p. 70). A third key strength of the IDI method—analyzability of the data—is a byproduct of the interviewer–interviewee relationship and the depth of interviewing techniques, which produce a granularity in the IDI data that is rich in fine details and serves as the basis for deciphering the narrative within each interview. These details also enable researchers to readily identify where they agree or disagree with the meanings of codes and themes associated with specific responses, which ultimately leads to the identification of themes and connections across interview participants.

Limitations

The IDI method also presents challenges and limitations that deserve the research-er's attention. The most important, from a TQF standpoint, has to do with what is also considered a key strength of the IDI method: the interviewer–interviewee relationship. There are two key aspects of the relationship that can potentially limit (or even undermine) the effectiveness of the IDI method: the interviewer and the social context. The main issue with respect to the interviewer is his/her potential for biasing the information that is gathered. This can happen due to (a) personal characteristics such as gender, age, race, ethnicity, and education (e.g., a 60-year-old Caucasian male interviewer may stifle or skew responses from young, female, African American participants); (b) personal values or beliefs (e.g., an interviewer with strongly held beliefs about global warming and its damag-ing impact on the environment may "tune out" or misconstrue the comments from interviewees who believe global warming is a myth); and/or (c) other factors (e.g., an interviewer's stereotyping, misinterpreting, and/or presumptions about the interviewee based solely on the interviewee's outward appearance). Any of these characteristics may negatively influence an interviewee's responses to the researcher's questions and/or the accuracy of the interviewer's data gathering. A result of these interviewer effects may be the "difficulty of seeing the people as complex, and . . . a reduction of their humanity to a stereotypical, flat, one-dimensional paradigm" (Krumer-Nevo, 2002, p. 315).

The second key area of concern with the IDI method is related to the broader social context of the relationship, particularly what Kvale (2006) calls the "power dynamics" within the interview environment, characterized by the possibility of "a one-way dialogue" whereby "the interviewer rules the interview" (p. 484). It is important, therefore, for the researcher to carefully consider the social interac-tions that are integral to the interviewing process and the possible impact these interactions may have on the credibility of an IDI study. For example, the trained interviewer will maximize the social interaction by utilizing positive engagement techniques such as establishing rapport (i.e., being approachable), asking thought-ful questions that indicate the interviewer is listening carefully to the interviewee, and knowing when to stay silent and let the interviewee talk freely.

Section 3.3 of this chapter provides a more detailed discussion of these strengths and limitations from the perspective of applying a TQF approach to the IDI method.

3.2 FOUR MODES OF THE IN-DEPTH INTERVIEW METHOD

An IDI can be conducted using various modes. In this section, we discuss the four most common ways to conduct IDIs: face-to-face, telephone, online, and mobile device. Each of these modes provides benefits and may have drawbacks, depend-ing on the research objectives, the particular target population under study, the availability of resources to conduct the research, and the timeframe of the research process. This section briefly discusses the unique strengths and limitations of each IDI mode from a quality design perspective. A summary comparison of these strengths and limitations is shown in Table 3.1.

Face-to-Face Mode

Strengths of the Face-to-Face Mode

Face-to-face IDIs are at the core of most qualitative research. When qualitative researchers across various fields of study talk about interviews or interviewing, they traditionally have been referring, implicitly or explicitly, to the face-to-face mode. One reason for this is purely historical given that other "technology" channels for accessing potential interviewees were in the past nonexistent or may have been limited (e.g., according to the U.S. Bureau of the Census [1994], only two-thirds of the households in the South had a telephone in 1960). The nonuniversal worldwide penetration of landline or cellular telephone services (World Telecommunication/ICT Indicators, 2014) continues to make face-to-face interviewing, for both qualitative and quantitative research, the most frequent mode of interviewing in some parts of the world.

A more important reason for the enduring prevalence of face-to-face IDIs is the naturalness the method has traditionally brought to the research experience. The absence of technological devices, or other conveniences, mediating the interviewer–interviewee's conversation creates an environment conducive to a social conversation, compared to a more formalized research atmosphere. For instance, the face-to-face method readily facilitates the presentation or sharing of stimuli relevant to the research and allows the interviewer and the interviewee to spend dedicated time together to establish some level of rapport and build a relationship that can lead to a free flow of in-depth information that addresses the issues or concerns that lie below the surface. As an example, geographers Baxter and Eyles (1999) discuss a face-to-face IDI study conducted among residents of a rural Canadian community concerning the environmental risk associated with the proposed siting of a solid waste facility. The researchers chose the face-to-face IDI method because they wanted to get beyond the usual stated concerns of risk, such as threats to personal health or water quality, and understand the more profound associations that underscore these perceptions. In this manner, the face-to-face mode enabled researchers "to understand the role of deeper issues, like community values and ways of life, and the meaning of risk from hazards . . . in the context of everyday life" (Baxter & Eyles, 1999, p. 309). The benefit of this research was in the ability to develop appropriate risk communication strategies that addressed the deeper issues that drove residents' concerns.

The "naturalness" of the face-to-face interview ideally fosters a trusting environment that results in extended conversations on a specific topic, allowing the researcher to elicit meaningful responses by way of follow-up and probing questions, while giving the interviewee the satisfaction of providing sufficiently detailed responses. Irvine (2011) compared the level of engagement (or "floor

TABLE 3.1. IDI Mode Comparisons: Key Strengths and Limitations of the Four IDI Modes			
Face-to-face	**Telephone**	**Email**	**Mobile**
Strengths			
• Most similar to natural, social conversation. • Ability to share stimuli. • Ability to build rapport and a trusting environment. • Can use nonverbal and visual cues to add meaning and gain more in-depth responses.	• Potential cost and time savings. • Can cover a wide geographic area. • Convenience (scheduling, location). • Relieves the pressure of direct social interaction.	• Detailed, thoughtful responses from participant. • Participant can control the process, instilling a sense of empowerment and engagement. • Can potentially help to access hard-to-reach population segments. • Potential cost and time savings, especially due to built-in transcriptions.	• High incidence of mobile device and/or smartphone use, especially among younger people. • Participant has multiple ways to respond—voice, text, visual image, video. • Participant is "in the moment," not relying on memory recall. • Incorporates advantages of other modes (e.g., sharing stimuli, geographic coverage, convenience).
Limitations			
• Physical presence may distort how the interviewer conducts the interview and how the participant responds. • Cost and time requirements that may limit the research scope. • Inaccessibility to participants (e.g., due to closed facilities, scheduling problems, participants' reluctance).	• Weakened ability to establish interviewer–interviewee rapport. • Absence of nonverbal, visual cues from the participant. • Shortened interview length.	• Weakened ability to establish interviewer–interviewee rapport. • Absence of verbal, nonverbal, and visual cues from the participant. • Text as the primary form of communication. • Challenge to maintain participant engagement and flow of the interview. • Selection and coverage bias (e.g., due to issues of literacy, computer and email access).	• Weakened ability to establish interviewer–interviewee rapport. • Limited opportunity for the researcher to ask follow-up questions, explore meanings. • Participant's control of what is and is not shared with the researcher. • Selection and coverage bias (e.g., due to issues of literacy, computer and email access).

holding"[7]) among participants in the face-to-face mode with those interviewed on the telephone on the same topics and concluded that "there was [on average] 25 minutes more participant floor holding in face-to-face interviews" (p. 209). This higher level of engagement, including more detailed input from the interviewee, is partially attributed to the length of a face-to-face IDI, which is typically longer than in other synchronous modes (i.e., the interviewer and interviewee participate simultaneously, e.g., as in telephone IDIs), often running 1–2 hours in length.

Another unique advantage of the face-to-face IDI method is the ability to more readily gain knowledge from what is *not* said because of the nonverbal and visual cues that can be observed in real time. These cues can range from aspects specific to the interviewee—for example, an interviewee's body movements or facial gestures, or the manner of response (e.g., a hesitancy or long pause in responding)—to environmental factors, such as the state of living conditions during an in-home IDI, or the particular location an interviewee selects for the interview (Herzog, 2005). The interviewer ideally uses these nonverbal cues and contextual feedback to tactically hone each interview—such as knowing when to move to another subject matter, as well as how to gain a more complete understanding of the interviewee's world, which can lead to new lines of questioning and aid in data interpretation.

Limitations of the Face-to-Face Mode

The personal relationships afforded by the face-to-face IDI method pose both a potential strength and potential liability to the approach. For all the positive effects that can and should result from this relatively natural social context between interviewer and interviewee, there exists the real concern that the face-to-face encounter may unwittingly influence (and distort) the manner in which the interviewer conducts the interview, the depth and breadth of an interviewee's responses, and, consequently, the quality of the data. Berg and Lune (2012) talk about the "performance" of the face-to-face IDI and how "the interviewer and the interviewee simultaneously send and receive messages on both nonverbal and verbal channels of communication." Therefore, "each participant is aware of the other's presence and . . . says something and/or acts in certain ways for the other's benefit" (p. 141). It is this awareness of the "other's presence" that can exacerbate what Brinkmann and Kvale (2015) call "an asymmetrical power relation" (p. 37) in the face-to-face IDI, which can lead the interviewee to "more or less deliberately express what they believe the interviewer authority wants to hear" (p. 38). And, as discussed on page 83, this visual awareness can also trigger conscious or unconscious personal bias from the interviewer as well as the interviewee.

The cost and time required to complete a face-to-face IDI study is no small matter. Research design in the real world of finite budgets necessitates serious practical considerations that can force the researcher to narrow the objective and limit the scope of the research. As an example, the board of education members in a particular state may want to conduct face-to-face IDIs with high school principals to hear their reactions to proposed changes in the qualifications required for new teachers, but the travel and interviewer costs associated with interviewing a sample of principals within each school district, as well as the extended time in the field to complete the interviews, exceeds the available resources and will delay input from the principals. In order to move forward with the research and gain some meaningful information, the board members may be compelled to restrict the study to one or two districts that they believe will adequately represent their school system overall and, within a district, include schools that character- ize a range of "best-to-worst performers." These practical limitations to face-to- face IDIs have implications for the quality of data, particularly the **coverage bias** resulting from the exclusion of geographically dispersed population segments.

Along with issues of geography, coverage bias in face-to-face IDI research also occurs due to the inaccessibility of the target subjects. Problems with access may arise because (1) potential interviewees are located in a closed site (e.g., military facilities, correctional institutions, private medical clinics, religious communi- ties); (2) members of the target population are hard to identify and, therefore, to reach (e.g., drug users, victims of domestic violence, people with disabilities) or are "elites," such as top corporate or government executives with limited access to them; and/or (3) the safety of the interviewer(s) is in jeopardy (e.g., the partici- pants of interest reside in a high-crime urban neighborhood). Under these condi- tions, the researcher may be able either to redefine the research objective around a segment of the population that is more easily accessible or to switch modes (e.g., replace a face-to-face research design with telephone IDIs). (Note: Coverage bias is discussed in more detail in Section 3.3.)

The recruitment of interviewees for a face-to-face IDI study can also be a limi- tation of the method. For any number of reasons (e.g., scheduling conflicts, incon- venience of the location, sensitive nature of the subject matter, the social aspect associated with the interviewer–interviewee interaction), potential interviewees may be reluctant or unable to participate in a face-to-face interview, but they may be willing to participate via a different mode.

Telephone Mode

Strengths of the Telephone Mode

Although face-to-face interviewing has been the most widely used IDI mode in the social and health sciences, the telephone mode offers several advantages and is the mode of choice in certain circumstances. From the standpoint of resources, a telephone IDI study is typically less expensive compared to face-to-face research (particularly if extensive interviewer travel is involved), and often the study can be completed in an appreciably shorter amount of time (especially compared to on-site face-to-face IDIs). There are also quality-design considerations that make telephone IDIs a good methodological option. For instance, a telephone IDI sam- ple can potentially include people from any and every geographic region (in the United States and worldwide) that includes the target population as well as indi- viduals who might otherwise be inaccessible due to problems in gaining entry (e.g., a closed facility, unsafe neighborhood). For this reason, many researchers have added telephone IDIs to their studies when "potential respondents were reluctant to participate in face-to-face interviews" (Sturges & Hanrahan, 2004, p. 109).

The telephone mode also provides the convenience of location. Whereas face-to-face interviews require the attendance of both interviewer and interviewee at a particular location at a particular point in time, telephone IDIs afford some amount of flexibility. Interviewees who might otherwise be unable or unwilling to meet for a face-to-face IDI may find time to meet on the phone. And, although IDIs conducted by way of cell phones are often not ideal (e.g., due to distractions and the typical weak time commitment of many cell phone users, poor or inconsistent voice quality, potential cost burden for the interviewee), the high incidence of mobile phone use has further added to the convenience factor of telephone IDI research. This greater convenience often facilitates recruitment by reducing refusals and enabling the researcher to engage a wider, more representative sample of the target population (Lavrakas et al., 2010).

Telephone IDIs also remove the direct social interaction between the interviewer and interviewee that is at the center of face-to-face IDIs. The telephone acts as a social intermediary that creates a distance which actually may be desirable for some interviewees and in some IDI studies. As a remote form of communication, a telephone IDI relieves some of the intensity or social pressure interviewees may experience in a face-to-face IDI (i.e., they may feel more relaxed), while giving them a certain sense of anonymity and privacy. In providing a more private context for the interviewee, the telephone IDI may be a particularly good mode for acquiring data on difficult topical areas, especially sensitive, highly personal issues.

Although there is little solid evidence to support the possible advantage of the telephone mode to discuss sensitive issues, Kavanaugh and Ayres (1998) found that telephone IDIs allowed interviewees to "talk freely" about the sensitive subject of perinatal loss. The literature generally, however, suggests that interviewees are willing to give as much, but not necessarily *more*, input on the telephone compared to face-to-face. For example, Maliski, Rivera, Connor, Lopez, and Litwin (2008) conducted an IDI study with male cancer patients and found "no evidence of differences in information shared between those interviewed in person versus those interviewed by telephone" (p. 1611). Similarly, Jendrek (1994) found in her research with grandparents who have custodial care of their grandchildren that switching from face-to-face IDIs (due to poor-quality audio recordings) to telephone interviews made no noticeable difference in the outcomes. Jendrek's finding that "the quality of the data was comparable using either interview mode" (Jendrek, 1994, p. 209) is important because, like Maliski et al., the subject matter was often sensitive in nature (e.g., asking grandparents to talk about their adult children's emotional or drug-related problems that led up to gaining legal custody of the grandchildren). More definitive research on this and on other data quality issues in the telephone IDI method is needed.

Limitations of the Telephone Mode

Telephone interviewing cannot duplicate the positive aspects of the interviewer–interviewee rapport dynamics in the face-to-face mode, partly due to the mechanism of the telephone and distance between the interviewer and interviewee, but, most importantly, due to the inability to detect nonverbal or visual cues in non-webcam-enabled phone interviews. As discussed earlier with respect to face-to-face IDIs (see p. 60), these visual data serve a critical function in IDI research by enabling the interviewer to observe the interviewee's bodily movements and gestures in response to various moments in the interview as well as the context of the interview environment. The lack of this type of input in telephone IDIs may hamper the interviewer's attempts to build a constructive relationship with the interviewee, which in turn may lower the quality of data (i.e., the validity and reliability of outcomes).

The limitations associated with interviewer–interviewee rapport in telephone IDIs are also apparent in the interview length along with the depth of content in the conversation. Although researchers have reported telephone IDIs of an hour or more (Irvine, 2011; Maliski et al., 2008), interviews in the telephone mode are typically shorter in duration than face-to-face IDIs. The shorter length of the telephone IDI is a function of (a) the agreed-to time commitment made by the interviewer and interviewee (e.g., an interviewer may agree to a shorter interview in order to facilitate the recruiting of participants); (b) the relative ease and abruptness in which an interviewee can choose to end an interview; and (c) the barrier of the telephone itself, which can inhibit an interviewee's spontaneity and willingness to elaborate on responses. Irvine (2011) found that telephone IDIs actually included more questions than similar face-to-face interviews, but were shorter in length because interviewees offered less detailed responses to interviewers' questions.

Online Mode

Many of the online Web platforms that are used to conduct group discussions—including the use of online "bulletin boards" (see Chapter 4)—are equally adequate for conducting IDIs. However, qualitative researchers (particularly outside the field of marketing research) do not often use them for IDIs and, indeed, there are few documented accounts in the literature concerning Web-based or Internet IDIs (e.g., via Skype).

Instead, many researchers opt for a text approach to online IDIs, specifically, **asynchronous email messaging**. Asynchronous email interviewing involves multiple email exchanges that are not conducted in real time but at the convenience of the sender. Asynchronous email IDI studies can be conducted in a fairly short (1 week) period of time or for a longer duration (lasting a couple of months or more); for example, Karchmer's (2001) email IDI study among 13 K–12 teachers was conducted over a 3-month period. Due to the more likely use of email interviewing, and the fact that a Web-based approach to the interview method is covered in Chapter 4, the focus of our discussion in this chapter concerning online IDIs is on the email method.

Strengths of the Email Mode

There are a number of benefits to conducting an online IDI study by way of asynchronous email messaging. One of the most important advantages to this method, which positively impacts the quality of the data, is the opportunity it affords the interviewee to elaborate responses with detailed information, including information that someone may have to look for and consult about prior to responding. It is the opportunity to reflect and provide thoughtful explanations to the interviewer's questions that, unlike other qualitative research methods, empowers the participant (e.g., allowing the participant to reread a response and to edit and refine it before it is sent).

In this regard, the email interview approach has proven to be particularly effective with hard-to-reach populations (e.g., people with disabilities) and/or on sensitive topics. For example, Beck (2005) received responses ranging from a total of one to 38 typed pages in her email IDI study among women worldwide who had experienced posttraumatic stress disorder after childbirth. She discovered, through IDI participants' comments, that these long, detailed responses were partly the result of the "cathartic" effect of the email method both in terms of providing the opportunity to thoughtfully reflect on their birth trauma experiences as well as instilling a sense of gratitude for the researcher's willingness to listen to their lengthy life stories.

On a related topic, McCoyd and Kerson (2006) compared IDI modes and found that, in a study among women who had terminated pregnancy after being diagnosed with a fetal anomaly, the email IDIs produced "more extensive communications" and "detailed, rich data" (p. 397), averaging three to eight pages more text compared to the face-to-face IDIs and six to 12 pages more text compared to the telephone IDIs. Egan, Chenoweth, and McAuliffe (2006) report similar outcomes with survivors of traumatic brain injuries, who "enhanced the quality of the data" (p. 1288) by providing unsolicited follow-up email messages so they could expound on their earlier responses. In these situations, the email mode becomes more like an electronic diary by which participants can detail their life activities and thoughts. Although it could be argued that the personal nature of the health-related topics and ordeals noted here are particularly well suited to eliciting engaged, verbose participation via email IDIs, Stacey and Vincent (2011), Curasi (2001), Gibson (2010), and others document comparable results in studies of less sensitive issues in education, marketing research, sociology, and other disciplines.

The breadth and depth of interview participants' responses to email IDIs indicates a certain level of commitment to the research process and participant engagement that directly impacts the accuracy and, ultimately, the credibility of the research findings. Researchers such as Egan et al. (2006) suggest that this engagement is, at least in part, a product of participants' "greater control of the interview process" (p. 1288) in the email IDI. Along with the ability to give lengthy, thoughtful responses (discussed above), the email participant is further empowered by the ability to control the process itself. Interview participants' control of the process stems principally from (1) the flexible nature of the online mode that allows participants to respond to researchers' questions at a location and in an environment of their choosing; and (2) the asynchronous aspect of the method, which gives IDI participants the opportunity to decide when to respond and to take the time they need to read and edit their responses as they feel necessary. In light of these realities, email IDI interviewers are forced to abandon the position of power they might assume in face-to-face and telephone IDIs and enter into a more collaborative relationship where interviewers' predetermined agendas and time schedules are replaced by a more adaptable approach that is responsive to each participant's situation. This shift of control over to participants can have an empowering effect that allows them to be more fully engaged in the research.

This aspect of control may also explain why some interview participants opt for email over face-to-face IDIs. Gibson (2010) conducted a study among music fans 30-plus years of age and found that 55 out of the 70 research participants opted for an email rather than a face-to-face IDI. She also discovered that the email IDI participants were more likely to reveal sensitive information, such as drug use, compared to face-to-face interviewees. The email interview participant's ability to control when and where responses are given may create a safe environment in which to discuss highly personal or confidential matters.

The email IDI approach also affords the interviewer a few unique capabilities. For instance, the extended duration of an email IDI study (e.g., Beck [2005] collected data for 18 months) gives the researcher sufficient latitude to integrate depth and complexity into the interview. The researcher might accomplish these goals by (a) assigning the interview participant particular tasks or "homework" to complete prior to responding to interview questions; (b) adding file attachments (e.g., images) to an email message for the IDI participant to view and think about; (c) sending a URL link for the participant to click in order to review a Web page; or (d) taking the time to read through an interview participant's responses and designing a new question or new series of questions that go deeper into the circumstances of that particular individual. Although the email IDI method also gives interviewers the opportunity to ask multiple questions on closely related issues in one email message, too many questions at one time may confuse or frustrate the email IDI participant (see p. 87 for a discussion of the appropriate approach to email IDI questions from a TQF perspective).

The email mode can be particularly cost effective, and, in some instances, an email IDI study can be completed in a shorter amount of time than either the face-to-face or telephone mode. For instance, recruiting willing-to-cooperate interviewees for an email IDI study often requires less effort—and therefore less time to recruit and less expenditure on recruiters—because, unlike face-to-face and telephone IDIs that demand a commitment on a specific date/time within the allotted timeframe of the study, the email mode offers greater flexibility in when (and where) the participant can respond to the interviewer's questions. And, the added cost and time that are necessary to travel from one face-to-face IDI to another is absent in the email IDI method.

One of the greatest contributors to the efficiency of cost and time in the email IDI method is the built-in transcriptions of the participants' input. This aspect constitutes a considerable advantage to email IDIs, given not only to the reduced cost and time but also the potential inaccuracies associated with transcriptions typed from audio or video recordings. This built-in transcription feature not only decreases cost, time commitment, and potential inaccuracies in translated transcripts, but also provides an easily accessible, ongoing account of participants' responses during the interview process, which in turn allows the researcher to monitor feedback and modify or design a new line of questioning as appropriate.

Limitations of the Email Mode

For someone to participate in an email IDI, they must have access to the Internet, have an email account, and be able (e.g., have an adequate level of literacy) and willing to use this mode of communication. There are, for instance, tens of millions of people in the United States and Canada (15% of the population as of 2013) and several billion people in the world (61% of the total population as of 2013) without Internet access and thereby unable to participate in an email IDI study (*www.internetworldstats.com/stats.htm*). This segment of the population will continue to decrease in size, but as long as it exists, it will differ in many ways from the rest of the population that is contactable via email for an IDI study.

As with telephone IDIs, the quality of an email interviewing approach is restricted by the fact that the interviewer is unable to see relevant body movements or gestures, the participant's appearance, and other visual information that might be useful in rapport building as well as in the gathering and interpretation of data. Likewise, the context of the interview from the participant's perspective is unknown by the researcher, making it impossible to record and evaluate the circumstance or environment in which the participant's responses are given. For example, a researcher conducting an email IDI study concerning the daily activities among the unemployed might interpret a participant's failure to mention any job-seeking behavior as a sign of laziness or other personality trait, when, in fact, this participant is without a car and resides in a location that is inaccessible by the public transportation that would enable him to get to a job interview. Unless the interviewer specifically asks about these circumstances, the data will reflect an erroneous interpretation of the situation.

There is another limitation related to cues that is highly particular to the email IDI method and that revolves around text as the form of communication. Because the written word is the only direct form of contact the researcher has with the participant, the participant's use of words and the manner in which text responses are typed become the cues from which impressions and assumptions about the participant are made. As Markham (2004) states, "the very existence of the online persona being studied is comprised solely by the pixels on a computer screen" (p. 340), leaving the researcher to use his or her own frame of reference to interpret a participant's writing style. Even on an unconscious level, the interviewer may form an opinion about a participant who, for example, types in all lower case, misspells words frequently, or uses poor grammar. There may be "an irresistible tendency to leap to conclusions" (p. 340) about such a person without any knowledge of the accuracy of these assumptions. The impressions that participants give through their text can negatively impact the quality of the analysis and interpretation of the data.

The third key challenge to the email IDI method is the potential difficulty of maintaining meaningful dialogue and keeping the interview on track. This difficulty is due, in large part, to the physical remoteness of the participant from the interviewer and the effort required of the interviewer to sustain a relationship. For instance, there may be long lapses in the interaction when the participant is slow to respond to the interviewer's question(s). The interviewer is left wondering what is causing the delay and whether the participant intends to respond (e.g., is he/she in the hospital, on vacation, etc., without informing the interviewer) or has self-selected out of the research (i.e., terminated the interview without informing the interviewer). It is for this reason that the interviewer may have to devote extraordinary effort to foster the interviewer–participant relationship. In fact, researchers such as Kivits (2005) have argued that it is the strength of the relationship, not the length of participants' responses, that is important to the success of the email IDI method, and that the primary task of the interviewer is "maintaining interviewee's interest in the interview process and in the topic discussed" (p. 44).

This potential difficulty of building and maintaining researcher–participant relationships in an email IDI study has implications not only for the flow of the interview process but also the content of the interviews themselves. The probing and follow-up questions that are essential components of face-to-face and telephone IDIs are cumbersome in the email IDI method because, in the time between question and response, participants may change their minds or not readily recall why they answered in a certain manner. The interviewer may further confound the problem by asking multiple questions in a single email message, hoping that the participant will use these probes to elaborate on his/her responses. As discussed earlier, the use of multiple questions in one email message can be an advantage of the email mode; however, data quality will suffer when multiple questions are used inappropriately and serve to confuse and/or frustrate the participant to the point of terminating the interview. The issue of multiple questions in the email mode is discussed further in Section 3.3 (see p. 87) pertaining to the TQF approach.

As mentioned above, an additional limitation to the email IDI method is the potential for selection and coverage bias. Individuals who have difficulty with reading and/or writing (due to problems in literacy or the language in which the study is being conducted) will not be capable of providing full and accurate data in an email study, as is also true for people who do not have regular access to a computer and an email account. For example, Bowker and Tuffin (2004) examined the viability of the IDI online mode among people with physical and sensory disabilities and resorted to face-to-face IDIs for three deaf participants who did not have online access. Likewise, an IDI study that is conducted only in English where the target population is an urban, mostly Hispanic, neighborhood may not be best suited for the online mode due to an inability to write (e.g., form complete thoughts and spell words) in the English language or because some residents in this community may simply be uncomfortable with their English-writing skills. This is just one illustration of why it is good practice for the researcher to learn as much as possible about the study population during the design phase to establish the appropriate mode for the IDI method.

A final concern about email IDIs, in the extreme, is that the interviewer/researcher may never be certain of the identity of the person who actually has composed, written, and sent back the email responses. This is a concern of all forms of research that use the Internet to gather data; and, indeed, quantitative researchers have found the use of fictitious identities to be a major problem in online panel research (Baker et al., 2014). Qualitative researchers should also be on the lookout for this possibility and keep it in mind as they are gathering data and interpreting any email IDI study.

Mobile Mode

Strengths of the Mobile Mode

The evolution of smartphone technology and the increasing ownership of smartphones worldwide have made mobile qualitative research a viable method for conducting IDIs. Although conducting IDIs by way of a smartphone may seem far afield from traditional methods such as face-to-face and landline telephone interviews, there are several advantages to mobile IDIs. One of the greatest advantages of the mobile mode for IDIs is that mobile or smartphone devices have become ubiquitous among the younger adult population—nearly 79% of those 18–24 years of age in the United States owns a smartphone, compared to 56% of all adults (Smith, 2013)—and similarly, almost 80% of tweens and teens own a mobile phone (Lenhart, 2012). Although it can be extremely difficult to gather information from people under the age of 30 via other modes of contact because they are inaccessible or unwilling to cooperate (Lavrakas et al., 2010), many of these same young adults and teenagers may agree to participate in an IDI study conducted on their smartphone.

An equally important strength of the mobile IDI mode is the quality and breadth of the input that can be captured due to the various types of responses that interview participants can give to the researcher's questions, including voice, text, and visual. The ability of an IDI participant to use the smartphone to provide audio feedback (via a voice mail message or live discussion with the researcher), use the keyboard function to send a text or email message, and use the still and/or video camera to send relevant images provides the researcher with a multisided understanding of an issue from the participant's perspective. For example, Civi-com (West, 2012) conducted a study among female consumers concerning their shopping behavior and use of a particular brand of body wash. In this research, 60 women gave details of their shopping experience by using the smartphone to (a) call a voice mail system to record their answers to specific questions provided on a user card (e.g., "What store are you at and how easy or difficult is it to find the body wash section?"); (b) take a still photo of anything in the body wash area of the store that was "particularly helpful in making your final decision"; (c) record a video of something that influenced the purchase decision (e.g., a video of the entire beauty/bath area and where the purchased product was located relative to other products); and/or (d) send a text or email message. Thirty of these women also used their smartphones *while in the shower using the body wash*[8] to give their opinion of its effectiveness and their satisfaction with the product. This approach gave the researcher multiple ways to analyze the consumer experience as well as a way to verify the data by comparing and contrasting participants' input across the various forms of communication (i.e., voice, text, and visual).

A unique and important aspect of the mobile IDI mode is that much of the data is not based on memory recall of an experience. Unlike other methods that rely on the participant's (fallible) recollection of a certain event, the mobile approach can capture the experience *as it happens*, with the participant relating his/her behavior and what he/she is thinking in situ. This immediate input may lack the depth or thoughtfulness of other methods (that enable the interviewer to sufficiently probe with follow-up questions), but it does enhance the validity of event-specific details.

This multifaceted response capability in the mobile IDI method also has the advantage of incorporating certain benefits typically associated with other modes, such as face-to-face, telephone, and email IDIs. For instance, like the face-to-face mode, mobile IDIs give the interview participants an opportunity to share stimuli and explain their experiences by actually showing what is going on (i.e., by way of still photographs or video). In this way, the researcher reaps some depth of understanding that comes from verbal, nonverbal, and contextual cues not unlike face-to-face IDIs. Similar to the telephone and email modes, mobile IDIs present the opportunity to sample from a broad geographic region, reduce the potentially negative impact of the interviewer–participant social interaction inherent in face-to-face IDIs, and offer interview participants convenience and privacy. With respect to convenience, the opportunity to give feedback in the moment of an experience may be considered preferable to scheduling an interview time at a later date, particularly among people who are technologically savvy and enjoy being engaged constantly with their smartphones. And, although the idea that mobile IDIs give participants a sense of privacy is not fully supported in the literature, there are reported cases of using the mobile mode to conduct IDIs on sensitive topics such as the personal use of medication for depression (Civicom, 2011).

Limitations of the Mobile Mode

Even more so than is the case with email IDIs, a relatively small proportion of the world's population, particularly outside the United States, uses a smartphone

(Rainie & Poushter, 2014), and the segment that does not use one may be different in demographics, behaviors, knowledge, and attitudes than the segment that does use one. Mobile IDI researchers therefore need to take special and explicit care in deciding whether this mode is appropriate to use for the target population of their IDI study.

From the standpoint of data quality, there are two important limitations to the mobile IDI method. The first concerns the restricted opportunity the researcher has to ask follow-up questions and explore the meanings behind participants' actions and thoughts. Although a smartphone approach gives the researcher a varied description of an experience, it may fail in providing a full and nuanced understanding of this experience based on other factors in a person's life. The researcher may learn, for instance, that product packaging and the shelf display led a participant to purchase a particular body wash, yet be left with little elaboration or insight regarding other (unstated or unseen) influences, such as the participant's past experiences with the competitive brands or her particular mood (or emotional state) at that moment in time. Relatively short responses without adequate follow-up by the researcher are likely to undermine the quality of the data.

A related serious concern with the mobile IDI method is the fact that the interview format is typically unstructured with the participant in nearly complete control of what is and is not passed to the researcher. Although the participant-driven model of mobile IDIs provides one perspective of human nature at a given point in time, the **selection bias** built into the process makes it unclear if the researcher is collecting thorough and accurate data. Unless the participant chooses to mention (or capture on the camera) the entirety of the environment (e.g., the in-store shopping experience), it is impossible for the researcher to understand the manner in which the participant may have been selective and then to analyze the impact of that selectivity on the data.

3.3   APPLYING THE TOTAL QUALITY FRAMEWORK APPROACH TO THE IN-DEPTH INTERVIEW METHOD

This section examines the IDI research method from the perspective of the TQF. The discussion focuses on how to design, implement, and interpret an IDI study based on the principles of the TQF with its associated four pillars of Credibility, Analyzability, Transparency, and Usefulness. We present guidelines to follow for each pillar/component to maximize the quality of the outcomes and produce IDI research that is ultimately of value to the end user. This discussion tackles some of the biggest limitations of the IDI method mentioned earlier in this chapter, including interviewer bias, the social context, and rapport building, as well as suggesting specific strategies related to interviewer training, interviewee recruitment/scheduling, the interview guide, reflexivity, triangulation, transcriptions, and coding. We also identify the unique differences among the various modes and how those differences impact the IDI process.

Credibility

The IDI method is potentially a very powerful research design for qualitative researchers. There are, however, potential threats to the credibility of the resulting data that researchers should proactively guard against in order to reduce or possibly eliminate their impact. These risks to credibility should be taken into account when researchers are planning their studies, implementing them, interpreting their findings, advancing implications, and thereby addressing the usefulness of their IDI study.

As with all qualitative research methods, the Credibility component of an IDI research design rests within the two broad areas of Scope and Data Gathering. *Scope* deals with representation, specifically addressing the issue of how well the group of interviewees included in the study reflects the larger target population of interest. The second area of Credibility, *Data Gathering*, centers on the issue of the reliability and validity of the data collected in the IDIs as far as capturing the essence of the constructs the researcher purports to have addressed in the study.

Scope

In an IDI research study, Scope pertains to factors related to (a) coverage of the target population, (b) the sampling approach used to select which persons will be contacted during the recruitment phase, (c) the extent to which all selected interviewees actually complete the interview and thereby are included in the final research data, and (d) whether interviewees who were selected but did not complete interviews would have provided data that is materially different from those who did complete the IDI.

Coverage

To cover the target population of an IDI study, the researcher must work with a list that accurately represents the population of interest. Therefore, the quality of a list that enumerates the persons that make up the population being studied is critical. The researcher can create this list, access or purchase it from an existing source, and/or use a list provided by a client. For example, if the study population is all staff at the management level within a nonprofit organization, the researcher will need to get a current list of those persons from the organization's human resources (HR) department. Ideally, this list will include accurate contact information on each staff member from which the researcher can select the appropriate number and type of staff people (as relevant to the study) for the recruiting phase. If the study population is the current and recent past members of inner-city street gangs, for example, the researcher may need to partner with local community organizations that work with these gangs to create a list of all these individuals, including how best to locate them. If the study population is the homeowners in an upscale census tract in suburban Chicago, the researcher may seek their names from the Cook County property tax records. In each of these examples, and for any target group, it is imperative that the researcher use one or more lists that contain all the members of the study population, to ensure that the interviewees included in the final data truly reflect the population of interest. An unrepresentative list of the population may well bias the outcomes of the research and, in some instances, this bias may be so large as to completely invalidate the credibility of the IDI study findings and interpretations. The researcher, therefore, needs to be committed to obtaining and assembling a comprehensive listing of all the persons in the population being studied. Anything short of this opens the door to possible bias resulting from an incomplete list.

Sample Design

Assuming that the list is not so small that everyone on the list will be asked to participate in the study, an equally important step to the compilation of a current and accurate list of population members is the method for selecting potential interviewees from the list. Selecting this sample of potential participants should be done in a systematic and, ideally, random manner. The researcher should begin by looking carefully at the list to determine whether there is an underlying order in how the persons are or should be listed (e.g., alphabetical, geographical, job title, age, longevity). The representativeness—and, hence, the credibility—of the study may be in jeopardy if the researcher fails to consider this orderliness of the list when selecting potential interviewees. It is a best practice, even in the absence of any inherent ordering within the list, to select persons across the entire list rather than to start at the beginning and proceed one consecutive person after the other (e.g., the first person, the second person) until the desired number of interviewees has been selected. By selecting a sample of potential interviewees across the entire list, the researcher is assuring that the quality of the final data will not be weakened by biases associated with the set of persons chosen for the IDIs.

More complex approaches for IDI participant selection may be appropriate depending upon the nature of the list. For example, if the gender, age, and educational attainment of all the persons on the list are known in advance, and if these demographic characteristics are expected to be related to the behaviors, attitudes, and knowledge specific to the subject matter of the interviews, the list should be sorted (stratified) prior to sample selection. The sorting in this example could start by grouping all women and all men into two separate subgroups, followed by arranging persons within each gender subgroup by age, and then sorting everyone within each gender–age subgroup by educational attainment. This newly sorted list can then be used to select potential interviewees systematically. For example, if the list contained 100 persons belonging to a school's parents club, and the researcher wanted to complete 25 IDIs (and had reason to believe that essentially every one of those selected would agree to an interview), every fourth person on the sorted (stratified) list would be chosen. In this way, the researcher is guaranteed that the group of people interviewed in the study is representative of the list in terms of gender, age, and educational attainment. By not sorting the list, even if the selection were random, the final outcomes may be biased due to the unrepresentativeness of chosen participants.

NUMBER OF INTERVIEWS. Another factor associated with sample design and the credibility of an IDI study is the number of interviews to be completed and, therefore, the proportion of interviewees on the list that needs to be selected. Unlike sampling decisions in quantitative research where sample size is statistically linked directly to the degree of confidence associated with the study findings, qualitative researchers who conduct IDI studies need to be able to provide a logical rationale (justification) for why the number of interviews they completed was sufficient (i.e., "fit for purpose") for the needs of the study. A researcher should give a priori attention to deciding how many IDIs will be completed and think carefully about the circumstances under which that number may need to be increased or decreased. Although it is also very important to evaluate the appropriate number of interviews while in the field (see below), by considering this factor at the beginning of an IDI study, before the onset of fieldwork, the qualitative researcher takes the high road in preparing to address problems that may arise in the field (e.g., incomplete or no interviews with one or more recruited individuals and/or unanticipated differences across interviewees that may require additional IDIs to better understand these differences) as well as being able to clearly document decisions that are made regarding the number of interviews and the group of interviewees represented in the final data.

In sum, the appropriate number of interviews to conduct for an IDI study needs to be considered at two key moments in the research process: (1) during the initial research design phase and (2) during the field execution phase. At the initial design stage, the number of IDIs is dictated by four considerations:

- The breadth, depth, and nature of the research topic or issue (e.g., a face-to-face study on how drought conditions in the Midwest are impacting farmers' operations will likely require a greater number of IDIs than investigating drought issues only among dairy farmers in a particular county in Wisconsin).

- The heterogeneity or homogeneity of the population of interest (e.g., in a study of Midwest farmers, more IDIs will be required if the study population encompasses dairy, poultry, and crop farmers compared to just dairy farmers).

- The level of analysis and interpretation required to meet research objectives (e.g., in the study among farmers in the Midwest, a greater number of IDIs will be needed if the researcher wants to contrast and compare the impact of the drought among farmers in Wisconsin from those in Kansas and Iowa).

- Practical parameters such as the availability of and access to interviewees, budget or financial resources, time constraints, as well as travel and other logistics associated with conducting face-to-face interviews.

These factors present the researcher with the difficult task of balancing the specific realities of the research components while estimating the optimal number of interviews to conduct. Although the number of required interviews tends to move in direct step with the variation of the target population and the level of diversity and complexity in the research design (i.e., the needed number of interviews increases accordingly with the complexity of the topic, population, and analysis scheme), there is little guidance in choosing "the right" sample size for the researcher at the planning stage. Thomson (2011) reviewed 100 articles pertaining to research studies utilizing IDIs and found that the average number of interviews conducted is 25. Baker and Edwards (2012) present a compilation of thoughts from "renowned social scientists" in answer to the question, "How many qualitative interviews is enough?", citing recommended sample sizes ranging from six (Adler & Adler, in Baker & Edwards, 2012, p. 8) for hard-to-reach or deviant subgroups (e.g., corporate executives or members of a motorcycle gang) to over 100 (Doucet, in Baker & Edwards, 2012, p. 25) when the objective of the research is to gain a deeper understanding of the interviewees that goes beyond the findings from just one interview (e.g., interviewing fathers who are primary caregivers over time and in different locations because "different settings produce different stories" [p. 26]).

The other key moment when the researcher should explicitly and carefully consider the adequacy of the sample size is during the field phase when interviews are actually being conducted. This has been the most widely discussed temporal issue by many researchers because it is then, when in the field, that the optimal number of interviews ultimately is determined. Specifically, researchers utilizing **grounded theory** rely on the notion of **saturation** or the moment when "the researcher has collected sufficient data, in the sense that additional data collection does not reveal fresh insights" (Robson, 2011, p. 532). On this basis, the researcher deems that a sufficient number of interviews has been conducted when no new themes or stark variations in interviewees' responses are coming to light. There are few guidelines for determining the number of interviews by way of saturation, and some have questioned the pervasive discussion of saturation among qualitative researchers when the idea itself has various meanings and offers "limited transparency" to the research process (O'Reilly & Parker, 2013, p. 191).

From a TQF perspective, it is not good enough to simply evaluate interview completions in the field for the point of saturation. Although it is important to determine the degree to which interviews are or are not reaping new meaningful information, there are many other quality concerns that need to be resolved. In utilizing the TQF to assess the number of IDIs at the field stage, the researcher should review interview completions based on the answers to the 10 questions listed in Box 3.3. These questions pertain to issues regarding the consistent coverage of the research objectives, the clarity of input obtained in the interviews, and the emergence of valid insights.

**BOX 3.3. Number of Interviews: 10 Questions
to Evaluate Interview Completions at the Field Stage**

1. Did every IDI cover every question or issue important to the research, or are there critical areas that were not discussed with all interviewees?

2. Did all interviewees provide clear, unambiguous answers to key questions or issues, or does the researcher need to go back to some interviewees for clarification?

3. Do the data obtained thus far answer the research objective?

4. To what extent are new ideas, themes, or information emerging from these interviews?

5. Can the researcher identify the sources of variations and contradictions in the data and the extent of unexplained differences?

6. Does a review of the researcher's reflexive journal reveal any concerns about objectivity and interpretations of the data?

7. Do the data confirm or deny what is already known about the subject matter?

8. By way of triangulation (e.g., interinterviewer, peer review), do the data confirm or deny the researcher's preliminary interpretation?

9. Do the data obtained thus far tell a story? Do they make sense and do they describe the phenomenon, life story, culture, or other subject of the study? Are there sufficient data to tell a story about each of the subgroups or sample segments?

10. Are new, unexplored segments or avenues for further research emerging from the data?

Gaining Cooperation

A third major Scope-related aspect related to the Credibility component of an IDI study is the proportion of selected interviewees not interviewed or only partially interviewed. This is the domain of research that is often termed "nonresponse." If this proportion is large and/or if the group that is selected but not interviewed differs in meaningful ways from those who are interviewed, bias can infiltrate the final data of an IDI study and compromise the credibility of the research.

To avoid this, qualitative researchers need to give serious a priori thought to how they will gain high and representative levels of cooperation from the persons they have selected to interview, and how individuals who do not cooperate may differ in past experiences, attitudes, behaviors, and knowledge compared to interviewees. The researcher must keep in mind that bias may enter into the outcomes, and the credibility of the study's findings and interpretations thereby weakened, if the characteristics of those in the sample who do not cooperate with an IDI study are correlated with the key topics the study is investigating. Likewise, qualitative researchers using the IDI method should also constantly monitor the representativeness of the group of selected participants that *does* cooperate and watch whether the characteristics of that group deviate from the characteristics of the target population. This may be difficult in the case of the email IDI where the interviewer must stay alert to the consistency of participants' responses and recognize when the identity of the interviewee may have changed (i.e., someone other than the recruited research participant is the one now responding). For instance, in an email IDI study among unemployed men, the interviewer may become suspicious when a participant who frequently misspells words and has stated that a chronic health problem prevents him from looking for a job writes in a later email, with no spelling errors, that he spends most of the day outdoors exercising or socializing with friends.

In trying to reduce or eliminate nonresponse as a potentially biasing influence on the final outcomes of an IDI study, the researcher should attempt to identify ameliorative approaches that would bring representativeness back into balance. There are several factors that researchers should consider when thinking about how to gain cooperation from a representative set of IDI interviewees, or when attempting to "fix" a lack of representation that is emerging during the field period. These include:

- How the purpose of the study will be explained to an interviewee, without biasing what is learned during the interview (e.g., explaining the purpose of a study concerning television viewership as a study to learn about at-home activities).

- The nonmaterial motivations that will be used to achieve cooperation from the selected interviewees (e.g., emphasizing that the study's ultimate goal is to improve some aspect of people's lives).

- Whether any material incentives (e.g., cash, a gift card, prized tickets to a sporting event, donation to a favorite charity) will be provided, including their nature and value, and whether they are given in advance of the IDI (i.e., a **noncontingent incentive**) and/or after the IDI is completed (i.e., a **contingent incentive**).

- The effect that knowing the identity of the study's sponsor may have on a participant's willingness to participate (e.g., corporate financial decision makers may be reluctant to participate in an IDI if the sponsoring bank is revealed up front, due to negative preconceived attitudes toward the bank or an assumption that the research is actually an attempt to sell products and services).

- The nature of any advance notice—both its substance (e.g., amount of detail) and form (e.g., a personalized letter in the U.S. mail on the research sponsor's letterhead vs. a generic email message)—that will be provided to interviewees before the IDI interviewer directly makes contact.

- What the recruiter/interviewer will do to tailor (i.e., target, modify, adjust) the recruitment effort to the specific interview participant, as opposed to using a "one-size-fits-all" approach (e.g., taking time to reiterate the purpose of the study and personalizing the benefits of participation to someone who initially refuses). The success of tailoring is clearly linked to the quality of the rapport the recruiter/interviewer is able to build with the potential interviewee.

Location, or where the interviews are conducted, impacts the level of cooperation in face-to-face IDI studies. A central location study, in which all interviewees are asked to travel to one central facility for interviewing, provides the researcher with a smaller, more narrowly defined population of potential interviewees compared to an on-site IDI study, where the interviewer travels to each interviewee's home, business, or other location that is convenient to the interviewee. The interviewer's flexibility in the interview location and time will minimize refusals due to scheduling conflicts, convenience, and other factors, and improve the overall success rate of recruitment. For example, recruiting residential building contractors for face-to-face IDIs is greatly facilitated by agreeing to conduct the interview at their respective construction sites; and Herzog (2005) found that it was easier to recruit female interviewees in Israel when they were given the option to be interviewed at home.

Any IDI study that asks interviewees to expend extraordinary effort, such as meeting at a specific location for a face-to-face IDI or transmitting photographs from a particular location for a mobile IDI, requires sound recruitment procedures. In addition to quality strategies already mentioned (e.g., tailoring the recruitment when needed, providing flexibility in location), the researcher can take the following steps to maximize the success of gaining cooperation from selected participants:

• The recruiter/interviewer for an IDI study should be very well-trained on the background, purpose, and rationale for the sample composition. This training will enable the recruiter to understand the importance of any screening criteria that may be deployed and correctly address issues that may be raised by potential interviewees during the recruitment.

• Particular attention should be paid to gaining access to interviewees in closed facilities (e.g., jails) or otherwise hard-to-reach interviewees. The researcher and recruiter/interviewer need to work together to identify and establish communication with possible gatekeepers or other key contact people who may be associated with providing access to the target population. For example, an IDI study with young drug addicts may require screening interviews with parents and/or rehabilitation supervisors. Access to members of community organizations is facilitated by establishing an interpersonal relationship with one or more community leaders or other source of authority. For example, Arcury and Quandt (1999) describe gaining access to community groups by way of a church pastor or the director of a health agency, and Kim (2010) recruited Korean Americans by way of a trusted, local Korean English newspaper.

• Although recruitment through gatekeepers may be necessary to safeguard access to and the successful recruiting of a representative sample of the target population, it is essential that the recruiter/interviewer—not the gatekeeper—maintain control of interviewee selection. Accordingly, the recruiter/interviewer should have expert knowledge in how to adhere to the sample design and be able to reject substitute recruits based on a gatekeeper's own preferences and recommendations.

• As noted above, a material incentive encourages participation and can be very important to a successful recruitment, especially when interview participants have no prior or ongoing "obligation" to the sponsor of the IDI project or the researchers conducting the study. Such incentives are particularly critical in studies among hard-to-reach populations or in IDI methods that ask interviewees to expend more effort, such as face-to-face and mobile IDIs. Unless forbidden (e.g., by regulatory authorities), it is not unusual to offer everyone recruited a cash incentive ranging from less than $50 (e.g., studies with children) to $200 or more (e.g., executive management and studies with physicians). In business-to-business research (e.g., a telecommunications company conducting an IDI study with its commercial customers), this incentive is often given in the form of a charitable contribution on behalf of the interviewee. However, it should be noted that monetary incentives may have the unwanted effect of skewing participants' responses. Although very little is written about this factor in the qualitative research literature, one small IDI study among low-income older adults concluded that cash incentives skewed participants' responses and led the participants to control what they would or would not reveal in the IDI (Cook & Nunkoosing, 2008, see Box 3.4).

Data Gathering

There are several important considerations pertaining to the Data Gathering facet of the TQF Credibility component that researchers need to take into account to maximize the quality of the data gathered and the overall credibility of their IDI studies. These include:

- How well the content of the interview includes (specifies) all aspects of the constructs the study purports to measure.
- **Interviewer effects,** specifically—
  o **Interviewer bias:** interviewer characteristics or values that bias responses. For example, an interviewer who shows any signs of personal agreement or disagreement with something the interviewee is saying would likely bias the information the interviewee is providing.
  o **Interviewer inconsistency:** the inconsistent manner in which the interviewer administers the interview that creates unwarranted variation in the data. For example, an interviewer who asks follow-up questions on a specific issue with some but not all interviewees will produce an inconsistency in the quality of the data gathered across all interviewees.
- The extent to which the interviewee is willing and able to provide fully accurate information about what is asked of him/her during the IDI.

BOX 3.4. Use of Monetary Incentives: Impact of Incentives with Impoverished Older IDI Participants

Cook and Nunkoosing (2008) conducted a face-to-face IDI study with 12 "impoverished elders" in Melbourne, Australia, to investigate community services for the poor among those "who are excluded or at risk of exclusion from their communities." Research participants could participate in up to two interviews and were given $20 for each interview.

In reviewing the key findings, the researchers observed many "interview interactions that were atypical." At least part of these irregularities was attributed to the monetary incentive, which, according to Cook and Nunkoosing, helped to create an interview environment where interviewees were motivated "to manage the presentation of self, retain control over the exchange of information, and reduce the stigma of poverty by limiting disclosure and resisting researcher questioning" (p. 421).

The importance of the incentive in the interview process became clear when interviewees volunteered comments such as "I need the $20 . . ." and critically compared the $20 to better (i.e., higher) cash incentives offered by other research studies. In this way interviewees were in effect "selling" their stories to the interviewer (and, some would say, at a bargain price), which, based on the researchers' analyses, tainted interviewees' responses with "stylized accounts" (or "rehearsed narratives") as well as "minimal disclosure," as seen in this excerpt from the transcripts (p. 424):

PARTICIPANT: What did you want to know?

INTERVIEWER: All about you.

PARTICIPANT: That's about it, like, there's not too much.

INTERVIEWER: Do you want to tell me a bit more? I don't really know who you are yet.

PARTICIPANT: You do.

INTERVIEWER: Tell me a bit about who you are, what you like, what you don't like.

PARTICIPANT: I don't like him (*gesturing toward the other agency client*).

Content of the Interview

In terms of the content of the interview, the credibility of what is being measured is linked to how well the researchers have identified and included all relevant constructs (see Chapter 2, pp. 30–31) in the interview guide on which the IDIs will be based, and whether all important aspects (attributes) of each construct have been included (the interview guide is discussed further on p. 80). Failure to do this will limit the quality of the information gathered in the IDIs, as it will neither be complete nor robust in capturing enough information about each construct of interest. To avoid this potential risk to credibility, researchers should plan the content of their interview by (a) building on past work on the topic (i.e., the researcher's own earlier work and/or a review of others' research on the topic published in the literature), (b) speaking with colleagues and other experts in the topic areas, (c) showing their draft interview guide to their clients and colleagues for review and feedback, and (d) to the extent that the schedule allows, taking a complete break from their development of the interview and going back to it a few days or a week later with a fresh mind.

For example, one of the most common mistakes researchers make in designing an IDI interview guide is the failure to fully discuss the relevant issues with each of the principal clients or sponsors of the research. These individuals have a vested interest in the success of the research and by failing to understand their particular perspectives on the subject matter, the researcher may remain ignorant of important ideas or concepts that need to be addressed in the interviews. So, for instance, an IDI study on renewable energy among customers of the statewide utility company would be remiss if the researcher did not consult with managers across all corporate departments that deal with the public (e.g., corporate communications, corporate responsibility, external affairs, marketing, and advertising).

INTERVIEW GUIDE. The interview guide is basically an outline of the topics or issues that the interviewer wants to be certain to cover in the interview, often highlighted in some way to designate each topic's priority in relationship to the research objectives. Within each topic area, the guide includes specific questions (and follow-up questions) to ask in the interview and/or a general idea of what needs to be covered. The interview guide is designed to be flexible. It typically begins with broad issues and then progressively narrows the focus to the primary subject areas (i.e., a "funnel" approach to interviewing), leaving the interviewer with opportunities to deviate from the guide as deemed appropriate. For example, Box 3.5 shows a portion of the interview guide used in a telephone IDI study conducted for an architectural and interior design firm with decision makers at budget hospitality properties. In this guide, the funnel approach begins with a general discussion of the decision-making process, followed by questions concerning the particular architectural or interior design objectives, from which the interviewer narrows the questioning to how these design objectives are currently met by architectural/interior design firms and, more specifically, the interviewee's preferences in design firms now and what design firms must do moving forward to meet future needs.

Pilot-testing of the interview guide is an essential step in the IDI method in order to ensure that the appropriate questions are asked and the research objectives met. If this guide is not comprehensive or an accurate representation of the constructs of interest, the usefulness of data gathered and the study's final recommendations will be limited and possibly undermined.

Interviewer Effects

The selection of an interviewer or multiple interviewers is of central importance to the quality of an IDI study. Each interviewer should have not only the interpersonal skills and interviewing experience required of any qualitative researcher but also be (a) highly organized (to maintain the interview schedule); (b) confident (to speak intimately and informatively with interviewees and, in the case

---

BOX 3.5. Example of an Interview Guide to Determine Architectural and Interior Design Considerations in the Budget Hospitality Market: In-Depth Qualitative Interview with Hotel Decision Makers

INTRODUCTION

The interviewer introduces herself and explains that the general purpose of the interview is to discuss the important considerations in the performance, service, and selection of a design firm. The interviewer encourages the participant to speak candidly about the issues, emphasizing that there are no "right" or "correct" answers to her questions. The interviewer also asks the participant's permission to take notes and audiorccord the discussion to assist in data analysis and report writing. The interviewee is given the opportunity to ask the interviewer for further clarifications as to purpose, etc.

NOTE: ALL QUESTIONS/PROBES ARE ASKED AS RELEVANT TO THE INTERVIEWEE'S DECISION-MAKING RESPONSIBILITIES.

I. Warm-Up/Background and the Decision-Making Process

A. My questions today will focus on recent or upcoming projects involving the new construction or renovation of budget hotel property. First, tell me about the property you have most recently completed or you are currently working on:
  - Where is it located, and is it new construction or a renovation?
  - What is your affiliation with this property?
  - [IF APPLICABLE] Where are you in the design process?
  - Were/are you involved in the architectural design, the interior design, or both?

II. Design Objectives

A. Let us now turn to a discussion about your particular design needs. I am interested in understanding what you are looking for in the way of design as it relates to your hotel property. What is your primary goal or design objective? [INTERVIEWER PROBES FOR CLARIFICATION.]
  - Can you give me an example of how this goal might be fulfilled?
  - How do your design objectives vary depending on the particular property?

B. What, more than anything else, helps you achieve this goal? What do you rely on more than anything else to reach this design objective? Explain.
  - What are some of the elements of the process?

C. What, if anything, has been (or could be) the biggest obstacle to achieving your design goals?

(continued)

III. Working with Design Firms

A. Let's talk about your goals in conjunction with design firms and help me understand how design firms help you reach your objective.

- What are the key qualities or attributes of a design firm that contribute the most to satisfying your objectives? [INTERVIEWER PROBES FOR CLARIFICATION AND IS SENSITIVE TO THE FACT THAT SOME OF THIS HAS ALREADY BEEN DISCUSSED IN RESPONSE TO SECTION II.]

B. What about: [INTERVIEWER PROBES EACH FOR DEFINITION AND CLARIFICATION.]

- Design capabilities?
- Knowledge of the hospitality industry?
- Knowledge of the needs particular to budget hotels?

C. Is there an area among design firms that, in your opinion, is relatively weak or missing? How could design firms, in general, improve their performance or services to clients?

IV. Preference in Design Firms

A. Now, I'd like to understand how your design goals and the importance you give to certain attributes impact decisions when it comes to selecting one design firm over another. What are the most important considerations when selecting a design firm for your properties? [INTERVIEWER PROBES FOR OTHER CONSIDERATIONS, SUCH AS COST/ FEES.]

- Is this universally true? How do priorities change from project to project?

B. Are there certain design firms that are better at meeting your goals than others? Who are they? Explain to me what differentiates these firms. What adjectives best describe each of these firms?

- With which of these firms are you currently working?
- With which of these firms have you worked in the past?
- With which of these firms do you hope to work in the future? Why is that?

C. Can you give me an example of the best working relationship you have had with a design firm?

D. And what about the worst, or most disappointing, relationship you have had with a design firm?

V. Future Design Needs

A. As you look to future design projects, what do you see as your greatest challenge?

- How can a design firm help you meet that challenge?

B. How will you go about selecting the firms to include in the RFP process? How does this selection process depend on the particular design project?

- Is there something a design firm can do to be included in your RFP process? Explain.

of face-to-face IDIs, meet with interviewees at unfamiliar locations); (c) flexible and tolerant (to effectively deal with unexpected changes to the schedule; e.g., an interviewee is suddenly not available to meet at the appointed time); (d) intelligent and creative (to adapt the interview guide in real time to pursue new threads of inquiry as they emerge, if they are relevant to what is being studied); and (e) have the ability to stay focused on the study's objectives. This last point—the ability to stay focused on the objectives—is particularly important to data quality because, although the flexibility of the semistructured interview is an important benefit of the method, it is equally important for the interviewer to stay targeted on the research objectives in order to come away from the interview with a thorough and reliable knowledge of the interviewee's attitudes and behavior as related to the key research issues. For example, in a study among chronic headache sufferers concerning their use of headache remedies, it may not be useful to the research goals if the interviewer allows the interviewee to give a long commentary concerning medications taken for leg cramps and stomach ailments.

INTERVIEWER BIAS. The outcome of an IDI study, regardless of mode, is greatly affected by the interviewer's conscious or unconscious influence within the context of the IDIs—that is, the absence or presence of interviewer bias. The interviewer's demographic characteristics (e.g., age, race), physical appearance in face-to-face IDIs (e.g., manner of dress), voice in face-to-face and telephone IDIs (e.g., a regional accent), and personal values or presumptions are all potential triggers that may elicit false or inaccurate responses from interviewees. For example, imagine that an IDI study is being conducted with a group of public school teachers who are known to harbor negative feelings toward the district's superintendent but who express ambivalent attitudes in the interviews as the result of the interviewers' inappropriate interjection of their own personal positive opinions of the superintendent. In this way, the interviewers have caused the findings to be biased. In order to minimize this potential source of distortion in the data, the researcher can incorporate a number of quality enhancement measures into the IDI study design and interview protocol:

- The IDI researcher should conduct a pretest phase during which each interviewer practices the interview and learns to anticipate what Sands and Krumer-Nevo (2006) call "master narratives" (i.e., the interviewer's own predispositions) as well as "shocks" that may emerge from interviewees' responses. Such an awareness of one's own predispositions as an interviewer and possible responses from interviewees that might otherwise "jolt" the interviewer will more likely facilitate an uninterrupted interview that can smoothly diverge into other appropriate lines of questioning when the time presents itself. In this manner, the interviewer can build and maintain strong rapport with the interviewee as well as anticipate areas within the interview that might bias the outcome.

For example, Sands and Krumer-Nevo (2006) relate the story of a particular interview in a study among youth who, prior to the study, had been involved in drug use and other criminal behavior. Yami, the interviewer, approached one of the interviews with certain assumptions concerning the interviewee's educational background and, specifically, the idea that a low-level education most likely contributed to the youth's illicit activities. Because of these stereotypical expectations, Yami entered the interview with the goal of linking the interviewee's "past school failures" to his current behavior and was not prepared for a line of questioning that was not aimed at making this connection. As a result of her predisposition, Yami failed to acknowledge and question the interviewee when he talked about being a "shy, lonely boy" and, consequently, stifled the life story that the interviewee was trying to tell her.

- The interviewer should use follow-up and probing questions to encourage the interviewee to elaborate on a response (e.g., "Can you tell me more about the last time the other students harassed you at school?"), but not in a manner that could be perceived as seeking any particular "approved" substantive response.

- Using a reflexive journal is an important and necessary feature of an IDI study design. This device enhances the credibility of the research by ensuring that each interviewer keeps a record of his/her experiences in the field and how he or she may have biased interview outcomes. The interviewer reflects carefully after each completed IDI and records how he or she may have distorted the information gathered in the interview (inadvertent as it may have been) and how the interviewee's behavior and other factors may have contributed to this bias. This "reflexive objectivity" (Brinkmann & Kvale, 2015) helps the interviewer gain "sensitivity about one's [own] prejudices, one's subjectivity" (p. 278) and consider the impact of these influences on the credibility of the data. This objectivity might also reflect on any personal characteristics of the interviewer (e.g., voice parameters, personality traits, demographics) that affected the interview and resulted in unintended variation across all IDIs. By way of the reflexive journal, the research is enriched with a documented firsthand account of any interviewer bias or presumptions as well as variations in the interviewer's handling of interviews throughout the study. An example of a reflexive journal format is shown in Chapter 2, Figure 2.2, page 42.

- A reflexive journal can also be used in the triangulation of interview data. From a TQF perspective, a best practice is to have an impartial research team member review the audio or video recordings from one or more IDIs to identify how and under what circumstance the interviewer may have biased interviewees' responses. In turn, this review can be used in cross-reference with the interviewer's reflexive journal and discussed with the interviewer to help him/her better understand lapses in self-awareness. And, as discussed later in this chapter, this journal becomes an important component of the study's audit trail and a tool in the final data analysis and interpretation.

INTERVIEWER INCONSISTENCY. As much as a researcher may take the steps outlined above to minimize potential bias associated with the interviewer, an additional source of vulnerability in the area of Data Gathering in the Credibility component of the TQF is an inconsistent manner in which an interviewer may administer the interview, leading to inaccurate assumptions concerning the constructs of interest. By "inconsistency," we mean the degree to which interviewers deviate from the interview guide in their questioning in a way that does not bias the findings (i.e., elicit an inaccurate pattern of responses in the aggregate) but does lead to variations in the data across individual interviewees that do not truly exist. For example, in the IDI study among public school teachers and their attitudes toward the district's superintendent, if the interviewers vary question wording or how they follow up on some responses, the data may ultimately show that teachers' attitudes about the superintendent are generally negative in the aggregate (as predicted) but may also depict a range in these attitudes, from slightly positive to very negative, when in fact they all had similar views.

Although flexibility—i.e., giving interviewers the latitude to modify IDIs as deemed necessary to reach the objectives—is central to all qualitative research and critical to a high-quality IDI study, interviewer behavior that mistakes the freedom of flexibility with an "anything-goes," sloppy, or careless approach to interviewing brings unintended variation to the outcomes, negatively impacting the credibility of the final data. One of the biggest reasons for inconsistency on the part of the interviewer is improper or insufficient training. The important areas of training play out in different ways across the different IDI modes, and these mode-related issues are interspersed throughout the discussion that follows. Specifically, interviewers need to be adequately trained to:

• Fully understand the interview content and why they should not ask about the same issue in a radically different way or in a different context across IDIs. A study concerning telecommunications use, for example, will result in unreliable outcomes if the interviewer varies the definition of "telecommunications" devices or equipment across IDIs—by failing to define it at all for one interviewee; defining it for another interviewee as only the use of landline phones and fax machines; as landline and wireless telephones for another interviewee; and as any type of telephone, radio, television, or Internet-access device for yet another interviewee.

• Stay alert and conscientious to the research objectives and the reasons why some questions on the issues are better asked in a particular way. For instance, to accurately gauge reactions to a new psychological assessment program, the interviewer must read the program concept statement exactly as written across all IDIs in the study.

• Recognize and deal successfully with the stress of one's job while paying sufficient attention to the flow of information from the interviewee, and follow up on important issues in a consistent manner across interviewees, even when the interviewer is overworked and emotionally fatigued.

• Know how to scale an IDI that was originally developed for the face-to-face mode for the typically shorter lengths of telephone interviews in order to maintain consistency in the conduct of the interview. Interviewers should be trained to carefully prioritize topics or questions (from those that are the most relevant to the research objectives to less important or peripheral issues), including follow-up questions, and, in this way, ensure that complete and accurate information is consistently obtained on the most important issues in the time allotted.

• Understand the particular skills required when asking follow-up questions in the email method. For example, because a follow-up question might be asked some time after the participant's response to the initial question, the interviewer is obligated not only to remind the interview participant of his/her earlier response but also to provide some context. For whatever reason, email IDI participants may have changed an opinion or not remember what triggered a particular response; however, by providing some context (e.g., reminding the participant of earlier comments on the issue), the interviewer assists the interviewee in clarifying his/her thoughts. In this regard, James and Busher (2009) discuss the importance of prompting email participants by asking them to "review previous events through consideration of texts from earlier parts of their conversations" (p. 25). To facilitate the ability of going back to earlier responses, the email IDI participant as well as the interviewer must agree to maintain the same subject line in their email messages for the duration of the study.

• Accept the researcher's monitoring and feedback concerning any inconsistencies in the interviewer's interviewing and receive the necessary retraining on how to avoid these inconsistencies. To ensure that quality standards are being met and that research objectives are being adequately addressed in the IDIs, debriefing sessions with the interviewer should take place throughout the fieldwork period. An experienced person on the research team should continually advise and educate interviewers on conducting quality IDIs by way of audio recordings of the interviews, live monitoring at the time of the interviews, or reviewing of email/text transcripts.

Any of these precautions should help to mitigate inconsistencies in the resulting data and bolster the credibility of an IDI study.

In some cases the inconsistent behavior on the part of an interviewer may be so extreme as to invalidate one or more of the IDIs conducted by him/her. The researcher then is faced with a difficult choice of whether to reinterview this interviewer's study participants or to simply select new members of the target population to be interviewed by another interviewer who is known to be reliable. In making this decision the researcher needs to balance several considerations, including (a) will it be possible for the interviewee who has already been interviewed to provide credible data a second time to another interviewer? (b) are there enough members of the target population left on the list who have not been interviewed to replace the interviewees whose interviews have been invalidated? and (c) is there enough time left in the field period to conduct more interviews without jeopardizing the timelines for the study? This decision is further complicated if the invalidated interviews are among interviewees who represent a special segment of the population (e.g., a particular age group or psychological condition or position within an organization), in which case, the researcher either has to reinterview these interviewees or replace them with other members from the same unique segment of the population.

Interviewee's Ability and Willingness to Provide Information

A final major source of measurement-related vulnerability to the credibility of the data gathered in an IDI study is the interviewee him/herself. Interviewees can affect the credibility of the information gathered in an IDI in two basic ways: (1) they may simply not know the information being asked of them and may be reluctant to admit this to the interviewer, or (2) they may know the information being asked but be unwilling to divulge it or may purposely give an inaccurate response (e.g., the reluctance to respond to questions on sensitive topics or giving socially desirable answers to emotionally charged issues, such as church attendance or one's own sexual preferences and practices).

The interviewer can potentially head off the problem of interviewees not knowing the answers to the interview questions by explaining the nature of the information sought prior to the interview. Although this is not generally considered a best practice, it can be useful when the IDI will be asking about specific details that are not necessarily in the interviewee's "head" and need to be retrieved elsewhere (e.g., from personal records). Of greatest importance is the interviewer's ability to build a strong rapport with the interviewee, one in which the interviewee feels comfortable simply telling the interviewer "I really can't recall anything about that" or "I've never thought about that before and I'm not at all sure what I think about it now." Without this level of comfort and rapport, the interviewee may fabricate an answer that may add bias and/or inconsistency to the IDI study findings.

A special consideration should be given to the email IDI when the participant may have difficulty in responding because the interviewer has asked multiple questions in one email message. Gibson (2010) found that email IDI participants "produced richer data" when given only one or two questions to answer at a time compared to "a full list of questions." Asking multiple questions within a single email message should be avoided or done only when the questions are closely related. For example, the questions, "How would you describe your last experience shopping for a car?" and "What can you tell me about your experience the last time you shopped for a car?" might be asked in the same email message. However, the questions, "How would you describe your last experience shopping for a car?" and "Did you shop primarily on the Web, or did you visit local car dealers?" may confuse, frustrate, or tire the email participant because whether shopping for a car was done online or offline may not be an important aspect of the experience.

There are situations when the interviewee knows the information being asked but is unwilling to provide it. Once again, the interviewer–interviewee rapport is essential to dealing with these situations. The interviewer should create an interview environment in which the interviewee is comfortable telling the interviewer "I am not willing to answer that question" or "I am not comfortable giving you that information." By building trust, assuring the strict confidentiality in which the interviewee's answers will be kept, and explicitly asking for their candor, interviewees should be encouraged to simply state their unwillingness to provide the information being sought rather than fabricating an inaccurate answer that will weaken the credibility of the study data.

With the appropriate building of interviewer–interviewee rapport, the interviewer can potentially deal with an interviewee who he/she suspects is not providing accurate information by asking about an issue in several different ways, including some that are direct and others that are indirect (e.g., getting at the effects of cancer treatment by asking, "How are things going at home with the family?"). This approach is time-consuming and may be costly, but these follow-up questions to inconsistencies can become the subject of additional conversation that may lead to new insights. On the other hand, this approach is not easy to do well without risking that the interviewee will be offended by being caught out in his/her inconsistencies, opening up the possibility that the rest of the interview will be tainted or even worthless.

BUILDING RAPPORT. It is essential that the interviewer have the necessary skills to build rapport with the interviewee. Rapport building begins early in the IDI process and continues through completion of the interview. The following are guidelines that IDI interviewers should consider using in order to establish a trusting relationship with their interviewees and maximize the credibility of their outcomes:

• Regardless of the mode by which the IDIs will be conducted, the interviewer should contact each recruited interviewee on the telephone at least once prior to the scheduled interview to begin establishing rapport. This preliminary conversation helps the interviewer and the interviewee make a personal connection, manage their respective expectations, and facilitate an open dialogue at the interview stage. In addition to building rapport, an early personal exchange with the interviewee also instills legitimacy in the research, which further aids in the interview process and makes the interviewee comfortable in providing detailed, thoughtful, and credible data. Although preliminary contact is important for the IDI method across all modes, this step is particularly critical to non-webcam-enabled telephone, email, and mobile IDIs when the interviewer and interviewee will not meet face-to-face. Other considerations pertaining to the preliminary contact are as follows:

o The interviewer's preliminary communication with the interviewee should make clear (a) the purpose of the study and the interviewer's association with the research; (b) the anticipated length of the study (i.e., a date when the research is expected to be completed); (c) the breadth of the interview (i.e., the range of topics that will be covered); (d) the depth of the interview (i.e., the level of detail that may be requested, either directly or indirectly); (e) the time commitment required of the interviewee (e.g., length of a telephone IDI, the frequency participants are expected to check email messages in an email IDI study); (f) the material incentive (e.g., cash, a gift card); (g) in an email or mobile IDI study, the frequency of reminder email/text messages to participants who are slow to respond; and (h) the importance of transparent communication throughout the process (e.g., the interviewee should tell the interviewer if a question is unclear).

○ Bias may occur if the preliminary communication reveals too much about the study hypotheses and purpose to the interviewee. To minimize response bias and maximize the integrity of the outcomes, the interviewer needs to moderate the specificity conveyed regarding the purpose of the study in advance of the actual interview. In particular, interviewees should rarely be told about the specific hypotheses being studied because, in doing so, interviewees may consciously and/or unconsciously respond to interview questions by telling interviewers what they think interviewers and researchers want to hear. Interviewers should therefore be skilled at deferring any of the interviewee's detailed questions about the purpose(s) of the study until the interview is completed. For example, the interviewer can reorient the interviewee away from the broader goal of the research and toward the more specific purpose of the IDI, emphasizing that the most important goal of the research *at that moment in time* is to learn everything there is to know about the interviewee as it relates to the subject matter.

○ Preliminary contact is particularly important in the email IDI method because it is essential to establish the ground rules and expectations prior to the first interview dialogue in order to reduce the likelihood that the recruited participant forgets or is unavailable on the agreed-upon date. The purpose of this preliminary communication is also to ensure that the interviewer and interviewee have a mutual understanding of what is expected and to circumvent delays in the interviewing process as well as incomplete responses from the participant. This approach will result in more complete, credible data from the interview.

• The interviewer should make a conscious effort to interject a sign of sincere interest in the interviewee's remarks, but do so in a nonevaluative (i.e., potentially biasing) fashion, without displaying either approval or disapproval with the sentiment being expressed by the interviewee (e.g., "Your comments interest me, please go on").

• Particularly in the telephone and online modes, the interviewer must be able to identify and respond to cues in the conversation—for example, the interviewee's audible hesitations or the background noise in a telephone IDI, or nonresponse from an email participant. The email interviewer also needs to be sensitive to the idea that he or she has misjudged the participant's intent. For instance, Bowker and Tuffin (2004) report on the potential difficulty in judging whether an email IDI participant has more to say on a topic or whether certain questions would be deemed redundant. In either case, these potential miscalculations on the part of the interviewer can interfere with the interviewer–participant relationship, with interview participants providing short retorts, such as, "Yes, that was the end [of my comments]!" (Bowker & Tuffin, 2004, p. 237).

• With telephone IDIs, the interviewer–interviewee relationship can be enhanced by adding a webcam and/or an online component. The ability to see the interviewee and/or present stimuli to him/her (e.g., new program service features, promotional concepts, audio and video clips) during the interview takes advantage of the benefits of face-to-face contact.

Analyzability

As noted previously, the Analyzability component of the TQF is concerned with conducting complete and accurate analyses, leading to reliable and meaningful interpretations of the outcomes. As explained in Chapter 2, Analyzability embraces the two key elements of all qualitative analysis: Processing and Verification. A TQF approach to the analysis of an IDI study incorporates quality standards specific to the creation of transcripts, coding, and the development of thematic categories (i.e., Processing), as well as the methodical scrutiny of alternative, supplementary input that serves to inform and enrich the primary data (i.e., Verification). By carefully considering Processing and Verification procedures, IDI researchers maximize the validity of their analyses and the ultimate usefulness of the outcomes.

Processing

The processing of IDI data is not unlike that for other qualitative methods in that it requires the transcription, coding, and theme development across all IDI audio recordings and/or interviewers' field notes. The accuracy and completeness of the transcriptions are obviously critical to the subsequent steps of coding and theme development. The email IDI method has the advantage of producing its own transcripts, but for face-to-face, telephone, and some aspects of mobile IDIs, researchers need to find one or more transcriptionists. Transcriptionists might be found within the organization (possibly even among the research team) or need to be hired from a firm specializing in transcription services. Although there are currently many such service providers from which to choose, the researcher should look beyond practical considerations, such as cost and turnaround time, when selecting a transcriptionist and consider the fact that transcriptionists can introduce several types of error. For example, MacLean, Meyer, and Estable (2004) mention processing errors associated with "misinterpretation of content"; emotion-laden content; class, cultural, and language differences; and "unfamiliar terminology" (e.g., mistaking the "Region of Peel" as the "Region of Appeal"). Poland (1995) classifies transcriptionists' errors as "deliberate" (e.g., a well-intentioned but misguided effort to "tidy up" the verbatim version to be more grammatical), "accidental" (e.g., misplacing the period or comma in a sentence, which changes the meaning of the sentiment), and "unavoidable" (e.g., the inaccessibility of nonverbal cues). A TQF approach to IDI research endorses the idea that "the transcriptionist is an important member of the research team" (MacLean et al., 2004, p. 119) and takes steps to bring the transcription process up to quality standards. To ensure accuracy and completeness, the transcriptions of IDI data should be conducted by someone who:

- Is knowledgeable about the subject category (e.g., K–12 education).
- Is trained and experienced working on the specific research topic (e.g., use of technology in the K–12 curriculum).
- Is sensitive to how people speak in conversation and will insert the correct

punctuation (periods, commas, etc.) as well as the "indicators of the pauses, overlaps, and stressed sounds that are part of everyday speech" (Silverman, 2013, p. 53) to reflect the interviewee's intention (e.g., "I use technology in the classroom when I can!" is not misinterpreted as "I use technology in the classroom, when I can.").

- Accounts for the entire interview even if some portions are difficult to hear (by inserting the appropriate codes or commentary as necessary).

- Understands the language (English or otherwise) and its regional variation, including the correct spelling, grammar, and use of slang, and can translate if necessary.

- Can detect a complete thought, and can distinguish between the continuation of one thought and the beginning of another.

The coding of IDI transcripts and theme development have become more automated over the years with the advancement of a number of computer-assisted qualitative data analysis software (CAQDAS) programs. Although the technology of CAQDAS gives qualitative researchers a variety of functions and capabilities, it would be wrong to assume that the use of CAQDAS alone is sufficient to create accurate and meaningful sense out of IDI data. Just as the interviewing format in an IDI study needs to emphasize a personal approach and remain flexible, so too the researcher must personally delve into the very important process of coding IDI transcripts. It is only by full immersion into the development of codes and the coding itself that the researcher can identify the appropriate themes in the data, recognize the appropriate connections between themes, and build the appropriate stories that effectively communicate the meaning of the study outcomes. So, although serving a supportive function, use of CAQDAS—even with the capability of finding emergent categories—is not "good enough" (not a sufficient condition) for the purposes of achieving reliable analysis of the data and useful interpretation of the outcomes. (Of note, the use of software in qualitative data analysis is discussed further in Chapter 6 with respect to content analysis; see pp. 248–253.)

A TQF approach to coding and theme development endorses an intercoder process by which, typically, two to four coders work independently on the identical subset of IDIs, developing particular codes for each interview as well as common codes across interviews. Under the supervision of the researcher, coders then compare their code labels and code definitions for each interview and look for similarities and differences in their results. This discussion among coders is an opportunity for each coder to explain why some aspect of an IDI was coded (or defined) the way it was and how it may be in contrast to another coder's interpretation. It is through consensus and authority from the primary researcher that any one code is adopted. Using multiple coders throughout the coding process is also important as an ongoing means of cross-checking the use of codes. For instance, in a study among low-income women concerning nutrition and, specifically, their food preferences, one coder might code the comment "I wish there was a better selection of fat-free products that I can afford at my local supermarket" as "need to improve the quality of available food products," whereas another might use the code "need to add more fat-free products," and a third coder might suggest adding a new code specific to affordability or product pricing. Utilizing two or more coders also provides checks and balances with respect to potential interviewer bias, thereby mitigating "concerns about researcher influence on the nature of analysis" (Berends & Johnston, 2005, p. 380).

Verification

Equally important to the processing of IDI data is the consideration of alternative sources of information that can serve to verify the study data while giving the researcher a different, more enriched perspective on an IDI's study outcomes. It is not important whether this additional input supports the researcher's conclusions from the primary data; and, indeed, contradictions in the verification process do not necessarily invalidate the study's findings. What *is* important, however, is that the researcher recognize how other points of view can contribute to a more robust and meaningful analysis. One verification device is the reflexive journal. The interviewers' reflexive journals can be extremely important for researchers because they are likely to identify topical areas where interviewers may have raised concerns about their objectivity and the possibility of inadvertently biasing the IDIs or IDI field notes due to their own thoughts, feelings, subjectivity, and expectations. By referring back to the reflexive journals, researchers become more sensitized to what actually occurred in each IDI and how it may have impacted the interview outcomes.

Qualitative researchers are also encouraged to utilize peer debriefing in the analysis process to gain independent, unbiased feedback on the data. For instance, a researcher might ask a well-informed but impartial colleague to review the field notes, transcripts, and/or audio or video recordings of interviews along with the researcher's interpretations from an IDI study and give an assessment on the researcher's findings. Regardless of how closely the colleague's takeaway from the data matches that of the researcher's, this peer debriefing is an important reflexive exercise for the researcher in that it shines a light on possible biases or areas of subjectivity that he/she may have introduced into the analysis.

Triangulation is another useful procedure for verifying IDI data. Triangulation can be conducted in any number of ways—the intercoder process of code development described earlier is one example of triangulation—but the purpose is always to compare and contrast the data from a different perspective. As an example of triangulation, a researcher might compare the outcomes from an IDI study among cardiac care nurses to data from other sources such as hospital administrators (i.e., data triangulation). Method triangulation looks at IDI data in conjunction with the findings from an independent piece of research conducted using a different qualitative method, such as observations, or possibly from quantitative survey results. It is this "mixed-methods" approach that Funk and Stajduhar (2009) consider in their research with family caregivers and, specifically, what it means to cope with the caregiving experience. These researchers contend that IDI data alone "might lead to erroneous assumptions about caregiving coping" (p. 862) and illustrate this point with the comments of one elderly caregiver, who admitted at the end of "many months" of interviewing (and at which point the husband she was caring for had died) that she had "deceived the researcher" and had hidden her true feelings in the interview because it was her way of coping (putting on a "brave face") as she faced the duties of caring for her dying husband. By adding a method (e.g., observations) to an IDI study such as this one, the researchers believe they gained a more accurate and robust account of the feelings underlying this caregiver's coping experience. And, indeed, Funk and Stajduhar assert that "our research experiences suggest that combining at least interview and observational methods in the study of caregiving . . . has greater potential to teach us more about the caregiving experience than interviewing alone" (p. 865).

An additional useful step in the data verification process is the seeking out and examination of instances when participants' responses or the interviewer's experience deviate from the mainstream findings. This deviant or negative case analysis approach allows the researcher to identify the "outliers" in the data and fully understand how and why a data subset is contrary to the broader outcomes. It is this ability to contrast and compare contrary IDI input with more typical responses that gives the researcher a more complete picture of the research matter as well as potentially stronger support for the plausibility of the final interpretations drawn from the study. As an example, an IDI study of state-run correctional facilities to explore the operational factors that make some facilities more cost efficient than others might reveal a best-practices "formula" that contributes to their high level of efficiency. It is not, however, an analysis of just the IDIs from the "best facilities" that allows the researcher to identify this "formula" but rather an equal appreciation and analysis of the least efficient (deviant) facilities, and the ability to contrast the two.

Transparency

The Transparency component of the TQF approach centers on the extent to which each IDI research phase, as well as each critical decision in the course of a study, has been documented. The goal is to provide an audit trail of the final outcomes that would allow another researcher to derive similar conclusions from the data as presented and/or apply the research to other similar contexts (i.e., transferability). A detailed or "thick" description of the thinking and processes involved with the study should appear in the final reporting document.

A detailed accounting for an IDI study should include varying degrees of information concerning the following:

THICK DESCRIPTION DETAILS FOR IDIs

- The researcher's assumptions regarding the sample population, data-gathering techniques, and expected outcomes.
- The adequacy (i.e., comprehensiveness) of the lists (sampling frame) that were used to represent the target population.

- The sampling rationale, especially the determination of the appropriate number of IDIs to conduct and the process of interviewee selection, including the efforts that were made to select a representative sample from the list(s).

- The failure to interview all interviewees sampled, efforts that were made to avoid this failure, and possible biases or weaknesses the absent interviews may have caused.

- The decisions, if any, that the researcher made while the study was in the field that modified the original research objectives or design elements. For example: Reasons for switching from face-to-face to telephone IDIs because of unexpected costs and time delays with the face-to-face mode, and the implications of this change in achieving the research objectives.

- The interviewers' reflexive journals, including examples of journal entries specific to their attitudes, beliefs (e.g., the researcher's theoretical orientation coming into the study), and behavior during the interviews that may have biased or influenced the data one way or the other.

  o For the email IDI method, this step includes documentation of any judgments or assumptions interviewers may have made about interviewees based on their writing styles, including relevant examples of interviewees' text responses.

- The field notes (e.g., note-taking procedures, examples from the field notebook).

- The transcription process (for face-to-face, telephone, and some portion of mobile IDIs).

- The coding procedures and justification for response categories.

- The verification procedures as well as the results and implications from these verification efforts.

This thick accounting of an IDI study not only allows others to live the experience of the researcher by comprehending the full extent of the process but gives other researchers the information they need to judge the strengths and limitations of the study as well as its transferability to different contexts (e.g., adapting a study concerning technology use among the disabled to study disabled people in different geographic locations or living situations).

Usefulness

The Usefulness component of the TQF addresses how well an IDI study advances the state of knowledge by way of new insights, actionable next steps, and/or transferability. Whether it is an academic, governmental, not-for-profit, or commercial proprietary study, the ultimate "acid test" of all IDI studies is the degree to which the research as a whole moves users and readers of the final documents forward in some regard.

For this forward movement to be the case, the Usefulness component relies completely on the other three units of the TQF model: Credibility, Analyzability, and Transparency. An IDI study is ultimately useful when the researcher has taken the necessary steps to (a) ensure representative coverage of the target population as well as reliable and valid data gathering (Credibility), (b) process and verify the data (Analyzability), and (c) fully document the life of the study and decision making in the final report (Transparency). By maximizing the concepts and steps toward applying the TQF, as discussed in this chapter section, the researcher is building support for why the design and execution of an IDI study has led to useful findings, interpretations, and recommendations.

In this manner, a TQF strategy enables the IDI researcher to take the high road by advancing knowledge in the subject area of the research as well as furthering quality standards in the IDI qualitative research design. The researcher's careful assessment and acknowledgment of the strengths and limitations of his/her IDI study, as well as the design features that make the study credible, analyzable, and transparent, increases the likelihood that the study is also, most importantly, useful. As a prudent measure to assess the usefulness of an IDI study, researchers are encouraged to conduct follow-up reviews subsequent to their final reporting, to evaluate if and how their research was applied to mitigate the research issue under study and/or to examine the research issue in other comparable contexts.

Case Study

A case study of an IDI project that was conducted for a provider of nonprofit information is presented starting on page 100. This research is an example of a TQF approach that resulted in highly useful outcomes for the sponsoring client and other researchers.

3.4   CHAPTER SUMMARY

✓ The in-depth interview (IDI) is central to most qualitative research, either as the sole method of data collection or in combination with other methods.

✓ The three types of IDI formats are structured, semistructured, and unstructured (the discussion in this chapter mostly refers to the semistructured format).

✓ Compared to group discussions, IDIs enable a thorough investigation that is less encumbered by social pressure and allows the interviewee to speak with greater candor about complex, sensitive, and/or yet-to-be-explored topics. IDIs can be particularly effective when conducting research with hard-to-reach and vulnerable populations.

✓ An IDI interviewer should have the ability to (1) build rapport with a vast range of interviewees, (2) practice active listening, (3) stay highly focused, (4) maintain heightened sensitivity to verbal and nonverbal cues, and (5) obtain an accurate and complete record of each interview.

✓ The primary strengths of the IDI method are (1) the close relationship that can and should develop between the interviewer and interviewee, which should increase data credibility; (2) the flexibility of the format, which empowers the interviewer to tailor the approach to maximize the value of the interviewee's data; and (3) the depth of interviewing that is possible, which yields highly granular, detail-rich data.

✓ A potential limitation of the IDI method occurs when an interviewer biases what the interviewee says due to the interviewer's own characteristics, mannerisms, values, and beliefs, or by overcontrolling the dialogue and failing to allow the interviewee to speak freely.

✓ There are four modes for conducting an IDI. The *face-to-face mode* has been at the core of most qualitative research. Its main strength is that it creates an environment conducive to a "natural" conversation, compared to a more formalized research atmosphere, and it provides the interviewer with nonverbal and visual cues that add meaning to the data. The *telephone mode* is typically less expensive and time-consuming than face-to-face IDIs. It does not suffer from the geographic and other logistical demands of bringing the interviewer and interviewee to the same location. In some situations, the telephone format provides a "comfortable distance" between the interviewer and the interviewee that may foster more candid thoughts about sensitive topics than an in-person IDI. *Online mode* IDIs often are conducted by way of asynchronous email messaging and have the advantage of allowing the interviewee to take more time to reflect on what is being discussed, to look up information that is not easily or accurately stored in memory, and to elaborate responses with rich details. Email interviewing also has the advantage of providing built-in transcripts at the completion of each IDI. The *mobile mode* IDI may be the best way to gain cooperation from those less than 35 years of age. The smartphones used for this mode allow the interviewee to readily communicate with the researcher via voice, text, and/or visuals about events *as they are happening*, thereby avoiding interviewee memory problems. The mobile mode also shares some of the advantages of the other three modes. However, both the online and mobile modes suffer from a lack of coverage of a portion of the general population due to older people being less likely to use these modes.

✓ From a Total Quality Framework perspective, the Credibility component of an IDI study is affected by how well the interviewees represent the target population, which is determined by (1) the quality of the list used to choose the interviewees, (2) how they are selected for the list, and (3) whether those selected, but who do not agree to be interviewed, are different from those who are interviewed. The number of IDIs to complete should be considered during the initial design phase and by evaluating 10 critical questions (see Box 3.3) while the study is in the field. Gaining cooperation from participants is important to obtaining quality data and can be particularly challenging when the study involves closed facilities or hard-to-reach segments of the population. When gathering data, there are three key areas to consider to maximize the quality of IDI outcomes: (1) interview content (including development of the interview guide); (2) interviewer effects (i.e., ways the interviewer may bias the data or conduct IDIs in an inconsistent manner); and (3) participants' abilities and/or willingness to answer the interviewer's questions. Interviewer training and monitoring are very important to building rapport and decreasing the chances of an interviewer biasing what an interviewee says or creating unwarranted data inconsistencies. IDI interviewers should use a *reflexive journal* to record what took place as they gathered data and their personal thoughts during the field period. Any of these precautions should help to mitigate uncertainty in the resulting data and bolster the credibility of an IDI study.

✓ The Analyzability of an IDI study relies on accurate and complete transcriptions of the interviews performed by a qualified transcriptionist with specific abilities discussed in this chapter (the exception is the email IDI, by which transcriptions are built into the process). Analyzability also hinges on various verification procedures such as peer debriefing, triangulation, and deviant case analysis.

3.5 EXERCISES AND DISCUSSION TOPICS

1. Select a published face-to-face IDI research study and discuss the design's strengths and limitations from the perspective of the TQF.

2. Consider a research issue that interests you and develop an email or mobile IDI study design utilizing the TQF approach. Discuss how you address each of the TQF components in your design.

3. What are the tradeoffs between the TQF components when designing a face-to-face IDI study, telephone IDI study, an email IDI study, and a mobile IDI study? Discuss how these tradeoffs might change depending on the research issue or objective.

4. Create a scenario where telephone IDIs would be the preferred method and design such a study based on TQF components.

5. Select a face-to-face or online IDI study from the literature and redesign it as a telephone or mobile IDI study and discuss the strengths and limitations of your design, compared to the original, from a TQF perspective.

6. Contrive an "ideal" scenario for a mobile IDI approach, design the study justifying each step via the TQF, and defend the design, compared to other methods, from a TQF perspective.

SUGGESTED FURTHER READING

Krumer-Nevo, M. (2002). The arena of othering: A life-story study with women living in poverty and social marginality. *Qualitative Social Work, 1*(3), 303–318.

This is a well-written and inspiring article that, among other things, provides an important discussion concerning the potential trap researchers may fall into by taking away stereotypical, "flat" interpretations from the research findings rather than "seeing people as complex characters/persons" (p. 314).

Kvale, S. (2006). Dominance through interviews and dialogues. *Qualitative Inquiry, 12*(3), 480–500.

As in the Brinkmann and Kvale (2015) book, *Interviews: Learning the Craft of Qualitative Research Interviewing* (cited in this chapter), in this article Kvale explores the "asymmetrical power relation" in the IDI. Because of the intimate, one-on-one nature of IDIs, Kvale's discussion of the power dynamics between interviewer and interviewee are especially relevant. Kvale contends that the IDI "is a one-way dialogue, an instrumental and indirect conversation, where the interviewer upholds a monopoly of interpretation" (p. 484).

Rubin, H. J., & Rubin, I. S. (2012). *Qualitative interviewing: The art of hearing data* (3rd ed.). Thousand Oaks, CA: Sage.

In this book Rubin and Rubin offer a style of IDI they refer to as "responsive interviewing." It is an interviewing style that "emphasizes the importance of building a relationship of trust between the interviewer and interviewee that leads to more give-and-take in the conversation" (p. 36). This book provides one example of how to design, conduct, analyze, and report IDI research that is *modeled after a specific type of interview.*

WEB RESOURCE

West, R. (2012). Lather, rinse, repeat: Getting into the shower and other private places with mobile qualitative. In *MRMW North America Conference*. Cincinnati, OH. *http://vimeo.com/49323073.*

This is an 18-minute presentation by Rebecca West concerning Civicom's mobile market research study for a beauty products manufacturer. This research studied the purchase and use of a body wash product among female "enthusiasts" by way of in-store visits and actual use in the shower. The presentation goes through the design considerations, the various ways participants communicated with the Civicom researchers at the store (i.e., voice, image, text, and video) and in the shower (i.e., voice), and research findings.

NOTES

1. Briggs proposes a four-phase approach to interview design: "learning how to ask" (determining how to ask research questions in various social situations within the research context), developing a methodology that incorporates appropriate techniques as well as supplemental sources of information, building reflexivity into the process, and analyzing the interviews.

2. In some instances the "researcher" may also be the person who conducts the IDIs (i.e., the "interviewer"). This is typically the case when the study is being conducted by a small research firm or group where the principal researcher assumes many duties, including the execution of all fieldwork. In other instances, the researcher may be the person who is responsible for managing a number of people on a research team, including one or more interviewers who conduct the IDIs. For this reason, we sometimes use "researcher" and "interviewer" interchangeably.

3. There are many examples of IDI studies among cancer survivors, patients, and caregivers, including Leydon et al., 2000; Mancini et al., 2011; Murray et al., 2002; Johansson et al., 2003; Osse et al., 2002; Ferrell et al., 1997b.

4. There are many examples of using the IDI method to examine health-related issues outside of those pertaining to cancer: for example, Mollen et al., 2008; Wahl, Gjengedal, & Hanestad, 2002; Veseth, Binder, Borg, & Davidson, 2012; Karp & Tanarugsachock, 2000; Provoost et al., 2010.

5. "Participant" and "interviewee" are used interchangeably throughout this chapter.

6. A discussion of projective techniques, including examples of various types, is provided in Chapter 4.

7. Irvine measured floor holding by the amount of time someone spoke "that in some way steered the conversation (namely questions, prompts and probes), or provided summation, assessment or evaluation of the participant's talk" (p. 208).

8. Research participants situated their smartphones just outside the shower or, when space allowed, resting on a ledge inside the shower.

IDI Case Study

PURPOSE

In 2009, an IDI study was conducted for a large firm ("Firm") that provides access to comprehensive information on more than one million nonprofit organizations in the United States to public and private entities who use this information for making grants and philanthropic-related activities. The purpose of this IDI research was to understand the current and future information needs among existing and former customers (i.e., users of their information services) to facilitate the development of new, "cutting-edge" service concepts that would be developed to meet these demands.

METHOD

Qualitative research and, specifically, the IDI method was deemed the appropriate approach, given that the Firm (a) had not conducted research with its customers (or potential customers) in the past and, therefore, had no historical data from which to draw to inform the current study; (b) needed in-depth feedback on a variety of service components; (c) wanted to show prototypes of possible new service products; and (d) caters to organizations that are widely dispersed throughout the United States.

DESIGN

Credibility

Scope

The Firm provided lists of its largest customers, its smaller but current customers, and former customers. All lists were sorted by revenue (to the Firm) and type of organization (e.g., private foundation, public charity, financial services, and "other" such as an educational institution). Organizations were selected from the lists on an nth-name basis across the entire lists, ensuring that research participants were representative of the lists provided.

A total of 86 IDIs were conducted for the Firm among individuals who make the decision within their organization to purchase and utilize the Firm's informational services. Twenty-eight of these interviews were conducted in the face-to-face mode with the Firm's largest customers (based on revenue to the Firm) because these multifaceted organizations have complex informational needs that required a more-involved, in-depth discussion. The remaining 58 interviews were conducted via telephone. There were two primary considerations in choosing to complete 86 interviews: (a) the required level of analysis—it was important to be able to analyze the data by type of organization, and (b) practical considerations—the Firm's budget (how much they had to spend on the research) and time restrictions (the Firm wanted to present the research findings at an upcoming board meeting).

Several steps were taken to achieve the highest degree of cooperation from current and former customers:

- A preliminary letter was sent (via email) to all contacts on the Firm's lists. This letter explained the purpose and benefit of participating in the research ("to better meet your information needs"), requested cooperation with the effort, and provided the name of the interviewer as well as the person who would be calling to set an appointment for the interview. This letter was signed by the president and CEO of the Firm.

- Because of the Firm's strong and positive reputation among nonprofit organizations in general, it was decided to identify the Firm as the sponsor of the research. Therefore, the Firm's letterhead was used for the preliminary letter, the executive recruiter mentioned the Firm's name during recruitment, and the interviewer openly cited the Firm during the interviews. The high level of cooperation witnessed in this IDI study is greatly attributed to identifying the research sponsor.

- Everyone contacted for the research was promised a summary of the research findings (i.e., a nonmonetary reward) upon completion of the research. This was an appropriate incentive, given that interviewees were interested to know how other decision makers were using nonprofit information and how they reacted to the Firm's proposed concepts presented during the interviews.

- The recruitment of interviewees was conducted by one professional executive recruiter who was highly trained on how to gain access to decision makers and to speak with them in a professional manner. This recruiter worked closely with the researcher to ensure that the scheduling needs of potential interviewees could be satisfied to the degree possible.

- Face-to-face interviewees were allowed to select any convenient location for the interview. The interviewer remained flexible when interviewees needed to make changes in the location or date of the IDI.

Data Gathering

The quality of the research data related to Data Gathering was maximized by the fact that the development of the interview guide and the completion of all 86 interviews were conducted by one professional researcher who was working with the Firm on a contract basis (i.e., she was not affiliated with the Firm). The researcher/interviewer maximized the credibility of the research results by:

- Meeting with various managers within the Firm who had a vested interest in the outcome of the research—for example, the president and CFO as well as the directors of research, programs, and communications—to gain a clear understanding of the research objectives and the constructs to measure.

- Learning as much as possible about the category via websites and literature particular to competitive providers of similar nonprofit information, how organizations use this information, and background details on each of the organizations that were included in the sample.

- Reviewing and deliberating with the Firm on multiple drafts of the interview guide for both the face-to-face and telephone IDIs.

- Prioritizing topics so that the issues of most importance to the research objectives were consistently discussed in every IDI—for example, opinions concerning other types of information providers and the usability of specific features on the Firm's website.

• Working (literally) side-by-side with an executive recruiter during the recruitment phase to ensure that the proper screening questions were being asked and that only qualified people were recruited for an IDI. For instance, it was determined in the recruitment phone call that a few people on the Firm's lists were not the appropriate decision makers. In those cases, the recruiter had to make an extra effort to track down the person within the organization who met the requirement of being the decision maker as well as the user of nonprofit information.

• Scheduling IDIs at least 2–3 hours apart so the interviewer could allow the interviewee to talk beyond the 30- to 45-minute initial time commitment (some face-to-face IDIs ran up to 2 hours and some telephone IDIs ran an hour).

• Building rapport with interviewees early in the process by way of emailing and telephoning them to confirm the interview appointment and introduce the interviewer, along with providing contact information for the interviewee to use in order to request a change in the schedule or otherwise communicate with the interviewer. Further, the interviewer encouraged interviewees to ask her questions about the research before, during, and after the IDI.

• Emphasizing at the onset of the interview that, even though the Firm was openly acknowledged as the sponsor of the research, the interviewee's candid opinions were essential to the success of the study. The interviewer reminded interviewees that she was not affiliated with the Firm and had no vested interest in the research outcomes beyond the quality of the data, analysis, and reporting.

Analyzability

With the interviewees' permission, all IDIs were recorded via a digital audio recorder. Two transcribers worked on the transcriptions, and audio recordings were given to them at the end of each day of interviewing. The transcribers were given complete background information on the Firm, the purpose of the research, the competitive providers, the organizations that would be participating in the research, and, to the degree possible, the particular terminology or language that was used in the IDIs. These transcribers had worked with the interviewer in the past and were known for their thorough and accurate approach to transcribing.

The researcher/interviewer developed codes from the transcriptions and created a spreadsheet that accounted for every IDI in terms of responses to key questions or topic areas as well as relevant organizational characteristics, such as the type of organization and primary use of the information. Interviewees' input was color-coded in the spreadsheet to signify the thematic emphasis of the response (e.g., the importance of a speedy information delivery system) and whether the response was intended as a positive or negative comment concerning the Firm and its information services. Adherence to the TQF would require that at least one other researcher be involved in the coding and thematic development. This may have enhanced the analysis; however, at the time, the researcher/interviewer felt that her unique knowledge of all aspects of the IDI study (as the sole researcher/interviewer involved) qualified her to perform all analytical functions. Inter-coder verification would have added validity to the research outcomes.

Verification procedures such as deviant analysis were conducted. For example, the researcher contrasted and compared the behavior and opinions of a few organizations whose use of information was unlike that of more typical organizations. The data corresponding to this analysis were given to the research director at the Firm for her independent analysis and interpretation.

Transparency

The Firm received an extensive report at the conclusion of the research documenting the details of the scope, data-gathering, and analysis processes. For instance, the report discussed the:

- Rationale of the sample design, the lists and list size (e.g., 28 of all 81 people on the large customer list were included in the sample and interviewed).
- Steps that were taken to encourage cooperation with the research and build rapport.
- Interview guide, including a copy of the guide in the report's Appendix.
- Fractured nature of the Firm's marketplace with respect to the types of information users both within and across organizations, and how this diversity translated into different information needs. The fact that this study was not able to interview everyone in any one organization who used the Firm's information services was discussed and stated as a precautionary note to the reader.
- Manner in which the interviews were conducted; for example, the unrestricted nature of the semiunstructured IDI and modifying the interview as necessary to remain relevant to the interviewee.
- Deviant cases, how they compared to the more typical organizations, and why the Firm might want to conduct further research with these "deviant" organizations.
- Comments made by interviewees that illustrated an interpretation of the data. Interviewees' statements were used (anonymously) throughout the report to emphasize research findings as well as "humanize" the data for the reader.
- Researcher's reflexive journal and the particular entries in the journal pertaining to possible sources of bias or undue influence on the data.

The transparency of this research, as exhibited in the documentation, was intended to enable the reader to understand how the research was conducted, how the researcher reached the final interpretations, and how others might apply the design in other similar contexts.

Usefulness

The research findings allowed the client to (a) create a more user-friendly website, (b) think differently about how information needs vary depending on specific user characteristics, (c) prioritize new product/service concepts for further development, (d) prepare for future opportunities based on interviewees' anticipated information needs, and (e) apply a similar research design for a follow-up study 3 years later.

CHAPTER FOUR

Interview Method

Focus Group Discussions

CHAPTER PREVIEW

Focus group discussions—also referred to in this chapter as "group interviews," "group discussions," or "group interviewing"—share a number of features with the in-depth interview (IDI) (discussed in Chapter 3), but also differ from it in many important ways. Although the depth and detail that can be gained via group discussions is generally less than what can be gained with IDIs, focus groups provide researchers with multiple perspectives as two or more persons become actively engaged in a "focused" discussion about the topics the researcher is studying. This discussion may take place face-to-face at a central physical location or via telephone or the Internet. Because the role of the focus group moderator is critical to the success of the group discussion process, this chapter addresses the many complex tasks in which quality moderators must be capable of engaging and juggling during a focus group discussion. Other important topics covered in this chapter from a Total Quality Framework (TQF) perspective include (1) the importance of using systematic approaches to selecting the individuals who will be invited to participate in the focus groups; (2) how to determine the "correct" number of discussion groups to carry out and how many persons should participate in each group; (3) whether to organize homogeneous or heterogeneous groups; (4) the wide range of operational logistics that must be coordinated to allow each discussion to be held while maintaining quality design standards; and (5) the key role that transcriptionists play in processing the recorded discussions into a format that researchers can use to reach valid interpretations of the data.

4.1 INTRODUCTION

Group discussions offer the researcher a unique and important interviewing method. Unlike in-depth interviews (IDIs; see Chapter 3), group discussions have the potential of providing the researcher with the insights and understanding of motivations and behavior that can come only from a dynamic, interactive discussion format. Whereas the IDI method gives researchers a highly individualistic, personal qualitative approach, group interviewing celebrates individuality by gathering people together and encouraging participants to talk about (even debate) their divergent and convergent thoughts or ideas. What group discussions may lack in the depth of information provided by IDIs at the individual level, they can make up for in the rich output to be gained from multiple perspectives in a group environment that often leads to "more spontaneous expressive and emotional views than in individual, often more cognitive, interviews" (Brinkmann & Kvale, 2015, p. 176). It is this spontaneity of viewpoints that can make the results from group discussions "greater than the sum of separate individual opinions gleaned from interviews" (Carson, Gilmore, Perry, & Gronhaug, 2001, p. 116). In a group discussion, the whole can become greater than the sum of its parts.

In qualitative research, group discussions are typically referred to as "**focus groups**." Although this terminology stems from the "focused interview" coined by Robert Merton and his colleagues (Merton & Kendall, 1946), Merton, by his own admission, "never used the term 'focus group'" (Merton, 1987) and, indeed, the focused interview is a well-defined IDI method with specific characteristics, purpose, and interviewer skills (Merton & Kendall, 1946). Modern-day focus groups evolved from the group interviewing work of Emory Bogardus (1926), Paul Lazarsfeld (see Merton, 1987), and even Merton with his group interviews of soldiers in World War II. Whether the method that is called "group discussions" should be called "focus groups" or "group interviews" has been a point of debate among researchers such as David Morgan (1996). For the purposes of this chapter (and throughout the book), however, we include all terminology—"group discussions," "focus group discussions," "focus groups," "group interviews," "group interviewing"—under the same umbrella to connote a qualitative research data collection method that involves interviewing two or more people simultaneously with the goal of fostering interaction among participants, resulting in an exchange of experiences and ideas. This definition, which emphasizes the interaction and dialogue between participants, excludes the less interactive, more structured, consensus-building formats such as the traditional **Delphi**[1] and **nominal group**[2] methods that emphasize gathering information or ideas at the individual level and then pooling these ideas for further consideration or discussion.

There are many variations in the design of a group discussion study. These variations primarily revolve around (a) the number of participants, (b) the type of participants, and (c) the mode of conduct. In terms of size, there are basically four levels of focus groups: (1) two participants (called "**dyads**"), (2) three participants ("**triads**"), (3) four to six participants ("**mini groups**"), and (4) seven to 10 or more participants ("full" focus group). Group participants can include any segment of the population under study. Marketing research, a particularly heavy user of the focus group method, typically conducts group discussions with consumers (e.g., people who use a particular brand of laundry detergent) and business people (e.g., electrical contractors who purchase their supplies from a particular

wholesaler). Similarly, researchers in other fields—for example, sociology, education, psychology, health care, and communications—conduct focus groups with
the people most affected by the research topic of interest (e.g., farming practices
among migrant farmers, eating habits among teenagers, cancer patients' employment experiences, child-raising information needs among young mothers, the
impact of a local natural disaster on school children from the perspective of their
teachers). Furthermore, employee group discussions are often conducted by large
organizations when management wants to understand, for example, employees'
reactions to a new policy (e.g., on paternity leave) or gain insights on what drives
employee satisfaction. Although the group interviewing method has most often
been conducted face-to-face, telephone and online modes are increasingly common.

Basic Design Considerations in the Group Discussion Method

There are several considerations that are fundamental to the method when
designing a group discussion study. In addition to the choice of mode and the
role of the moderator (discussed elsewhere in this chapter), the researcher needs
to pay particular attention to the (a) suitability of group discussions based on the
research objectives as well as the accessibility and receptivity of the target population, (b) format or size of the groups, and, (c) group composition. Unlike the
IDI method that benefits from the "naturalness" of the one-to-one approach, the
more contrived environment of the focus group discussion may make the method
less suitable under certain circumstances. For example, face-to-face focus group
research would not be appropriate for a state agency that wants to understand the
credit needs of low-income residents of a small town, because the community's
narrow pool of these residents would necessitate recruiting people who may know
each other and who may be reluctant or unwilling to share details of their lives,
particularly as those details relate to credit. For similar reasons, face-to-face focus
groups would not be advised for investigating sexual activity among teenagers in
a close-knit community. And, group discussions would not be suitable when the
objective of the research is to gain feedback on the *usability* of a new website (i.e.,
the ability to navigate the site and move easily around it to find needed information) because it is the individual interplay with this website that comes closest to
mirroring its eventual use in the real world, and this can better be learned in an
IDI setting, not a group discussion.

On the other hand, group discussions are ideal when the research topic is not
highly sensitive and the dynamics of the group interaction can foster important
insights relevant to the research objectives. For example, a researcher might use
group interviewing to investigate (a) reactions to a new mobile-phone concept in
order to identify its perceived strengths and weaknesses, (b) perceptions of risk
and risk-taking among firefighters, (c) material preferences and purchases among
people who knit or crochet, (d) eating habits and food preferences among young
people with diabetes, (e) attitudes toward changes in a nonprofit's annual fund-
raising event among its program volunteers, (f) coping mechanisms and in-class

techniques for calming elementary school students in emergency situations among teachers, and (g) informational needs among residents of a retirement facility. Other real-life examples of using focus groups are discussed on pages 109–110.

As mentioned earlier, there are four basic types of groups for the group discussion method based on size. The most common is the "full" focus group comprising anywhere from seven or more people but, most typically, eight to 12 participants. Some researchers (and particularly research sponsors) believe that a 12-person group is optimal because they assume that more input (i.e., from 12 participants) is always "better" than less (i.e., from a smaller group). Yet, from a Total Quality Framework (TQF) perspective, a more productive group discussion (in any mode) is smaller in size—ideally, no more than 10 people—because it gives the moderator sufficient time to gain substantive, useful feedback from each group participant while also reducing any intimidation participants may feel from speaking in a larger group setting. This factor is why smaller group formats such as dyads (two-person group) and triads (three people) can be particularly useful in some situations. Toner (2009), for instance, describes the "more intimate interaction" she experienced in conducting dyads with Native Americans and Latinas as well as the "incredibly rich data" that resulted from these discussions. Her research is an example of how a small group size has the potential advantage of reaping in-depth information, not too dissimilar from an IDI. The size of the group has implications related to the modes of the group discussion method, which we discuss in more detail in Section 4.2 (starting on p. 113).

Group Composition

Another important consideration that is fundamental to the design of a focus group study is group composition. Specifically, the researcher must determine the degree of homogeneity or heterogeneity that should be represented by the group participants. As shown in Box 4.1, there is any number of questions the researcher needs to contemplate, such as the extent of similarity or dissimilarity in participants' demographic characteristics, as well as in their experiences and involvement with the subject matter.

Whether or not—or the degree to which—group participants should be homogeneous in some or all characteristics has been at the center of debate for some years. On the one hand, Grønkjær, Curtis, Crespigny, and Delmar (2011) claim that at least some "homogeneity in focus group construction is considered essential for group interaction and dynamics" (p. 23)—for example, participants belonging to the same age group may have similar frames of reference and feel comfortable sharing their thoughts with people who have lived through the same experience. In the same vein, Sim (1998) states that, "the more homogeneous the membership of the group, in terms of social background, level of education, knowledge, and experience, the more confident individual group members are likely to be in voicing their [own] views" (p. 348). Even among strangers, there is a certain amount of comfort and safety in the group environment when the participants share key demographic characteristics, cultural backgrounds, and/or relevant experience.

**BOX 4.1. Focus Group Composition:
Questions When Considering Heterogeneity versus Homogeneity**

A few of the questions the focus group researcher might consider when determining the desired heterogeneity or homogeneity among group participants include:

- Should participants be in the same age range and/or stage of life?
- Should participants be the same gender, race, and/or ethnicity?
- Should participants be at a similar income, socioeconomic, or educational level?
- Should participants reside in the same community, be members of the same organization(s)?
- Should participants have similar professions or jobs (including job titles)?
- Should participants have a similar involvement, experience, or knowledge with the research topic, for example, the same types of problems with their 13-year-old boys? The same health care service provider? The same purchase behavior? The same level of expertise with a new technology?

A problem arises, however, if this comfortable, safe environment breeds a single-mindedness (or "groupthink") that, without the tactics of a skillful moderator, can stifle divergent thinking and result in erroneous, one-sided data. Heterogeneity of group participants (e.g., including users and nonusers of a particular child care service within the same focus group) potentially heads off these problems by stimulating different points of view and a depth of understanding that comes from listening to participants "defend" their way of thinking (e.g., product preferences). As Grønkjær et al. (2011) state, "a group may be too homogeneous; thus influencing the range and variety of the data that emerges" (p. 26). The tension that heterogeneity may create in a group discussion can serve to uncover deeper insights into what is being studied, providing the moderator is able to channel this tension in constructive directions. In addition to a heightened level of diversity, heterogeneous groups may also be a very pragmatic choice for the researcher who is working with limited time and financial resources, or whose target population for the research is confined to a very narrow group (e.g., nurses working at a community hospital).

Ultimately, the answer to the question of whether group participants should be homogeneous or heterogeneous is "it depends." As a general rule, group participants should have similar experiences with, or knowledge of, the research topic (e.g., using the Web to diagnose a health problem, weekly consumption of fat-free milk), but the need for "sameness" among participants on other parameters can fluctuate depending on the circumstance. Halcomb, Gholizadeh, DiGiacomo, Phillips, and Davidson (2007), for example, report that homogeneity of age is particularly important in non-Western countries where younger people may believe it is disrespectful to offer comments that differ from those stated by their elders. Homogeneous groups are also important when investigating sensitive topics, such as drug use among teenagers, where a more mixed group of participants with people who are perceived as "different" (in terms of demographics and knowledge/experience with drugs) may choke the discussion and lead to a struggle for control among participants (e.g., one or more participants trying to dominate the discussion).

Homogeneity of gender (i.e., an all-male group or an all-female group), on the other hand, may or may not be important to the success (usefulness) of a focus group study. For example, an organization conducting employee focus group research to explore employees' attitudes toward recent shifts in management would need to conduct separate groups with men and women in order to discover how the underlying emotional response to new management differs between male and female employees. In contrast, a focus group study among city residents concerning public transportation might benefit from including both men and women in the same discussion, among whom the varied use and perceptions of the transportation services would serve to stimulate thinking and enrich the research findings. The heightened level of dynamics in groups that are heterogeneous in gender and other aspects may also provoke conversations on taboo subjects (e.g., racism) that might not be forthcoming in an IDI. Group composition is discussed in Section 4.3, as it relates to sample design (see pp. 129–130).

Appropriate Uses of the Group Discussion Method

The focused interview approach used with individuals and groups as described by Merton and Kendall (1946) was never intended as a stand-alone research method. Rather, the purpose was to "test" certain hypotheses or assumptions that resulted from content analyses conducted on "a particular situation," such as reactions to a radio program. In other words, group interviewing, from the early days of Merton, served the purpose of supporting *quantitative* research by affirming or denying theories derived from survey data, or generating new ideas and hypotheses that could be verified by further survey research. To this point, Merton emphasized that from the results of group discussions, "there is no way of knowing in advance of further quantitative research which plausible interpretations (hypotheses) will pan out and which will not" (Merton, 1987, p. 558).

Focus group discussions today are, to some degree, used in conjunction with quantitative research (as prescribed by Merton) and, indeed, are an effective method for exploring new ideas and informing the design of a survey questionnaire (e.g., in terms of subject matter and language) as well as evaluating and deepening the researcher's understanding of the survey data. The work of O'Donnell, Lutfey, Marceau, and McKinlay (2007) on physician decision making is one example of how group discussions have been integrated with the research process to improve the quantitative component. Other examples come from Vogt, King, and King (2004), who conducted focus groups with Gulf War veterans concerning war-related stressors to aid in the development of their instrument to assess psychological status, and Alquati Bisol, Sperb, and Moreno-Black (2008), who conducted triads with deaf and hearing youth to assist in the development of a survey questionnaire concerning HIV/AIDS and sexual behavior.

Group discussions, however, are more often utilized as the sole qualitative method to investigate phenomena independently from quantitative research. In this respect group interviewing has been used for a broad range of topics or issues across the health care and social science disciplines. For example, Nicholas et al. (2010) conducted focus groups among children with chronic health problems to assess the viability of the face-to-face versus online mode for discussions with this target population, and Ferrell et al. (1997a) conducted group discussions with survivors of breast cancer to understand their perspectives related to quality-of-life issues. Sociologists have used group discussions to study gender violence among teenagers (Aubert, Melgar, & Valls, 2011). Researchers in the education field have used focus groups to examine the experiences of racism among Black students in predominantly White universities (Harper et al., 2011). Communication researchers have studied the phenomenon of cyberbullying by way of group discussions with 10- to 18-year-olds (Vandebosch & Van Cleemput, 2008). And the marketing research industry, easily the most frequent user of the focus group method, utilizes group interviewing extensively to research a variety of issues among consumer, business, and employee segments. For example, in the unpublished work of the first author, consumer group discussions have been conducted with homeowners concerning their do-it-yourself project material preferences and purchase behavior, with men concerning their experiences undergoing hair transplants, with mothers of young children concerning food preparation, with telephone customers concerning advanced telecommunication services, and with viewers of "The Weather Channel" concerning their weather-related information needs from the Internet. Among business people, group discussions have been conducted with small business owners about how they select one bank over another, with roofing contractors concerning their preferences in roofing materials, with utility commercial customers concerning the viability of a new business Web portal, with managers of top-tier hotels to discuss in-room amenities, with information technology (IT) and operations managers concerning the potential usefulness of new telephone technology, and with logistics managers concerning next-day courier service needs. Employee focus groups can address a number of corporate issues pertaining to communications, human resources, and customer service. Discussions with employees can also prove effective when a tragic or unfortunate event has occurred at the company; for example, the first author conducted focus groups with employees to understand their thoughts, emotions, and communication needs after a shooting incident at their corporate headquarters.

Moderator Skills

The moderator of a group discussion plays a unique and major role in the outcome of focus group research. More than any other qualitative method, the ultimate usefulness of group discussions relies on the complexity of skills honed by the person who interfaces with the participants and "guides" the discussion—that is, the moderator. These skills encompass the necessary abilities of any interviewer, such as minimizing bias, building rapport, active listening (see pp. 55–56), in addition to managing the **group dynamics** associated with various personalities, participant interaction, disruptive behavior (e.g., a domineering participant), and the potential of a "runaway" discussion that departs from the research objectives. The skillful moderator is one who can adapt to the uniqueness of each group situation and manage the dynamics while staying focused on maintaining a supportive group environment that encourages a spontaneous, interactive discussion that includes all participants and that addresses the research issues in a way that maximizes the credibility and usefulness of the outcomes.

Overview of the Strengths and Limitations of the Group Discussion Method

Strengths

The unique advantage of the group discussion method is clearly the participant interaction and what it adds to (goes beyond) what might be learned from a series of IDIs. When conducted to achieve its full potential, the back-and-forth dialogue among the participants benefits the researcher (and the quality of the data) in several important respects:

- A dynamic group discussion will often stimulate spontaneous ideas and personal disclosures that might otherwise go unstated in an IDI.
- A relaxed, interactive, as well as a supportive (e.g., homogeneous) group environment can be conducive to discussing sensitive topics (e.g., a discussion of the immigration process among recent Chinese immigrants to the United States).
- As participants exchange opinions, they consider their own views in relation to others'—which may encourage participants to refine their thoughts. In this way the group interaction gives the researcher insight into how people think about the topic(s) being studied and on what basis opinions may change. For example, in a focus group with college students who are considering various study-abroad programs, some participants might change their criteria for selecting one program over another after hearing other participants' considerations. This discussion would help the researcher identify the important aspects of study-abroad programs that may impact students' decision making.

Participant interaction, or the social aspect of focus group discussions, can be a particularly important advantage when conducting research with vulnerable and underserved population segments. For instance, women's studies researchers such as Wilkinson (1999) believe that focus groups offer feminist psychologists an important research approach over other psychological research methods because they (a) come "closer to everyday social processes" (p. 227) and are less "artificial" than other methods; (b) are highly interactive, which "produces insights that would not be available outside the group context" (p. 229); and (c) reduce the moderator's "exploitation" of the research by shifting control of the discussion to the participants. Other researchers have found the social nature of focus group discussions to be conducive to investigating societal constraints and health needs among Emirati women (Bailey, 2012; Winslow, Honein, & Elzubeir, 2002).

There are two other important strengths of the group discussion method: (1) it allows for the presence of observers, especially in the face-to-face mode; and (2) it increases the likelihood that a wide range of attitudes, knowledge, and experiences will be captured in one group session. Whereas most qualitative research methods can conceivably accommodate observers, observers take on a particularly special role in group interviewing. Face-to-face focus groups are typically conducted at a facility equipped with a one-way mirror, behind which members of the research team can view and hear the discussions. (Note: Group participants are informed of the presence of observers prior to the discussion.) Viewers often include people affiliated with the research sponsor who have a vested interest in learning firsthand about the attitudes and behavior of members of the target population. In addition to gaining clarity on participants' wants and needs, observers can be helpful in redirecting the discussion on the spot, if necessary, when participants make unanticipated comments that introduce a new way of thinking about the research topic. In these situations, it is important to be able to change course in the research or otherwise pursue new lines of questioning as unanticipated insights emerge from the discussions.

The range of opinions and behavior that can be represented in any one focus group is another important strength of the method because such a range is a factor in finding the "surprising insights" mentioned above. Even the most homogeneous group of participants will relate different experiences and thoughts, thereby giving the researcher an awareness and appreciation of the extent of divergent views on a particular issue. Unlike the IDI method that requires many separate interviews to uncover the spectrum of perspectives related to the subject matter, group discussions offer a time- and often cost-efficient method for revealing differing viewpoints.

Limitations

The interactive, dynamic nature of group discussions may also present a potential limitation to the method. The exchange of information and ideas may have the positive effect of eliciting new insights (as discussed above), but it may also have the damaging effect of unwittingly influencing responses from participants who are reluctant to voice dissenting opinions and just want to go along with the prevailing mood. Although a professional moderator can often identify the more introverted or shy participants in a group and use rapport-building techniques to encourage their candidness, these attempts are not always successful and the research outcomes may reflect more agreement on an issue than is actually warranted. Whether the nonexistence of differing attitudes among group participants is due to the reluctance of people to speak their minds or an honest reflection of personal points of view, some researchers can easily fall into the trap of believing that this lack of opposing attitudes is the same as a group consensus. As stated by Sim (1998, p. 348), "the absence of diversity in the data does not reliably indicate an underlying consensus" but is rather a possible product of the group environment, which may mask individual opinions.

Alongside the potential downside of group dynamics is the critical role of the moderator. Professional moderators trained in the complexities of group interviewing are essential to the success of the group discussion method. Although competent researchers are important to all qualitative methods, weak or not-fully-trained moderators pose a particular limitation to the focus group method where a myriad of factors can sway the outcomes one way or the other. The moderator not only has to deal with group dynamics, individual personalities, possible disruptive behavior, and potential runaway dialogue (as discussed on pp. 110–111), but must also have the ability to (a) spark conversation as needed; (b) exude a firm but gentle authority over the group with a relaxed, personable style; and (c) minimize potential bias from the influence of domineering participants and/or peripheral aspects, such as observers and audiovisual equipment in face-to-face discussions.

An additional limitation (or, at least, a real challenge) to the group discussion method involves ethical considerations, particularly the issue of guaranteeing confidentiality to the participants. There are many people involved in a focus group study, all of whom will be privy to the research subject matter as well as the comments made by individual members of the group. The research topic may be a guarded secret (e.g., a pharmaceutical company's new product concept) or, at the least, not for public knowledge (e.g., proposed policy changes to the county schools' education program for gifted children), yet all the relevant information is necessarily disclosed to everyone involved with the research: group participants, observers, recruiters, as well as facility personnel and audiovisual operators (as needed for face-to-face discussions). Likewise, participants are encouraged to be candid and may be asked to reveal personal or otherwise sensitive information, which they can be expected to provide only if they feel safe in the discussion environment. A signed consent form—stipulating the purpose, process, risks/benefits of the research, as well as the confidentiality of all participant information (or not, e.g., if a video recording of the discussion will be used in the final presentation) and the option to withdraw from the study at any time—from all group participants is important; however, the reality is that there is no way the researcher[3] can totally guarantee confidentiality.

4.2 THREE MODES OF THE GROUP DISCUSSION METHOD

Group discussions have traditionally been conducted in direct, face-to-face sessions with participants. Even today, when someone talks about conducting a focus group, they are most likely referring to the face-to-face mode. There are, however, other approaches to group interviewing. In this section, using a TQF perspective, we consider three modes of the group discussion method that are capable of producing credible and analyzable outcomes: face-to-face, telephone, and online. The key distinctive benefits and limitations that each mode offers are summarized in Table 4.1.

TABLE 4.1. Focus Group Mode Comparisons: Key Strengths and Limitations of the Three Focus Group Modes

Face-to-face	Telephone	Online
Strengths		
• Most similar to natural, social conversation. • Dynamic/interactive. • Provides nonverbal and visual cues. • Can use a broad range of moderating techniques. • Can share a broad range of stimuli with participants. • Allows for refreshments and immediate distribution of cash incentives.	• Cost and time savings compared to face-to-face. • Can cover a wide geographic area and remote locations. • Can access hard-to-reach population segments. • Easier to recruit than face-to-face due to the convenience of scheduling and location. • More focused discussions due to the shorter length and fewer participants compared to face-to-face. • Participants remain anonymous from each other. • May be better able to discuss sensitive topics compared to face-to-face.	• Gives participants flexibility on when/where they respond. • Detailed, thoughtful responses more possible from participants. • Gives participants a sense of anonymity. • Can cover a wide geographic area and potentially access hard-to-reach population segments. • Potentially a high level of interaction. • Can potentially discuss sensitive topics. • Cost and time savings due to built-in transcriptions. • Online platforms offer a high level of functionality and controls for the moderator.
Limitations		
• Group dynamics may not allow all participants an equal and fair opportunity to give input. • Moderator must be skilled to manage group dynamics/interaction, especially participants who dominate the discussion and those who are reluctant to talk. • Group interaction affects the direction of the outcomes. • Requires participants to be at the same place at the same time, which may lead to low levels of cooperation among those who are invited.	• Participants may be distracted or inattentive. • Less natural, more awkward form of discussion that may stifle engagement. • Moderator needs to expend extra effort to ignite and maintain a lively discussion. • Moderator needs to keep close track of which participants have spoken and those who have not.	• Text-based communication may prevent people with literacy problems from participating, or limit the depth of their responses. • Can be difficult for the moderator to ask follow-up questions for every participant response. • Ethical considerations, especially related to security and participant identity. • Coverage bias related to limited computer and Internet access, ability to use the online platform, and remembering to log in and participate in the discussion during the study timeframe. • Possible technical glitches.

Face-to-Face Mode

Strengths of the Face-to-Face Mode

Not unlike the IDI method, group interviewing in the face-to-face mode has the advantage of being a natural form of communication. The scenario of people sitting together and sharing their opinions and experiences is generally considered a socially acceptable form in the everyday lives of humans. And it is this natural way of communicating that ignites the dynamic, interactive environment of focus groups, as discussed on page 111. As the primary strength of the group discussion method, participant interaction is maximized in the face-to-face mode where the back-and-forth conversation can be spontaneous and easygoing. For example, Nicholas et al. (2010) found, in their study with children suffering from a chronic health problem (e.g., cerebral palsy), that "most preferred to express themselves verbally" (p. 115) in the face-to-face (vs. online) format because it allowed them to (a) give input immediately without waiting for typed responses, (b) gain feedback from the other participants straightaway, (c) show the emotional intensity of their feelings (i.e., display visual cues), and (d) potentially develop relationships with their peers beyond the confines of the specific focus group in which they participated. This last point is particularly relevant to group discussions conducted with a wide variety of target populations. In our experience, it is common for men who have recently hiked the Appalachian Trail, for example, to exchange tips on hiking gear or share photographs at the conclusion of a group discussion; or for special education teachers to swap contact information so they can continue to share teaching methods; or for business executives to stay after a focus group to chat and learn more about each other's work.

Also similar to the IDI method, face-to-face group discussions offer the moderator as well as participants and the observers the advantage of seeing the non-verbal signals—for example, a nod of the head, loss of eye contact, a blush, smile, frown, grimace—that people consciously or unconsciously exhibit in the course of discussion. Furthermore, like the IDI method, the face-to-face focus group mode significantly broadens the scope of the discussion interview, as well as the cache of interviewing techniques at the moderator's disposal, compared to either the telephone or online group discussion approach. The facilities where face-to-face focus groups are conducted are typically well equipped with (a) wall railings to display visual stimuli; (b) built-in audiovisual equipment for presenting videos, websites, and other material to participants; (c) easel pads to note participants' comments or illustrate a concept; and (d) an abundance of writing pads, pens/pencils, and other supplies for use by the moderator for participant activities during the discussion. The face-to-face mode also allows refreshments to be served to the participants, contributing to the relaxed social nature of the discussion; and, unlike the telephone mode, participants in a face-to-face discussion can receive their earned incentive payment (for participating) immediately upon completion of the session.

Limitations of the Face-to-Face Mode

As discussed earlier (pp. 111–112), the interactive, dynamic aspect of the group discussion method is its greatest potential strength as well as its greatest potential liability. This is especially the case in the face-to-face mode where the close physical proximity of participants can unleash any number of factors that will threaten data quality if left unchecked. One of the most important factors is the caliber of the discussion; specifically, the extent to which all participants have a fair chance of voicing their input. This is critical because the success of the group discussion method hinges on generating a true discussion where everyone present participates in a dialogue with the other group members and, to a lesser degree, with the moderator. A true participatory discussion, however, can be easily jeopardized in the social context of the face-to-face focus group because one or more participants either talk too much (i.e., dominate the discussion) or talk too little (i.e., are hesitant to express their views). In either case, the quality of the data will be compromised by the failure to capture the viewpoints of all participants, leading to erroneous interpretations of the outcomes. For instance, the following snippet from an all-male group, with a male moderator, discussing gender roles illustrates how quickly "John," an overly dominant group participant, commands the discussion and stifles dissenting opinions, which may have taken the discussion (and, ultimately, the final analysis of the research) in a misguided direction:

MODERATOR: Let's talk some more about the specific roles, if any, you associate with men and women in our society.

JOHN: I know this sounds old-fashioned but, uh, I think a woman's place is in the home . . . you know, having babies, taking care of the house, cooking the meals, that kind of thing.

MICHAEL: Well, I don't know . . .

JOHN: Really, think about it, someone needs to do those things, and men are just better at "bringing home the bacon" . . .

PAUL: Bringing home the bacon is just a man's job? You don't think women are capable of working at a good-paying job? That's . . .

JOHN: I'm just saying, women need to stick to traditional roles . . . like my mother . . .

GEORGE: But . . .

JOHN: Somewhere along the line, we lost the traditional male and female roles in our society and it's messed everything up . . . made it confusing, not knowing who is supposed to do what.

MICHAEL: Well, I guess I see your point.

John's domination in the above discussion and refusal to enter into a respectful dialogue with the other group participants promptly squelched the opinions of those who attempted to speak and never gave the more reserved group members a chance to overcome their reluctance and voice their views. In the absence of the moderator's intervention to make certain everyone was given a chance to express their own opinions fully, the researcher may very well conclude that these men agree that women should play more traditional roles in today's society.

The potentially negative impact that the face-to-face group interaction can have on data quality is an important consideration in qualitative research design, yet this impact—or, the effect of group interaction on the research—is often overlooked when conducting the analyses and reporting the outcomes. Researchers who have explored the role of interaction in focus group research include Grønkjær et al. (2011), Belzile and Öberg (2012), and Moen, Antonov, Nilsson, and Ring (2010). Grønkjær et al. analyzed the "interactional events" in five focus groups they conducted with Danes on the use and perceptions of alcohol and determined, for example, that "disagreements between participants can function as a catalyst to keep the focus group discussion going" (p. 26). As a way to build interaction into a focus group research design, Belzile and Öberg propose a "continuum of use" by which researchers can opt for a "low" level of interaction in the design (i.e., interaction is primarily addressed in the discussion, not the analysis), a "medium" level of interaction (i.e., some of the group interaction is included in the analysis), or "high" level of interaction (i.e., interaction is used equally in the group discussion and in the analysis). Moen et al. used an interaction "template" contrived by Lehoux, Poland, and Daudelin (2006) to analyze focus groups conducted with patients and physicians concerning their perceptions of multiple medicine use. The Lehoux et al. template (see Table 4.2) takes the researcher through a series of questions that is intended to touch on the critical areas of interaction from the standpoint of the group *process* (e.g., "What types of interactions occur among participants?" and "Which participants dominate the discussion?") as well as the group *content* (e.g., "What do dominant and passive positions reveal about the topic at hand?" and "What types of knowledge claims receive less support?"). In applying this analytical model, Moen et al. were able to identify "all the important aspects of the interaction," including the "domineering participants" and their impact on the final outcomes.

An important aspect of the interaction effect is the influence the moderator has on group dynamics. In addition to many factors associated with interviewer bias and training in IDI research (discussed in Chapter 3, pp. 83–86), there is also the issue of how the moderator manages the group interaction and how this management affects the direction of the outcomes. For instance, in their group discussions concerning alcohol use in Denmark, Grønkjær et al. (2011) emphasized the importance of the moderator's "continuous assessment of the interactions between various participants" (p. 25), while maintaining the status of moderator and resisting the urge to speak as a health professional by interrupting the interaction with expert knowledge.

Another limitation with many face-to-face focus groups is the low level of cooperation that is often achieved when recruiting people to attend a particular session. This may be because people are reluctant (or too shy or socially self-conscious) to agree to spend 90 minutes or 2 hours interacting with complete

TABLE 4.2. Lehoux's Analytical Template for Focus Group Research with Patients

Group processes	Epistemological content
Research design: Contrasting the researcher's purposes with those of participants	
• Who do participants represent when they speak (e.g., a member of a larger group, an individual sharing his/her own experience)? • What are the explicit purposes of participants? What could be their implicit purposes?	• To what extent do participants comply with the moderator's cues and/or seek to foster discussion on other issues? • Why do these issues matter? And to which participants? • What do participants' purposes tell about the research topic?
Interactive social space: Understanding interactions and what is shared as a result of the relational positioning of participants	
• What types of interactions occur among participants (e.g., limited–significant, empathic–challenging, educational–personal, negative–constructive)? • To what extent do these interactions reflect the broader social contexts (e.g., age, gender, status, authority)? • Which participants dominate the discussion? How does this affect the contribution of other participants? • Which participants adopt a passive role? How do other participants respond to this position?	• What do dominant and passive positions reveal about the topic at hand? • What types of knowledge claims (e.g., clinical–experiential knowledge, self-care skills, strategies and resources mobilized) are endorsed and/or challenged by participants? On what basis? • What types of knowledge claims receive less support? Why?
Moderator's role: Considering the extent to which the moderator participates in the construction of the patients' views	
• How does the moderator set the tone at the beginning? • How does the moderator succeed in making room for each participant to contribute to the common ground? • Do participants accept and/or challenge the leadership of the moderator? How and when is acceptance or defiance manifested? How does the moderator respond?	• How does the moderator respond to the validation and/or disputing of knowledge claims? • What is the overall impact on the focus group "common ground"? • Does the common ground remain stable over time?

Note. Reprinted from Focus Group Research and "the Patient's View" by Pascale Lehoux, Blake Poland, and Genevieve Daudelin, *Social Science and Medicine, 63*(8), 2091–2104. Copyright 2006, with permission from Elsevier.

strangers, or because face-to-face focus groups are held at a central location, mandating that all participants attend at the same place and the same time. There may be people in the target population who are invited to participate in a group discussion but who refuse (despite the offer of a cash incentive payment) because of scheduling conflicts or the inconvenience of traveling to a central facility. The logistics can be particularly troublesome for people with disabilities, health issues, or no means of transportation. Linked to this lower level of initial cooperation is the reality that people who do agree to participate in a face-to-face discussion may not actually show up due to unexpected scheduling conflicts, transportation difficulties, or just a last-minute unwillingness to venture from home or office to travel to the location of the group session.

The limitations of the face-to-face mode discussed here—that is, the moderator's undue influence on the output from a group discussion and the potentially low level of participant cooperation—as well as other limitations to face-to-face focus groups are discussed from the perspective of the TQF in Section 4.3 (see "Gaining Cooperation," pp. 132–136).

Telephone Mode

Strengths of the Telephone Mode

The telephone mode of the group discussion method shares many of the advantages of telephone IDIs, particularly the greater efficiency of available resources (i.e., cost and turnaround time), compared to face-to-face discussions, as well as the ability to include participants who are widely dispersed geographically or reside in remote (rural) locations, have limited mobility (e.g., those with disabilities), or represent a small population segment (e.g., human resource managers for the top automobile manufacturers in the United States). And like telephone IDIs, participants for telephone focus groups are typically easier to recruit—and more likely to show up—compared to face-to-face discussions, because the researcher can potentially offer participants a choice of dates and times that are most convenient to their schedules, and participants have greater flexibility in the location of the discussion (i.e., they can participate from anywhere they have access to a landline phone or good quality mobile phone connection). This higher rate of participation in the telephone mode may produce a more representative sample of the target population than would be the case with a face-to-face group discussion.

There are other advantages to the telephone mode that may make it the mode of choice for many research purposes. For instance, the smaller size (fewer than 10 participants), shorter duration (60–90 minutes compared to 90–120 minutes for face-to-face), and absence of visual stimuli associated with telephone groups often lead to more focused discussions compared to the face-to-face mode. Furthermore, the relative anonymity of participants can make telephone discussions an appropriate method for sensitive research topics. In this respect, Frazier et al. (2010) found, in their comparison of face-to-face and telephone focus groups among women diagnosed with gynecological cancer, that "certain topics such as sexuality were only brought up by women who participated by phone" (p. 624); and Appleton, Fry, Rees, Rush, and Cull (2000) report that women with an increased risk of breast cancer openly talked about their psychosocial anxieties because "the anonymity of the telephone conferencing system made them feel less inhibited about sharing their experiences" (p. 519). Telephone discussions are also becoming increasingly more efficient as the sophistication of teleconferencing technology continues to advance. Today, there are many providers with state-of-the-art teleconferencing capabilities, including online features (e.g., collaboration boards), webcam conferencing, call management (e.g., placing participants in subconferences), transcription services, online audio archiving (allowing researchers and clients to listen to the discussions at a later date), and translation services.

Telephone group discussions have been especially popular in the health care field, for example, to conduct research with primary care physicians in rural locations (Tolhurst & Dean, 2004) and physicians across the United States (Purvis Cooper, Merritt, Ross, John, & Jorgensen, 2004), as well as with nursing students (Reilly, Gallagher-Lepak, & Killion, 2012) and women with an increased risk of breast cancer (Appleton et al., 2000). Telephone group interviewing has also been utilized successfully across other fields of study, such as the forestry industry to investigate timber sale programs (Brown, Kilgore, Blinn, & Coggins, 2012), in library sciences to study technology skills among librarians (Partridge, Menzies, Lee, & Munro, 2010), in communication research to examine crisis communication in select populations (McGough, Frank, Tipton, Tinker, & Vaughan, 2005), in visual anthropology to explore cultural literacy (Gerber, 2007), in service marketing to explore the effect of scent on social interaction in common hotel areas (Zemke & Shoemaker, 2007), and with teenagers concerning their attitudes toward modes of transportation and climate change (Line, 2008).

Limitations of the Telephone Mode

While the moderator in a face-to-face focus group may have his or her hands full with exuberant participants who want to dominate the discussion, the moderator conducting telephone groups often has the opposite problem of participants who may become distracted or otherwise disengaged from the group discussion because they may, for example, be involved in other activities (i.e., multitasking) while on the telephone. Because the moderator and the participants are unable to see each other, there are few clues as to what other activities telephone participants may be doing instead of paying attention and contributing to the conversation. Furthermore, the telephone device itself, as well as the remote, less natural (i.e., compared to face-to-face) social context, can feel awkward to participants and stifle their spontaneity, making them hesitant or even reluctant to engage in an interactive discussion. Participants' distractions, inattentiveness, and timidity can cause the quality of the data from a telephone focus group to suffer appreciably unless steps are taken to mitigate the problem at the time of the discussion. Rather than subduing a dominant participant, as in the face-to-face mode, the telephone group moderator is more likely to make various attempts to ignite a dynamic discussion. For these reasons, the management of telephone focus groups requires a unique set of moderator skills, including the ability to ascertain when one or more participants are distracted or inattentive and knowing when and on whom to call for their input. One approach for managing participants' contributions to the discussion comes from Smith, Sullivan, and Baxter (2009) who utilized a "speaker grid" (e.g., with participants' names running across the top and discussion topics along the vertical) to "record responses, and cue and monitor participation" (p. 283).

The limitations of telephone focus groups are discussed in Section 4.3 in the context of moderator skills training (see pp. 147–148) and building rapport (see p. 152).

Online Mode

There are several approaches to conducting group discussions in the online mode: synchronous and asynchronous by way of specifically designed Web-based platforms, as well as the fairly new use of social media and/or online communities. **Synchronous** focus groups—in which all participants are simultaneously online—come closest to the real-time discussions of the face-to-face and telephone modes and can be conducted in a text chat or audio–video format. These online discussions—when all the participants and the moderator are present at the same time—have the advantage of generating spontaneous interactive conversations but may be difficult to manage, particularly when there are 10 or more participants. Gathering meaningful data from all participants (i.e., eliciting responses and comments for all questions from all participants) requires a moderator who is specifically skilled in effectively handling the fast pace of simultaneous engagement online.

Strengths of the Online Mode

Of all the online approaches, qualitative researchers are most likely to conduct **asynchronous focus groups** discussions, commonly referred to as "bulletin boards." These **bulletin boards** are not held in real time (which is the case with synchronous discussions) but extend over two or more days, with participants contributing to the discussion at their convenience within the allotted time period. The moderator poses questions each day and continually monitors responses in order to ask appropriate follow-up questions and encourage interaction among the participants. To ensure that participants are exposed, and have an opportunity to respond, to all the topical areas of the research discussion, they are asked to visit the online bulletin board site at a certain frequency (e.g., at least once in the morning and once in the afternoon for at least 15 minutes each time) and reply to the moderator's questions as well as to comments made by other participants, as appropriate. As an online mode, bulletin board groups can accommodate a large number of participants (30 or more); however, it is best to keep the group size to a manageable level (in terms of facilitating the group as well as for the purposes of the final data analysis) with no more than 15 participants and, ideally, a group size of 10 or less (not unlike the face-to-face mode).

The popularity of asynchronous group discussions has been bolstered by the increasingly sophisticated features and services built into the online platforms designed for bulletin board research. In an attempt to move closer to the face-to-face discussion experience, the providers of these online platforms have developed systems that allow:

- The moderator to incorporate various discussion activities, such as, asking participants to view a website, react to visual stimuli (e.g., concept boards, communication messages), and/or upload a video or photograph (e.g., depicting a typical night at home).

- Participants to mark up a virtual whiteboard in order to highlight their reactions to visual stimuli (e.g., circling the particular words in a communication message that most resonate with the participant).

- Participants to upload profile photos along with personal information to share.

- The moderator to view and respond to all participants' responses and comments from one screen and thereby manage the entire group from one location.

- The moderator to conduct private conversations with one or more group participants.

- For a virtual backroom where the research team can observe the discussion and carry on text chats with the moderator on an ongoing basis.

- The researcher immediate access to the discussion transcripts that can be organized (by keyword and other criteria) and downloaded.

- The researcher access to the multimedia stimuli (e.g., videos and photographs) that can be used (only after explicit permission from each participant) for presentation of the research findings.

Asynchronous online group discussions provide benefits to the participants as well as researchers. This online discussion format gives participants the (a) flexibility (i.e., the freedom) to contribute to the discussion at a time and place of their choosing (within the study timeframe); (b) opportunity to provide thoughtful, detailed responses to the researcher's questions; and (c) comfortable sense of anonymity. These benefits were clearly shown in the online qualitative research conducted by Tates et al. (2009) in the area of pediatric oncology, where the children and parents participating in the online discussions especially valued the flexibility and convenience of logging in at their own pace.

For the researcher, online bulletin boards allow access to very geographically dispersed or otherwise hard-to-reach populations, as well as typically robust group engagement. With respect to the latter, asynchronous focus groups, like the face-to-face mode but unlike telephone group interviewing, have the capability of eliciting a high level of group interaction, with participants freely commenting and posting visual examples. Online bulletin boards have also proven successful in engaging participants on sensitive topics that might otherwise be difficult to discuss in a face-to-face environment. These advantages of group interaction and willingness to discuss sensitive issues are illustrated in a 10-day bulletin board study conducted for the Crohn's and Colitis Foundation of Canada (Hancock, 2012). In this research, the moderator incorporated various activities—for example, asking participants to write or post photos/videos of "things that frustrate them" and of "items that help in coping with the disease"—which served to stimulate the discussion and create a supportive environment that fostered a willingness to share personal insights on this delicate subject matter.

Another important advantage to the asynchronous approach to online group discussions is the functionality and controls it affords the moderator, particularly in managing participants and the discussion itself. Not unlike the face-to-face mode, the moderator is able to (a) see which participants are contributing to the discussion and communicate with those who are not in order to motivate their participation; (b) show participants stimuli and elicit their reactions; (c) ask follow-up, probing questions to clarify participants' responses; (d) stimulate group interaction so that participants ask each other questions and comment on others' thoughts; and (e) engage participants in various activities.

The online mode (synchronous and asynchronous) also has the advantage of facilitating data analysis, especially as it relates to transcriptions and coding. This process is made easier, more efficient, and less costly than in the face-to-face and telephone modes because:

- The moderator and anyone on the research team have immediate access to the automated written transcripts.

- The transcripts are available for download for an extended period of time (in some cases, an unlimited period of time).

- The transcripts can be sorted or organized based on keywords or other criteria.

- The transcripts are an automated byproduct of the text discussion, and therefore no additional cost is incurred by the researcher.

Limitations of the Online Mode

The three primary limitations to asynchronous bulletin board discussions—the more common method compared to real-time, synchronous discussions—are associated with the text-based form of communication, ethical considerations, and potential coverage bias. As a discussion mode that relies mostly on text responses, outcomes from bulletin board groups can be limited by the literacy levels of the participants and by superficiality or lack of depth. Brüggen and Willems (2009), for instance, compared asynchronous online and face-to-face group discussions and found that participants used, on average, fewer words in the online mode.

The absence of depth can be attributed to the difficulty of following up each participant's response with the kind of questions that a moderator might ask in a face-to-face group to elicit greater details. This is also partly due to the fact that the online moderator is focused on the difficult task of maintaining (or even generating) interactivity among the participants and less so on deepening his/her own understanding of any one participant's comments.

Another limitation to the online mode revolves around ethical considerations. Although issues of confidentiality and anonymity are critical to all research, they are a particularly sensitive concern in the realm of online group interviewing. Online participants might harbor security and identity worries for any number of reasons. Even after signing a consent form, online participants may be skeptical or unclear about (a) where and for how long their input (written comments and uploaded material) will linger in data storage; (b) the security measures in place for the data storage and who will have access to these data; (c) who, other than the moderator, may be "observing" the discussion as it is taking place; (d) how much of their identity is actually known by the moderator, the observers, and the other participants; (e) whether their written comments will be kept confidential by the other participants; and (f) whether they will be identified with their input either in the reporting/presenting of the research results internally or publically (e.g., posting text snippets on an online blog or uploading a participant's video on YouTube).

Similar to the email and mobile IDI methods, researchers who opt for online group discussions need to pay attention to the possibility that the credibility of the outcomes may be jeopardized due to coverage bias. The online mode—whether synchronous, asynchronous, or by way of social media or online communities (see below)—necessarily excludes population segments that do not have access to a computer (of any kind) and the Internet during the study period; may have difficulty understanding how to use the online platform (e.g., the elderly); may have difficulty remembering to log into a bulletin board over the course of a multiday study; and have problems with reading, spelling, and/or using a keyboard. Online discussions are also susceptible to technical glitches (e.g., problems showing images from the online platform to participants' Internet-enabled devices) that may interfere with the flow and content of the discussion.

Special Case: Social Media Groups and Online Communities

Using social media (e.g., Facebook, Twitter) for online discussions (which may or may not be synchronous) is a fairly recent phenomenon that is particularly popular among marketing researchers who have begun experimenting with this online channel. At this very early stage, there are few examples of sound focus group research designs based around any of the social media platforms; so far, the bulk of marketers have been simply monitoring consumers' posts to identify popular products or trends, or using social media as a crowdsourcing tool to create new products by asking consumers to "vote" for their preferred beer ingredients or flavor of potato chip, for example (Clifford, 2012). One exception is the National Cattlemen's Beef Association, which conducted a 6-week discussion on Facebook with 13 30-year-olds concerning their beef consumption behavior. Participants were screened and selected based on specific demographic and psychographic characteristics (e.g., beef consumption and meal planning activity), and a special page on Facebook was created just for the purpose of this research. The result was a "rich, colorful, and dynamic dialogue" that provided insights on how to "motivate and educate the Millennials toward a desired [beef-eating] behavior" (Koenig & Neuman, 2012, p. 28). There are clearly limitations to conducting group discussions via social media today—not the least of which is that social media users seriously skew to the younger segment of the population (Duggan & Brenner, 2013)—yet new advancements in technology, and more widespread use of social media in the population may make this a viable mode in the future.

A more targeted variation in the realm of social media is the **online community**. Like social media, online communities have become particularly prevalent in consumer marketing research. These communities are typically created as private, invitation-only websites that include anywhere from 300 to 500 or more members. Members consist of highly targeted consumers (e.g., a retailer's best online customers) who are recruited into the community utilizing standard focus group recruiting procedures. Depending on the research needs of the marketer, an online community may exist for only a week or for several months. Marketers and marketing researchers use their online communities to observe the members' interactions and "listen" to the members as they discuss product- and service-related issues among themselves. Researchers intermittently ask the members questions or give them an activity to perform (e.g., to create a journal within the community that chronicles their daily experiences using the marketer's product), but otherwise may leave the members to get to know each other and form their own social circle. Examples of online communities include[4] (a) Scholastic Book Clubs, who utilized an online community of 200 teachers and 100 mothers in a "co-creation process" to improve the design of the Scholastic flyer sales piece; (b) Godiva, who used their online community during the 2009 economic downturn to listen to their members as they discussed how they had modified their purchase and eating of high-end chocolate, leading Godiva to ultimately create a new product line; (c) InterContinental Hotels Group, in partnership with Chase, who created a 300-member online community of frequent travelers to conduct a 12-month "ongoing conversation" to develop a new credit card; and (d) NASCAR who maintains their NASCAR Fan Council of more than 10,000 fans in order to "better understand your thoughts about our sport and to learn more about the NASCAR community" (*www.nascarfancouncil.com*).

The primary advantage of online communities is that, unlike other group discussion formats, they offer the researcher a more long-term, in-depth understanding of the members (as a group and as individuals) as well as the research topic. A couple of key limitations, however, are that online communities are relatively expensive to conduct—due to the group size, longevity, and continual need to engage members in order to minimize attrition—and, similar to social media (discussed above), vulnerable to the bias that may result from the target population's access to, and interest in, online communication/engagement.

APPLYING THE TOTAL QUALITY FRAMEWORK APPROACH TO THE GROUP DISCUSSION METHOD

Group discussions comprise one of the most important and frequently used methods in qualitative research. Regardless of format or mode, the group discussion method offers the researcher the unique opportunity to "listen" to a range of attitudes and behavior in an interactive context that provides data for the researcher to tease out a nuanced understanding of the research topic. In this section we discuss how to design, implement, and interpret a group discussion study based on the principles of the TQF's four components: Credibility, Analyzability, Transparency, and Usefulness. Here we consider both the strengths and limitations of the group discussion method (discussed in Section 4.2) and describe a best-practice approach toward maximizing the credibility, analyzability, transparency, and ultimate usefulness of this research method. The extent to which the application of the TQF varies by mode is discussed throughout this chapter section.

Credibility

The group discussion method can be an important and valuable approach to qualitative research. The value, however, can be undermined unless the researcher utilizing this method takes every measure possible to ensure credible outcomes. It is the researcher's responsibility to incorporate the necessary design features into his/her focus group studies in order to reduce the potential risks that can undermine focus group data and thereby strengthen the credibility of the data. The degree to which the final research design may have compromised the credibility of the data from a group discussion study should be fully acknowledged and utilized to temper the analysis, interpretation, and concluding implications or recommendations.

As with all qualitative research methods, the Credibility component of a group discussion research design rests within the two broad areas of Scope and Data Gathering. In the focus group method, Scope is directed at how well the participants involved in the group discussions represent the target population of interest. Data Gathering is concerned with the reliability and validity of focus group data and how well the research outcomes present an accurate account of the constructs the researcher set out to measure in the group discussion(s).

Scope

Within group discussions Scope relates to (a) the coverage of the target population (including the representativeness of the list used to draw a sample of potential group participants), (b) the sample design (how individuals on the list will be chosen for contact during the recruitment phase and the number of group discussions to conduct), and (c) the gaining of cooperation by way of the recruiting process (the ability of the recruiter to gain access to the sampled individuals and elicit their full cooperation, culminating in their participation in the group discussion).

Coverage

In order to reduce or eliminate coverage bias in the group discussion method, the researcher must obtain a quality list that accurately accounts for the individuals who make up the target population. Often the list will be provided by the sponsoring client who wants focus groups to be conducted with a well-defined target population of the client's choosing—for example, a board of education wanting information from parents of recent high school graduates, a hospital CEO wanting information from patients undergoing cancer treatment, a store manager wanting information from frequent customers, a YMCA Board of Directors wanting information from members of the YMCA, or a telecommunications company vice president of marketing wanting information from customers who have purchased the company's new mobile phone device. Although recruiting from lists such as these can be a challenge (due to inaccuracies or incompleteness of the lists), this may be the only way to obtain a list of the population segment of interest. In other situations, the researcher can create a list or access/purchase it from an existing source.

For example, in a group discussion study to be conducted for a hospital that was interested in learning how to improve satisfaction and the rate of retention among its certified nursing assistants (CNAs), the researchers would receive a complete list with accurate contact information for all CNAs who are employed by the hospital at the time of the study. The researchers would then randomly sample from the list and contact those selected to invite them to participate in the discussion group(s). Assuming the list was complete and included accurate contact information, this approach would be representative of all CNAs at the given hospital. However, if the list was incomplete or inaccurate because not all departments within the hospital (e.g., intensive care) provided contact information on their CNAs—and if the experiences of CNAs who work in intensive care are different from those who work in the emergency room and other departments within the hospital—then the resulting focus group(s) may yield biased data because the full population of interest was not actually covered by the list the hospital provided the researchers.

As another example, consider a focus group study among persons in the metro San Antonio area who are planning to purchase a new car in the next 24 months. In this case, there are several ways that a listing of such persons could be compiled. For example, one option would be to access the State of Texas automobile registration lists for that metro area and identify everyone with a car more than 5 years old. Then a random sample of these car owners could be contacted via U.S. mail (if there was sufficient time in the research schedule) or telephone and screened to determine if they expect to buy a new car in the next 24 months. Using this approach, however, is problematic because the list that is used to cover the population of interest will contain a number of people who do not expect to purchase a car in the next 2 years and therefore would need to be screened out. In addition, this approach to covering the target population is weakened by the fact that the list excludes people who currently own a car that is 5 or fewer years old but nevertheless may be planning to purchase a new car in the next 24 months. For this group discussion study, a more complete, albeit more expensive, approach to covering the target population in the San Antonio metro area would be to create a random sample of San Antonio landline and mobile telephone numbers and call these to screen for people who planned to buy a car in the next 24 months.

These two examples illustrate the importance of taking seriously the issue of how researchers choose to cover the population their focus groups purport to represent. Researchers may be inclined to use a haphazard, convenient, or least expensive procedure for creating the list from which to choose their participants (e.g., using a recruiter's existing database of people who have participated in group discussions in the past or have asked to be put in their database in the hope of being contacted for a future study). However, prudent researchers will think carefully about the various threats that may result to the credibility of their group discussion findings if they do not start with a fully representative list from which to sample their participants.

Sample Design

Once the researcher has compiled a current and accurate list of members in the target population, it is then important to develop the correct method for selecting the persons from the list who will be contacted and asked to participate in the group discussions. Selecting a sample of potential focus group participants ideally should be done in a systematic and random manner, beginning with a careful examination of the list to identify if there is a fundamental order in how the persons are listed (e.g., are they listed alphabetically, by age or other demographic variable, by geographic region, by job title, or by some other criterion?), or if such an order could and should be created. The representativeness of the group participants—and hence the credibility of the group discussion study—may be threatened if the researcher does not consider this orderliness of the list prior to the selection of potential participants. Regardless of any built-in order within the list, however, focus group researchers should select a sample of potential participants from across the entire list rather than simply starting at the beginning and proceeding one consecutive person after the other (e.g., the first person, the second person) until the desired number of sampled participants has been reached. Selecting from across the list ensures the representativeness of the focus group participants (i.e., representative in terms of the list from which they are selected), which bolsters the quality of the final outcomes. If the list accurately reflects the population, and the selection of participants reflects the list, then the selection of participants will also accurately reflect the population.

A more involved approach for selecting group discussion participants might be used if personal or *firmographic* (i.e., company-related information on businesses) information is available on the list. For example, if the gender, age, and race of all the persons on the list are identified, and if these demographic characteristics are expected to be related to the behaviors, attitudes, and knowledge specific to the subject matter of the focus groups, the list should be sorted (stratified) on these characteristics prior to sample selection. The sorting in this example could start by grouping all women and all men into two separate subgroups, followed by arranging persons within each gender subgroup by age, and then sorting everyone within each gender–age subgroup by whether they are Asian, African American, or White. This newly sorted list could then be used to select potential group participants systematically.

For example, assume that a researcher wants to conduct a focus group study for a county health department among county residents to learn about the attitudes and behavior associated with the use of alcohol. The researcher wants to conduct six face-to-face discussions with eight to 10 participants in each group and has obtained a list of 1,000 persons that has been sorted by gender, age, and race. If the researcher needs to recruit 12 participants for each group (to ensure that eight to 10 people actually show up), and it is expected that approximately one out of four of those invited to participate will agree to do so, then $6 \times 12 \times 4$, or 288 of those 1,000 persons on the list, would need to be sampled. A little less than one of every third person on the sorted (stratified) list would be selected for the recruitment phase. It is only by way of this approach that the researcher can be sure that the people sampled for the six focus groups are representative of the entire list of county residents in terms of gender, age, and race. It is the sorting of the list prior to sampling that allows for this representativeness and strengthens the credibility of focus group data.

The researcher may, however, logically assume that county residents' attitudes and behavior regarding alcohol use may differ across demographic variables, particularly age. In that case, the researcher might decide to recruit by age group in order to create an element of commonality or homogeneity among participants. The researcher would therefore want to conduct a group discussion for each specific age range, with one focus group for each of six demographic cohorts, such as females 21–34 years old, females 35–50 years old, females over 50 years old, males 21–34 years old, males 35–50 years old, and males over 50 years old. The sampling would need to be done separately for each cohort. For example, if there were 145 females between 21 and 34 years of age on the stratified list, then randomly sampling every third one of these women would yield the 12 persons who would be expected to agree to participate in the group discussion for women in the 21–34 age range. And, if there were 475 males 35–50 years old on the stratified list, then randomly sampling every tenth person on this list would yield the 12 individuals who would be expected to agree to participate in the focus group with 35- to 50-year-old men.

It behooves qualitative researchers who plan to use the group discussion method to think carefully about how they will choose those persons in the target population who will be invited to participate in the focus group(s). It takes a little more time and effort in planning and implementing a systematic approach to selecting who gets invited to participate in a group discussion, but not doing so may bias the results to an extent that the credibility of all the other aspects of the project is threatened.

NUMBER OF GROUPS. Another important decision that researchers need to make when using the group discussion method is the *number* of such focus groups that will need to be conducted. As with the IDI method, researchers are faced with a cost–benefit tradeoff for which they may need to remain flexible as they begin conducting their group discussions. This tradeoff is the tension between neither wanting to conduct too many nor too few focus groups. The decision of how many group discussions to conduct is based on any number of factors and will vary depending on the situation for each study. However, there are some common critical factors that prudent researchers will need to think about when considering the number of discussions at the outset for any focus group study:

- Geographic range of the target population (e.g., whether the target population for face-to-face groups is located in one city or spread across the United States).

- Depth of the discussions in terms of the number of topics/issues and questions expected to be covered to satisfy research objectives. For example, fewer group discussions may be necessary if the primary research objective is to learn mothers' preferences for shelf-stable baby food, whereas a greater number of groups may be needed if the objective is to understand mothers' preferences across all types of baby food and, specifically, to investigate the priority they place on nutritional and organic foods.

- Homogeneity or heterogeneity of the group participants. Using the example above, more groups will be required if the mothers of interest range in age from 25 to 40 years old, as well as in income level, and if there is reason to believe that attitudes and behavior vary across these demographic characteristics.

- Variation in results that is expected to occur across the different focus groups that will be conducted. If there is little variation expected from one group to another (e.g., if group participants are highly homogeneous, or the attitudes among participants in New York are not expected to be different from those in Dallas), then only a few focus groups may suffice. If there is a great deal of variation expected, then many focus groups will be required to fully measure the range of experiences, attitudes, and knowledge the participants are likely to impart in the discussions.

- Project schedule and amount of available time to complete the study.

- Research budget that is available to fund the study.

It is this assortment of factors that causes qualitative researchers to generally disagree on the optimal number of focus groups. Krueger and Casey (2009, p. 21) state that "the accepted rule of thumb is to plan three or four focus groups with each type or category of individual." However, Kitzinger (1994) and her colleagues conducted 52 group discussions concerning the media coverage of AIDS among broad, diverse population groups across England, Scotland, and Wales; and Peek and Fothergill (2009) reported conducting 23 discussions with Muslim

American students, due, in part, to the need to segment groups by gender. Yet others, such as McLafferty (2004), use the concept of saturation[5] (i.e., conducting group discussions only to the point when no new information is being gleaned) as their "guiding principle" when determining if the appropriate number of groups has been conducted.

Although the list of considerations above may assist the researcher during the research design phase to establish the number of groups to conduct, it does little to help evaluate the set-upon number when one's study is in the field. To be clear, it can be expensive and disruptive to the research process to cancel or add group sessions to a focus group study that is under way (particularly, when conducting face-to-face discussions that require reserving and making arrangements with brick-and-mortar facilities); however, it is important for the focus group researcher to assess the components of his/her research design—including the number of group discussions—throughout the process. Like with an IDI study, the question of how many research events (in this case, group discussions) to conduct raises a host of issues associated with data quality. And, like IDIs, the researcher's assessment of the number of focus groups while in the field examines such issues as the degree to which:

- All questions and topic areas have been covered in all discussions.
- The moderator clearly understands the feedback and responses obtained in each discussion.
- Research objectives have been met.
- New ideas, themes, or information are emerging from the discussions.
- Variations in the data can be explained.
- Reflection reveals that the moderator maintained objectivity throughout all discussions.
- The data inform the subject matter.
- Triangulation confirms or denies the researcher's initial hypotheses.
- The discussions have divulged a story that explains the research question for each of the population segments or subgroups.
- Opportunities for further research have emerged from the discussions.

An important additional component to this assessment in the group discussion method is the degree of interactivity or group dynamics within the discussions. Specifically, the researcher needs to carefully consider the degree to which participants in all groups equally shared their experiences and thoughts during the discussions. If, for instance, one or more focus groups were dominated by a small number of participants who were outspoken on the issues, the researcher should be cautious when assessing the value of these groups (in terms of the credibility of measurement) and consider these dominant participant groups in the determination of the number of groups to conduct.

Gaining Cooperation

In addition to assembling a comprehensive and accurate list of their target population and determining the optimal sample design, group discussion researchers are faced with the very important considerations of (1) how best to contact the sampled persons and (2) how best to convince them to attend and participate in the focus group to which they are assigned. The ability to contact and gain cooperation from the research sample falls within the domain of research that is often termed "nonresponse" that deals with how to minimize the proportion of people who are invited and agree to participate in a focus group but fail to appear at the appointed time. If this proportion is very large or if the people who never agree to participate in the first place or who initially agree to participate but do not show up for a group discussion differ in meaningful ways—for example, if characteristics of those who do not cooperate are correlated with the key topics the focus group study is investigating—from those who do participate, the final results of the focus group(s) will likely be biased and will jeopardize the credibility of research data. This is why qualitative researchers should continually assess the representativeness of the focus group participants who *do* cooperate and examine the degree to which characteristics of these participants are the same or different from the characteristics of the overall target population. By identifying problems in representativeness, researchers can take corrective measures that will likely result in a participant sample that more closely mirrors all people within the population of interest.

Take, for example, a focus group study that is gathering data about the attitudes and behaviors of adult suburban women who are or are not members of a large fitness center in the central city. Let's assume that participants were contacted by sampling their telephone numbers from suburban telephone directories, invited to attend a face-to-face focus group session at the central city fitness center at 4:00 P.M., and that they were offered $75 to participate in a 90-minute focus group discussion. This approach to gaining cooperation would likely yield biased findings that undermine the study's credibility for several reasons. First, there is the issue of coverage because using a telephone directory (either a printed version or online) will miss all those women who do not have a listed telephone number. The individuals who are missed will be disproportionately from upscale households and from minority lower-middle-class households because these types of households are least likely to list their phone numbers in a local phone directory (Lavrakas, 2010). Women from these types of households may hold different attitudes and engage in different fitness-related behaviors than those women listed in the local directories.

Second, another coverage problem is that all those women who live in a household with a mobile telephone but not a landline telephone (which is approaching 40% of all U.S. women; Blumberg & Luke, 2013) will be missed because mobile phone numbers are not printed in a local telephone directory (or its online version) in the United States. These women will be disproportionally younger and minority adults, and their own attitudes and behaviors will likely differ from suburban women with a listed landline telephone number.

Third, $75 might be considered a more-than-adequate incentive by some women, but others may feel that it is not an equitable or attractive amount given the time burden on a person from the suburbs to travel to the central city and participate in the focus group. So, for example, the promised incentive may appeal disproportionally more to suburban women with lower household incomes whose attitudes and exercise habits may be different from upper- and middle-income women.

Fourth, women with child care or other family responsibilities at home may be less likely to participate in the group discussion than women without such responsibilities; yet, these subgroups of female suburbanites may hold different attitudes and exhibit different fitness-related behaviors, which this study would fail to capture.

Fifth, the 4:00 P.M. time may be inconvenient or extremely difficult for women who work at a job that ends at 5:00 P.M. or mothers who need to be home when their children return from school. In this way, the focus group study would be missing some portion of working women and mothers whose attitudes and behavior may not match that of other women.

Sixth, if the research design did not include separate groups for members and nonmembers (i.e., if only one group discussion was planned with a mix of both members and nonmembers as participants), women who already belong to the central city fitness center (i.e., members) may be more likely to cooperate due to their familiarity with and positive disposition to traveling to the fitness center to participate in the discussion than women who do not belong to the center (i.e., nonmembers).

For all these reasons, this approach to gaining cooperation from a representative sample of suburban women would fail badly. The data produced from the suburban females who did participate in the focus groups would be biased (unrepresentative of the target population) and would thereby weaken the credibility of the study. However, as discussed below, there are many approaches these researchers could take to gain a higher level of cooperation and minimize threats to the credibility of the data.

Gaining cooperation from a representative set of sampled focus group participants requires the consideration of a variety of factors in the recruiting process, including:

- The communication of the purpose of the study, which should arouse interest in participating without introducing details that may influence participants' feedback in the discussion (e.g., the suburban women being recruited for the central city fitness center study might be told that the purpose is to identify attributes of an enjoyable fitness experience—which would be a true statement—without specific mention of the pertinence to the fitness center itself).

- The communication of a personal benefit or nonmaterial motivation (e.g., telling suburban women that their participation in the discussion is their opportunity to contribute to the creation of an improved fitness environment).

• The material incentives, such as the nature of the incentive (e.g., cash, a gift card, prized tickets to a sporting event, donation to a favorite charity) and the value (e.g., if, during recruitment, suburban women expressed interest in attending the discussion group but mentioned that $75 was too small for them to take the time to travel to the central city, the researcher should consider increasing the incentive).

• The effect of identifying the study's sponsor (e.g., women may be more likely to cooperate with the research if they knew that their input would help restore the landmark, flagship building in which the fitness center is located).

• The particular circumstance of the people on the sampled list (e.g., cooperation in the study among suburban women might be improved by offering day care or babysitting services to young mothers, or switching from a 4:00 P.M. weekday to a 11:00 A.M. Saturday discussion time to accommodate working women).

• The logistical details that are given to the participant so that showing up for the focus group is easy and uncomplicated (e.g., giving clear, detailed directions to the central city fitness center will encourage nonmembers who do not typically travel to this location and help them find the room where the discussion is being held).

• The steps that are taken to minimize inadvertently recruiting individuals who do not qualify for the discussion group based on the screener specifications (e.g., recruiting a suburban woman for the central city fitness center study who only works out at home and would never consider belonging to a fitness center), including "professional participants" such as "repeaters" and "cheaters." Repeaters and cheaters are individuals who have made attending focus groups a source of income and attend as many discussions as possible in order to earn the cash incentive. In the screening interview, repeaters will misstate how long it has been since they last participated in a group discussion in order to be accepted into the study, and cheaters will purposely misrepresent themselves as it relates to specific usage or attitude questions on the screener.

OTHER CONSIDERATIONS. One of the other considerations in the recruiting process that can affect participants' level of cooperation is the mode by which they are contacted. If recruitment is by way of telephone, it is advisable to make advance contact with the participants via U.S. mail (if there is sufficient lead time in the research schedule) or email (when email addresses are available for the listing of the target population). Advance notification is preferable to the recruiter placing "cold calls" to the sampled participants because it gives participants time to warm to the idea of the focus group and it legitimizes the authenticity of the study (e.g., by the use of professional-looking letterhead) prior to the recruiter's phone call. When the research budget and scheduling requirements of the study are not too restrictive, advance contact may also provide the opportunity to send the sampled participant a noncontingent incentive (e.g., a cash payment or other gift sent in an advance letter that the sampled participant can keep regardless of whether he/she participates in the group discussion) to further develop a sense of trust toward the researchers and encourage cooperation with the study. All other things being equal, telephone recruitment will be more persuasive in gaining cooperation than relying solely on mail or email recruitment (Lavrakas, 2010).

The location where an in-person focus group will be held may greatly impact the level of cooperation that can be achieved from those invited to participate. Using only one location, where all participants are required to travel some distance, may provide the researcher with a much smaller, more narrowly defined (and less reflective of the target population) segment of potential participants compared to offering (a) a location within close proximity to participants or (b) when the research budget will allow, a choice of sites among which the participants can choose. In the example of the focus groups with suburban women, cooperation may be appreciably higher, and the resulting group of participants more representative of the target population, if the group discussions are hosted in a suburban neighborhood near to where the participants actually live, or if these women were given a choice between a focus group facility in a suburban location and the central city fitness center (which might be more convenient to women who work downtown).

As mentioned earlier, the time of day as well as the amount of the incentive can affect cooperation levels and therefore the success of the recruitment process. If, for example, the focus groups are held only during the week at daytime hours, those who are employed will not participate as readily as those who are not. And, to be effective, the value of the incentive paid to participants must take into account the time (e.g., a 90-minute focus group may take 3–5 hours out of a participant's day) and out-of-pocket expenses associated with traveling to and from the location of a face-to-face focus group discussion, as well as other financial burdens for some participants, such as paying for a babysitter. If what is being studied in the group discussion study is correlated with any of the reasons people find the time of day inconvenient or the incentive amount insufficient, then the research will lead to biased outcomes that are not representative of the target population.

A final very important consideration to gaining a relatively higher cooperation rate from a representative sample of the target population is the follow-up contact that is used with those who initially have agreed to participate in a focus group. The proportion of people who are no-shows can be kept low by strategically using follow-up contacts after initial cooperation is gained, much along the lines of what has become routine practice by medical practitioners who strive for a very low level of no-shows among patients who have made office appointments. For that reason, and if the research schedule allows, a follow-up letter or postcard should be sent to recruited participants (via U.S. mail or email) that arrives about a week before the date of the focus group session. (If the lag in time between when cooperation is first gained and when the focus group will be held exceeds 2 weeks, then it is advisable to also send an initial follow-up letter or postcard immediately after gaining cooperation to thank the participant for agreeing to attend the focus group.) A day or 2 before the date of the group discussion, telephone contact should be made with each participant, and every recruited participant should receive a confirmation phone call the day of the focus group.

The persons doing these contacts should be trained in how to be persuasive in overcoming the reluctance they will encounter in some participants to follow through on their pledge to attend. This will help keep the back-out rate among recruited participants on the low side. It should be noted, however, that, no matter what the researchers do in their follow-up communications, there will be individuals who do not show up for the discussion. It is, therefore, prudent for focus group researchers to overrecruit their in-person, telephone, or online groups by gaining cooperation from more than the minimum number of participants that are needed in each focus group. Researchers typically overrecruit by around 20% (e.g., recruiting 12 people to ensure a discussion with 10 participants). Overrecruiting may be particularly necessary when the target population is a minority or low-income segment in which weak confidence or low self-esteem may dampen the level of cooperation (Rabiee, 2007).

RECRUITING HARD-TO-REACH AND VULNERABLE POPULATION SEGMENTS. The recruitment of hard-to-reach and vulnerable segments of the population requires special considerations that will vary for each type of population group, the research topic, and the research mode. Table 4.3 presents three examples of recruiting issues pertaining to focus group research with (1) South Asian men and women on a sensitive topic (Culley, Hudson, & Rapport, 2007); (2) people who have disabilities (Kroll, Barbour, & Harris, 2007); and (3) gay, lesbian, bisexual, transgender (GLBT) persons (Matthews & Cramer, 2008).

Data Gathering

Data quality and the overall credibility of a focus group study rely on three essential facets of Data Gathering: (1) the content of the discussion, (2) the group interviewer (i.e., the moderator), and (3) the group participants. The most important aspect of the content revolves around the topics, issues, and particular questions selected for inclusion in the discussions, and, specifically, how well the outcomes from the focus groups measure the constructs set down in the research objectives. This issue is discussed further starting on page 139.

The second critical factor in measurement is the moderator who, similar to an IDI interviewer, can affect the quality of the data by the manner in which he/she conducts the discussions. The two primary **moderator effects** are:

1. **Moderator bias**, that is, behavioral and other characteristics of the moderator that may bias responses. For example, a moderator who tells participants they have given the "right" answer or otherwise indicates that some responses are more "right" than others would unduly bias the research outcomes; or a moderator

TABLE 4.3. Focus Group Recruitment: Examples Pertaining to Hard-to-Reach and Vulnerable Population Segments

Author(s)	Population segment(s) and research topic	Recruiting issues and strategy/approach

Culley et al. (2007)	• Three South Asian communities in England; separate groups conducted with:
	  ○ Indian Hindu
	  ○ Indian Sikh
	  ○ Bangladeshi Muslim
	  ○ Pakistani Muslim
	  ○ Members of an ethnoreligious community
	• Topic: Infertility and infertility services
		• Recruitment for all 14 group discussions took almost three times as long as anticipated (i.e., 11 months instead of four), primarily due to issues related to "insider status" and sensitivity of the topic.
		• Participants were generally recruited from community centers.
		• The White female researchers recruiting female participants achieved insider status by way of their perceived roles as "experts" and affiliation with a university, as well as their gender.
		• Male participants were difficult to recruit because (a) men in these communities rarely meet in groups, (b) infertility is considered a woman's, not a man's, topic of discussion, and (c) work and other commitments made scheduling a challenge. For these reasons, "the intervention of the male community facilitators was vital to the recruitment" (p. 108).
		• To build trust during recruitment, the researchers made many visits to the group venues to meet "key people" and discuss the purpose of the focus groups.
		• Because "group conveners" were involved in assembling the groups, the researchers faced an ethical concern related to informed consent; specifically, whether all participants understood what was going to be discussed prior to attending the group.

Kroll et al. (2007)	• People with various types of disability conditions (e.g., mobility, visual, or learning impairment) • Topic: Issues related to the type of disability or disease, the use of the mobility device, or the daily activities of living, among other themes.	• Although convenient, recruiting by way of independent living centers and disability organizations is discouraged because participants recruited in this manner may be atypical in that they may (a) have a better support network, (b) have greater knowledge of their disability, (c) be more outspoken, (d) have repeatedly participated in focus group research (becoming "professional subjects"), and (e) not be representative of ethnic, social minority, and low-income groups. • Added time and cost are necessary for a "proactive" and all-inclusive approach to recruitment. For example, "it is crucial that all recruitment material, such as information sheets and flyers, be available in alternative formats (e.g., Braille, large print)" (p. 692) and go through cognitive testing when the research involves participants with cognitive and intellectual disabilities.

(continued)

	TABLE 4.3. *(continued)*	
Author(s)	**Population segment(s) and research topic**	**Recruiting issues and strategy/approach**
Matthews & Cramer (2008)	• Gay, lesbian, bisexual, and transgender (GLBT) persons • Topic: None specifically. The authors refer to several studies, including a group study with single, gay adoptive fathers. The article focuses on the use of the Internet to conduct research, including focus groups, with hard-to-reach people such as the GLBT population.	• The ability to include large numbers of geographically dispersed people who are typically "hidden" or hard-to-reach, such as GLBT persons, is made easier by creating dedicated online group communities via an online service such as Yahoo!. • The "welcome" screen and other features of the Yahoo! group site can be customized to enhance the credibility of the group and encourage participants to join. • Invitations to join the group can be promoted via the Yahoo! directory of groups. The researcher has the ability to approve all participants who ask to join the group. • Building trust is important in recruitment. Disclosing a GLBT researcher's sexual orientation as well as explaining why a particular research topic is being studied (and how the results will be used) can instill trust. However, revealing the location of the researcher (e.g., in the South) may impede recruitment. • In the group with single, gay adoptive fathers, participants were allowed to remain anonymous and not required to share identifying information. • Recruiting is made easier by the fact that online groups give "hidden populations . . . the ability to connect with others who may have life experiences similar to their own" (p. 309).

whose demographic characteristics are so at odds with the demographic mix of the focus group participants that it biases the resulting discussion (e.g., an African American focus group moderator conducting a face-to-face discussion with an all-Asian group of participants who are asked to discuss race relations in their Los Angeles neighborhoods).

2. **Moderator inconsistency**, that is, unwarranted and unrepresentative variations in the data as the result of the moderator's inconsistent manner when conducting the group discussions. For example, a moderator who does not adequately manage the allotted time for the discussions and is forced to skip one or more topics in some, but not all, groups will introduce inconsistency in the data and jeopardize the study outcomes; or, if two moderators are separately conducting a series of focus groups on a contentious subject for a particular study, and one of the moderators is much more adept at keeping the discussions at a civil level whereas the other moderator has a tendency to allow the discussions to become disruptive and out of control, then these substantively different moderating styles will result in an inconsistency in the quality of the data gathered across the series of focus group discussions.

The third key factor that can influence the quality of the data that are gathered in the group discussion method involves the group participants and their ability and willingness to provide complete and accurate information. Participants' engagement and forthrightness in the discussions is a function of whether they (a) know the information being asked of them and (b) are comfortable sharing this information with the moderator and other participants.

Content of the Group Discussion

Quality measurement in the group discussion method leans heavily on an accurate assessment of the topics and issues associated with the constructs of interest (see Chapter 2, p. 30). Before the moderator can conduct a meaningful and credible discussion, it is imperative that the researcher and moderator, along with any other members of the research team, ensure that the discussions include the entirety of topical areas that define the underlying constructs of the research objectives as well as the various aspects of importance within each construct. To do this, the focus group researcher needs to practice all the steps outlined in Chapter 3 for building content in the IDI method (see pp. 79–80), with a particular emphasis on meeting with various individuals among the clients or sponsors of the research who have a vested interest in the outcomes. So, like the researcher preparing the interview guide for an IDI study, the researcher who is developing content for focus group discussions must (a) review and build on the proprietary and academic research that has been conducted on the topic in the past, (b) consult with experts on the topic areas, (c) prepare a **discussion guide** (the guide is discussed further below) in collaboration with the client/sponsor, and (d) allow sufficient time in development to take a break from, and come back to, the discussion guide for further revisions.

Compared to IDIs, focus group research typically attracts an above-average amount of attention within a client/sponsor organization and may necessitate the involvement of a greater number of interested parties. This is especially true for the face-to-face mode where 10 or more individuals from the client/sponsor organization may attend the discussions to observe behind a one-way mirror. With this being the case, the focus group researcher needs to be sensitive to the possibility that any number of people, apart from his/her direct contact within the client/sponsor organization, may want to be engaged—both before and during the field period—with the development of content as well as the peculiarities of the discussion guide itself. For instance, a focus group study among undecided independent voters being conducted for a politician's reelection campaign would be remiss if the researcher did not reach out beyond the immediate research team and consult with other members of the politician's election staff across all levels, including strategic planning, communications, marketing, and advertising.

DISCUSSION GUIDE. A critical component in the reliability and validity of the content in group interviewing rests with the moderator's outline that guides him/her throughout the discussion. The organization of the outline (typically, organized in a "funnel" style, with broader, more general issues leading to specific questions relevant to the research topic) as well as the content related to the actual components—i.e., comprehensiveness of the topics to be covered, pertinence of the primary and follow-up questions to ask, and use of particular enabling or projective techniques (see below)—play a significant role in determining the ultimate credibility and usefulness of the focus group research outcomes. In every respect, throughout the design of the discussion guide the researcher has to ask "Will the order and pace (i.e., the time allotted to each topic area) of the content be reasonable across all discussion groups so there is a 'sameness' that allows us to evaluate the reliability of the data?", "Is this [topic, question, technique] relevant to the construct we are investigating?", and "Does this [topic, question, technique] measure the aspect of the construct that we think we are measuring?" For example, in the instance of conducting focus groups with independent voters so that an incumbent politician can increase his/her chances of being reelected, suppose the discussion guide was heavily slanted toward inquiring about voters' propensity to vote for the politician's opponent. If the content of the discussion guide did not also plumb the reasons why these voters may or may not want to vote for the politician him/herself, the information learned from the focus groups could be completely off-target and lead to a flawed strategic plan for the politician's reelection. This would be an example of the discussion guide failing to specify all the relevant constructs related to the purpose of the research that needed to be addressed in the group discussions to provide credible data.

DISCUSSION GUIDE: ENABLING AND PROJECTIVE TECHNIQUES. A moderator's guide will often include group exercises or facilitation techniques as alternative approaches to direct questioning. Although many of these alternative tactics are not unique to the group discussion method, they have become a popular device in focus groups. These alternative approaches can be broadly categorized as either "enabling" or "projective" techniques, the difference being whether the moderator's intent is to simply modify a direct question to make it easier for group participants to express their opinions (**enabling techniques**) or delve into participants' less conscious, less rational, and/or less socially acceptable feelings by way of indirect exercises (**projective techniques**). Examples of enabling techniques are:

- *Sentence completion*—for example, "When I think of being happy, I think of _____." or "The best thing about the new city transit system is _____."
- *Word association*—for example, asking prospective college students, "What is the first word you think of when I say, 'first day of college'?" or asking hospital administrators, "When I say 'patient care,' what is the first word or words that come to mind?"
- *Storytelling*—for example, "Tell me a story about the last time you visited your local library for any reason."

Projective techniques strive to depersonalize the discussion by moving away from direct questions specific to the research topic and instead ask participants to project their feelings by imagining the thoughts of others, role playing, or describing visual stimuli (e.g., images). Catterall and Ibbotson (2000), for example, asked a group of postgraduate students to complete two "thought bubbles" on a cartoon drawing depicting faceless (and genderless) characters (a teacher speaking in front of a class of students), asking them to speculate what a student in the class and the teacher were thinking. The results of this exercise led to "previously untapped responses" regarding the projected thoughts of the teacher. Another example of a projective technique, "associative imagery," is provided by Gong et al. (2012), who used the method with home care givers and the recipients of home care services ("consumers"). In a series of 10 focus groups, participants were shown a stack of 19 photographs and asked to "pick the best picture that represents how you feel when you are interacting with your homecare worker/consumer" (p. 1417). This study revealed the impact of imagery in stimulating reminders of the giver–consumer relationship as well as particular metaphors (e.g., a picture of dolphins represented harmony and friendship), and, in this way, "demonstrated that associative imagery can be used effectively in focus groups to elicit emotional and descriptive responses so that participants can express difficult and complex concepts" (p. 1423).

Projective techniques have also proven effective with marginalized segments of the population, as shown by Fine and Sirin (2007), who asked Muslim American youth (and young adults) to draw "identity maps" depicting how they saw themselves. Fine and Sirin used focus groups to explore deeply the meaning of these maps and to "witness the collective existential challenge posed to self by engagement with others" (p. 30).

Projective techniques are used heavily among marketing researchers who increasingly (with the growing capabilities of online research) devise new variations of projective exercises. Hofstede, van Hoof, Walenberg, and de Jong (2007), for example, looked at consumers' perceptions of beer brands via a couple of personification techniques that asked participants (in individual interviews, not group discussions) to match brands of beer with (1) pictures of celebrities and the perceived personality type for each celebrity; and (2) a type of job (e.g., minister, gym teacher, or gardener) and the personality trait associated with that job type. Similarly, it is not uncommon for marketing researchers to ask group participants to personify a brand by asking, "If the popular brands of coffee represented a family, which family member does this particular brand represent?" A few of the other techniques include:

- *Eulogy and birth announcements*—that is, asking participants to write the obituary for the "death" of a brand or an announcement of the "birth" of a new member of a product line.

- *Guided imagery*—for example, asking participants to close their eyes and imagine walking into an electronics store and describing their reaction when they do not find a sought-after computer brand.

- *Psychodrawing*—for example, asking participants to draw their depiction of what it would be like to be without a mobile phone.

- *Picture sorts*—for example, using the social media site Pinterest to share images found online that answer the question, "How do you feel when you are in a big social gathering with people you do not know well?"

From a TQF perspective, the use of projective techniques can be problematic and begs the question of whether or how much projective techniques bring added value to the group discussion. Whereas enabling techniques are extensions of direct questioning that fall within the researcher's natural skill set, the indirect method of projective exercises drifts into the little-known realm, among many social science researchers, of clinical psychology. Regardless of whether focus group participants are given the opportunity to explain their own interpretation of their thought bubble, drawing, or picture sort, or whether the interpretation is left for the researcher, the inherent subjectivity of the meanings that are ultimately associated with participants' output threatens the validity of these techniques. The credibility of qualitative research data partially rests on knowing what is being measured, yet the moderator's qualifications and/or the short duration of a focus group session may make valid interpretations of the data (and linkages back to the research objectives) from projective techniques a challenge. What, for example, has the researcher measured from a collage exercise resulting in a collection of seemingly unrelated images from each of 10 group participants? The moderator can investigate each participant's interpretation of his/her "artwork," but the reality is that the focus group moderator does not have the capability of knowing whether the collage exercise tapped into an unconscious realization important to the research objectives, or if the exercise measured aspects of the participant related to (for example) motivations, cultural background, or social awareness. Humans are remarkable in thinking that they can "make sense" from all sorts of things that really have no sense to be made of. Therefore, the challenge to researchers who are subjectively interpreting the data from projective techniques is to not overinterpret them beyond the bounds of credibility.

To maximize the credibility of focus group data stemming from the use of enabling and projective techniques, researchers must carefully select which techniques to use based on their ability to interpret the results in conjunction with the in-session time the moderator will be able to give to these exercises. For instance, the researcher might opt for a smaller discussion format, such as dyads and triads, to accommodate the necessary time to complete a projective technique involving a picture sort, including a thorough examination of each participant's reasons for the photographs he/she selected as well as those that were rejected. The careful use of these techniques will not only enhance data credibility but also increase the overall quality of the research by allowing the researcher to perform necessary verification procedures (e.g., triangulation) in the analysis phase (see Analyzability, p. 152).

Moderator Effects

Focus group moderators who have the crucial task of conducting the discussions in the group interviewing method also have a direct role in determining the outcomes of the research. Similar to the IDI interviewer, the group moderator must be a professional researcher with a high level of interpersonal skills. However, unlike the role of the IDI interviewer, the role of the focus group moderator requires additional abilities related to the control and facilitation of group dynamics as well as multitasking activities, chiefly in the face-to-face mode, such as responding to the needs of observers and managing logistics at the facility where the discussions are taking place. For these reasons, it is particularly important that a focus group moderator be:

- Highly organized, with very good time management skills to ensure coverage of the discussion guide in each group within the agreed-to timeframe of the discussion.
- A leader, someone who can manage the discussion without being overbearing and exhibit control, as necessary, in terms of knowing
  - How long to spend on a given topic and when to move on.
  - What topic to move on to.
  - How and when to speak firmly to manage the flow of the discussion, but doing so in a respectful way that does not alienate the participants.
- Open-minded and flexible in order to deal with
  - Observers' requests (e.g., asking the moderator at the midway point in a discussion to interject a new topic or question).
  - Unanticipated events (e.g., participants who do not show up for the discussion by the appointed time, or someone in a discussion who gets very angry or upset and starts to cry).
  - Managing logistics (e.g., the discussion room setup for face-to-face groups, the look and capabilities of the online platform for online bulletin boards, or the teleconferencing connections for telephone focus groups).
- Attentive, with the ability to "think on your feet" during a discussion in order to identify, evaluate the importance of, and discuss new topics as they emerge.

These key moderator skills are summarized in Box 4.2.

All of these skills are at work when the moderator, for example, is conducting a discussion on a contentious topic, such as a focus group discussion about environmental issues among individuals who are active in environmental causes. In this instance, it would be natural for each participant to have a strong personal view of the most important issues to be discussed, possibly leading to a very fragmented and argumentative group discussion that may not touch upon the specific

> ## BOX 4.2. Four Key Moderator Skills
>
> A focus group moderator must be:
>
> - **Highly organized**
> - **A leader** who knows
>   - When to move on in the discussion
>   - Where to move to in the discussion
>   - How to manage participants and maintain the flow of discussion
> - **Open-minded and flexible**, responsive to
>   - Observers' requests
>   - Unanticipated events
>   - Logistical requirements of the discussion venue
> - **Attentive**, with the ability to
>   - Identify and incorporate new topics as they emerge

topics the researchers need to study. Such a situation also could lead to an impasse in which no productive exchange of ideas is occurring. For a potentially contentious focus group to be productive in generating credible data, it is critical that the moderator manage the flow of the discussion in a way that does not squelch the expression of individual views, but at the same time does not allow individual expression at the expense of neglecting the research objectives—which, in turn, would prevent the research team from gathering useful information from the discussion.

MODERATOR BIAS. Like an IDI interviewer, the focus group moderator can negatively impact the quality of data that are gathered and therefore the credibility of the research outcomes via a variety of ways that may bias the data. The moderator, for instance, may influence the participants' responses, thereby weakening the credibility of the data by behaving in a certain manner (e.g., affirming a response or favoring one participant over another), displaying particular demographic or physical characteristics that may be obvious depending on the mode (e.g., apparent racial differences in face-to-face groups, or varying manner of speaking the English language in telephone discussions), or, in face-to-face groups, dressing in a certain manner (e.g., wearing jeans and a tee-shirt to a discussion with business managers).

Another example of moderator bias is a focus group study being conducted with groups of White police officers who were known to harbor negative feelings toward racial minorities in their jurisdiction, but who expressed ambivalent attitudes in the group discussion as the result of the moderator's inappropriate interjection of her own personal opinions of the minority groups. In this example, it is the moderator's verbal behavior that caused the discussion findings to be biased.

The potential impact of moderator bias can be reduced by proactively integrating quality-control measures in the design of a focus group study, as follows:

• A pretest phase is not typically conducted in the group discussion method due to reasons of practicality (e.g., the additional cost a pretest adds to the research budget and the additional time it adds to the research schedule). However, pretesting is always a best practice because it reveals ways in which the moderator may be overly influencing responses, and pretesting has proven effective in determining the "most appropriate" group interviewing technique. For instance, Kenyon (2004) conducted pretest focus groups among teenagers 16–17 years old to "critically evaluate" two group interviewing methods—semistructured and nondirective—and identify the method that was more likely to stimulate greater "experiential intertextuality" when participants gave their interpretations of media advertisements for alcohol. The result of this pretest—which included analyses of the audio and video recordings of the discussions conducted using the semistructured interviewing method and other discussions conducted using nondirective interviewing—"showed that the nondirective questioning technique was more appropriate" (p. 432).

• The researcher moderating a group discussion must know when and how to follow up on participants' comments and to probe responses that may be unclear or inconsistent with remarks made earlier in the discussion. The moderator has the additional responsibility of keeping track of the group dynamics and identifying if and how individual attitudes may have shifted as the result of the group interaction (e.g., exploring why mothers, who stated early in the discussion that they buy fast food for their children because it is easy and convenient, talk about purchasing healthy food for their children after hearing other group participants espouse the virtue in giving children a nutritional diet).

• The researchers should observe the first few focus group discussions each moderator conducts in real time (e.g., by way of a one-way mirror in face-to-face groups or the virtual backroom in online bulletin boards; Note: Group participants are informed of the presence of observers prior to the discussion), listen or view the audio or video recordings, and/or read the transcripts of these discussions very soon after they have been conducted. There are many reasons to do this, but in the case of potential moderator bias, it is imperative that the researchers detect its presence and provide instructive, unambiguous feedback to the moderator to help him/her eliminate any future bias. Even with experienced moderators, it is prudent that the researchers commit the time required for this quality assurance phase.

• As noted in Chapter 3, a reflexive journal is an important and necessary feature of an IDI study design, but this quality-control measure has not become a routine practice in the group discussion method. *We believe that this needs to change.* Focus group moderators who keep a reflexive journal enhance the credibility of the research by way of maintaining a record of their experiences and how they may have biased the discussions. Moderators can create reflexive journals by listening to audio recordings (or watching video recordings) of focus groups they have just conducted and giving firsthand accounts of how they may have unduly influenced participants' comments and the ultimate outcome of the discussion. This self-evaluative exercise is meant to help moderators gain insights into their behavior and other factors that affected the discussion as well as consider the impact of these on the credibility of the data from this discussion as well as all the group discussions these moderators are conducting for a given study. Reflexive journals also provide the researcher with invaluable information to consider when analyzing and interpreting the study's findings. An example of a reflexive journal format is shown in Chapter 2, Figure 2.2, page 42.

For example, a reflexive journal can be used in the group discussion method as a way of triangulating the data. A TQF best practice is to have someone from the research team who understands the research objectives yet who is impartial examine two or more focus groups by way of the audio or video recordings and consider if and how the moderator may have prejudiced the outcomes in one way or the other. This review should then be shared with the moderator and examined in conjunction with the moderator's own reflexive journal in order to identify similarities as well as discrepancies between the two accounts. The independent review, the moderator's reflexive journal, and the comparison of the two should be used thoughtfully in the analysis and interpretation of the data and become an essential part of the final research reporting document. As noted previously, this level of quality control is not at all a routine practice in focus group research, but we strongly recommend that it become so to help raise the level of credibility by which group discussion research is carried out.

MODERATOR INCONSISTENCY. Moderator inconsistency can be a real problem, from a TQF perspective, in the group discussion method because of the extreme multitasking with which the moderator has to contend. More so than in the IDI method, the group interviewer has to manage multiple points of view and ensure the full engagement of all group participants within a well-defined slot of time (typically, 90–120 minutes for a face-to-face discussion). Because of these challenges and the inherent unpredictability of the group dynamic process, the moderator may find it difficult (if not impossible) to cover all areas of the discussion guide across different focus groups and/or practice consistent behavior in the articulation of research questions in each group. This inconsistency across groups does not necessarily lead to *inaccuracy* in the research data (i.e., biased outcomes) but may result in *variations* in the data that do not actually exist.

For example, the series of focus group discussions among people who are active in environmental causes (mentioned earlier) might include some groups that were easily managed by the moderator, who was able to cover the entirety of the discussion guide, thereby providing a well rounded and informative perspective of the issues. Other groups within the series, however, might have been especially contentious, dominated by a few highly vocal environmental activists who were disruptive to the point that the moderator had difficulty maintaining control of these groups and was ultimately forced to skip some of the important areas of the discussion guide. As a result of this inconsistency in group dynmics and management, the final outcome of the research might accurately reflect participants' positions on the research topics of interest, but the final data may also indicate a wide variation of personal opinion on the issues when, in reality, this variation does not exist. (This example speaks further to the importance of managing participants when moderating group discussions while, at the same time, giving participants sufficient latitude to speak their minds.) In the worst case of moderator inconsistency, one or more focus groups may be invalidated. The researcher is then faced with the costly prospect of scheduling new focus groups (with all new participants) to replace the ones that were nullified.

Moderator inconsistency may also be the result of inadequate training, including a lack of on-the-job monitoring and retraining during the field period. Too often clients and researchers hire focus group moderators on the assumption that they will do a very fine job even if the client or researcher does not get involved in overseeing the progress and quality of the focus groups. This may well be the case for many moderators, but certainly not all. For this reason, it is advisable that any client or researcher who sincerely cares about the quality of data gathered in his/her focus groups allocate the time necessary to monitor all moderators, no matter how experienced each moderator is.

Moderators may need slightly different skills depending on the mode (as noted below), but moderator training should generally strive to maximize moderator consistency by giving moderators the ability to:

• Discriminate between the topical areas or questions that must be stated in the same manner across all group discussions (e.g., concept statements) from the remaining areas of the discussion guide where such exactness is unnecessary or not possible (e.g., follow-up questions that probe for clarification). A study concerning racial prejudice, for example, will result in unreliable outcomes if the moderator varies the definition of "prejudice" across the group discussions—that is, failing to define it at all for some groups, defining it in one way for some other groups, and defining it in another way for still other groups.

• Manage discussion time and topical priorities to ensure that there is consistent coverage of the discussion guide across groups.

• Maintain focus during each discussion, asking follow-up questions and pursuing emerging ideas, even though he/she may be overwhelmed with stress and fatigue. Particularly in face-to-face group studies when travel is involved, but in all multigroup projects to some degree, the mental acuity of the moderator can be weakened due to the high level of social interaction (related to working with the group participants as well as various individuals from the client/sponsor).

• Learn the special skills required to conduct telephone group discussions. In particular, the moderator of telephone focus groups must (a) shorten and reprioritize the discussion guide to guarantee that the most important topics or issues can be discussed within a 60-minute discussion, and (b) develop a method to identify who is speaking and track each participant's engagement so that the moderator can adequately follow up on specific comments and be certain that all participants have contributed to the discussion. The "speaker grid" used by Smith, Sullivan, and Baxter (2009) is one such method.

● Conduct online group discussions (asynchronous or synchronous) in a consistent manner and fully engage group participants by way of the online platform. Moderators need to learn how to shorten the discussion guide so that only four to six questions are asked on any particular day, ask questions as simply and clearly as possible in order to not confuse participants' interpretations of the questions, and develop a method for tracking participant engagement (many online platforms have features that make this easy to do) as well as the moderator's follow-up activity (questioning) with participants.

Group Participants' Ability and Willingness to Provide Information

Beyond the content of the discussions and the effects of the moderator, there is a third critical component that threatens the quality of data gathered in the group discussion method: the participants themselves. The participants in a group discussion face a more daunting social environment than IDI interviewees—an environment in which participants are typically expected to meet (face-to-face, on the phone, or virtually) and engage with a set of strangers. At the minimum, participants in a dyad find themselves among two other individuals they have never met (the moderator and other participant); and, in the opposite extreme, participants in an online bulletin board may be one of 10 or 12 people who have been asked to join the discussion. As with the IDI method, focus group participants in any mode (i.e., face-to-face, telephone, or online) can negatively impact the quality of the data that are gathered and therefore the credibility of group discussion data by their (a) inability to divulge certain information accurately because they do not know or are not aware of the information being asked for; or (b) unwillingness or reluctance to divulge certain information that they do know, leading them to say nothing or to make an inaccurate statement (e.g., participants may be unwilling to comment on sensitive or highly personal topics such as personal hygiene, or may feel compelled to give socially acceptable responses to questions that are laden with societal norms, such as alcohol use, or they may say something untrue simply to try to "impress" others in the group).

Researchers can proactively try to avoid the problem of participants not knowing about the topics to be discussed in the focus groups by having each participant adequately screened for relevant knowledge and/or experience during the recruitment stage (a step that will also help to identify "repeaters" and "cheaters," discussed on p. 134). When appropriate, this process can screen out individuals who would not be likely to make credible contributions to the group discussions.

In some focus group studies, what people do *not* know (or have not done) is a central part of what the study is exploring (e.g., recruiting people who have not been involved with a local nonprofit organization to learn about their awareness and perceptions of this organization). When this is the case, the moderator must use his or her rapport-building skills not only to help participants feel comfortable with him/her but, importantly, to also make participants feel comfortable with each other so that less aware or knowledgeable participants are not afraid to comment. Establishing rapport in the socially more complex research environment of the group discussion is essential to creating an atmosphere where participants feel free to express their doubt or lack of awareness, where they are comfortable admitting to the moderator and to the other participants, "I am not aware of any urgent care medical facilities in our city" or "I don't recall seeing or hearing anything about that organization." Participants' lack of knowledge on any topic of interest is an important research finding, but it is one that is unlikely to be detected accurately without the support and rapport fostered by the moderator. By capturing the "I don't know" response, when it is an accurate reflection of a participant's position on an issue, the moderator has added to the credibility of the final outcomes.

What about the participant who *does* know the answer to the moderator's questions but is unwilling to share that information? This may happen if the participant believes that the questions being asked or the topic area is of a highly personal or sensitive nature, or a subject matter governed by certain social norms—such as alcohol use, racial profiling, church attendance, and healthy eating—that may pressure the participant to respond in a socially desirable (or acceptable) manner. As with the IDI method, rapport building (discussed on the next page) plays an important role in creating a trusting environment (whether it is face-to-face, on the telephone, or online) in which group participants feel safe in speaking about sensitive issues or in simply saying, "I would prefer not to talk about that."

A trusting focus group environment is one that should relieve some of the pressure participants may feel to give socially desirable responses to the moderator's questions. A socially desirable response may be face-saving for the participant, but it introduces inaccurate, untruthful information that undermines the quality of final data. One way for the moderator to deal with the possibility of inaccurate or false information from participants is to wait for a moment in the discussion when participants would not sense that the moderator was singling out any one participant and interrupt the discussion to remind all participants that the focus of the discussion is on honest and accurate feedback and that it is better not to say anything, or say "I don't know," than to say something that is not accurate. This type of reminder is a common practice among moderators, even when there is no suspicion that one or more participants may be giving false information. When inaccuracies among participants do occur and the moderator can identify participant(s) who may have fabricated one or more responses, the moderator should document his/her suspicions as soon as the focus group has ended and the participants have left (e.g., in a reflexive journal). In this way the researchers can be put on notice that a specific participant's (or participants') input in the discussion may not be reliable and valid. This does not invalidate the entire group discussion but allows the researchers to filter out what is likely to be credible in the data from what is not.

In addition to building rapport with the participants, the moderator can use a variety of discussion facilitation techniques, previously discussed, that can help draw out participants' opinions or knowledge on a subject area. These enabling and projective techniques (detailed on pp. 140–142) modify the style or type of questions to make it easier for participants to express their thoughts or to reveal information that is not readily available to the rational mind.

BUILDING RAPPORT AND KEEPING CONTROL OF THE DISCUSSION FLOW. The ability to quickly build rapport with group participants and then maintain it throughout the discussion session is a necessary skill of all moderators. Regardless of mode (face-to-face, telephone, or online), focus group moderators must learn how to effectively engage participants to generate accurate and complete information. Rapport building for the moderator begins even before the start of a group discussion, when he/she welcomes the participants as they arrive at the facility (for a face-to-face discussion), on the teleconference line (for a telephone focus group), or in the virtual focus group room (for an online discussion), and it continues beyond the introductory remarks during which the moderator acknowledges aspects of the discussion environment that may not be readily apparent (e.g., the presence of observers, the microphone or other device being used to audiorecord the discussion), states a few ground rules for the session, and allows participants to ask any questions or make comments before the start of the discussion. In the face-to-face mode, the moderator's rapport building goes beyond what he/she says to participants to make them feel at ease to also include the physical environment. For example, business executives might feel comfortable and willing to talk sitting around a standard conference table; however, in order to build rapport and stimulate engagement among a group of teenagers, the moderator needs to select a site where teens will feel that they can relax and freely discuss the issues. This might be a standard focus group facility with a living or recreation room setup (i.e., a room with couches, bean bags, and rugs on the floor for sitting) or an unconventional location such as someone's home or the city park.

Another aspect of the physical environment in face-to-face discussions that impacts rapport and consequently the quality of the data gathered is seating arrangement. For instance, Krueger and Casey (2009) recommend that the moderator position a shy participant directly across from his or her seat in order to "maximize eye contact." Other moderators prefer to keep particularly talkative and potentially domineering participants in seats close to them so that they can use their proximity to better manage these participants as needed. The "ideal" seating arrangement will vary depending on the physical environment; the number, type, and homogeneity of participants; and topic of discussion (e.g., for a potentially "explosive" topic such as women's rights, individuals who are particularly active and opinionated on the issues should not sit together where they may form a subgroup or coalition that could end up dominating and skewing the discussion).

A few of the more critical considerations in building rapport to maximize the credibility of group discussion data include the following:

- Group participants should be contacted on behalf of the researcher(s) at least twice after they have agreed to participate in a focus group—once immediately after recruitment to confirm the date and location, and again via telephone the day before the discussion. This advance/reminder contact helps the participant better understand what to expect in the focus group and, in a sense, can begin the process of rapport building between the participant and the moderator by instilling trust and legitimacy in the research process. Preliminary contact is important across all modes of group discussions. Other important aspects of the preliminary contact are:

   o The information given to the participant, which should include (a) the purpose of the study, but usually not in great detail; (b) any preparation or "homework" required of the participant prior to the discussion (although this is not a common requirement); (c) the format of the discussion, including the role of the moderator and the participants; (d) the date, time of day, logistical information— that is, location for a face-to-face discussion (including directions for travel), call-in information for a telephone focus group, and URL/log-in information of an online discussion—and the anticipated length of the session; and (e) the incentive amount that will be given to the participant and when this will be given. When the preliminary contact is made by way of telephone, the recruiter should also use the opportunity to seek a reaffirmation from the participant that he/she is still fully committed to attend and participate in the scheduled session. When the recruiter encounters a participant who does not appear fully committed to participate (which is bound to happen with some), the recruiter needs to use polite but persuasive communication to increase the chances the participant will in fact attend the scheduled focus group.

   o How much of the research purpose and study hypotheses that is revealed to the participant, with a caution not to reveal too much information. This applies not only to the advance communication but also to the moderator's comments at the start of the discussion. By divulging too many details of the research, the moderator runs the risk of influencing participants' thoughts, which may lead the discussion in a biased direction that otherwise it would not have gone. When the moderator concludes his/her introductory remarks in the focus group and asks for participants' questions or comments, it is not unusual for at least one participant to ask for clarification as to the specific purpose of the discussion. The moderator can often deflect these questions by honestly stating that the particular focus of the discussion will become clear soon after the discussion begins.

   o In addition to the URL and log-in information for online group participants, the preliminary contact should also provide brief instructions on what to do when participants log into the online platform, including the mention of a few key platform features. For instance, participants should be told how to create a personal profile and, if they wish, upload a profile photograph that the moderator and other participants will see.

• Not unlike the IDI interviewer, a necessary ingredient to building rapport with group participants is the moderator's ability to show genuine interest in the discussion as a whole and with each participant's contribution to the discussion. Demonstrating this interest involves frequent and relevant follow-up probing questions as well as helping participants engage with each other—for example, "Susan, it sounds like you had a much better experience than George at the City fine art museum. Why don't you tell George what you liked about the museum and maybe even try to change his mind about it."

• The moderator should be attuned to any verbal and nonverbal cues that signal participants' level of engagement and, hence, the extent of rapport among the participants. In the face-to-face mode, the moderator should be able to recognize both visual cues (e.g., frowns and grimaces, lack of interest, downright inattention) and audio cues (e.g., audible hesitations, drawn-out sighs, under-the-breath remarks) from each participant and respond to those, as appropriate, to keep a comfortable and productive level of discussion going among participants. In the telephone mode, these cues are only available audibly and the moderator must be particularly alert to the pauses or sounds (e.g., the sound of a participant typing on a keyboard) that may signal a distracted, disengaged participant. The telephone mode can be moved closer to the face-to-face experience by the addition of a webcam or other online feature to allow the moderator to pick up on visual as well as audible cues.

• Rapport building is especially difficult in the online mode (without a webcam) because the moderator does not have direct visual or verbal contact with the participants and therefore has less control over the rapport-building process. The online moderator can, however, identify participants who are not logging into the discussion very often or are leaving only short, nondescriptive responses to the moderator's questions. In these cases, the moderator can send each of these participants a private email to inquire why he or she has not been more active in the discussion and offer to assist with any difficulties the participant may be having with logging in or otherwise accessing the discussion. The moderator may also choose to call this participant on the telephone in an attempt to establish a more personal connection that may encourage the participant to become more active in the session.

Analyzability

Analyzability is the component of the TQF that deals with the processing (i.e., the transformation of data into usable form, such as transcripts, from which a coding system can be developed to uncover themes and meanings) as well as the verification (e.g., by way of triangulation and peer reviews) of research data. Like all qualitative research, the group discussion method deserves and demands a thorough and strategic analysis of the outcomes to ensure the validity of the final interpretations of the data, the transferability of the research (i.e., the ability to apply or transfer the research to other contexts), and the ultimate usefulness of the study.

Processing

The Processing facet of the Analyzability component, as it relates to focus group data, includes the transcription, coding, and theme development using all available data sources, including audio and/or video recordings and written transcripts. The simplicity or the complexity of these processing procedures is, in part, a function of the number of group discussions that are completed for any particular study. For example, in the case of a study that involves only one focus group on a fairly straightforward topic (e.g., a discussion among Little League coaches concerning ways to improve baseball camp), the researcher may listen to the audio recording, view the video, and/or read the transcripts shortly after the focus group is completed, spending only a few hours taking notes and identifying one or more themes. The researcher might then be able to review these notes and report on the findings within a 24-hour period.

It is more likely, however, that the researcher is conducting a study consisting of several (possibly, many) group discussions. In this case, the researcher will need to allow for adequate time to gather the data sources for each group (most likely a recording, transcript, and/or images), take notes, and develop a way to systematically code or organize the data in order to capture each occurrence of the factors being studied. (Developing and applying such a coding scheme are not unlike doing content analysis, described in Chapter 6.) Only then will the researcher have the information consolidated in such a way as to engage in theme building and other sense making. This process could take several weeks to complete, depending partly on the number of focus groups that were completed, practical considerations (e.g., the available time in the researcher's schedule and funding), and the complexity of the substantive data resulting from the discussions.

The complexity of the substantive data in the group discussion method is no small matter. For one thing, more and richer data sources typically stem from focus group research compared to the IDI method. Video recording, for instance, is more common in the face-to-face focus group method and needs special attention because it may include important nonverbal information beyond the substance of the words that were spoken. For example, the participants' facial expressions may provide valuable insights in addition to what is manifest by the spoken words themselves. However, a more profound contributor to the complexity of processing group discussion research is not a data source but a component that is the essence of the method: that is, the interactivity of the group participants. It is *participant interaction* that sets this method apart from the one-on-one IDI approach, yet focus group researchers are typically lax in their attention to this all-important area of analysis. From the TQF perspective, complete and accurate analyses and interpretations of group discussions are achieved by expending the necessary time and effort to consider the group members' interactions with each other and with the moderator.

Whether it is by way of video or transcriptions of the discussions, the dynamic interaction fostered by the group environment has the potential of offering the analyst views of the research outcomes that go beyond what is learned from the process of developing codes and identifying themes. Grønkjær et al. (2011) talk about analyzing "sequences of interactions" (e.g., "adjacency pairs," a comment from one participant followed by a response from another participant), stating that the analysis "revealed a variety of events that impacted on content" (p. 27). Other suggested means of studying group interaction include the template from Lehoux et al. (2006), discussed earlier in this chapter (see p. 117); asking relevant questions during the analysis, such as, "How did the group resolve disagreements?" (Stevens, 1996, p. 172); and, as espoused by Duggleby (2005) and complementing the work of Morrison-Beedy, Côté-Arsenault, and Feinstein (2001), the integration of participants' interactions into the written transcripts, for example, incorporating both verbal and nonverbal behavior that more fully explains how participants reacted to each other's and the moderator's comments.

Like the IDI method, written transcripts of focus group discussions are an integral data source for the researcher to mine. Whereas online discussions have the advantage of producing their own transcripts (i.e., the text is captured by way of the online platform), the face-to-face and telephone modes require one or more transcriptionists to commit the discussions to text. Chapter 3 (see p. 90) discusses the necessary qualities of transcriptionists and the importance of embracing these people as members of the research team. In addition to the six required characteristics outlined in Chapter 3—(a) knowledge of the subject category, (b) experience working in the specific topic area, (c) sensitivity to how people speak in conversation, (d) ability to account for the entire discussion, (e) grasp of the language and regional variations, and (f) ability to detect a complete thought—the transcriptionist in the group discussion method must be particularly attentive to the dynamics and interactivity of the discussion. To accomplish this complete task, the requirements of the transcriptionist need to go beyond his/her knowledge of the subject matter and extend to his/her know-how of the focus group method. Ideally, the person transcribing the discussions will be someone who has at least some experience as a moderator and can readily isolate interaction among participants and communicate, by way of the transcripts, what the interaction is and how it may have shifted the conversation. For example, going back to the discussion of women's role in society (see p. 116), a qualified transcriptionist would include in that transcript any audible (or visual, if working from a video recording) cues from the group participants (e.g., sighs of exasperation or expressions of acceptance or agreement) that would provide the researcher with a clearer understanding of the dynamic environment than simply the words that were spoken.

Coding and theme development in the group discussion method is not unlike that for IDIs. The process—including the use of automated procedures—is partially discussed in Chapter 3 (see pp. 90–92) and more fully in Chapter 6. It should be mentioned here, however, that the use of computer-assisted qualitative data analysis software (CAQDAS) for the coding and thematic development is particularly troublesome as applied to focus group research. As a stand-alone aid in the analysis process, CAQDAS will fail to provide the researcher with the nuanced dimensions of the discussions or the dynamic interactions between/among participants that inform the outcomes. More so than in the IDI method, the complexity of group discussions, by the mere fact that the method involves more than two (and typically many more) people, requires analysts who are fully engaged with the entirety of what transpired in the group environment, and on that basis, build meaningful connections that inform the final interpretations of the data. CAQDAS simply cannot do this sophisticated level of information processing that is commonplace for the human brain.

As also discussed in Chapter 3 (see pp. 91–92), the TQF approach to coding and thematic development utilizes an intercoder process that relies on contrasting and comparing the work of two or more coders. This is a time-intensive process (e.g., not all coders will work at the same speed and efficiency) but an important one that strongly contributes to the ultimate validity of the conclusions and recommendations—and therefore to the usefulness of the research. When using multiple coders, the procedure should dictate that each coder undertake identical steps in developing codes, including a complete reading of the written transcripts, a review of video recordings (if available), as well as an examination of ancillary material such as images uploaded by online participants, in-discussion activity work by face-to-face participants, the outcomes from enabling and projective techniques, and/or notes from the debriefing sessions with observers. Unlike the IDI method, the complexity of the focus group data demands a multifaceted approach that looks at various data sources and goes beyond what is said by way of considering participants' interactions in the group setting. Clearly, for this level of analysis to take place effectively, the people who code should ideally be the moderators involved in the study or the moderator and his/her assistant(s) who were present at the time of the discussions. Once coders complete the procedures, they should discuss their results and identify areas of agreement as well as disagreement. For instance, in the discussion on women's societal roles (see p. 116), John's comment, "a woman's place is in the home" might be coded by one coder as expressing "traditional values," by another coder as "intolerance," and by a third coder as the "importance of home and home life." When such differences arise, it is the study's primary researcher who determines the final coding scheme.

Verification

Verification is the other basic element to the TQF Analyzability component. The quality of the final interpretations of focus group data will only be as good as the analyst's ability to substantiate (or not) the information on which the interpretations are made. The researcher is not in pursuit of evidence that necessarily agrees with his/her findings but rather is partaking in due diligence to uncover additional information that may support, and still other information that may contradict, those findings. The moderator's paraphrasing of participants' comments throughout a focus group is a particular form of verification called *member checking* (i.e., confirming with the participant that the moderator has correctly heard the intended meaning of his/her comment) in the group discussion method. Deviant case analysis, which examines data for possible "outliers" or contrary data to help understand the prevailing outcome, is another example. Let's say that a series of group discussions are conducted with men over the age of 75 years who reside at a local retirement facility. The researcher may determine that the overwhelming need among these men is to participate in a greater variety of exercise activities, conveniently located at the facility. The researcher may learn more by conducting a richer analysis that examines the input from participants who are not in favor of a greater variety in activities, which may lead to the discovery of an underlying need among these residents that transcends the exercise proponents as well as detractors. In this way, the researcher can ensure the accuracy and meaningfulness of the final analysis.

As with any qualitative method, there is a considerable responsibility and burden on the person or persons who analyzes the data. Ideally more than one individual will do this and ideally it is done independently of anyone else. Having at least two skilled individuals independently analyzing the same data goes a long way toward increasing the likelihood that the findings from the focus groups will be reliable and valid. This conclusion follows from the reasoning that if two independent people extract the same findings from group discussion recordings or transcripts, then much more confidence can be placed on those findings. Ideally, one of the analysts should be one of the moderators who worked on the study.

The following are the characteristics of other people who are capable of analyzing focus group data at a high-quality level and extracting meaning that is reliable and valid from the discussions. These are individuals who:

- Are knowledgeable in the subject area and in the exact purpose(s) of the study.
- Have broad and social savvy language skills, which range from understanding dialogue that uses a very high level of vocabulary to the use of jargon that is particular to a specific region, culture, and/or demographic cohort.
- Have advanced social perception skills that are sensitive to accurately "reading" both the manifest and latent content in human communications, including both the verbal and nonverbal components of those communications.
- Are highly attentive to all aspects of the conversations, including the minutiae.
- Are highly organized and committed to quality so that the effort made to extract meaning from each focus group in a study is consistent, comprehensive, and recorded in a uniform fashion.

The foundation of verification is the process of triangulation. As discussed in Chapter 3 (see p. 92), triangulation involves any number of ways to contrast and compare research data with another source, investigator/coder (not unlike the intercoder process outlined earlier), and method. Observer and peer debriefings also play an important role in the group discussion method because they offer observers' and peers' analyses of the discussion data, which can then be compared to the researcher's interpretation of the outcomes. Traulsen, Almarsdóttir, and Björnsdóttir (2004) advocate for a variation of peer debriefing, namely, interviewing the moderator. Traulsen et al. found that "the interview forces the moderator to reflect on the [focus groups] and communicate a deeper, more articulate response than self-reporting" (p. 715). The interviews typically take place shortly after the completion of each discussion and focus on the moderator's reflections on specific content, participant interactions, and other factors contributing to the discussion outcome. The results of these interviews are then added to the transcripts as another data source in the analysis. This approach adds a third-party element to the reflexive journal contents and transcription account of a focus group, adding another measure of verification to the data.

Transparency

The final documentation of each aspect of a study utilizing the group discussion method is essential to the TQF approach in qualitative research design. The Transparency component of the TQF brings together all of the activities under Credibility and Analyzability and lays out in detail the *what, how,* and *why* of the research design. The purpose is to provide the reader of the final document with a thick description of the research—including obvious accounts of processes as well as decisions that were made along the way that may have altered the outcomes—so that the reader can (a) be informed enough to come to similar (or dissimilar) interpretations and recommendations from the research, and/or (b) transfer the research design to investigate similar issues in other compatible contexts (e.g., adapting a focus group study that investigates community activities among inner-city young people in New York City to design a series of group discussions with inner-city young people in Chicago).

To offer a thick description of a group discussion study and create transparency by way of complete disclosure in the final document, the researcher should provide details concerning the following:

THICK DESCRIPTION DETAILS FOR FOCUS GROUPS

- The researcher's assumptions regarding the sample population, data collection techniques, the rationale for the group composition (e.g., homogeneity vs. heterogeneity), and expected outcomes.
- The adequacy (i.e., comprehensiveness) of the lists (sampling frame) that were used to represent the focus groups' target population.
- The sampling rationale, especially the determination of the appropriate number of

focus groups to conduct and the number of participants to include in each group (e.g., dyads, triads, or full groups), and the process of participant recruitment selection and the recruitment procedures used to gain a representative sample of the target population.

■ Any failures to gain cooperation from all the potential participants that were sampled, efforts that were made to avoid such failures, and possible biases or weaknesses these omissions may have caused.

■ Possible decisions that were made while the focus groups were being fielded that modified the original research objectives or design elements. For example, changing the discussion guide because it was not sufficiently addressing the research objectives or the information being sought from participants.

■ Moderator's reflexive journal, including samples of journal entries specific to self-identified behaviors (verbal and nonverbal) during the group discussions that may have biased the data.

■ Operational logistics that were used for the focus groups, including the type of room in which discussions were conducted for in-person groups, the type of system that was used to record the sessions and the fidelity of the recordings, whether (and how many) observers were present (especially in the face-to-face mode) and, if so, how their presence may or may not have been obtrusive to the participants and affected the outcome of the discussion.

■ Transcription process (if used) and possibly copies of the transcriptions (with all comments that would identify an individual participant in any way removed).

■ Participants' interactions and how they impacted the group dynamics and final outcomes.

■ Enabling and projective techniques that were used to stimulate discussion and interaction in the discussions.

■ Coding procedures and justification for response categories.

■ Verification procedures as well as the results and implications from these verification efforts, including peer debriefings and moderator interviews.

Usefulness

As noted previously, the Usefulness component of the TQF approach to planning, conducting, and interpreting qualitative research revolves around, and follows directly from, the other three components of the TQF model: Credibility, Analyzability, and Transparency. A group discussion study is credible when researchers achieve a representative sample of the target population through their approaches to sampling and the recruiting of participants, as well as the development and implementation of a discussion guide that fully specifies all the important constructs that should be measured. In this way, Credibility adds to the Usefulness of the study by giving researchers needed confidence that their study sample is fair and balanced and that all the key issues that are central to understanding the research topic have been measured.

Furthermore, the Analyzability component of the TQF allows researchers to gain considerable confidence that their findings will be useful to the goals of the research by way of its focus on a systematic, objective, and thorough approach—including built-in reliability checks for possible bias—to the processing and verification of group discussion data. The third component contributing to Usefulness is Transparency, which has been achieved when the focus group researcher provides a complete and "thick" documentation of the design elements, the field and processing procedures, as well as the steps taken to verify the data and derive interpretations from their focus group research. Transparent documents provide the kind of useful information that enables researchers to take the next steps in their own studies as well as assist others who may want to transfer or adapt the research to study a compatible issue in another context.

Case Study

A case study of a focus group project that was conducted for a major retailer by the first author is presented starting on page 164. This research is an example of taking a TQF approach to produce highly useful outcomes for the sponsoring client and other researchers.

4.4 CHAPTER SUMMARY

✓ Focus group discussions (also called "group interviews," "group discussions," or "group interviewing") as a qualitative research method involve two or more persons actively engaging in a "focused" discussion on topics that the research is studying. The discussion, which should be led by a skilled moderator using a discussion guide, is recorded in an audio format (for in-person and telephone groups), a video format (for in-person and webcam-enabled telephone groups), and via built-in transcripts in asynchronous online groups.

✓ Focus groups can be an especially effective qualitative method to gather valuable data about hard-to-reach and vulnerable populations.

✓ There are many variations in the design of a group discussion study, based on the number of participants, the type of participants, and the mode of conduct. There are basically four levels in the size of focus groups: (1) two participants ("dyads"), (2) three participants ("triads"), (3) four to six participants ("mini groups"), and (4) seven to 10 or more participants ("full" focus groups).

✓ In-person discussion groups have the advantage of providing a natural setting for conversation among participants, and they provide visual cues about the participants as part of the data that are gathered. However, managing the group interaction so that all participants are heard can be a challenge, and face-to-face discussions can be difficult to schedule because people are reluctant to meet with strangers and/or participants must be at the same physical location at the same time. Telephone discussion groups are easier to schedule, but unless they are webcam-enabled, visual cues are missing from the data. Asynchronous online discussion groups ("bulletin boards") are often carried out over several days or weeks and, although there are no real-time visual cues about the participants as in an in-person discussion and the mode excludes people with low technology and/or literacy skills, bulletin boards have the advantage of allowing participants more time to consider their responses and provide thoughtful answers, and written transcripts of the discussions are built into the process.

✓ Many focus group researchers fail to use systematic methods to select and recruit their participants. As a result, and from the perspective of the Total Quality Framework (TQF), they often gather data from participants who do not accurately reflect the target population the focus group is meant to study, and thereby lower the credibility and usefulness of their studies' findings and recommendations.

✓ To enhance the credibility of the data that are gathered, focus group researchers must make careful decisions about (1) the number of discussion groups to conduct, (2) the number of participants to have in each group, (3) the degree of homogeneity or heterogeneity of participants to build into each group, (4) the mode in which the discussion will be conducted, (5) the content of the guide that will be used to "focus" what the participants discuss, and (6) how to select and train skilled moderators.

✓ It is often impractical (because of cost) to pilot-test focus groups, including pretesting the discussion guide. However, a TQF approach is one in which focus group researchers take responsibility for immediately and carefully reviewing the focus groups that are conducted early in the field period, so as to have an informed basis on which to modify, as needed, the content of the discussion guide and correct the behavior of moderators.

✓ The quality of the data generated in a focus group will be no better than the quality of moderator who conducts the group. From a TQF perspective, a skilled moderator must be able to quickly build rapport with all participants so that they feel confident that their contribution to the discussion is valued and will be kept in confidence by the researcher, moderator, and other participants. The moderator must also have excellent time management skills, as focus group participants have a fixed duration of time they have agreed to commit to the group discussion, and the moderator must cover all the topics in the discussion guide during that fixed time (typically 90–120 minutes), but in a way that allows all participants a fair chance to speak their minds.

✓ It is highly recommended that focus group moderators keep a reflexive journal, which includes their own self-evaluation of anything they might have done in a discussion session to bias the discussion.

✓ In addressing the Analyzability component of the TQF, researchers should think carefully about the transcriptionists who work with the recording of each face-to-face or telephone group discussion because they must be very skilled in both capturing an accurate record of the verbal exchanges within the group, and also recording information about participants' behavior, including observable behavior (e.g., gesticulations, grimaces) in video recordings of the session and any audio cues (e.g., hesitations in speaking, snickering, under-the-breath comments).

4.5 EXERCISES AND DISCUSSION TOPICS

1. Select a published face-to-face group discussion study and discuss the design's strengths and weaknesses from a TQF perspective.

2. Consider a research issue that interests you and develop a face-to-face group discussion study design utilizing the TQF. Briefly discuss how you would address each of the TQF components in your design, and the strengths and limitations of your design within each component.

3. Take the study design described above and create a discussion guide, including the enabling and/or projective techniques the moderator will use.

4. Describe the tradeoffs between the TQF components when designing a face-to-face group discussion study and give examples of the conditions under which the researcher would be better off, from a TQF perspective, opting for the telephone mode.

5. Design a bulletin board study utilizing the TQF. Include a discussion of the research objectives, target population, the moderator's questions to be asked on each day, and the rationale for this mode. Discuss how you would address each of the TQF components in your design.

SUGGESTED FURTHER READING

Fine, M. (1994). Working the hyphens: Reinventing self and other in qualitative research. In N. K. Denzin & Y. S. Lincoln (Eds.), *The handbook of qualitative research* (pp. 70–82). Thousand Oaks, CA: Sage.

Fine, M., & Sirin, S. R. (2007). Theorizing hyphenated selves: Researching youth development in and across contentious political contexts. *Social and Personality Psychology Compass, 1*(1), 16–38.

These two articles (the first a book chapter and the other, a more recent journal article) discuss the concept of "the Other" and, specifically, "hyphenated selves" (e.g., Muslim-Americans) and how the hyphen "separates and merges personal identities with our inventions of Others" (1994, p. 70). In the first, Fine focuses on the role researchers play in constructing the "other" and advocates for researchers to better understand their relation to the research context and their participants. This point is further illustrated in the 2007 journal article, which details the authors' use of focus groups to explore meanings of hyphenated selves depicted in "identity maps" drawn by Muslim-American youth.

Krueger, R. A., & Casey, M. A. (2009). *Focus groups* (4th ed.). Thousand Oaks, CA: Sage.

This is an introductory book that provides an overview of the focus group method, considerations for planning a focus study—including question development and recruiting of participants—as well as those related to moderator skills, analysis, and reporting. Krueger and Casey also discuss unique applications of focus groups, such as discussions with youth and ethnic groups, telephone and online groups, and employee focus groups.

Merton, R. K. (1987). The focussed interview and focus groups: Continuities and disconti-nuities. *Public Opinion Quarterly, 51*(4), 550–566.

In June 1986, Robert Merton gave a talk at the New York AAPOR (American Association for Public Opinion Research) meeting where the subject of the panel session was on "How Did We Get from 'Focussed Interviews' to 'Focus Groups'?" For anyone who is associated with, or interested in, the focus group method, it is both enlightening as well as entertaining to read Merton's firsthand account of the historical framework and true background of the focussed approach. Back in 1946 (when he coauthored "The Focused Interview and Focus Groups" with Kendall), Merton had no con-cept of focus groups and, indeed, Merton stated early in his AAPOR talk, "The truth of the matter is that there can't be many people in the field of social science and certainly none in the related field of marketing research who know less about focus groups than I" (p. 550).

Morgan, D. L. (Ed.). (1993). *Successful focus groups: Advancing the state of the art.* Newbury Park, CA: Sage.

As an edited volume, this book covers a variety of issues pertaining to the rationale for conduct-ing focus groups, quality threats and controls, utilizing focus groups to assist in survey questionnaire design, and special uses of group discussions (e.g., low-income populations and sensitive topics). In addition to Morgan, the book's contributors include Richard Kreuger, Robin Jarrett, and many others.

WEB RESOURCES

Directories of Focus Group Facilities and Services

ESOMAR Directory
http://directory.esomar.org/service8_Focus-groups

GreenBook Directory
www.greenbook.org/market-research-firms/focus-group-facilities

MRA Blue Book
www.bluebook.org/about.cfm

Quirk's Directory
www.quirks.com/directory/focusgroup

Online Bulletin Board Platforms and Services

Dub
http://dubishere.com

FocusForums
www.focusforums.net

Itracks
www.itracks.com/our-tools/bulletin-board-focus-groups

Revelation
www.revelationglobal.com/applications

20/20 Research
www.2020research.com/tools/qualboard-overview

Reporting Resource

Adobe Creative Cloud (*www.adobe.com/creativecloud.html*) is an online resource that provides a suite of Adobe apps (Photoshop, Illustrator, Premiere Pro, etc.) that can be used for the creation and sharing of various media and image content. This is a potentially very useful tool for researchers, especially, focus group researchers who may have a great deal of content to report, who can, among other things, use Adobe Creative Cloud to edit video, audio, and photographic images for their final research document or to otherwise share with the research sponsor.

NOTES

1. The Delphi method typically is used to find consensus on a particular problem or issue by way of a series of rounds (or a back and forth process) in which a selected panel of experts or knowledgeable people give their written opinions/agreement based on the outcome of each round. The panel never meets as a group, and the identities of panel members remain anonymous to each other.

2. The nominal group technique typically is used to find consensus on a particular problem or issue by way of a highly structured group format consisting of a panel of experts and a facilitator knowledgeable on the topic. The specific stages of the group process are (1) each participant writes down his/her ideas concerning the issue, (2) the facilitator records these ideas, (3) each idea is openly discussed, and (4) each participant writes down his/her ranking or rating of the ideas. This technique was developed as a modified approach to group discussions to circumvent group interaction effects, specifically the domination of one or two individuals.

3. In some instances, the "researcher" may also be the person who conducts the focus groups (i.e., the "moderator"). This is typically the case when the study is being conducted by a small research firm or group where the principal researcher assumes many duties, including the execution of all fieldwork. In other instances, the researcher may be the person who is responsible for managing a number of people on a research team, including one or more moderators who conduct the group discussions. For this reason, we sometimes use "researcher" and "moderator" interchangeably.

4. All the examples of online communities are from Communispace (2011).

5. Saturation is discussed in Chapter 3.

Focus Group Discussion Case Study

PURPOSE

A U.S.-based retailer of construction tools and supplies ("Retailer") was transforming itself from its traditional focus on the contractor trade toward a strategy that would appeal to consumers. As part of this effort, the Retailer was considering what and how to modify certain aspects of its stores—such as merchandising, store format, and overall operations—in order to soften its hard-edge, contractor-only image and appeal to consumers generally and homeowners specifically. The Retailer decided to take an innovative approach in the early stage of concept development and use qualitative research—specifically, the group discussion method—to learn what consumers associate with their "best shopping experiences" and utilize this information to help shape the Retailer's new consumer orientation. The purpose of this focus group research was to examine homeowners' shopping experiences across a variety of retail categories and identify those experiences that might be adapted by the Retailer to create a new way of consumer shopping for construction tools and supplies.

METHOD

The group discussion method was considered the appropriate approach for this research because it: (a) enabled consumers to freely share their shopping experiences and tell meaningful stories of particularly positive and negative experiences; (b) fostered a dynamic exchange of information that would not have happened in the IDI method; and (c) allowed the moderator to use enabling exercises, such as guided imagery, to stimulate consumers' memories of their experiences.

DESIGN

Credibility

Scope

Ten face-to-face focus group discussions were conducted for the Retailer, with two discussions conducted in each of five major U.S. metropolitan markets. Participants in all groups consisted of homeowners who regularly shopped at large, consumer-oriented stores such as Crate & Barrel, Best Buy, and Bed Bath and Beyond, as well as a construction-type store similar to the Retailer. One group in each location was conducted with women and the other group was conducted with men. The homogeneity of the participants in terms of gender was deemed important, given that men and women typically have very different types of shopping experiences. And, although the shopping experience may also vary across age and income levels, the research budget was not sufficient to accommodate additional discussions with age and/or income subgroups and, therefore, various age ranges and household incomes were represented in each group.

Group participants were selected from a list of homeowners, purchased from a list provider, within each market area. Each list contained address, landline and mobile telephone contact, and demographic information for 100 male or female homeowners. The lists were sorted by age and then income levels. To achieve eight to 10 participants in each focus group, 12 people were selected from each list on an every eighth-name basis. In order to gain cooperation among the sampled homeowners, the recruiting process involved several components.

- A postcard was sent in the U.S. mail to all 100 homeowners on each list. The postcard briefly mentioned the purpose of the research and that the home-owner might receive a phone call from the recruiting firm inviting him/her to participate.
- Sampled participants received a phone call approximately 2 weeks prior to the focus group in order to give them sufficient time to arrange their schedule so they could attend.
- Because the new-store concept was still in development, the Retailer did not want to identify themselves as the sponsor of the research. However, to encourage cooperation, the recruiter for each group emphasized the "fun" participants would have sharing shopping experiences and how they might learn something new about stores in the area.
- All participants were offered $75 for their participation in a 90-minute focus group.
- The focus group facility utilized in each market also offered babysitting services (someone who would come to the facility to sit with children while their parents were in the discussion) as necessary.
- Complete, detailed instructions on how to get to the facility were given on the initial recruiting phone call, on a confirmation postcard sent directly after the initial phone call, and during a confirmation phone call the day before the group discussion.

Data Gathering

All 10 focus groups were designed and conducted by the first author who had worked with the Retailer on many and varied research studies. She developed the moderator's guide, which was used to conduct all 10 discussions, and worked with the client (i.e., the Retailer) to maximize the quality of the research data related to measurement by:

- Utilizing her knowledge of the Retailer and the industry to incorporate relevant topic areas/questions in the moderator's outline and identify key comments in the discussions that required additional follow-up questions.
- Meeting repeatedly with the Retailer's research manager as well as managers from operations, merchandising, and architecture/design departments to ensure that everyone was in agreement on the research objectives, the discussion guide, and the final written documents needed from the research.
- Prioritizing the topics, issues, and questions that would be asked in terms of relevance to the research objectives. This included allocating the approximate amount of time that the moderator should spend on each area within the discussion. Although flexible, the time allocation ensured that all topic areas—particularly the ones of highest priority—were covered in each discussion.
- Conducting daily communications with the recruiters and their supervisors to discuss the status of the recruiting effort (including a disposition of the calls

made and the level of cooperation experienced) as well as any questions or issues raised by those contacted. A spreadsheet detailing the recruited participants (in terms of responses to screening questions) was updated daily. These were quality-control measures to safeguard the representativeness and qualification of group participants.

- Rescreening participants twice prior to the discussion (i.e., participants were asked a series of questions similar to those asked in the initial recruiting phone call during confirmation as well as when they arrived at the facility) to identify anyone who may have been recruited but in fact did not qualify.

- Establishing moderator–participant rapport prior to the discussions was begun when the moderator visited with participants in the waiting room prior to being seated in the discussion room. This approach comforted the participants and helped them be forthcoming early in the discussion.

- Taking the participants through a guided imagery exercise. The moderator asked the participants to think about their "best shopping experience" and then had all participants close their eyes and imagine reliving that experience. The moderator guided participants through the exercise by telling them first to imagine themselves walking through the entrance door of the retailer and describing what they see and how they feel, then asking them to describe where they go in the store after entering, to explain why and what they experience at that point, then proceeding in the same manner incrementally until the shopping experience is completed. This exercise was possible because of the rapport that had been established and was very useful is substantiating participants' comments made at other moments in the discussion.

- Consulting with the six managers from the Retailer who attended all the discussions to observe. The moderator consulted with these observers continually before, during, and after each discussion which served as a way to verify interpretations of the data on an ongoing basis while also keeping the research aligned with the research objectives.

Analyzability

A video and audio recording was made of each discussion (with the participants' consent). Two transcribers—who had experience working in the retail category and were briefed on the Retailer as well as the objectives of the research study—used the audio recordings to transcribe the discussions. The transcriptions, as well as the video recordings, were used to identify thematic variations in the data, specifically those associated with the research objectives related to consumers' shopping experiences. By utilizing the video recordings, the moderator relived the focus groups (and recalled important moments in the discussions) and, along with the transcripts, verified the context in which particularly relevant statements were made. A spreadsheet was used to input participants' ideas and poignant verbatim comments on specific topic areas, and to sort, group, and connect information within and across group discussions. Insights were shared with the client research team throughout the analytical process and met with the team to discuss alternative interpretations of the outcomes.

An important component of the verification procedure was to identify the factors that all "best" shopping experiences had in common (e.g., the organization of the merchandise) and examine instances when these factors were in place but consumers actually had a bad shopping experience (e.g., if the organization of merchandise is important to a good experience, why did some consumers have a negative experience even when they described the merchandise as well organized and tastefully displayed?).

Transparency

The final written report documented all aspects of the research, including the interpretations and implications for next steps, with the intention of providing the reader with a sufficient accounting of the research so that the study could be used to develop action steps and/or transfer the study design to another context. The report discussed:

- Why the group discussion method was chosen and its ability to gain rich insight on consumers' shopping experience overall as well as specific things particular stores have done to create the "best" shopping experience.
- The recruiting process, the level of cooperation, the composition of the groups, and the impact this composition had on the data.
- How the moderator's guide was developed and the rationale for the selection of topics/issues (a copy of the guide was included in the Appendix to the report).
- The moderator's style and techniques used in the discussions.
- Group dynamics and interaction, including the biasing influence of participants who dominated discussions and/or the reluctance of some participants to speak their minds.
- How the analysis was conducted.
- Steps that were used to verify the data, including deviant cases, peer review and examples of good and bad shopping experiences (including participants' verbatim comments) across a variety of store types that illustrated the interpretations. A limitation to the verification process was the absence of a reflexive journal. The research would have benefited from the moderator's personal account concerning the decisions that were made and what transpired in the discussions as they were happening in the field period.

In addition to the written report for the client, a video containing short clips of all 10 group discussions was created. This video highlighted the moments in the discussions that exemplified the final interpretations of the data as well as gave viewers of the video a firsthand look at what had occurred in the focus groups, including the emotions and manner in which participants expressed themselves.

Usefulness

The focus group data provided the client with an in-depth understanding of the variety and nuances that contribute heavily to a positive, "best" shopping experience. For example, the research findings did not just reveal that attractive, real-life displays are important to the shopping experience but supported such claims with consumers' stories and descriptions of retailers who are "doing it right." These details allowed the Retailer to learn more by visiting these other retailers through the consumers' lenses as well as to determine which aspects of the preferred experience were most compatible with the Retailer's construction tools and supplies business. From this research, the Retailer was able to design a prototype of a new store concept that was the subject of additional research.

CHAPTER FIVE

Observation Method
Ethnography

CHAPTER PREVIEW

Ethnography began more than two centuries ago as the sole domain of cultural anthropologists, who traveled to remote locations where "primitive" cultures could be studied through extended observations that required ethnographers to immerse themselves in those cultures. Our approach to examining ethnography views it as using "in-context immersion" to gather in-depth information about the beliefs, attitudes, and behaviors of those being observed, ultimately to understand the motivations behind their thoughts and actions. Ethnography, especially when conducted covertly (i.e., without the awareness or express consent of those being observed), poses many ethical challenges, and these issues are an important focus of the chapter. In addition, the chapter discusses the various modes of ethnography (in-person, online, and mobile) as well as the range of involvement an observer can take (from being a complete nonparticipant in what is being observed to becoming a complete participant), all the while striving to maintain one's objectivity in recording what is observed. More so than any other qualitative method, ethnography provides the researcher with the opportunity to "live and breathe" all that is experienced by those being observed. However, a tradeoff that ethnographers (conducting in-person observations) often must make is working with small and narrowly defined target populations due to how labor intensive the research can become. There are many other important considerations from a Total Quality Framework (TQF) perspective that are discussed in the chapter, including (1) how to decide on the number of people to observe and how many observations to make; (2) the skill set of knowledge, experiences, and "talents" that make an observer reliable and effective; (3) the importance of maintaining a reflexive journal; and (4) how other qualitative methods, including in-depth interviews (IDIs) and focus groups, often play important supplementary roles within an ethnographic study by complementing the observational data that are gathered.

5.1 INTRODUCTION

Ethnography has long been the subject of controversial discussions centering on its *meaning* (i.e., how to define the term "ethnography") as well as its *breadth* (i.e., what is involved in conducting ethnographic research). A core issue in the controversy concerning the meaning of ethnography has to do with whether it constitutes a discipline (i.e., field of study) or a set of methods. This issue poses a fundamental distinction that often pits cultural anthropologists (the originators and defenders of traditional ethnography) against sociologists and other social scientists, who have adjusted the anthropological approach to examine a myriad of matters in contemporary society. In this regard, Wolcott (2008) has made the distinction between "doing ethnography" and "borrowing ethnographic techniques," with the former referring to researchers who adhere to the traditional intent and goals of ethnography, that is, to study nonliterate people within a cultural, site-specific milieu, and the latter referring to the use of the typical procedures or methods employed in ethnographic research to gather data "without imposing on how they are to be used" (p. 44). As a field of study, ethnography is discussed as a unified discipline, as in "We conducted an ethnography," or "Ethnographies have been conducted in many educational environments." In contrast, a methodological view of ethnography typically emphasizes the main method of observation, often replacing the term "ethnography" with "observational methods," "participant observation," or "observational research."

So, what is this research approach called ethnography?

Ethnography began as the sole domain of cultural anthropology where researchers traveled far from home to immerse and possibly entrench themselves in the unfamiliar environs of "primitive" cultures for extensive periods of time in order to describe the beliefs, values, customs, and behavior of "others" within their social context. However, as ethnography has evolved and been adapted by researchers outside of anthropology, the focus has shifted in a number of ways. Examples of these shifts are from a focus on

- A society's culture to smaller studies examining one point in time.
- The location or where the study is conducted (e.g., studying an indigenous tribe in New Guinea) to a focus on a particular societal problem (e.g., compulsive gambling).
- The study of "others" or strangers in an unfamiliar setting to the study of the familiar (e.g., study environments located close to home, in a subject area familiar to the researcher, such as elementary school education).
- Discovery by way of immersion and inductive analysis to "a robust, disciplined empiricism" (Mills & Ratcliffe, 2012, p. 148).
- Ethnography as a field of study, in and of itself, to a collection of methods for data gathering.

It is, therefore, no wonder that anthropologists such as Michael Agar (2006) ask, "Is *qualitative* research *really* ethnography?" (p. 4, emphasis in original).

The orientation to ethnography that we take in this book might best be described as a combination of both the traditional and contemporary approaches. Our attention is on maintaining the integrity of the original intent of ethnographic research to describe the beliefs, attitudes, processes, and "meanings behind the acts" (Berg & Lune, 2012) of others by way of an in-context immersion or a form of prolonged reality-based researcher–participant engagement. At the same time, we take a methodological perspective with the emphasis on maximizing the credibility, analyzability, transparency, and ultimate usefulness of ethnographic research in its various manifestations, whether large or small studies, culturally remote or neighborhood-based, using traditional or new (e.g., online) modes.

Beyond the controversy surrounding the meaning of ethnography, there is a discordant understanding among researchers concerning what is involved in conducting ethnographic research. Although it is generally accepted that ethnography encompasses multiple methods (e.g., observation and IDIs), there is not necessarily agreement on the optimal design elements or scope of ethnographic research. For instance, researchers grapple with design issues such as (a) whether to conduct nonparticipant or participant observation, and whether this observation should be covert or overt; (b) the directedness of the observations (e.g., should the researcher begin the fieldwork with an open-ended, unstructured observation of events or enter fieldwork with predefined targets for observation); (c) the use of public versus private site locations; (d) the number of site locations and whether to focus on a single location or multiple sites; and (e) the type of interviews to incorporate with observations (e.g., "formal" IDIs or informal, "casual" conversations). Even the terminology researchers use when discussing their ethnographic studies can vary from one researcher to the next, with the people who are observed in these studies referred to as "participants," "informants," "subjects," "insiders," or "social actors."[1]

Ethical Considerations

Ethical considerations play a particularly important role in ethnography. More so than in most other qualitative methods, the ethnographer may be faced with difficult ethical considerations and decisions that have a direct impact on the study design and dissemination. For instance, the researcher utilizing observation as his/her principal method may have (depending on the nature of the research objective and study population) critical choices to consider regarding (1) whether to conduct the observation as a participant or nonparticipant, and (2) whether to reveal his/her identity to participants (i.e., conduct **overt observation**) or not (**covert observation**) before or during the study. As discussed later in this chapter, there are several well-documented covert ethnographic studies, some of which became highly controversial for their use of deceptive tactics. For example, Ellis (1986) conducted a 9-year observation of a Guinea (traditional watermen) community in the tidewater region of Virginia whose townspeople befriended her unaware that the sole purpose of her visits was to further her research endeavor; and Leo (1995), in his study of police interrogation procedures, "consciously reinvented" his persona in order to "fit the attributes, biases, and world view of my subjects" (p. 120).

Like the practice of ethnography itself, researchers and those who consume ethnographic research findings do not necessarily agree on whether or not deception is acceptable and about the need (some would say "obligation") to debrief those who have been observed by covert researchers; however, most do believe that there should not be an outright ban on covert observation (Allen, 1997). Even the "Use of Deception in Research" clause in the *Code of Ethics* from the American Sociological Association (1999) states that there are a number of conditions under which "deceptive techniques" are permissible. And similarly, the American Psychological Association (2010) acknowledges in their *Ethical Principles of Psychologists and Code of Conduct* that there are valuable research studies that could not be conducted without the use of deception.

These issues and other matters pertaining to the design of ethnographic research (sometimes called "ethnographies") are addressed in this chapter and, more specifically, in Section 5.3 on applying the TQF to ethnographic studies. The remaining portion of this chapter section discusses the variations in ethnographic research design, the instruments utilized to conduct fieldwork, examples of the many ways in which researchers have used ethnography, and an overview of the strengths and limitations of ethnographic research.

Variations in Ethnographic Research Design

Observation, as a form of gathering information, is at the core of ethnographic research. With this as a starting point, there are two key considerations in observational research designs:

1. How the observations will be conducted, especially, the role of the observer in the research context.
2. The ancillary methods, if any, that will be employed to support the observations and contribute to the quality of the data, interpretations, and conclusions.

The various forms of observation (discussed below) are similar in their purpose. The goal of all observation in qualitative research—whether it is the observation of a group of people (which is rooted in traditional anthropological ethnography) or the observation of a single individual (which has become popular across the social sciences)—is for the observer to utilize as many of the five senses as possible in order to recognize and document the totality of the naturally occurring research environment. Two of the five senses—sight and hearing—are of the utmost importance in face-to-face ethnographic observation, given the relative objectivity to be gained from these observations compared to that from other senses, such as smell, where the observer's subjectivity (based on personal experiences or associations) is more likely to bias a true accounting of the observed. For example, by looking and listening, a researcher[2] conducting an ethnography concerning the activities of daily living (ADLs) among people with disabilities living at home might record (e.g., using an observation grid, as discussed on p. 206) the following observations during a home visit:

1. What the observer could see, including the:
   - Home context, such as the location and type of dwelling, the condition of the home, furnishings and decoration, and specific accommodations that have been made for the disabled person.
   - Size and usability of the living areas, such as the kitchen, living room, den, bedroom, and bathroom (the observation would likely include sketches of the spaces).
   - Age, gender, and physical condition of the other household members present in the home at the time.
   - Interactions of the other household members with the disabled person and the roles they play related to assisting with ADLs.
   - Body language that communicated frustrations, anger, impatience, satisfaction, pleasure, appreciation, etc.
   - Degree to which the disabled person can handle ADLs independently of household members or other assistance.
   - Particular routines or processes enacted specifically for the benefit of the disabled person (e.g., related to meal preparation and mealtimes).

2. What the observer could hear, including:
   - Household members talking about when/how to coordinate particular ADLs.
   - Discussions between the disabled person and household members concerning changes to ADL routines.
   - Words of praise or frustration from the disabled person and/or household members.
   - Discussion of activities that are not performed because they are considered too arduous.

Observer Roles

Central to the variations of observational methods is the role of the researcher/observer. This role is defined by the *physical* and *psychological* or emotional distance the observer puts between him/herself and the observed—ranging from remote, off-site observation (e.g., online observation of Sierra Club members via a public discussion forum) to being immediately present in the observed environment, including complete immersion and participation in the activities being studied (e.g., joining the Sierra Club and fully participating as a club member in the discussion as well as activities outside the forum). This range of distance between the observer and the observed constitutes five levels of observation, two forms of **nonparticipant observation** and three variations of **participant observation**.

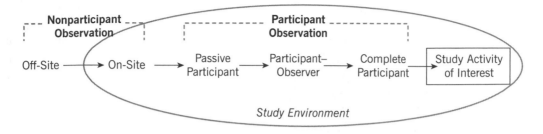

FIGURE 5.1. Observer roles.

Figure 5.1 illustrates the role of the observer at each of these five levels of observation in relationship to the observer's distance from and level of engagement with the research participants.

Nonparticipant Observation

As a nonparticipant, the researcher's role is to strictly observe in a completely unobtrusive manner, without any interaction with the research participants, either remotely (i.e., off-site) or within the study environment (i.e., on-site). In some cases, those being observed in nonparticipant observation are entirely unaware that someone is observing them for research purposes. Examples of **off-site nonparticipant observation** include Internet ethnography (similar to the remote Sierra Club example above) and observations of the teaching methods used in college medical training via remote monitors in an off-campus building. **On-site nonparticipant observation** moves the observer physically closer to (into the same space as) the observed activity but, like off-site observation, is purposely devoid of observer–participant engagement. For example, Griffiths (2011) worked as a change attendant at an amusement arcade in order to observe gambling behavior, and Lyall and Bartlett (2010) conducted an on-site nonparticipant observational study at a medium-secure forensic psychiatric unit where Lyall was able to unobtrusively observe how psychiatrists made decisions regarding patient leave by accompanying the clinical team on the ward rounds.

Nonparticipant on-site observation can be covert in nature, wherein the true identity of the researcher is not divulged (as was the case in the Griffiths study); however, this observation method can also be overt, in that those being observed know the observations are taking place and who is doing the observing, but the observer does not have any direct interactions with those being observed (as was the case in the Lyall and Bartlett study mentioned above). Two examples of nonparticipant on-site observation that were carried out with full knowledge of the participants include a Williamson, Twelvetree, Thompson, and Beaver (2012) study that followed advanced nurse practitioners as they worked in their hospital wards, and an in-classroom observation to examine students' interactions with the teacher and other students (Cotton, Stokes, & Cotton, 2010).

Participant Observation

The three variations of participant observation are (1) *passive participant* (or what Adler [1990] called "peripheral" or "marginal" involvement ["membership"] in the research study activity); (2) *participant–observer* (or what Adler called "active membership"); and (3) *complete participant* (what Adler called "complete membership"). As shown in Figure 5.1, each of these forms of observation move the observer closer to full immersion in the "study activity of interest" where those being observed are engaged in the events under investigation. Unlike the nonparticipant observer status discussed above, participant observers are on-site in the research context in every case and engaged, to some extent, with the participants at some level beyond mere observation.

Passive participation requires the observer to play a role that is primarily that of an observer but one who also interacts with participants by way of asking questions or becoming involved in activities beyond or even unrelated to the critical areas of study. For example, a **passive participant observer** who is conducting research on how team members cooperate with each other on the soccer field might ask the players questions about the experience when off the field or help out by providing water and towels at the end of a game. The observer in a passive participant observation may observe overtly (i.e., with participants' full knowledge that they are being observed) or covertly (i.e., when the true identity of the observer is not revealed to the participants, such as in the Adler [1990] study of drug trafficking).

In the **participant–observer** role the researcher becomes more engaged with the research participants, even to the extent of participating in key areas under study and sparking friendships. Using the soccer team example, the researcher assuming a participant–observer role might go out on the field with the team to hear firsthand what is discussed in the huddle. In this case, the observer may be conducting an overt observation (i.e., the soccer team is aware that the observer is not a regular team member and is there only temporarily to observe); however, like other forms of observation, the participant–observer might observe in a covert manner (e.g., the observer might be introduced to the soccer team as a newly recruited member of the team).

Staying with this soccer example, the researcher assuming the role of a **complete participant observer** would be someone who actually has qualifications as a soccer player and joins the team as a player and is involved in all the associated team activities on and off the field. Of all the observer roles, complete participants willingly "go native" by becoming a full-fledged member of the study group. This type of observation can be overt or covert in nature; however, the overt–covert distinction is less clear in complete participant observation in that it is difficult to maintain the status of an objective research observer (as in overt observation) when the observer ultimately becomes a fully integrated group member. A good example of this type of research is the Schouten and McAlexander (1995) study with the motorcycle subculture (discussed next).

It is not uncommon for researchers to transition from one observer role to another role; for example, to begin fieldwork as a nonparticipant on-site observer but then move to a passive participant role with greater engagement and possibly go on to become more involved with the participants by way of a participant–observer or complete participant role. An example of how the status of the researcher can change and evolve over time in ethnographic research is the study that Schouten and McAlexander (1995) conducted with owners of Harley–Davidson motorcycles to understand the biker subculture. At the outset, these researchers took the role of nonparticipant observers accompanying a local motorcycle club to two annual rallies. This status changed when the researchers allowed two of the chapter members to befriend them and involve them in the club activities, transforming the researchers' roles to that of participant–observers. The researchers' observer status changed again when they determined that their study design was lacking "an empathetic sense of a biker's identity, psyche, and social interactions in the context of everyday life" (p. 46) and, on this basis, made the decision to purchase Harley–Davidson motorcycles, make it their primary mode of transportation, and become immersed in the biker subculture. This "process of progressive contextualization" (p. 44), from outsiders to insiders, led the researchers to insights that may not have been gained otherwise: for example, the research finding that biking is considered a form of *performance* and how bikers' perception of themselves as performing to an audience impacts the biker experience.

Covert and Overt Observation Roles

As mentioned earlier (see "Ethical Considerations," p. 170), in determining the type of observer role to assume for any given ethnographic study, the researcher must also consider whether the observer's status will be covert and therefore unobtrusive in nature (i.e., secretive and "undercover," by which those being observed are acting without knowledge of the observer's true identity or purpose) or overt and hence obtrusive (i.e., participants are made aware of the research and the identity of the observer prior to the onset of fieldwork). Researchers such as Cotton et al. (2010) assert that covert observation "is rarely ethically acceptable!" (exclamation in original), yet the American Sociological Association (1999) and American Psychological Association (2010) as well as others such as Berg and Lune (2012) contend that "there are situations in which covert research is both necessary and ethically justified" (p. 86). One example of when the covert approach is justified, according to Berg and Lune, is when studying "powerful and elite" groups (e.g., politicians, corporate executives) who would otherwise be difficult to observe due to gatekeepers who protect access to them or who may only agree to participate if allowed to review and edit the researcher's field notes. As discussed on page 171, researchers generally believe that some form of covert observation may be necessary in order to gain unbiased data and, indeed, much of the ethnographic research conducted on the Internet is covert in nature, with "a disproportionate number of covert versus overt projects [online, particularly those related to] sex and deviance" (Murthy, 2008, p. 839). Murthy cites, for example, covert studies of activity on paid-for-sex and pornographic websites as well as chat groups.

There are a number of documented studies—such as the research from Ellis (1986) and Leo (1995) mentioned earlier—where deception played a key role in the research design. In addition to conventional subject matter, such as Ellis's observational study of a small fishing community, deviant and subculture groups have also been the target of covert ethnographies. For instance, Humphreys' (1970) classic study on male homosexual bathroom trysts involved the researcher acting as a watchdog for quick sexual liaisons in public bathrooms between male strangers. It could be argued that using "passive deception" to conduct his observations did no harm; however, "what he did with his observations . . . is another matter" (Bernard, 2011, p. 330). Subsequent to the observations, Humphreys obtained the names and addresses of the observed men by using public records to look up their automobile license plate numbers. Then, 1 year later, Humphreys visited these men, pretended to be conducting survey research on mental health, and, in so doing, conducted 50 interviews that appeared to have nothing to do with the men's earlier bathroom sex activities. Despite generating interesting findings, this study was extremely controversial in terms of its ethics and, among other things, created an upheaval within the sociology department at Washington University (where Humphreys had received his doctorate degree).

Other covert ethnographies involving deviant groups include the work of Adler (1990), who justified her covert passive participation in a study investigating drug trafficking by the "illegal nature of the activity and the degree of suspiciousness" (p. 102) she witnessed among the participants (i.e., the drug dealers), as well as the "necessity for maintaining relationships with our key informants" (p. 107); Tewksbury (2002), who used covert observation to investigate the "social and sexual dynamics" of two gay bathhouses as a complete participant (i.e., as a real member of the bathhouses), justifying his covert strategy based on earlier work in this area; Andriotis (2010), who studied a gay nude beach in the context of an "erotic oasis" as a covert on-site nonparticipant observer; and, as discussed earlier, Griffiths (2011), who justified his covert on-site nonparticipant observation of gambling behavior based on the fact that the researched sites were public venues.

As these examples show, covert observation has been conducted across all observer roles and with a variety of population segments. The question of whether to conduct an ethnographic study in a covert or overt manner is an issue for all ethnographers to consider very carefully, regardless if the observation is off- or on-site or the observer is acting as a passive or complete participant in the study activity. The implications of covert versus overt observation to the design of ethnographic research are discussed in Section 5.3 on conducting ethnographic research using the TQF approach.

Ancillary Methods of Observational Data Collection in Ethnographic Research

As noted, observation is the principal method of gathering data in ethnographic research; however, it typically is supported by the use of other research methods, and, by definition, ethnography requires "multiple methods" (American Anthropological Association, 2004). By incorporating other ways of understanding participants and the topic of interest, researchers gain a richer, more nuanced knowledge that enhances their inductive powers to find meaning in the culture or phenomenon under study. Ethnographic researchers are most likely to supplement their observations with IDIs, group discussions, and/or documentary review.

For instance, Russell et al. (2012) conducted a study to investigate organizational practices within Canadian family care facilities by way of on-site nonparticipant observations of clinical and administrative staff, IDIs with patients and key informants, and a review of documents such as business plans, internal communications, and clinical records. Some ethnographers have augmented their observations utilizing relatively new technologies such as small and affordable video cameras as well as smartphones and global positioning systems (GPSs). In their research on the student experience, Cotton et al. (2010) equipped students with video cameras, voice recorders, and notebooks to facilitate their keeping a diary of their field study experience in South Africa. Christensen, Mikkelsen, Nielsen, and Harder (2011) cast a wide net in their study examining children's everyday mobility, incorporating into their research design on-site nonparticipant observations along with IDIs among children (conducted as a child gave the researcher a "guided tour" of the neighborhood) and their parents, as well as GPS tracking of the participants' location during the day and a mobile survey that the children were asked to complete five times a day via their smartphones. Each survey included five items and asked the children questions such as, "What are you doing?" and "Where are you?" In this way, the mobile survey became a "travel diary" of the children's everyday experience.

Appropriate Uses of Ethnography

Ethnography is used across the health and social sciences where the goal is to gain an in-depth understanding of the meanings associated with particular customs or behaviors by living the experience to the degree possible. Anthropologists have traditionally conducted lengthy and entrenched ethnographic studies among native tribes in distant lands; however, beginning in the early 1970s, anthropologists such as Spradley (1972) put their ethnographic skills to work closer to home, researching social groups on American soil, such as men on skid row (and, specifically, the "culture" of alcoholism). The observation method (along with ancillary methods) has since been utilized by anthropologists to study a host of Western social groups and phenomena, expanding even into the virtual online world with, for example, Internet-based research to examine the expatriate experience in Buenos Aires (Freidenberg, 2011). Researchers in the health sciences have used on-site nonparticipant observation coupled with IDIs to study the level of advice and knowledge pharmacists impart in their interactions with their customers (Cramer, Shaw, Wye, & Weiss, 2010), the obstacles nurse board members face in impacting community health care policy (Hughes, 2010), and the treatment of older people with dementia in the hospital setting (Jurgens, Clissett, Gladman, & Harwood, 2012). Ethnography has been used in the field of psychology in work that ranges from on-site nonparticipant observation of decision making in closed facilities of the mentally ill (Lyall & Bartlett, 2010) to planting covert observers in psychiatric hospitals (i.e., complete participant observation) to study the environment in which psychiatric diagnoses are made (Rosenhan, 1973). Sociologists such as Haenfler (2004) and Williams (2006) have used the methods of complete participant observation and online ethnography, respectively, to study the youth "straight edge" subculture in order to understand the values and belief system of this group as well as the personal experiences and meanings in identity associated with belonging to this subculture, including the pledge to abstain from recreational drugs, alcohol, and tobacco. Researchers in education have used ethnography to investigate the in-classroom experience, specifically teachers' approaches to educating school-age children on topics such as environmental issues (Cotton et al., 2010), as well as values and morality (Thornberg, 2008). With the advent of digital communications, journalism researchers have conducted ethnographies to study how newsrooms are dealing with the transition from print to online publication (Robinson, 2011) as well as the use of new technology (Mabweazara, 2010).

Ethnography has also become popular among corporate and marketing researchers. "Corporate anthropologist" Brigitte Jordan, for example, conducted an ethnographic study for Intel Corporation in their assembly plants in Costa Rica and Malaysia to study the interaction, communication, work-flow issues, and productivity among employees (Jordan & Lambert, 2009). Mariampolski (2006) has adapted ethnography for marketers to observe consumers and business customers going about their daily routines in their natural environments. These ethnographic studies have included the investigation of diabetes patients' use of glucose measurement devices; at-home use of paper towels and potential new uses of paper towels; decision making at the retail level for a variety of consumer goods manufacturers (e.g., shelf-stable Mexican foods) by way of "shop-along" observation (i.e., the researcher shops with the consumer participant as a passive participant); consumer behavior associated with seasonal and year-round barbecue grilling; and how various types of businesses compile reports for their customers utilizing specific office equipment.

Another obvious use of ethnography is in the study of open spaces. This includes research into such areas as the public spaces at a university library and how these spaces impact students' learning experiences (May, 2011), as well as the design and social implications of the coffee shop as a community gathering space (Waxman, 2006).

Although ethnography is not typically associated with research on delicate or sensitive topical areas, there are instances when ethnographers have successfully completed nonparticipant observational studies on sensitive issues. One example is the work Mariampolski conducted for faucet manufacturer Moen, Inc., to observe showering behavior among consumers (see ElBoghdady, 2002). In that study, the researcher recruited "social nudists" to be videotaped (using a specially devised video recording system) while going through their usual showering routine. As another example, Forbat, White, Marshall-Lucette, and Kelly (2012) report on a study involving on-site nonparticipant observations of clinician–patient consultations with men in various stages of prostate cancer treatment. The purpose was to learn what is spoken (and what is implied but not spoken of directly) in these consultations by the clinicians with patients (and their partners who also attended these consultations); and, specifically, the content and manner in which the topic of sexual functioning was discussed.

Observer Skills

For ethnographic research to generate good quality data the person doing the observing must be skilled in a number of ways, which are associated with three broad areas impacting the outcomes of observation. These are the:

- Mechanics or operational aspects.
- Personal characteristics or traits of the observer.
- Observer's sensibilities to the research participants and the study environment.

The first two (i.e., the mechanics and observer's characteristics) are particularly relevant to on-site ethnographies, whereas the third (i.e., sensibilities) pertains to both on-site and off-site (i.e., off-site nonparticipant and Internet) observations. With respect to operational issues, there are any number of concerns that the observer has to address in the field that require the ability to adapt quickly and smoothly to the participants, the particular situation under investigation, and the multiple responsibilities of the observer necessary to meet research goals. These include:

- Dressing appropriately to "fit in" with the research participants (e.g., dressing in business attire when observing the daily routines in a corporate office environment).
- Adapting to an unsafe or potentially dangerous study environment (e.g., the observation of deviant behavior such as drug dealing and activities of street gangs).
- Working in suboptimal conditions (e.g., living among residents in Appalachia or on Native American reservations where some communities may be without modern conveniences such as running water).
- Working long or "odd" hours for a prolonged period of time (e.g., conducting a 6-month observation of a farmers' market that operates from 6:00 A.M. to 6:00 P.M.).
- The ability to coordinate and use a variety of recording tools and devices in order to create site diagrams (mapping), audio and/or video recorded observations in an unobtrusive manner, and to conduct systematic inventories (e.g., of an at-home patient's medicine cabinet) as well as organized field notes.
- Strategies for exiting the field (e.g., the difficulty of severing emotional attachments that may have been made between the observer and participants in a complete participant observation).

Not unlike the IDI and group discussion methods of qualitative research, the on-site observer in ethnographic research must also consider carefully his/her own characteristics or traits that can bias or unwittingly influence participants' behavior and the study environment. The observer's age, gender, race, and ethnic identification can potentially cast a certain stereotype that can affect the relationships—and therefore the observations—with research participants. Although, in some circumstances, this effect can work to the observer's advantage—for example, "status as a foreigner can allow some distance to be created" from societal rules that would otherwise limit the observer's access to the people of interest (Hammersley & Atkinson, 1995, p. 93); or the case of female observers who effectively gained entry into the masculine world of automotive "customizers" by playing the role of "admiring female" (Mariampolski, 2006)—it is more likely to interfere with gaining a full and clear understanding of the study environment. A female observer, for example, may be restricted from observing participants in some areas of an all-male facility. It is therefore essential that the observer be keenly aware of his/her personal characteristics and have the necessary skills to reduce, if not eliminate entirely, the impact of these traits on the final data that are gathered.

The most important of all observer skills is the sensibility of the observer. It is this skill that can compensate for the potential negative effects related to operational missteps and an observer–participant mismatch in terms of personal characteristics. The observer's capacity to be aware of and to reflect on his/her surroundings, the actions of the participants, and how the observer may be influencing the outcomes from the observation is critical to the success of an ethnographic study. An essential component of this sensibility is the observer's analytical competency; that is, the ability to apply analytical skills while in the field that deepen the researcher's understanding of the culture and events from the participants' point of view. A few of the primary required skills along these lines are discussed below.

The central analytical skill that is imperative of all ethnographic observers is what Stacey and Eckert (1999) called "dual perspective" or the ability to derive meaning from participants' activities (as well as the study environment) by internalizing the viewpoint of the research participants while maintaining an "outsider's" objectivity. In this way, the observer is mentally placing him/herself among the participants while at the same time (i.e., at the same moment of observation) looking out for the connections that give meaning to the group. A dual perspective demands that observers have the ability to actually "put themselves into the shoes" of unfamiliar cultures and social groups, sensing and recording events from the participants' vantage point while also reflecting on the meanings as well as on the observer's own values and possible biases. This ability distinguishes the untrained observer from the experienced and skilled ethnographer who "attempts to maintain a self-conscious awareness of what is learned, how it is has been learned, and the social transactions that inform the production of such knowledge" (Hammersley & Atkinson, 1995, p. 101).

The observer's job is made particularly difficult because a dual way of thinking is only one of the analytical sensibilities required from an ethnographic observer. In addition, an observer's analytical sensibilities also need to include the ability to:

- Notice and record (during observation) participants' body language (e.g., posture, gestures, eye contact), spoken language and word choices, seating or standing positions, relative interaction with others, as well as various aspects of the physical setting (including a map of the physical space and the participants' positions within it).

- Gain participants' trust by managing assumptions and expectations (e.g., patients in a drug detox facility might alter their behavior under the assumption that the observer is an undercover agent, or students in training may believe that the observer is there to offer expert advice rather than just observe).

- Focus attention on what is happening *now* in the study environment rather than trying to anticipate what will happen next; that is, "being in the moment."

- Reflect on observations during the field period, construct hypotheses or begin to identify patterns, and investigate nascent theories with participants while still in the field by way of IDIs and/or activities.

- Maintain an appropriate level of naivety when in the role of complete participant (e.g., an observer who is an experienced sailor would need to make a conscious effort to be self aware of his/her expertise and control what he/she knows about the subject matter to objectively study the daily lives of fishermen).

There is an additional sensibility that is peculiar to the complete participant observer that can prove critical to the lasting "success" of an observation event. This is the skill of knowing *when* and, particularly, *how* to withdraw from participation/observation, which effectively ends the observer's association with the group. Observers typically expend a great deal of effort developing trusting relationships with participants, but, as many ethnographers have found, disengagement from the group can be much more difficult than rapport building. Snow (1980), for example, recounts the tensions that arose when he attempted to withdraw from a Buddhist "movement" that he had willingly joined in order to conduct an 18-month ethnographic study. His membership withdrawal was generally regarded with disfavor and he found that the "committed members engage[d] in a type of 'rallying action' aimed at turning the straying member back into the fold" (p. 110). Indeed, Snow's withdrawal was met with equal resistance and pressure for him to seek guidance from other members. As he wrote in his field notes: "While I was thus trying to curtail my involvement and offer what seemed to be legitimate reasons for dropping out, I was yet being drawn back in at the same time" (p. 110).

Overview of the Strengths and Limitations of Ethnography

The following sections provide a brief discussion of the strengths and limitations associated with ethnographic research. This discussion pertains to ethnography overall and does not specifically delve into the advantages and disadvantages of the five separate levels of observation (see Figure 5.1, p. 173). However, the implications of these varied observer roles in the design of ethnographic qualitative research are discussed in Section 5.3 within the context of the TQF.

Strengths

There are several strengths important to the ethnographic approach in qualitative research. These strengths revolve around the fact that ethnography is (a) reality-based, (b) a process of immersion, and (c) a multi-method approach.

Reality-Based

The focus on the natural course of events as experienced in the reality of the moment is the critical differentiator of ethnography from other qualitative research methods. The reality-based approach of ethnography gets at the heart of what it means to conduct qualitative research: that is, to gain a meaningful and nuanced understanding of behavior, attitudes, and values by getting close to the lives of the target population. The researcher benefits from the *in situ* approach of ethnography in three important ways:

1. The observation of people's actual experience makes it true and accurate to their lives. Although the observer can potentially bias this account (see Section 5.3 for a discussion on the potential biases), the reality of the experience contributes highly to the credibility of the data. And although participants who are aware that they are the subjects of a research study may behave differently than if they were not aware, myriad past experience with ethnography provides convincing evidence that participants soon forget that they are the subjects of research, especially in complete participant observation when the observer becomes a full-fledge member of the study group.

2. The fact that the fieldwork is primarily directed by the participant, not the researcher, adds to the quality of the outcomes. This participant-guided approach is made possible by the inherent flexibility of ethnography—which allows the observer to switch roles, to intervene with questions as appropriate, and to devise new observation or participation strategies as necessary to accommodate the participant-led experiences as they unfold—and its underlying goal of discerning meaning inductively, from the inside out, by thinking and living like participants.

3. Unlike IDIs or group discussions, the reality basis of the collected data in ethnography is intended to sidestep the potential error introduced by the faulty recall among those observed of past events and information, as well as the possibility that researchers may "favor particular ways of interpreting what people are saying" (Silverman, 2013, p. 55).

In turn, those being observed are not burdened by being the subjects of an ethnographic study in that they are not required to travel to the study environment (e.g., as is necessary for a face-to-face focus group) and, indeed, the research is being conducted in a location that is natural and familiar to them (e.g., in the classroom during normal school hours, at home with family members, on the street corners where they normally hang out, in bars or lounges where they go after work).

Process of Immersion

An additional strength of ethnography is the level in which the researcher consumes him/herself with the people and events of interest. It is this process of immersion—a process that may begin with off-site nonparticipant observation and escalate to active or complete participation—that provides the opportunity for the researcher to gain a sensibility and depth of understanding of the contextual, emotional, and social factors that define meaning within a group or for an individual. This sensibility brings with it a comprehensive and, most likely, a complex view that can reveal patterns in behavior and stimulate new insights. The typical length of ethnographic studies contributes greatly to the immersion process. An ethnographic observation may last only 1 day but is often conducted over long periods of time, such as Haenfler (2004), who studied the straight edge movement for nearly 15 years. The extended period of ethnographic fieldwork has the added advantage of often mitigating observer/researcher bias (this too is discussed in Section 5.3).

A Multi-Method Approach

Complementing the immersion process is the fact that ethnography is not an observation-only approach. Although observation typically represents the key component to an ethnographic study, true immersion and absorption in the study environment is derived from gaining participants' input on many levels. Researchers often use observation as a starting point in the field from which they form an idea of where they need clarification or follow-up. This often leads to IDIs or group discussions with participants and, in some instances, influential others (e.g., parents of the children participating in the Christensen et al. [2011] study discussed earlier). Unlike the multi-method approach discussed in Chapter 7 (see p. 287), the utilization of multiple data sources in ethnography is squarely focused on augmenting the researcher's observations, with the observations serving as the primary data. For example, an overt observer's targeted questions may allow participants the opportunity to contribute their interpretations of what is going on in the study environment, help to clarify observed events for the observer, and enhance the observer's ability to ultimately find patterns or themes in the study activities along with the meanings that participants associate with their actions. For a covert participant observer, this same process of augmenting observational data has to play out much more subtlety and with continued subterfuge, since the observer must avoid "blowing cover" while, at the same time, probing for information to help identify the patterns or themes without appearing to be doing so.

An ethnographic researcher studying the use of skiing equipment, for instance, might ask the skiers who are being observed (during a ski trip the researcher is taking with them) to discuss the circumstances that resulted in their switching helmets or the reasons they made particular adjustments on their skis. For the overt researcher these queries would be done explicitly and directly, whereas for the covert researcher they would be worked into what otherwise would appear to be normal conversation with other skiers. Other ancillary methods such as the review of relevant documents can also enrich observations and strengthen an ethnographic study overall. Russell et al. (2012), for example, were better able to understand their observations of team interaction among clinical and administrative staff in primary care offices by analyzing the internal communications and minutes from office meetings.

Limitations

The major limitations of ethnographic research fall into three broad categories: (1) the potential for bias and weakened credibility of the data that are gathered, (2) logistical and practical issues in implementing an ethnographic study, and (3) the narrow target populations that can be studied well using this method of research.

Potential for Bias

The possibility of bias creeps into ethnography by (a) the mere presence of the observer who may distort the very behaviors of the participants being studied; and (b) the observer's own preconceptions, attitudes, and expectations, which may bias the information the observer gathers and interprets. Even in the case of covert observers, their immersion into a group may be the catalyst that materially changes what subsequently happens in the group. Unless observers are carefully trained and well experienced on how to maintain objectivity in the field, and unless they use their analytical abilities to think and record solely from the perspective of the participants, they can harm the integrity of research outcomes. Observer bias can actually pose a greater threat to ethnographic research than interviewer bias poses in the IDI method or moderator bias in group discussions. This is because, unlike these other methods, the observer in an ethnographic study may take on the role of a complete participant who is fully engaged with the social group under study or may otherwise have some affinity for the situation being investigated. In either case, there exists the *potential* for bias by way of the observer "going native"—as illustrated by Schouten and McAlexander (1995) in their study for Harley–Davidson (see p. 175)—or imposing his/her own knowledge and experience, which may (a) impede the observer's ability to sense what is going on in the study environment from the participants' points of view or (b) change the group dynamics in material ways from what would have happened had the observer not become a member of the group. Ethnographic research is particularly susceptible to this type of bias when the researcher has used "opportunistic" or **convenience sampling**, which is the practice of selecting a study environment and/or research participants that are easily (and inexpensively) available and familiar to the observer. For example, a researcher studying how people behave and interact in confined spaces might decide to take advantage of his daily ride on the local subway to observe other commuters, or a study to observe the staff–patient dynamic in a geriatric facility might be conveniently conducted at the facility where the researcher regularly visits her parents. Bernard (2011) used his vacation in Mexico to track the use of "beach space" by American and Mexican families.

Logistical and Practical Issues

There are also logistical design issues that limit the practicality of ethnography. By definition, the study period for ethnographic research can be considerably longer than for other methods, such as IDIs and group discussions. Whereas a marketing researcher may spend only a few hours or a day observing and interviewing any one consumer at home or during a retail shopping event, that is typically not the case in most ethnographic research. Recall that health care researchers such as Williamson et al. (2012), educational researchers such as Cotton (2006), psychologists such as Griffiths (2011), and sociologists such as Haenfler (2004) have studied research subjects anywhere from a week (Williamson et al.) to 2 years (Cotton and Griffiths) to nearly 15 years (Haenfler). These prolonged periods of time in the field are meant to advance the credibility and analyzability of the research outcomes, but the real world of deadlines and researchers' busy schedules can make these time requirements impractical for any but a very limited number of researchers.

The time factor also has other consequences. In addition to making unrealistic demands on the research schedule, the extended period of field time for an ethnographic study may add significant cost to the research (e.g., employing observers over time and training new observers, as necessary, to replace observers who move on to other assignments or become ill), which may make a quality ethnographic approach well beyond the fiscal limits of the available research funds. The limitations associated with time and cost often restrict the scope of ethnographic research as far as the number of observations the researcher can afford (in terms of time and/or cost) to complete.

Another practical matter is the training of observers. A credible ethnographic study resulting in quality data requires an observer who has been professionally trained and possesses the skills discussed in this chapter section (see p. 179) and in Section 5.3 (see pp. 207–213). The researcher not only needs to find and train new observers as existing observers become unavailable but also must supervise and retrain observers, as required, to maintain optimal data collection standards.

INSTITUTIONAL REVIEW BOARDS AND INFORMED CONSENT. Obtaining approval to conduct ethnographic research from institutional review boards (IRBs), as well as gaining **informed consent** from the research participants (when that is required), can be a logistical limitation to the approach. Although it is critical to maintain the highest ethical standards, and approvals may be essential to the process, the practical matter of gaining authorization may impede the research and cause unacceptable delays. Approval from IRBs may be a particularly involved and lengthy process due to (a) a tendency to use medical research as a model for review of research proposals rather than social science research, despite the view that "the research of most social scientists involving human subjects does not pose a threat of physical or mental harm" (American Association of University Professors, 2000); (b) the *sui generis* nature (i.e., uniqueness) of individual ethnographic studies (e.g., the topic being studied, the purpose behind the approach, the observation method, longevity in the field); and (c) particular concerns associated with covert observation in which the observed are not aware of the researcher's disguised or hidden presence (Baker, 2006).

In theory, devising a means of providing the necessary information to, and gaining informed consent from, all research participants (and proxies, e.g., parents, legal guardians) is also a necessary step in the ethnographic research process. Informed consent requires that, in advance of making a decision of whether to participate in a research study, participants be made aware of the following (National Research Council, 2003):

- Research objectives.
- Activities and duration in the field (i.e., what the participant is being asked to participate in and for how long (e.g., a 3-day observation and a 2-hour interview).
- Likelihood and level of risk or inconvenience the participant may experience.
- Benefits to the participant as a result of participation (monetary compensation is not considered a "benefit").
- Confidentiality of the data (i.e., participants' identities will not be associated with the data).
- Voluntary nature of participation (i.e., the person can refuse to participate).
- Option to participate only partially or to withdraw from the research at any time.
- Contact information for the principal researcher, the IRB chair, or other authority.

Additionally, those being observed in an ethnographic study should be informed regarding:

- Compensation or incentive (if any) to be paid for consenting and/or cooperating.
- Data storage, including who will see the data and how they will be used.

As a practical matter, obtaining informed consent may be fairly simple in a small study involving just a few participants who may have previous experience with research protocol; however, a larger study with a social group that is totally unfamiliar with the idea of research (possibly a subculture, such as bikers, who have never been approached to participate in research) may require extensive communications and explanations before consent is given.

In obtaining informed consent, the researcher can present the basic components (as outlined on p. 186) to study participants either orally or in written form. Although an IRB may require a written and signed consent form, this is not always the case; and, indeed, there are situations when the necessity for written informed consent may be waived by IRBs. Typically, these are research studies in which (a) the primary risk is a breach of confidentiality; (b) there is no more than minimal risk of harm to participants, and the research involves acts that would not, under normal circumstances, require written consent; or (c) the consent form would be the only record connecting the participant to the research.[3] Yet, even when the research does not meet these stipulations for waiver, written consent is not always obtained and, indeed, oral consent is not uncommon (the Conn, Oandasan, Creede, Jakubovicz, and Wilson [2010] study is just one example). Further, there are research conditions that circumvent IRB approval altogether (i.e., neither written nor oral consent is required), such as research conducted in public spaces (e.g., parks, restaurants, street corners) where individuals "should not have an expectation of privacy" and the data gathered from an unobtrusive observer "would scarcely permit identification of individual participants if it became known to others, and disclosure would not likely place the participants at risk of any legal, economic, or social harm" (National Research Council, 2003, p. 152). Regardless of whether participants give their written or oral consent (in those situations when consent is requested), researchers should, ideally, always explain to participants what the consent form states. This is particularly important with certain study groups such as the illiterate or mentally ill. As the American Anthropological Association (2012) notes, "It is the quality of the consent, not its format, which is relevant."

When doing overt observations (i.e., studies where the participants are aware of being observed), an ethnographer can obtain **active consent,** by which participants sign and return a form agreeing to participate (i.e., they actively opt in to the study), or **passive consent,** by which nonparticipants sign and return a form refusing to participate in the research (i.e., they actively opt out of the study). Although active consent is more typical, there are situations when passive consent is preferable for the sake of the credibility of the study. For instance, an ethnographic study among a hard-to-reach or lower-income minority segment of the population may achieve a higher level of participation (resulting in a more representative sample) from passive rather than active consent because it does not require an action from the participants. However, passive consent has been deemed ethically questionable because it places the onus on the participant to opt-out of the study when, for any number of reasons (e.g., poor literacy skills, lack of access to the U.S. mail or other form of delivery), the participant is incapable of doing so (cf. Jason, Pokorny, & Katz, 2001).

In the case of covert observation, when the participant–observer has secreted his/her true identity, obtaining active or passive informed consent in advance from those who will be observed is inappropriate. Because of this, a special responsibility should be assumed by ethnographers who use covert methods; a responsibility to hold a formal debriefing session with those who have been secretly observed shortly after the completion of all the covert observations. Although it is not uncommon in ethnography for covert observers to fail to debrief the observed individuals, the ethical ethnographer is obligated to uphold the highest research standards and, in so doing, inform those who were observed of the research project and the role(s) they were unknowingly playing in it.

The debriefing session with the participants of the research should:

- Fully explain the purpose of the research, why the deception was necessary, and what will be done with the findings.

- Assure the persons who were secretly observed that the data gathered about them will be kept entirely confidential.

- Ask about their experiences and, specifically, if they suspected deception and whether they believe they were harmed in any way.

- Encourage those observed to ask questions about the research, such as, why they were selected, why deception was used, and what happens to the data.

- Thank the observed individuals for their unwitting cooperation with the study and provide them with the researcher's contact information.

In instances where anyone who was observed believes that harm resulted to him/her or to others, it is the responsibility of the researcher to make a sincere effort to undo that harm, even if the researcher disagrees with the person who reported the harm being done.

Obtaining informed consent when conducting ethnography in the virtual world is generally lacking. Although some researchers conducting overt observations may present participants with an online consent form with the option to click "I agree to participate in this research" (i.e., opt-in), Internet-based ethnographic research typically meets one of the waiver conditions mentioned on page 187 (e.g., minimal risk of harm).

Narrow Target Populations and Subject Matter

Because ethnography is frequently very labor intensive and highly focused on the concentrated study of relatively small groups of people, by definition it is limited in the range of target populations that can be studied well. This is especially true for in-person (compared to online) observation because the cost and time required to gain coverage of even modestly sized target populations is far beyond the means of most qualitative researchers who do ethnography. Take, for example, a desire to conduct an on-site passive participant study of male prostate cancer support groups in Cleveland. It would not be unusual for an ethnographic approach to study only one group over time. In some cases it may be feasible to study more than one group, but a researcher could not possibly conduct an ethnographic study that adequately covered the wide range of prostate cancer support groups that actually existed. It is therefore impossible for the researcher to make credible statements about all prostate support groups in Cleveland (or conjecture about those outside of Cleveland) when he/she intensively studied just one or a couple of these groups. Ethnography is very good for studying specific groups when the interest in the research is just that—those groups—but it is often too limited to study larger populations.

It is also important to consider the fact that ethnography is not appropriate for all subject matter. For instance, an observational study to examine decision making in an office environment may be ill-conceived, given that many decisions are not the result of an explicit series of actions within a well-defined timeframe, but rather a complicated process that may take place over many months or years and at many different levels of employee involvement. It is important, therefore, for the researcher to think carefully about the research topic and critically evaluate the appropriateness of the observational method.

5.2 ETHNOGRAPHY IN THE DIGITAL AGE

In this section we discuss two ways in which ethnographic research has evolved in the digital age: (1) the study of virtual worlds or online contexts and (2) ethnography in a mobile society. The increasingly ubiquitous use (and capabilities) of digital technology has made the online environment and the mobile smartphone mode important considerations in the design of ethnographic research. There is little doubt that the use of new technologies is changing the course of fieldwork and, specifically, the role of the researcher/observer, from the naturalistic observer who lives in the "ebb and flow" of "real people in real circumstances" to someone who takes part in defining participants' realities by, for example, easily disseminating images and video (Angrosino & Rosenberg, 2011, p. 472). What follows is a brief overview of the online and mobile approaches from the standpoint of producing quality ethnographic data outcomes. A summary of the strengths and limitations of these approaches is presented in Table 5.1.

The Study of Virtual Worlds or Online Contexts

In Section 5.1 our discussion of ethnography was implicitly or explicitly directed at the observation of real-world social groups, events, or activities at one or more locations where the participants are physically present. But nowadays, the study of groups, events, and activities in the virtual or online environment is often a necessary component to gaining a complete understanding of the subject matter.

TABLE 5.1. Ethnography Mode Comparisons: Key Strengths and Limitations of Online and Mobile Modes

Online	Mobile
Strengths	

• Overall efficiency and practicality, including cost and time considerations.
• Taps into the online extension of people's lives offline.
• Acknowledges the virtual world as an important cultural dimension.
• Access to special and hard-to-reach population segments (e.g., migrants, subculture groups).
	• When used with other methods, can support and more robustly inform the researcher about participants' experiences.
	• Provides an added dimension (in conjunction with other methods), including:
	  ○ Real-time accounts of events, with less chance of memory-related biases.
	  ○ On-the-go feedback on a specific aspect of experience.
	  ○ Researcher can ask clarifying questions in the moment.
	  ○ Participant input regarding multiple locations, events, etc.
	  ○ Partial replacement of a face-to-face method may reduce time and cost.

Limitations	
• Participants' identities can be fluid and "innovative" (using text and images) depending on how someone wants to be perceived. • Researcher's role demands certain skills to understand context and interaction. • Lurking without participants' consent. • Excludes people without Internet access or who are unable to actively participate in online social media. • Lacks visual and verbal cues. • Weak anonymity safeguards for participants.	• Utilizing a mobile device disrupts and potentially alters some of the participant's natural behavior and experience. ○ Use of a mobile device may be an unnatural act, especially for older segments of the population. • Because the participant decides what behavior or experience to share or not share with the researcher, the data quality may be jeopardized; the researcher is not necessarily observing all relevant behavior or experiences. • Excludes people without a mobile device and/or Internet access or who are unable to actively participate using all mobile technology features.

Ethnography conducted in the virtual world has been given many labels, including "virtual ethnography," "online ethnography," "digital ethnography," "netnography," "cyber-ethnography," and "webnography." This terminology, however, suggests a novel mode or method—that is, ethnography conducted online—when, in fact, ethnography for the virtual space is not unlike that of conventional ethnography in that multiple methods and modes are integrated around the core method of observation. For example, researchers employing ethnography in the virtual context enhance the observation of online chats or the computerized personalities of avatars with the use of offline methods (such as face-to-face IDIs) in order to complement and deepen their comprehension of the phenomena under study. Orgad (2006), for instance, conducted 11 face-to-face and one telephone IDI with breast cancer patients whose communications she had observed on cancer websites to better understand "the experiences of using the Internet in the context of their illness" (p. 9). Schrooten (2012) used face-to-face and email IDIs to "fill gaps" and validate her online observations of Brazilian migrants living in Belgium who were participating on a particular social networking site. And Hughey (2008) conducted IDIs in various modes to understand the "contextual meanings" woven into his observations of an online forum for African American fraternity and sorority members. Other researchers—such as Gatson and Zweerink (2004) and Wilson (2006)—have gone offline to more fully immerse themselves in the culture under study. Gatson and Zweerink, for example, attended face-to-face "gatherings" for fans and online community members of *Buffy the Vampire Slayer*; and Wilson augmented his online observations of the rave subculture by attending various rave dance parties and conducting IDIs (via face-to-face and online) with DJs, promoters, and ravers.

Strengths Associated with Ethnography in the Virtual World or Online Context

Conducting an ethnographic study in the online environment presents the researcher with several advantages, including (a) overall efficiency and practicality, (b) an important cultural dimension that has become a part of people's everyday experience and an extension of their lives offline, and (c) access to special populations or subcultures that otherwise may be very hard-to-reach. The observation method in the online context can be highly efficient compared to fieldwork in the physical environment from the standpoint of breadth (e.g., the ability to observe multiple sites due to no geographical boundaries); access to participants (e.g., with the exception of closed forums, few if any gatekeepers or key informants are required for entry); and researcher involvement (e.g., multiple researchers/observers can collaborate and contribute to the fieldwork). Further, similar to the online modes for IDIs and group discussions, the turnaround time to complete the research may be shorter (e.g., due to the time saved because observers need not travel to physical locations or because text data are archived online, eliminating the necessity of transcriptions), and fewer financial resources may be required (e.g., due to the cost and time savings from reduced travel).

An additional strength of conducting ethnographic research in the participants' online world is that it acknowledges that "virtual reality is not a reality separate from other aspects of human action and experience, but rather a part of it" (Garcia, Standlee, Bechkoff, & Cui, 2009, p. 54). Whether it is by way of social networking sites such as Facebook and Twitter, or forums and listservs for special-interest and professional groups (e.g., the American Anthropological Association's listserv for members of its Association of Black Anthropologists), or consumers' reviews of products and services on sites such as TripAdvisor (*www.tripadvisor.*

com), the Internet has ushered in a pervasive communication and socializing channel that has become fully integrated in the everyday experience of most people in the developed countries of the world. In this way, "there is one social world which contains both traditional and technologically advanced modes of communication and sites of social activity" (Garcia et al., 2009, p. 54). The virtual domain has become a new yet fundamental cultural dimension that ethnographers can embrace and explore as a complementary extension of participants' lives offline.

A third important strength of the virtual environment to ethnographic research is the opportunity it offers the researcher to study particular, and often rare, segments of the population. For example, ethnographers have found the online world an appropriate context to study mobility, specifically mobile population groups such as migrants and expatriates. Schrooten (2012) used the online social networking site Orkut (in addition to offline IDIs) to study Brazilian migrants living in Belgium, emphasizing the idea that "we are no longer in the age of the uprooted migrant" (p. 1798) as well as the key role that the virtual context plays in maintaining transnational cohesiveness among these groups. Freidenberg (2011) found in her study of expatriate communities living in Buenos Aires that "a central characteristic of these populations was their heavy reliance on virtual communication as if it was an integral component of the expat transnational persona" (p. 265). The online context has also increasingly given researchers access to subcultures, such as the straight edge movement, for whom the Internet has become "a new social space for subcultural identification and change" (Williams, 2006, p. 175).

Limitations Associated with Ethnography in the Virtual World or Online Context

The primary limitations of ethnographic research conducted in the virtual environment fall into the three broad categories of (1) participant identity; (2) the researcher's role; and (3) typical online mode issues related to coverage (i.e., the fact that not all segments of the population are accessible online because they do not have access to or use the Internet), visible cues, and confidentiality. The identities that participants choose to portray in an online context can be problematic for the researcher and potentially undermine the credibility of the research data. The idea that "identity is fluid and potentially multiple on the Internet" (James & Busher, 2009, p. 35), and that the creation of an identity can be an ongoing process of innovation, leaves ethnographic researchers with an uncertainty about the realities they are observing. Online participants not only create their identities by way of text but also through images and video diaries that "ultimately reflect how the participants want to be viewed or represented" (Murthy, 2008, p. 843). This uncertain reality should lead researchers to ask themselves questions such as, "What aspects of these people's identities are they self-selecting to convey in this virtual space?", "Am I actually observing some form of reality or rather imaginary characters made up by participants?", and "How does an individual's identity in a particular online environment compare to his/her identity in an offline or other online context?" These types of questions make it important for ethnographers in the virtual realm to extend the scope of their research designs by incorporating face-to-face IDIs or other interactions with those being observed in order to triangulate the data and provide stronger support for their final interpretations.

Another aspect that potentially weakens an ethnographic approach in the virtual sphere has to do with the researcher—that is, the role he/she plays in the study environment as well as the particular skills required to discern the contextual underpinnings that shape the observed interactions (e.g., observing an online forum by learning as much as practicable about the people being observed, how their lives or relevant factors shape their comments, and how the aggressiveness of some forum members has changed the course of the observed event). As in conventional ethnography, the observer/researcher in the online study environment can decide how involved to be with those who will be observed, with many researchers opting for a nonparticipant or participant role. A nonparticipant role is particularly easy to adopt online, and, in fact, it is so easy that it calls into question whether unannounced "lurking" on the part of a researcher is ethically justified. Even though ethnographers in the online context often begin their observations as nonparticipants, they—like ethnographers in the physical world—may gradually assume a more participatory role and make the observed group aware of their identities (Orgad, 2006; Isabella, 2007) However, it is not always the case that observers reveal their identities. Sugiura, Pope, and Webber (2012), for example, utilized nonparticipant, covert observation to study the purchase activity and use of illegal "slimming drugs" among people engaged on three Internet forums, never identifying themselves to those observed. And participant observation in graphical online environments has given researchers the ability to "hide" behind different personas by way of adopting one or more avatar identities (Williams, 2007). The all-too-convenient (and seductive?) option of lurking without people's consent represents a potentially serious ethical limitation to ethnographic research in the virtual context.

As with online IDIs and group discussions, ethnography in an online environment is limited as a research design due to the potential for (a) a lack of representation of one's target population due to the nonuniversal access to or use of the Internet (e.g., among people in the United States without a high school diploma; Zickuhr, 2013) and the inability of some portion of the population to negotiate various websites; (b) the absence of visible cues such as body language; and (c) potentially weak safeguards for participants' anonymity. The issue of anonymity is becoming an increasingly problematic limitation to ethnographic research in the virtual world because of the ever-growing technological capabilities that enable others to identify people's online presence by way of "cookies," IP (Internet protocol) addresses, and server logs; and that enable people to display their portrait photos, pseudonyms, and other characteristics that may reveal their identities. For these and other reasons, it is difficult to guarantee anonymity in the online context to those being observed.

"Mobile Ethnography" and the Mobile Mode

In 1995 anthropologist George Marcus used the phrase "mobile ethnography" when he talked about "tracing a cultural formation across and within multiple sites of activity" (Marcus, 1995, p. 96). In this sense, mobile ethnography refers to "multi-site ethnography" in which researchers examine the "paths" and "juxtapositions" of multiple locations within the scope of the study frame in order to deepen their understanding of cultural meanings and the role that sites (collectively and independently) play in the cultural context. The study of migration across geographical territories is one example of multisite ethnography, as is ethnographic research in the online environment (discussed on pp. 190–191) where observations in the virtual space can be contrasted and compared to participants' activities in offline locations. The "go-along" approach espoused by Kusenbach (2003) and the community "guided tour" used by Christensen et al. (2011) in their study of mobility among children are variations of Marcus's mobile or multisite ethnography in that the focus is not on any one field site but rather the various places that hold meaning and import in participants' lives.

Today, the phrase "mobile ethnography" has been popularized, particularly among marketing researchers, to refer to the process of data collection by way of participants' mobile phone devices. In many cases, however, it is questionable whether these are true ethnographies. For example, the consumer products firm Proctor and Gamble conducted a 3-month study with mothers of young children to "understand the process mom goes through when switching" diapers (Sauer & August, 2012). Participants used their smartphones to relay back to researchers images of children "testing" diaper products, participants' retail experiences when shopping for diapers, and text/email messages capturing participants' thoughts at specific moments in time. Although the length of time in the field and the research methods employed (the study also included IDIs and group discussions) are design features that make the research "ethnographic-like," it falls short of true ethnographic research because of the undue guidance (and potential influence) from the researcher by way of the "immersive exercises" and "weekly assignments" demanded of the participants that most likely altered their natural behavior in various ways.

This and similar work underscore the inherent problem with attempting to conduct ethnographic research *solely via mobile technology*. By asking research participants to interrupt their usual activities to send or upload images, video, or text, the researcher has disturbed the study environment and distorted the natural behaviors and experiences of the participants. By definition, an ethnographic approach must enable the researcher to observe unadulterated events as they naturally unfold, from which appropriate hypotheses are formed and next steps in the research are determined. Yet the unnatural act[4] of using a mobile device to record events makes a mobile-only strategy in ethnographic research untenable from the standpoint of the credibility and analyzability of the final data.

In addition to disrupting the natural course of the participant's behavior and experience, relying on a mobile device in an ethnographic study also means that the researcher is being provided only that aspect of behavior or experience that the participant wishes to reveal. Not unlike our discussion of the mobile mode in Chapter 3 (see p. 70), the ultimate quality of the data is at the mercy of what the participant chooses or does not choose to share with the researcher.

There is, however, clearly a role for mobile phone technology in conducting ethnographic research. This is the important supportive role that the mobile mode can play in helping to inform the researcher about participants' meanings. When used in conjunction with other modes and methods (e.g., face-to-face observation and IDIs), input from mobile devices can make significant contributions to the research outcomes. A case in point is the Christensen et al. (2011) study (discussed on p. 177), which integrated a brief (five-question) mobile survey into a multifaceted research design, serving to enhance their understanding of children's daily mobility and associated experiences. Utilizing the mobile mode in combination with other modes and methods may add an important dimension to an ethnographic study and offer the researcher certain advantages, including:

- In-the-moment, real-time accounts (via photos, videos, voice, and text) of an event or situation.

- Feedback on specific aspects in on-the-go situations (e.g., reactions to billboard advertising while riding on public transport).

- The researcher's ability to ask participants questions (via text or voice) to clarify in-the-moment situations.

- Coverage of multiple sites; that is, participants can relay feedback from more than one site location, which may allow the researcher to analyze the data by contrasting and comparing site locations (e.g., a college student's experiences at various student facilities on campus, such as the library, athletic center, student union, and main dining hall).

- A reduction in the overall time required to complete the research (e.g., mobile images will likely reduce or eliminate the need for visiting physical sites).

- A reduction in the overall cost of the study (e.g., due to reduced travel for the researcher).

5.3 APPLYING THE TOTAL QUALITY FRAMEWORK APPROACH TO ETHNOGRAPHY

In this section we take a critical look at ethnographic research from the standpoint of the TQF. As with the other qualitative research methods discussed in this book, we concentrate this discussion on how to maximize the quality of the research design for ethnographies by adhering to the principles of the TQF defined by its four main components—Credibility, Analyzability, Transparency, and Usefulness. Our discussion further addresses both the strengths and limitations of ethnography, and pays particular attention to the areas of research design that are most central to ethnography and where quality design standards can have the most impact on the usefulness of outcomes from ethnographic studies (e.g., considerations such as sampling, observational techniques, observer training and skills, as well as mode and ethical considerations).

Credibility

Ethnographic research is a classic paradigm for qualitative researchers because it allows them to gain considerable understanding, both deep and rich, of the phenomena that are being observed. However, there is a distinct tradeoff typically made by ethnographers—that is, in gaining this detailed understanding, ethnographers (knowingly or not) must accept a variety of threats to the credibility of their resulting data. As with other qualitative methods, these risks should be taken into account when a researcher is interpreting his/her findings, advancing implications, and thereby addressing the usefulness of their ethnographic study, by tempering the research outcomes as needed.

The Credibility component of an ethnographic research study is founded upon the areas of Scope and Data Gathering. In ethnography, Scope addresses the issue of how well the individuals or group that is observed represents the target population of particular interest to the research objectives. The credibility associated with Data Gathering in ethnographic research rests on the reliability and validity of the data that are gathered and how well the researcher's observations have actually addressed the constructs of interest.

Scope

The Scope of an ethnographic study encompasses many of the coverage, sample design, and cooperation issues discussed in Chapters 3 and 4 pertaining to IDIs and group discussions, respectively. Ethnography, however, presents the researcher with many unique design considerations that need to be taken into account. For instance, in this chapter section we discuss **purposive sampling**, which is the deliberate selection of particular individuals or groups of people for observation because of their relationship to the research problem. Although purposive sampling may be utilized by other qualitative research methods, the observational researcher often has reason to employ this highly directed approach. And, although this form of sampling may be highly attractive to the needs and interests of ethnographic researchers, it brings with it a number of threats to a study's Credibility. These and other Scope-related issues are discussed in the material that follows.

Coverage and Sample Design

An ethnographic approach to research often differs from IDI and group discussion methods in how the researcher goes about securing the "list" of the target population from which people will be chosen to be observed. Although a list may be readily available for the needs of some ethnographic researchers, it is often the case that no such list of the population of interest exists or is accessible. An example of an ethnographic study for which the researcher could easily obtain a listing of the target population would be a study being conducted for the police chief of a large urban police department concerning race relations between mixed-race pairs of police officers, whereby the ethnographer plans to observe these officers by way of ride-alongs. In this case, an exhaustive list that fully covered the population of interest (mixed-race officer dyads in the city's police department) would be available directly from the police chief. In contrast, an example of an ethnography for which no list of the target population could possibly be created would be a similar ride-along study that, in this case, was investigating the citizens' reactions to mixed-race versus same-race pairs of police officers among city residents seeking police assistance. Unlike the previous case, there would be no way anyone could anticipate where the police dyads would travel or what forms of assistance would arise in a given day, thereby precluding the possibility of the researcher obtaining an a priori list of the target population (i.e., city residents in need of police assistance). Instead, in this example, the population would be sampled by a process of "natural occurrence" on a daily basis—by happenstance.

It is not uncommon in ethnography for the researcher to use purposive sampling to select the individuals or particular group of people to study. Purposive sampling is used when (a) the research objectives are aimed at a very finite, specific type of individual or well-defined group; (b) only certain people have the knowledge or expertise related to the research topic the ethnographer wants to observe; and (c) the researcher is studying all or most of the population of interest because that population is very small in size and it is therefore feasible to study it in its entirety. Examples of purposive sampling include (1) deliberately selecting cancer patients in varying stages of treatment to observe patient–physician consultations (Forbat et al., 2012), (2) the work of Williams (2006) with the straight edge subculture, (3) choosing specialists to study the use of poison in insecticides (Tongco, 2007), and (4) sampling from the limited number of online consumer forums (i.e., websites) that chat about the use of weight loss medication to investigate how people obtain and use slimming drugs (Sugiura et al., 2012). In each of these cases, the focus is on how well the sample addressed the research problem, not necessarily the representativeness of the sample to the larger population (although it could be argued that in instances of a very-low-incidence population group, representation may not be a high-priority concern).

Another example of purposive sampling would be an ethnographic study in a small school district, concerning the manner in which principals conduct faculty meetings, where the target population would consist of the principals and faculty in this one district, thereby raising little concern that those selected for observation would not be representative of the population of interest. In contrast, if the same study were being conducted for the Chicago Public Schools, with more than 600 principals and their respective faculty, the ethnographic researcher would need to receive a listing of all principals/schools within the district in order to make certain the entire target population was fully covered. An incomplete listing could lead to the poor representation of the population of interest, and therefore less credible findings, if those principals missing from the list had different styles of interacting with their faculty compared to those on the list.

When ethnographers choose to represent their target populations by studying a group or set of individuals that is merely convenient (i.e., chosen primarily because they are easily accessible), the credibility of the study may be seriously threatened. Convenience sampling—using the examples of the daily subway commute to study confined spaces, and visits to the researcher's parents' nursing home to investigate staff–patient relationships at geriatric facilities—was discussed briefly with respect to the potential for biasing ethnographic research. Unlike purposive sampling, which may be necessary (e.g., because of a low population incidence) and/or beneficial (e.g., because of the particular expertise of those sampled) to achieving the research objectives, convenience sampling is difficult to justify.

From a TQF perspective, convenience sampling does not enable the confident transferability of the research to other contexts, which is a vital aspect to the framework's Transparency component. For example, a graduate student who is conducting ethnographic research for his dissertation, concerning the roles played by clergy in the lives of their congregation, might decide to study a church two blocks from his/her university. As part of this study, the researcher plans to observe the various members of the clergy and congregation at church as well as during off-site clergy activity such as visits to parishioners' homes and hospital visitations. In addition to observations, the researcher will also conduct IDIs with clergy and church members. This is a labor intensive study and if done well, the researcher will learn a great deal about the clergy and congregation *at this church*, including the inner workings of their relationships and interactions. The grave limitation of this study, however, lies in the fact that the basis of the research rests on a church that was selected, not because it is representative of the population of churches (or religious organizations) important to the research objectives, but rather because it was conveniently located on the student's route to and from school. Not knowing how this church relates to any other church in the population will impede attempts by any consumers of this research to apply this ethnography to other contexts, ultimately limiting the overall usefulness of the study.

When the ethnographer is not working with a purposive sample—a group of people intentionally selected due to some characteristic that is highly relevant to the purpose of the study—but has obtained some sort of listing(s) of the target population, systematic sampling is necessary for the resulting data to be credible. Take, for example, an ethnographic study that is investigating seatbelt usage in Scottsdale, Arizona. As part of this study, the researchers will directly observe drivers and passengers in various intersections of Scottsdale. For the series of observations that will be made for this particular study, the selection of the intersections and the times of the observations are very important so as to be representative of what actually is occurring in Scottsdale. This selection should be conducted in a thoughtful, systematic manner. A decision should be made first about choosing a geographically representative sample of intersections at which to observe autos passing by, and then a decision should be made regarding a day of the week and time of day or night for each intersection observation. A more robust study would select multiple days and times to observe at each intersection. And, an even more sophisticated and representative approach to this selection would be to use the findings of a recent traffic flow study to disproportionally stratify the intersection selection by the amount of vehicular traffic it experiences, with heavily traveled intersections having a greater chance of selection than lightly traveled ones. (Once the ethnographic part of this study is completed, IDIs and/or focus groups could be conducted with Scottsdale residents, asking them about their experiences in using, or not using, seatbelts when driving or riding in a car in Scottsdale.) This example of sampling illustrates that for certain ethnographic studies, systematic selection of what is being observed and when it will be observed is very important to the credibility of the research.

"Missing" observations can also negatively impact research quality in ethnographic research. From a TQF perspective, the failure to complete all observations as prescribed by the research design (or subsequently adjusted when in the field; see "Number of Observations," below) may weaken the credibility and the analyzability of the research. For all observer levels, with the possible exception of "complete participant" (when the researcher is immersed and participating in the observed activities on an ongoing basis), the ethnographer will need to determine (in collaboration with those being observed, as appropriate) the schedule for observation. The integrity of the research will be jeopardized when observations are missed due to scheduling changes or other reasons. If, among the set schedule of observations for the seatbelt research example in Arizona, mentioned above, observations are missing that are related to times when the behavior under study changes compared to the times when the scheduled observations are carried out, then bias will result in the data, which may seriously threaten the study's credibility. To avoid this, the researcher ideally should have more than one person trained to conduct the observations so that a substitute observer can fill in if the primary observer is not able to keep to the assigned schedule. In the event that it is not possible for another trained observer to help keep to the scheduled observations, the burden rests on the researcher to give careful consideration to whether the observations that were missed may have biased the data. If there is reason to suspect this could have happened, then the researcher should exercise additional caution when the results are analyzed so as to take into consideration the possible effects of such bias on the study's findings and final interpreted implications.

NUMBER OF OBSERVATIONS. Another important decision that ethnographic researchers need to make is the number of observations to conduct, or, more accurately, the number of:

- Sites to observe.
- People within sites to observe.
- Observational events (e.g., how often to revisit a particular site).

This question can be complex to address—a process of both art and science—or fairly straightforward. In the simplest case, the number of sites to observe and observation events will be dictated by the (1) breadth and depth of the research objectives, (2) breadth and depth of the target population, and/or (3) practical realities of the research (e.g., the accessibility of the target participants, financial resources, and time available to complete the study). If, for example, the research objective is to examine the implementation of new procedures at a county free clinic, the number of sites to observe is just one (the clinic) and the frequency of observations will be determined by such factors as the fluctuation in the patient load (i.e., the slow- and high-volume hours in the clinic) and level of procedural details the observer wants to capture. A more complex situation arises when the focus of the research is on a broad target population such as consumers. For instance, ethnographic research to study how consumers shop for vitamins would most likely require many observations of the same or different individuals within a variety of retail environments (e.g., supermarkets, drug stores, and superstores such as Target or Walmart). As a consumer researcher, Mariampolski (2006) recommends that the ethnographer observe no less than 15 sites; however, it is the expansiveness of the research objectives and target population, as well as practical matters, that may ultimately serve as the prime bases in the decision of how many sites to observe and how often.

In addition to the number of sites to observe, the ethnographer also wants to carefully consider how many individuals as well as the "type" of individuals who will be observed. As an example, is the observer interested in studying everyone on staff at the county free clinic (e.g., the receptionist, the nursing assistants, the nurses, and the physicians), or are the new procedures under investigation only pertinent to one aspect of the clinic, such as patient registration and check-in?

For all ethnographic research, the overriding "goal is to get at the meanings behind the acts" (Berg & Lune, 2012, p. 197) as they relate to the constructs under investigation. Not unlike the decision of how many IDIs are sufficient for a particular type of research study (see Chapter 3, pp. 73–75), an ethnographic researcher must consider the number of observations (site and individual) at both the design and fieldwork phase. Ultimately, the researcher wants "enough" observations to be confident that the range of variation in what is being studied has been captured by the observations; however, the number that is anticipated when developing the research design may need to be adjusted when in the field. If there is more variation than expected, the researcher will need to extend the number of observations; otherwise, the lack of additional observations may threaten the credibility of the study by missing something important in the behaviors of interest. A study concerning visitor attendance to the state park, for example, may need to expand the number of observations originally planned to include unexpected variations in behavior that occur during different weather conditions. In turn, if there proves to be less variation than expected— for instance, if park visitors behave very similarly regardless of weather, demographics, or other factors—the prudent researcher will want to make an explicit decision about whether or not to end the field period sooner than had been planned. The caveat should be added that, although the researcher's confidence in the variations of behaviors being observed is important, the decision to either extend or cut short the observations may also boil down to the practical or logistical realities of the study itself (e.g., safety concerns for a researcher observing in a high-crime area of the city, travel plans that cannot reasonably be changed, other types of ancillary research such as IDIs that are also being conducted for the study and whose timing cannot be changed, and meeting others' expectations to complete the research as planned).

Although there may not be an exact way to decide how many observations to conduct, a TQF approach guides (and compels) the researcher to explicitly address a number of questions while in the field to assess this issue. These questions are not unlike those posed for IDIs (see Chapter 3, Box 3.3, p. 75):

- How well have the observations provided insight on the constructs of interest?

- Is it clear to the observer what has been observed? What is the extent of the ambiguity?

- At what level can the observer explain or anticipate variations in the observations?

- Does the observer's reflexive journal reveal any biases or concerns with objectivity?

- Have the observations provided the necessary input to facilitate next steps (i.e., the ancillary methods such as IDIs)?

Gaining Cooperation

As in all qualitative research, gaining and maintaining cooperation with those being observed in an ethnographic study are critical to data quality. The level of cooperation the researcher can foster with his/her participants has a direct impact on the credibility, and ultimately the analyzability and usefulness, of ethnographic research. The importance of participant cooperation in an ethnographic study with overt observation is not just in the simple fact that it facilitates the ability to conduct observations, allowing the researcher to complete the research assignment, but in the fact that a high degree of cooperation preserves the representativeness of the study sample. The Credibility component of the TQF defines the Scope of the research not only by the representative coverage and sample design considerations discussed above, but also by the recruitment and retention of the sample representation throughout the course of the research. The credibility of ethnographic research that uses overt observations is undermined when cooperation is weak and the individuals or groups that *are* observed are somehow different in their behavior and/or attitudes compared to those who were chosen but end up not being observed. In this way, the analysis and final interpretations from an ethnographic study with overt observation may be biased. A diligent effort to obtain access to and cooperation of research participants who will be observed—*as well as maintain high levels of cooperation*—will go a long way to mitigate this threat of bias.

In the case of ethnographic research in which the observations are covert, there is no process whereby a researcher attempts to gain direct (explicit) cooperation from those who will be observed. Therefore, the issue of "missing" observations on those who decide not to cooperate—as well as the concern that their behavior would be materially different from those who did agree to participate, and thereby lead to biased data—is essentially moot. There is, however, a somewhat parallel concern in covert ethnographic research having to do with achieving secrecy in observing and the possibility of having to infiltrate the group being studied. To the extent that a covert observer does not carry out his/her role successfully, it could cause some of those being observed to be less likely to participate in the group or less likely to participate as "energetically" as they had been doing before the observer started observing. For example, some group members may simply not like a covert participant–observer (e.g., there may be a clash of personalities) even though they are unaware of what the observer is really doing in the group. This clash may cause them to participate less or cease their participation in the group altogether. It is thereby possible in covert observation for people to change their behavior and thereby bias the observational data being gathered.

Explicitly gaining access and cooperation in some ethnographic research principally rests on two functionaries: gatekeepers and key informants (see Box 5.1 for a summary of the roles each plays in gaining access and cooperation). **Gatekeepers** are typically people who hold some type of authority or control over the access to one or more other individuals. A gatekeeper may be a receptionist or administrative assistant in an office environment, the director at a primary care facility, a community leader, a school principal, a manager at a coffee shop (Waxman, 2006), a college dean (Magolda, 2000), or the owner of a website (Paechter, 2013). Because the gatekeeper has the power to give or deny access to the population of interest, the ethnographer is wise to develop a strong, positive relationship with any gatekeeper associated with the study participants. In contacting the gatekeeper, the researcher should introduce the purpose of the research as well as how the research will benefit the people or organization that the researcher is hoping to gain access to observe. For example, an ethnographer studying a community's homeless population might contact the manager of the local shelter for permission to observe its patrons, emphasizing that the final outcome of the research is expected to help improve services for the homeless in the community and larger city. The researcher may need to work hard to secure this researcher–gatekeeper relationship (and, therefore, access), including being willing to negotiate with a gatekeeper who may be skeptical and hesitant to cooperate with the researcher's request.

Ethnographers conducting participant observation also rely heavily on **key informants**. These are generally people who are associated and involved with the research participants (e.g., a nurse in the maternity ward, a member of the local Al-Anon support group, or a union member at the manufacturing plant), and act as the ethnographer's advisors and supporters throughout the study. Key informants

---

BOX 5.1. Gaining Access and Cooperation: Gatekeepers and Key Informants

GATEKEEPERS

- Control access or otherwise have authority to permit/deny access to the people the ethnographer wants to study (e.g., director at a facility, school principal, an administrative assistant in a corporate office, parents of young children).
- Require a special effort by the researcher to establish a strong, positive relationship.
- Need to be convinced of the importance of the research and how it will benefit those being studied and/or the organization.
- Need to be assured of the researcher's identity, legitimacy of the study, and safety of the participants (i.e., no harm will come to those being observed).
- Require the researcher's negotiating (bargaining) skills in order to persuade gatekeepers who are skeptical or hesitant to cooperate by way of providing access.
- May bring special challenges in keeping secret a covert research study.

KEY INFORMANTS

- Are associated or involved with the research participants (e.g., a nurse in a maternity ward, a member of a support group or union).
- Need to be assured of the researcher's identity, legitimacy of the study, and safety of the participants (i.e., no harm will come to the research participants).
- Advise and support the researcher throughout the study.
- Develop a close, trusting relationship with the researcher that may lead to a true, long-term friendship.
- May collaborate with the researcher on the analysis and reporting of research outcomes.
- May be particularly useful when conducting covert research.

---

are invaluable, and the researcher must make a concerted effort to develop a trusting relationship. Unlike gatekeepers, who may or may not fade from significance once access is given, the ethnographer's relationship with key informants may extend over a lengthy period of time and culminate in true friendships, not uncommonly resulting in researcher–informant collaboration on the analysis and actual write-up of the research. Because of their intimate association with study participants, key informants need to be assured of the researcher's identity, the legitimacy of the research endeavor, and that the research will not result in any harm or otherwise negatively affect the participants.

Key informants can be particularly useful in covert observation and/or studies with deviant populations or subcultures. Adler (1990) and her husband depended heavily on key informants in their 6-year participant–observer ethnographic study of the drug trafficking trade. Their informants not only advised them on approaching the group of drug dealers being observed, but also supported them when altercations erupted during observation and widened their set of contacts by letting them know "when someone we might be interested in was planning on dropping by, vouching for our reliability as friends who could be included in business conversations" (p. 102). This example illustrates many critical functions of key informants and the important role they play in gaining and maintaining participant cooperation. Regardless of whether the ethnography is overt or covert, key informants facilitate:

- The introduction to participants and other relevant individuals.
- The participants' trust by assuring them of the ethnographer's credentials, integrity, and legitimacy of the research effort (in overt observation).
- The cooperation among participants with words of encouragement and reasons why they should participate (in overt observation).
- The rapport between the ethnographer and participants by helping the participant–observer understand the group experience, and advising him/ her on how to deal with particular situations.
- The covert nature of the observations (i.e., maintaining the observer's cover).

In the case of a covert style of observing, the researcher must think carefully about how the covert nature extends to the gatekeepers and key informants. In essentially all cases, the researcher will benefit from (i.e., gaining access and cooperation will be easier) disclosing to the gatekeepers and key informants that he/she is doing observational research. When the researcher does this, an additional challenge is faced: The researcher must convince the gatekeepers and key informants his/her need to conduct covert observations and, in so doing, the gatekeepers and key informants must agree to keep the researcher's cover secret. The success of these negotiations will depend on the degree to which the gatekeepers or key informants are convinced of the importance of the research as well as the researcher's ability to establish rapport. Of course, by disclosing this information to people outside the research team (i.e., the key informants and gatekeepers), the researcher is taking a risky step because the possible inability of the key informants or the gatekeepers to maintain secrecy may well undermine the entire ethnographic study.

Data Gathering

In addition to Scope, Data Gathering is the other broad area of the Credibility component that affects ethnographic research. There are three primary aspects concerning the gathering of data in ethnography that require serious consideration by the researcher in the development of the study design. To optimize the measurement of ethnographic data, and hence the quality of the outcomes, researchers must pay attention to:

- How well the observers have identified and recorded all the information (e.g., verbal and nonverbal behavior, attitudes, context, sensory cues) pertinent to the research objectives and constructs of interest.

- **Observer effects**, specifically—

  - *Observer bias*, that is, behavioral and other characteristics (e.g., personal attitudes, values, traits) of the observer that may alter the observed event or bias his/her observations. For example, an observer as a complete participant would bias the observational data if there was an attempt to "educate" participants on a subject matter for which he/she had personal expertise or knowledge.

  - *Observer inconsistency*, that is, an inconsistent manner in which the observer conducts the observations that creates unwarranted and unrepresentative variation in the data. For example, an on-site nonparticipant observer conducting in-home observations of the use of media and technology would be introducing inaccuracies in the data by observing and recording the use of television and gaming in some households but not in others where television and gaming activities took place.

- **Participant effects**, specifically, the extent to which observed participants alter a naturally occurring event, leading to biased outcomes. This is often called the **Hawthorne effect,** whereby the people being observed, either consciously or unconsciously, change what is being measured in the observation because they are aware of the observer. For example, an ethnographer conducting an overt, on-site passive observation of teaching practices in a school district would come away with bad data if one or more school teachers deviated from their usual teaching styles during the observations in order to more closely conform with district policies.

Capturing Relevant Observations

An obvious yet paramount concern in the area of data gathering in ethnographic research revolves around the researcher's ability to capture all the aspects of an observed activity that are relevant to the objectives and constructs of interest. Relevant observations should be well defined prior to fieldwork and continually refined, as necessary, during the course of observations. Not unlike the development of an IDI or discussion guide, the ethnographer seeks to identify those observable events—including the specific individuals (or types of individuals), the verbal and nonverbal behaviors, attitudes, sensory and other environmental cues—that will further the researcher's understanding of the issues. Isolating the observations of interest in the design development phase can be achieved by:

- Looking at earlier ethnographic research on the subject matter and/or with similar study populations.

- Interviewing the clients or those who have requested the research to learn everything they know about the topic and their past work in the area.

- Consulting the literature or other experts concerning the behaviors and other occurrences associated with particular constructs.

- "Shagging around" (LeCompte & Goetz, 1982) the observation site(s) to casually assess the environment and begin to learn about the participants.

For instance, a researcher conducting an observational study of travelers at a major airport might visit the airport two or three times before the onset of the fieldwork to consider various physical spaces as potential venues for observation, map out the observation venues to contemplate traffic flow, and get a feel for what goes on within the observation venues (e.g., the types of travelers, behaviors, and contextual factors related to the research objectives).

OBSERVATION GUIDE. After the relevant observations have been identified and agreed to by the research team, the ethnographer can begin developing the **observation guide**. Similar to the content guides utilized by interviewers and moderators, the observation guide is an outline of the most pertinent observational components along with questions or issues related to each component. This guide serves two important functions: (1) It reminds the observer of the key points of observation as well as the topic of interest associated with each, and (2) it acts as the impetus for a reflexive exercise in which the observer can reflect on his/her own relationship and contribution to the observed at any moment in time. For example, the observation guide for the Cramer, Shaw, Wye, and Weiss (2010) study of consumers seeking pharmacists' advice on over-the-counter medications covered such areas as the physical environment, daily routines and customer traffic, interactions between staff and customers, and "researcher reflexivity" (e.g., how the observer was affected by the observations). An observation guide should be developed for all ethnographic research regardless of the observer's role. Nonparticipant and passive participant observers will have no problem in referring to the guide, as needed, during their observations, whereas participant–observers and complete participants (especially in covert research) will need to consult the guide and make notations at a scheduled time subsequent to the observation period.

As an adjunct to the observation guide, it is recommended that researchers involved in ethnographic research also utilize an **observation grid**. The grid is similar to the guide in that it helps to remind the observer of the events and issues of most import; however, the observation grid is a spreadsheet or log of sorts that enables the observer to actually record and reflect on observable events *in relationship to the research constructs of interest*. The constructs or issues should be broadly defined so as to not discourage the observer from taking in all observable events in an unrestricted manner. This grid might show, for instance, the relevant constructs or research issues across the top (as the column headings) and the specific foci of observation along the side (as the row headings). Using the airport study mentioned above as an example, the three key research issues related to activity at the gate might be "waiting" for departures, "delays" in departures, and "boarding" the plane, which are used as the column headings, with the various areas of observation (e.g., behavior, conversations heard, contextual information such as the fact that there is a rainstorm outside, overall mood) as the row headings (see Figure 5.2). This grid gives the observer a convenient way to make sure that the principal issues as well as other important components of the observations (e.g., ancillary information such as the weather) have been recorded. By using this grid (either during or immediately following observation), the observer is not only enhancing the quality of the data gathered (and therefore its credibility) but also facilitating the analytical process by way of organizing the outcomes from observational events by research issue or construct.

Observer Effects

In qualitative research, the researcher—including the IDI interviewer, focus group moderator, coder in content analysis, and observer—is the instrument, meaning that the qualitative researcher wields substantial control in the design content, the outcomes, and interpretation of the research. Ethnography is no different in that the observer—albeit, not controlling participants' natural environment—plays a central role in creating the data for the study by way of recording observations. In this respect, the credibility of an ethnographic study as it pertains to measurement issues essentially rests on the observer's ability to identify and record the relevant observations. Section 5.1 (see pp. 179–181) discusses three broad areas associated with observer skills: operational aspects, the observer's personal traits, and the observer's sensibilities in studying participants and the context/environment. The observer's personal characteristics and sensibilities are particularly significant to the potential problems in measurement associated with observer effects, that is, observer bias and inconsistencies.

In combination with the skills discussed earlier and below, the observer's impact on data quality will be determined in part by his/her natural abilities. The appropriate natural skills that an observer brings to an ethnographic study will vary from study to study and from observer to observer. But there is one personal characteristic that is especially valuable to all who act as observers in ethnographic research, whether they are doing so as nonparticipants or participants in the events being studied. This characteristic is being "people smart"; that is, possessing the ability to quickly and accurately understand (sense) the *latent motivations* and meanings that underlie the *manifest behaviors* that other people display and that are to be (and can be) directly observed. Although observer training is always of the utmost importance in ethnographic research, some researchers are naturally skilled in relating to participants and absorbing all the elements of

Site location: | **Date:** | **Start time:** | **Stop time:**

Research Issue

Area of Observation	Waiting	Delays	Boarding
Behavior (What? By whom? Where?)			
Conversation (What? By whom? Where?)			
Context (What else is going on? What is the weather? Is it a holiday?)			

Type of traveler (alone, families, business companions)		
General mood (What? How conveyed? By whom?)		
Other areas of observation:		
Reflexive comments:		

FIGURE 5.2. Observation grid: Airport travelers example.

an observable event (i.e., the individuals involved, the context, and other factors impinging on the environment), coming away with a realistic understanding of what is going on beyond what participants simply say and do. This natural ability is especially helpful to mastering the skill of dual perspective (see p. 180) by which observers internalize the participants' viewpoints while maintaining objectivity. The researcher should pay particular attention to individuals undergoing observer training who may have less of this natural ability than others and are in need of more extensive tutoring in such areas as thoughtful listening and nuanced observation (i.e., picking up on slight, nonverbal behavior such as body language), and provide more opportunities for role playing along with independent assessments of their observations.

The potential observer effects of bias and inconsistency (discussed below) can be mitigated not only by the observer's ability to relate to the participants and the situation but also by the skills required of all qualitative researchers: the ability to attend to details and organize various aspects of the research. The challenges of generating credible data with the measurements taken in ethnography are very complex, and the ability to attend to many things simultaneously and keeping those multiple happenings well organized contributes to high-quality data collection and credible outcomes.

Lessons learned from prior experience in ethnography may improve someone's skills in conducting high-quality ethnographic studies—ones in which the data are credible. But typically this is a very slow process toward improvement. Nevertheless, it is likely the most effective way, in the long run, to gain skill as an ethnographer. Anyone who seeks to make ethnography a principal method for their research is well-advised to serve one or more "apprenticeships" with more experienced ethnographers and to commit themselves to a lifetime of self-evaluation and improvement in conducting ethnographic research.

OBSERVER BIAS. Without the proper skills, an observer has the potential of biasing the data, which in turn will negatively impact the analysis, interpretation, transferability, and ultimate usefulness of an ethnographic study. The potential for bias exists regardless of observer role. An off-site, nonparticipant observer may knowingly or not impose subjective values on an observed event—for example, ignoring certain comments the observer finds personally offensive in a study of an online forum discussing alcohol use—and an on-site observer, operating either overtly or covertly, may bias results by way of personal characteristics (e.g., age or racial identity) and/or inappropriate behavior (e.g., personal commentary during the observed event). For example, an on-site passive observer who makes a point of greeting patients as they arrive for their doctor appointments would be interfering with the normal procedures for patient registration at the clinic and thereby jeopardizing the credibility of the data.

The effects of possible observer bias should be anticipated and controlled for by the integration of certain quality features in the design of ethnographic research. These features are detailed below and summarized in Box 5.2.

> **BOX 5.2. Quality Features to Mitigate Possible Observer Bias**
>
> - Match on-site observers with study participants.
> - Observers must be trained to play the dual role of "insider" and "outsider."
> - Continually monitor observers' objectivity.
> - Adequate training in "acting" skills and the "art of deception" are important, particularly in covert observation.
> - Observers must engage in constant and detailed self-evaluation.

- Onsite observers should be "matched" to the study participants to the extent warranted by the study environment and objectives. In most instances, observers who are similar in age and other demographic characteristics will be less obtrusive and more likely to gain rapport with participants.

- As discussed on page 180, observers must learn to play a dual role as both "insider"—observing events from the participants' perspective—and "outsider"—observing events with an objective, value-free frame of mind. This is a critical skill; if the observer were to learn only one skill in training, this is the skill on which to focus. A dual perspective bolsters the credibility of the data because it fosters honest accounts of the observed events as the observer internalizes participants' meaning, while, at the same time, minimizing the possibility of observer bias by holding an objective, nonjudgmental perspective.

- Objectivity is paramount in all research, but particularly in ethnography, where the researcher/observer may spend an extraordinary amount of time in the field and, depending on the observer role, operate among the participants. For this reason, an ethnographic study needs to be continually monitored and controlled for the possibility of inappropriate value judgments and other groundless interjections in the data by observers.

- Participant observation requires a certain amount of "acting" from the observers. The ability to step outside oneself to take on and maintain a different persona while "in character" as a participant in ethnographic observations is an important skill. The abilities to "blend in" and "not make waves" help minimize observers' effects on the behaviors and events they are observing. In this way, observers are less likely to bias (i.e., change in a distorting way) what they are trying to observe objectively.

An observer's acting skills are particularly important in covert participant observations where the observer is concealing his/her identity from the participants. Covert participation also requires an observer who is comfortable with the idea of deception. Covert observation may cause considerable tension for many people, which may manifest itself in ways that cause observers to behave awkwardly (including a compulsion to confess their true identity), distorting the behaviors and other aspects of the observed event. To minimize observer bias in these situations, the researcher must select observers who are completely accepting of the covert role while engaging with participants so as to not negatively affect the credibility of the data they gather for their study.

• It is the responsibility of the observer to engage in constant and detailed self-evaluation, such as maintaining a reflexive journal, about how he/she may have changed the outcomes being observed. This self-evaluation becomes a critical tool in formulating (and tempering) conclusions about the study and thereby enhancing the credibility of the study through disclosure of this self-critique process. An example of a reflexive journal format is shown in Chapter 2, Figure 2.2, page 42.

OBSERVER INCONSISTENCY. To safeguard the credibility of the data generated from ethnographic research, it is important that the observer conduct observations in a consistent manner. Whether as a nonparticipant or participant, overt or covert, the observer must be trained to understand why consistency matters and how inconsistency may result in unacceptable levels of unwarranted variation in the data. Maintaining consistency can present a particular challenge in ethnography, where the unpredictability of naturally occurring events can make it difficult to maintain constant focus on the key variables related to the research objectives. Although the participants and the specific activities themselves will change from observation site to observation site, it is critical to the quality of measurement that for each observation, the observer concentrates on identifying and recording the behaviors, conversations, contextual factors, and the like pertaining to the priority areas of observation (determined in the research design phase) and constructs of interest. If, in the earlier example of airport travelers, the observer focused attention at one site on only passengers waiting to board their flight to the exclusion of observations related to passenger delays and the actual boarding process, while at another site fixating on just the boarding process, the resulting data would be distorted and of poor quality. In this example, the researcher would need to review the observer's field notes and most likely retrain or even replace the observer (and discard these observations).

Although the ever-changing, unpredictable nature of ethnography—and its ability to challenge the observer's attention to key variables—is a leading cause of inconsistent data collection, the quality of an observer's observation may also vary due to inadequate training or personal reasons such as sickness, exhaustion due to lack of sleep, or a mental preoccupation with personal problems unrelated to work. Regardless of the cause, the ethnographer should strive for consistency across all observations by making sure that observers understand and are trained on the following:

• Research objectives, including background information on the topic and how the results of the research will be used.

• Specific areas of observation that are prioritized, including the rationale for their priority status.

- Specific constructs or issues that are prioritized, including the rationale for their priority status.

- Observation grid, including how it is designed to be used (as both a recording and a reflexive device), how to complete the grid, and how to add important but unanticipated observational components to the grid.

- Types of observation sites the observer will be working in and how identifying the particular observations of interest may be difficult in some instances—for example, an observation site in the airport study example (mentioned above) may be very small and congested—requiring the observer to work rigorously to stay alert and, in addition to taking in the scene as a whole, be ever mindful of the observations related to waiting, delays, and boarding.

- Ways to deal with stress and fatigue on the job.

Participant Effects: Effects Caused by Those Being Observed

Unlike qualitative methods such as IDIs and group discussions (when problems in the data may arise when participants do not respond to the interviewer's or moderator's questions), the persons who are being observed and behaving naturally in an ethnographic study are generally not a source of threat to the credibility of the information that is gathered. However, there is a circumstance when participants may constitute a major threat to the credibility of an ethnographic study: if the participants are too aware that they are being observed and, unconsciously or consciously, alter their behaviors because of this knowledge. As discussed earlier (see p. 205), this reaction to the observer's presence is often referred to as the "Hawthorne effect." In altering their behavior, participants may change the observed event to the extent that the observer's data is no longer a credible (valid) representation of what actually would have occurred had the participants not been aware that they were being studied. Regardless of whether the observations are conducted on- or off-site (face-to-face or on the Internet), participants' knowledge that they are the object of observations by an "outsider" may change their behavior in ways that negatively alter the credibility of the data that are gathered.

To guard against undue participant effects, the observer must remain vigilant for indications that this is happening: for example, people tending to stop conversations when the observer comes near them, other signs of reluctance or discomfort interacting with the observer, and discrepant/inconsistent information coming from the same members of the group being studied. Even if the observer is vigilant, it is best to debrief the participants after the field period of observations to learn the extent to which they may have been behaving differently because they sensed they were being observed for the research study. If a researcher learns that this was the case, it is incumbent upon him/her to take this knowledge into account when drawing conclusions about what was learned from the data and to disclose these participant effects (and the potential implications of these effects) when reporting the study's findings.

In ethnographic studies that deploy covert observation, there should be (in theory) no effects due to those who are being observed. But, of course, in practice, this may not always be the case. That is, even though an observer may be conducting secret observations, the observer may nevertheless cause those being observed to suspect that "something just isn't right" with the behavior of the secret observer and thereby change their behaviors. This is why, as discussed earlier, a postobservation debriefing is so important in covert observation. In addition to ethical reasons (e.g., to determine if any inadvertent harm was done to anyone secretly observed), it is important to conduct a debriefing with those observed to ascertain whether the observer's "cover was blown" and, if so, how that may have altered the behaviors or other activities that were observed, distorting the data that were gathered. If the identity of the secret observer is discovered by participants during the study field period, the challenges the researcher may face to overcome this deception-in-the-name-of-research may be so severe as to entirely undermine the credibility of the data that would be collected if the researcher were to try to continue the study beyond this point.

Analyzability

Analyzability is the component of the TQF that is concerned with the Processing and Verification of the research data. The purpose of the Analyzability component is to guide the researcher toward a complete and accurate analysis of the data, from which he/she derives valid and meaningful interpretations of the outcomes. As in all qualitative research, the quality standards defined for Analyzability—in conjunction with that for Credibility and Transparency—empower the ethnographer to ultimately produce research that advances new theories, proposes next steps, and/or can be applied in other contexts; that is, it furthers the researcher's ability to provide ethnographic research that is useful. We focus our attention on the processing and verification of observational data, as the principal method in ethnography.

Processing

There are five primary data sources in ethnographic research: (1) field notes, (2) observation grid, (3) audio and/or video recordings, (4) photographs/images, and (5) Internet-based data, such as text, recordings, and images (e.g., photographs, avatars, screen shots) obtained by way of online ethnography. A sixth data source—the observer's reflexive journal—is another important data document; however, this journal need not be processed as are the other sources (i.e., subject to transcription and content analysis) but is more of a personal diary to which the observer can refer throughout the data-gathering and the analytical phases of the research.

Not unlike the data from IDIs and group discussions, the observer's field notes and the observation grid need to be transcribed. However, unlike IDIs and focus groups, it is strongly recommended that the observer—*not a transcriptionist or other person*—do the transcribing. It is further recommended that the transcription be made *as soon after the completion of an observation as possible* to take advantage of the observer's sharp memories of recent events. Although it may be necessary, due to practical reasons (e.g., the timeframe in which the research report is due), to hire a transcriptionist or other person to transcribe the field notes and grid, it is discouraged. The observer is the person with intimate knowledge of what happened during the observation, and he/she is the person who can most accurately decipher for transcription the notations made in the field notes and observation grid. This transcription process may also offer the observer an opportunity to reflect more fully on the observations and add, as warranted, relevant comments to the field notes and/or observation grid. For similar reasons, the observer should be directly involved in recording (via text or audio) the meanings associated with any photographs or other images captured during the observed event (e.g., an observer studying gang violence may have taken a photograph of street gangs congregating at the observation site to illustrate how close or distant gang members keep from each other). At the very least, the observer needs to brief the principal ethnographer on the research team and explain where the images came from, how they fit in with the observed activities, and why they are meaningful to the research goals.

Audio and/or video recordings of the activities that were observed will also need to be transcribed and, depending on the quality of these recordings (i.e., the sound and visual clarity), the transcription can be done by either the observer or another qualified person. The qualifications for a transcriber, other than the observer, are not unlike those discussed in Chapter 3 (see pp. 90–91), including having knowledge of and experience in the research topic, and sensibilities regarding language and discourse. If the recordings are few or short in duration, transcriptions may not be necessary. In this case, the researcher can simply listen or view the recordings one or more times and, in the process, take new or additional notes to extract meaning. Even for rather long recordings—that is, when a recording has been made of an entire observation period—the researcher may elect to listen or view the recording in its entirety without note taking in order to first formulate a "big picture" assessment of the main themes that were displayed by the observed individuals. Once this broad perspective is formulated, the researcher will benefit by going back through the recording and thinking about the details of the observation from the vantage point of the bigger picture. In this way the researcher can identify the best details that illustrate and help flesh out the big picture, as well as the important details that are at odds with the big picture and how to handle these contrary findings.

Ethnography in the online context can potentially generate a great deal of textual, audio, visual, and graphical data. The textual data may not need to be transcribed; however, the other data forms will need to undergo very similar transformation as that produced in the off-line mode.

The general steps related to the processing of ethnographic data are as follows:

Soon after Each Observation Event

• Nonparticipant or passive participant observers should review and edit the field notes and observation grid.

• Participant–observers or complete participant observers should record field notes and complete the observation grid.

• All observers should reflect on the observation and annotate the field notes and grid accordingly, for example, adding noteworthy quotes, personal thoughts on the experience, thoughts on common threads, or points of difference compared to earlier observations.

• Observers should create a site folder that brings together and organizes all data types for that site; for example, field notes, completed observation grid, recordings, photographs/images, a spreadsheet tallying frequency counts of certain activities, a site map or drawings that were made by the observer, and the observer's entry from the reflexive journal (which may be separate from the reflexive comments made on the observation grid) for that site.

After Every Two or Three Observation Sites

• Observers should meet with the principal ethnographer and other members of the research team for a debriefing to review the observations conducted thus far in terms of observed activities, what has been learned and insights gained (or lack thereof), whether the observer needs to revisit an observation site (if practicable) to broaden or deepen understanding, and any changes that may be needed in the research design to better address the research objectives (e.g., with the observation guide or grid).

After All Notes and Recordings Have Been Transcribed

• A content analysis (see Chapter 6) should be conducted in order to organize, categorize, code, and identify meaningful patterns or themes in the data. To increase the reliability and validity of the process, it is recommended that at least two researchers independently conduct the analysis. This multiple-analyst approach, however, may be impossible for some ethnographic studies, especially those that are participant–observer in nature. In those cases, unless there is more than one participant–observer or complete participant observer involved in gathering the data for the study, only the one who actively participated can have the unique in-depth understanding that "living the experience" of the group being studied makes possible. In such cases, that unique experience and the insights it brings to understanding the data cannot be replicated by someone else who has not "been there and done that." Therefore, replication of the analyses of the ethnographic data by another independent person makes no sense in such instances. However, in ethnographic studies where there is more than one observer with comparable involvement with the study, it is strongly recommended that the analyses, at least initially, be carried out separately by at least two of those persons for the sake of cross-checking the sense-making processes that will extract meaning from the data. Furthermore, being able to report in the final research document that this cross-checking was done at the start of the analysis phase of an ethnographic study will bolster the confidence that consumers of the research can (and should) place on the findings and recommendations.

For a study that includes many observation sites and separate observations of one or more people over an extended period of time—such as Rowe and Wolch's (1990) ethnographic study of homeless women in Los Angeles, which focused on five sites over a 2-year period—the researcher will need to allow for a long period of time to engage in theme building and other sense making. This process could take several weeks or months to complete, depending in part on the volume of ethnographic information that must be processed and reviewed, and the complexity of the behaviors that are being studied.

The researchers assigned to the processing of ethnographic data should be carefully considered in order to achieve reliable and valid outcomes. Similar to the qualities discussed for group discussions (see Chapter 4, p. 154), the people (observers and other researchers) involved with the processing of ethnographic data (a) should be knowledgeable in the topic and study objectives, (b) should have participated directly as a participant–observer or complete participant (when applicable), (c) should possess sufficient "people smarts" to make them sensitive to assessing manifest as well as latent content, and (d) should be extremely organized, consistent, and comprehensive in the extraction of meaning from the data.

Verification

The other critical element in the TQF Analyzability component in ethnographic research is Verification. It is by taking specific steps to corroborate the collected data that the researcher has helped to maximize research quality. The verification tools at the ethnographer's disposal go beyond those identified for the IDI and group discussion methods (see Chapters 3 and 4) in that they include expanded observation. For example, Lincoln and Guba (1985) stated that it is "more likely that credible findings and interpretations" will come from ethnographic data with "prolonged engagement" in the field and "persistent observation" (p. 301). The former refers to spending adequate time at an observation site to experience the breadth of stimuli and activities relevant to the research, and the purpose of the latter (i.e., persistent observation) is "to identify those characteristics and elements in the situation that are most relevant to the problem or issue" (p. 304)—that is, to provide a depth of understanding of the "salient factors." Both prolonged engagement and persistent observation speak to the idea of expanding observation in terms of time as well as diligence in exploring variables as they emerge in the observation. Although expanding observations in this way may be unrealistic due to the realities of deadlines and research funding, it is an important verification approach unique to ethnography. When practicable, it is recommended that researchers maximize the time allotted for observation and train observers to look for the unexpected or examine more closely seemingly minor occurrences or variables that may ultimately verify (or contradict) the observer's dominant understanding.

The ultimate usefulness of expanded observation in verification is not unlike deviant or negative case analysis discussed in earlier chapters. In both instances, the goal is to identify and investigate observational events (or particular variables in these events) that defy explanation or otherwise contradict the general patterns or themes that appear to be emerging from the data. For example, a researcher conducting in-home observations of young mothers may find that infants are typically put back in the crib when they begin to cry, which seems to be a routine behavior among the mothers observed. The observer may come to the assumption that mothers equate crying with fatigue and place their infants in the crib so they can rest. But observations of mothers who do not respond to their crying infants yet put them to bed at similar times of the day may give the observer a different point of view and lead him/her to explore other factors, such as, the mother's fatigue and need to be away from the baby. It is this ability to always question assumptions and look for factors that disprove these assumptions that enhance the quality and ultimate usefulness of ethnographic research.

As in all qualitative research, triangulation is an important procedure for verifying ethnographic data. The purpose of triangulation, similar to deviant case analysis, is to integrate other ways of looking at the data into the analysis. One example is researcher triangulation, which might include collaborating with other members of the research team in the data collection and processing phases (discussed above), or asking someone on the research team to review transcripts or the observer's reflexive journal to give his/her own assessment. As with deviant case analysis, any differences that may surface between the researcher's and the colleague's interpretations should be treated as an opportunity to learn more about the underlying meanings from the observations.

The most frequently used form of triangulation in ethnography is built right into the approach. Although observation is the primary method in ethnography, other methods (typically IDIs) are part and parcel of an ethnographic study. It is by way of method triangulation that ethnographers are able to gain a richer, more nuanced understanding of the research outcomes than would be possible from using any one method by itself. In this way, one method informs the other, which together informs the final interpretations and implications. The most common method used in ethnography other than observation is, by far, interviews. These interviews are often in-depth (i.e., IDIs); however, ethnographers will frequently conduct casual or informal interviews during the course of observation, such as the informal interviews Griffiths (2011) conducted with patrons at the gambling venues. This more casual form of interviewing may be necessary particularly in covert participation observation, when the observer does not want to reveal his/

her identity and therefore chooses to casually engage in everyday types of conversation with one or more of the people being observed.

Another triangulation-like consideration is offered by Dicks, Soyinka, and Coffey (2006), who discuss the variation of meanings in ethnographic research derived from different media. The idea is that the meaning of an observed event is transformed by the different modes of capturing the data. So, for instance, the researcher needs to consider what meaning in the data is lost or gained by listening to the spoken word in an audio recording compared to reading the written word in text. This "media triangulation" becomes particularly complex in an online context, where hyperlinking makes it nearly impossible to decipher the participant's experience. For example, as Dicks et al. state, "How does a piece of video film change when linked to a piece of written text? And what kind of reading or interpretation is produced by that linkage when the reader can pursue an almost infinite number of traversals and linkages of his/her own?" (p. 94).

Transparency

The Transparency component in the TQF brings together the Credibility and Analyzability parts of the framework to give the reader of the final document a complete and thick account of every design, decision, and executional aspect of an ethnographic study. It is by way of this full disclosure that the user of the research has sufficient information to draw similar conclusions from the data as presented and/or transfer the study design to other comparable ethnographic contexts (e.g., applying many of the data-gathering and analysis features in a study to observe operations in an automobile assembly plant to design research investigating assembly plants in other industries, or adapting an online ethnographic study of the survivalists subculture to study another cultural subgroup active in the virtual environment).

In earlier chapters, "thick description" was defined strictly in terms of detailed descriptions of each aspect of the research process. Among ethnographers, the term "thick description" pertains primarily to the detailed portrait of the cultural or social "scene" that the observer takes away from an observation site. It is these detailed accounts that are at the center of what it means to conduct ethnographic research. For this reason, Geertz (2003) asserts that "ethnography *is* thick description" (p. 156, emphasis added), given the "multiplicity of complex conceptual structures" (p. 150) the ethnographer must identify and find meaning from. For the ethnographer to "bring us into touch with the lives of strangers" (p. 156) requires the utmost in detailed thick descriptions. In this sense, conducting ethnographic research *is* thick description.

The final research document for an ethnographic study should satisfy the need for thick description across, as well as within, each step of the research process. To achieve this transparency and give users what they need to evaluate the strengths and limitations of the study, the ethnographer should include the following details in the research report:

THICK DESCRIPTION DETAILS FOR ETHNOGRAPHY

▓ Research objectives, hypotheses, and constructs under investigation and why ethnography was considered the best approach.

▓ Target population.

▓ Sampling, especially how the appropriate number of individuals or groups to observe was determined and the process for selecting the individuals who were observed, including a discussion of purposive sampling (if applicable).

▓ Individuals or group(s) that were chosen for the study, those who actually participated, and their representativeness of the target population.

▓ Rationale for choosing the particular level of observation (e.g., level of nonparticipant or participant-observer role status) and mode (e.g., conventional or online).

▓ Choice of overt or covert observation.

▓ Observation sites (e.g., public or private, location, characteristics of the physical space or online environment).

▓ Number of scheduled observations and the rationale.

▓ Status of the scheduled observations (e.g., which/how many were actually completed, specific actions that were taken to gain cooperation, reasons why not all observations were completed and the possible biases or weaknesses any omissions may have caused).

▓ Ethical considerations, including the provisions for informed consent, the IRB, participant debriefing (if applicable), and justification for covert observation (if applicable).

▓ Ancillary methods that were used in addition to observation (e.g., why these other methods were chosen and not others, how they added new insight).

▓ Decisions that were made while the research was in the field that modified the original research objectives or design elements. For example, expanding the number and duration of the observations because it was found that more variation in behaviors was observed than had been anticipated. An example of a very clear account of fieldwork activity in an ethnographic study is presented in Box 5.3.

▓ Observer training and specific skills training associated with mitigating observer effects.

▓ Role gatekeepers and key informants played, if any, in the completion of observations, including the relationships between observers and informants and any friendships that emerged.

▓ Observers' reflexive journals, including examples of journal entries (and comments from the observation grid) specific to their self-identified behaviors (verbal and nonverbal) or thoughts/attitudes during observations that may have biased the recorded data.

▓ Activities that may have occurred in one or more observations that were unanticipated (e.g., participants' discovery of a covert observer's identity).

> ### BOX 5.3. Transparency:
> ### Example of Ethnographic Fieldwork Description
>
> Small, Kerr, Charette, Schechter, and Spittal (2006) report on a participant–observation study that was conducted to complement a broader study concerning the impact of enforcement on illicit drug-use-related behavior. Their description of what went on in the field is a good example of giving the reader a clear understanding of the field activity:
>
> > Trained observers spent time "hanging out" in and around locales where drug sales and injecting took place, talking to and interacting with drug users. Discussions, occurrences, and observations were documented in fieldnotes. Observational data recorded in extensive fieldnotes included: location and character of public injection venues; syringe acquisition, availability, and disposal; public drug consumption patterns for injection and noninjection drugs; and description of public drug users. . . . Each observational field visit incorporated two hours of participant–observation conducted in streets and alleys as well as time spent writing fieldnotes to document observations and discussions. A target area and schedule of observations was devised, drawing on previous ethnographic research examining needle exchange practices. . . . The observations targeted both street-side and in the alleyways along 10 blocks of Hastings Street, where numerous clusters of drug market and consumption activity were identified by ethnographic mapping techniques. . . . Observations were distributed between morning, afternoon, and evening hours, with an increased number of observations occurring around monthly welfare payments when public drug scene and police activity increases. As some drug market and using locales shifted and new ones emerged, ethnographic data collection activities were altered accordingly to survey the largest portion of the open drug using scene, including areas far outside the central Hastings corridor. (pp. 86–87)

■ Expanded observations that were used as measures of verification (e.g., which/how many sites were subject to expanded observations, what the extended duration at these sites added to the final outcomes).

■ Operational logistics that were used for the observations, including the type and fidelity of any recordings that were made and the observer's use of mapping and the observation grid.

■ Particular steps that were taken for an Internet-based ethnography (e.g., use of emoticons and other devices to build rapport, involvement with participants off- and online, analysis techniques).

■ Members of the research team (e.g., how many were on the team and the roles they played) directly involved in the observations and analysis, including specific discussion of the observers' involvement with analysis and interpretations.

■ Transcription processes (if used).

■ Coding procedures, including the documents that were used in coding (e.g., field notes, observation grid), and justification for particular response categories.

■ Thematic and pattern-building process in analysis.

■ Specific verification efforts utilized beyond expanded observations (e.g., multiple methods, deviant case analysis).

■ Observed events and related evidence (e.g., journal entries) that exemplify the researcher's final interpretations and implications from the data.

Usefulness

An ethnographic study is only as good as it is useful to the people who will actually apply the research (a) to move the sponsoring client forward on a particular issue by way of actionable next steps; (b) to support or reject standing hypotheses or to generate new hypotheses; or (c) to enable other researchers to address new research problems in comparable contexts. Usefulness is the lynchpin of the TQF, as it is of ethnography and all research, yet reaching the goal of "useful" research depends entirely on the framework's other three components—Credibility, Analyzability, and Transparency. The final outcome of an ethnographic study is ultimately useful when all the necessary steps have been taken (1) to represent the target population and implement reliable and valid measures that serve, for example, to mitigate observer and participant effects (Credibility); (2) to completely and accurately process the data sources as well as verify the data by way, for example, of multiple researchers and methods (Analyzability); and (3) to fully document the life of the study, including the decision making, by addressing the details outlined above in the final report (Transparency). In this way, the ethnographer has not only justified the final interpretations and implications from the data but also provided the support required to ultimately deem the research useful.

A TQF approach to ethnographic research is intended to heighten quality standards and give the users of the research (i.e., the sponsors and other ethnographers) confidence in applying the results with full awareness of the study's underlying strengths and limitations. The framework encourages the researcher to take a methodical, thorough, and objective approach to all phases of ethnography that deepens the researcher's commitment to the process and goes way beyond the act of observing or simply reporting "this is what we saw in the observations." The TQF model for ethnography strives to articulate an intricate understanding of the observed events that reliably informs users of the research.

Case Study

An ethnographic case study is presented beginning on page 227 that exemplifies a study incorporating many of the standards advocated by the TQF approach.

5.4   CHAPTER SUMMARY

✓ The question of exactly what constitutes "ethnography" has long been the subject of controversy. Our chapter takes the view that ethnography is qualitative research that uses "in-context immersion" to gather in-depth information about the beliefs, attitudes, and behaviors of those being observed, ultimately to understand the motivations behind their thoughts and actions.

✓ Although observational methods are the central information-gathering techniques of ethnography, other qualitative methods (including IDIs and focus groups) often are used to supplement what is learned in the observations.

✓ There are five roles an observer can assume: off-site nonparticipant, on-site nonparticipant, passive participant, participant–observer, or complete participant. Sometimes the observer shifts roles during a study. Each role has its strengths and limitations. The decision of which role best serves a particular ethnographic study is extremely important.

✓ Ethnographic observations can be *overt* (whereby those being observed are aware of the observer's research presence) or *covert* (whereby those being observed are unaware of the observer's research presence). With overt observations, informed consent should be secured from participants, who thereby give their a priori permission in advance of the research. Ethnographers using covert observations should debrief the persons who were unknowingly observed soon after all the observations have been completed. These debriefings are primarily meant to determine if any harm was done and, if so, to try to undo the harm, as well as ascertain whether those observed were aware of being observed and may have altered their behavior as a result of this knowledge.

✓ Observers need special skill sets to enable them to accurately observe and record what happens while, at the same time, remaining objective about recording observational data. An observational grid can help the observer record information in each observation about all the constructs that are important to the ethnographic study. Observers record much more information than simply what they see and hear from those who are being observed. This ancillary material includes information about the environment within which the observations are taking place.

✓ Observers who engage in covert observations must have the skills to "act out" various personas and "keep their cover," both of which allow them to blend into the group that is being observed with the hope that they are not changing the behavior of the group members. Covert complete participant observers must also be at ease keeping their true purpose secret and be willing to deceive the other people in the group being observed, possibly for a very long period of time.

✓ Real-time observations typically are done in person, but may also be done remotely via a mobile phone device (in real time) or the Internet (typically not in real time). Internet ethnographies may include the observations of virtual persons who exist only on the Internet.

✓ A TQF approach to ethnography raises many considerations for the researcher. For instance, because in-person ethnographic studies are usually very labor intensive, they may frequently be limited in the number of individuals or groups being observed. This limitation, in turn, may severely narrow the breadth of the target population for these studies.

✓ Sampling for ethnography is often purposive, whereby the researcher deliberately selects particular individuals or groups of people for observation because of their relationship to the research problem. From a TQF perspective, convenience sampling is difficult to justify. The ethnographic researcher should always have clear and logical theoretical reasons for his/her selection of those who will be observed.

✓ A TQF approach to ethnography places an emphasis on gaining the cooperation of gatekeepers and key informants, who are very important to ensuring that those selected for observation are ultimately included in the study, thereby adding to the Credibility of the data.

✓ Unlike IDIs and focus groups, the observational data gathered in ethnographic studies do not suffer from the fallibilities of human memory because the phenomena being studied are typically happening in real time and not subject to recall error.

✓ Observers must constantly and proactively guard against introducing bias into the data they record. From a TQF perspective, this requires that specific steps be taken to mitigate bias, such as "matching" on-site observers with study participants, the demonstration of proficient observational skills by the observers, and the use of a reflexive journal as a self-critiquing method by observers.

✓ In terms of the Analyzability component of the TQF, it is strongly recommended that the person directly involved in the observations (i.e., the observers) transcribe the field notes and observation grid. And, as part of the verification process, it is recommended that researchers maximize the time allotted for observation and train observers to look for the unexpected by closely examining minor activities in their observations that may ultimately verify (or contradict) observers' dominant understandings.

5.5   EXERCISES AND DISCUSSION TOPICS

1. Define the five roles of ethnographic observation and contrast and compare when to use each by giving examples.

2. Select and evaluate a covert observation study from the literature and discuss (1) the appropriateness of the covert design (i.e., was a covert approach the only reasonable choice), (2) the particular ethical issues pertaining to this study, and (3) the manner in which the researcher addressed these issues.

3. Consider a research issue that interests you and develop a nonparticipant ethnographic study design utilizing the TQF. Discuss how best to address each of the quality components in your study design.

4. Design an on-site nonparticipant observer study to conduct observations in a public space (e.g., a park). Develop the objectives, constructs, observation guide and grid, scope, and measurement considerations (e.g., minimizing observer effects).

5. Select a subject area and topic scenario that are particularly suited for ethnography using the participant–observer method. Defend the approach, design the study utilizing the TQF, and discuss potential learning from the outcomes around the quality framework perspective.

6. How and why would you conduct an ethnographic study in the virtual world? Give examples.

SUGGESTED FURTHER READING

Adler, P. (1990). Ethnographic research on hidden populations: Penetrating the drug world. *The Collection and Interpretation of Data from Hidden Populations, 98*, 96–112.

This article, included in the National Institute on Drug Abuse Research Monograph Series #98 focusing on hidden populations, provides a concise and informative overview of participant observation generally, as well as an account of Adler and her husband's 6-year ethnographic study on a drug-dealing and smuggling community. Adler discusses how they became involved with this study (upon the discovery that their next-door neighbors were drug dealers) as well as the "strategies and tactics" they used to develop and maintain their "research relationship" with participants while assuming a "covert posture." This is a fascinating read that highlights the hurdles faced by complete participant observers as they juggled their undercover status while also taking the appropriate measures to ensure the quality of the data they were gathering.

Bernard, H. R. (2011). *Research methods in anthropology: Qualitative and quantitative approaches* (5th ed.). Lanham, MD: AltaMira Press.

In this 600-page book, Bernard presents a thorough discussion of both the qualitative and quantitative methods used in anthropology. The qualitative researcher will find his chapters on participant observation (direct and indirect observation), as well his chapter on field notes, particularly informative. The latter, for example, discusses how to write field notes and gives a detailed understanding of four types of field notes: jottings, a diary, a log, and "field notes proper." Bernard writes in a scholarly yet engaging manner, making the book's content highly accessible to the reader.

Humphreys, L. (1970, 1975). *Tearoom trade: Impersonal sex in public places.* Chicago, IL: Aldine.

This book provides the details of a classic (and what some consider to be "notorious") ethnographic study that we referenced in Chapter 5: Humphreys' research on homosexual behavior in a public setting (i.e., a public restroom). In addition to the study details, Humphreys provides the background of the "tearoom trade" and the facilities that attracted "a great number of men who wish, for whatever reason, to engage in impersonal homoerotic sexual activity" (1975, p. 9). Undoubtedly due to the controversy Humphreys' study stirred (see our discussion in Chapter 5), the 1975 volume is an "enlarged edition with a retrospective on ethical issues."

Spradley, J. P. (1980). *Participant observation.* New York: Holt, Rinehart & Winston.

In Chapter 5, Spradley is mentioned as one of the earliest anthropologists who, in the 1970s, began using his skills as an ethnographer to observe social groups "closer to home," that is, on American soil. In particular, we cite his investigation of alcoholism among those who lived on skid row (Spradley, 1972). Spradley was a strong believer in the *doing* of ethnography, and the practical applications provided in his 1980 book make it an excellent resource toward achieving that aim. In less than 200 pages, Spradley takes the reader through the underlying principles and "cycle" of ethnographic research followed by his 12-step "research sequence"—from the selection of an observation site to the final "writing of ethnography" (where he advises that "the only way to learn to write is *to write*," p. 160). Spradley is an engaging and enthusiastic author who has a great deal to teach the student of ethnography.

WEB RESOURCES

Statements on Ethical Standards and Professional Responsibility

American Anthropological Association
www.aaanet.org/profdev/ethics/upload/Statement-on-Ethics-Principles-of-Professional-Responsibility.pdf

American Educational Research Association
www.aera.net/Portals/38/docs/About_AERA/CodeOfEthics%281%29.pdf

American Psychological Association
www.apa.org/ethics/code/principles.pdf

American Sociological Association
www.asanet.org/images/asa/docs/pdf/CodeofEthics.pdf

NOTES

1. Throughout this chapter we refer to those who are being observed as "participants" when discussing observational studies wherein the individuals are aware that they are being observed. We do this because we believe that being a "participant" implies that someone has consented to taking part in a research study. In contrast, we refer to people who are unaware they are being studied as "those being observed" or some other language to that effect. When no distinction is being made between those who are or are not aware of being observed, we most often use the word "participants."

2. In some instances, the "researcher" may also be the person who conducts the observations (i.e., the "observer"). This is typically the case when the study is being conducted by a small research firm or group where the principal researcher assumes many duties, including the execution of all fieldwork. In other instances, the researcher may be the person who is responsible for managing a number of people on a research team, including one or more observers who conduct the observations. For this reason, we sometimes use "researcher" and "observer" interchangeably.

3. The reader is referred to the National Research Council (2003) publication for a complete discussion of informed consent requirements under the "Federal Policy for the Protection of Human Subjects," known as the Common Rule. "The Common Rule lays out a set of protections and related requirements applicable to all research on human participants that is conducted, funded, or overseen by federal agencies or conducted at institutions receiving federal funds that have agreed to these protections for all research at their sites" (p. 9).

4. The increasing use of smartphone applications may make the use of mobile phones a natural way of completing some functions, mitigating the oddity or unnaturalness of this mode.

Ethnography Case Study

PURPOSE

Religious networking organizations are structured groups consisting of people from multiple religious congregations that meet regularly to discuss common interests. The primary purpose of this study was to examine how and why these organizations work for social justice in their local community and how religion is integrated into the organizations' work in social justice.

METHOD

An ethnographic approach was considered appropriate because of the distinctive insight it could give into the organization members' personal experiences, as well as the proven benefit of ethnography, by other researchers in community psychology, in identifying and understanding the storied lives of individuals and social processes within community-based environments.

DESIGN

Credibility

Scope

Two networking organizations were included in this study. Both organizations are located in the same Midwestern community. The researcher became aware of, and was introduced to, these organizations by way of contacts (gatekeepers) within the community. The researcher assumed the role of an overt participant observer, attending monthly 2-hour meetings at both organizations for approximately 1½ years. The ethnographer's involvement with the organizations ended (i.e., his observational study concluded) when common patterns or themes in the data reappeared and no new observations were witnessed (i.e., when the researcher believed he had reached a saturation point).

The researcher discussed his research and interest in conducting participant observation with key informants (organizations' leaders and group members). He received approval from both organizations as well as from the university IRB. In lieu of written informed consent, the researcher obtained passive assent by reading a short script at the beginning of each network organization meeting. This script stated the researcher's university affiliation; his role as an ethnographer (specifically, participant observer); his intent to take field notes and write one or more academic papers at the conclusion of the study; and his contact information with instructions to notify him or a key informant (an organization leader) if any member did not want notes taken of his/her activity. The researcher took the added ethical precaution to brief any member who arrived at the meeting after his script was read and omitted the member from the field notes if his/her assent was not obtained.

_____

Source: Todd (2012).

Data Gathering

Observations at each meeting were directed by an observation guide that focused on the core construct of interest—how networking organizations understood and worked for social justice in the community—along with the topics/issues discussed, manner in which decisions were made, interaction among members, key events or incidents during the meeting, variations or deviant patterns, manner in which members attached meaning to their own behavior, sensory cues such as sights and sounds, physical layout of the meeting room (mapping), members' language during discourse, use of anecdotes and quotes, and the researcher's personal, reflective reactions or thoughts.

The ethnographer was mindful of the potential for observer bias. One concern was the brevity of the script he read at the start of each meeting, which was purposely kept short so as to not disrupt the meeting. Still, the researcher questioned whether it was sufficient to explain his role and intentions (however, there was no indication from the members that this was a problem). The researcher was careful to refrain from interjecting questions or statements into the meeting that would only serve his research purpose. He was also careful to limit his involvement during the group meetings. In his report, the ethnographer (someone with a graduate degree in theology as well as psychology) acknowledged that his own assumptions prior to involvement with the organizations were potentially biasing his analysis, and, with this awareness, he continually reflected on his interpretations of the data.

Analyzability

The ethnographer reflected on the field notes throughout the study, and his personal reflections were integrated with the field notes. By continually reviewing and assessing these notes, the researcher used this information and insights to better understand future meetings where past observations were either affirmed or denied. This iterative, grounded analytical approach became a form of "focused coding" that identified key concepts and categories that were confirmed, or not, by additional observations. During analysis, the field notes were reread many times and organized by themes, patterns, processes, group activities, and around the key construct: how and why these organizations understood and worked for social justice in the community.

In addition to the observations, the researcher triangulated his data during analysis with the meetings' agendas, handouts, announcements, and minutes. Other triangulation techniques included deviant case analysis (e.g., looking for and exploring observations, relationships, or categories that were contradictory) and member checking by debriefing members after the initial observations and presenting a report to each organization after the analysis and interpretation, asking for member feedback on the findings.

Transparency

As shown in this brief account, the ethnographer provided a detailed report of the research covering the scope, data-gathering, and analysis processes. Importantly, the researcher was very forthright and specific on particular issues regarding the construct of interest, participant consent, his own prejudices and the potential for bias, and the limitations of the study (e.g., the differences between the organizations). By way of the researcher's documentation, the reader is able to understand (a) how the research was conducted, (b) the obstacles or issues that may have impacted the data, (c) the process the researcher went through to reach the final interpretations, and (d) how the research might be applied in similar contexts.

Usefulness

The findings from this ethnographic study broadened the existing research on religious organizations and introduced a new religious setting—the religious networking organization—as an important entity in the shaping of positive behavior and attitudes. In particular, this research contributed to the literature the idea that these organizations work for social justice in the community and create social capital. This research called on community psychologists to partner with religious networking organizations to better their local communities and "create a more just and equitable society" (p. 243).

CHAPTER SIX

Qualitative Content Analysis

CHAPTER PREVIEW

Content analysis is both a qualitative and a quantitative method for conducting research. This chapter focuses on the qualitative approach. Our definition of qualitative content analysis is *the systematic reduction (i.e., condensation) of content, analyzed with special attention on the context in which the data were created, to identify themes and extract meaningful interpretations.* When qualitative researchers are engaged in *primary* content analysis, they are focused on a body of existing content that is typically in textual form (e.g., newspapers, books, emails, government documents), but may also include any body of content created by people, such as paintings, videos, and audio recordings (e.g., songs or speeches). At times, qualitative researchers conduct *secondary* content analysis on transcripts that were generated by other qualitative methods, such as in-depth interviews (IDIs) or focus groups. Qualitative content analysis includes the coding of *manifest content*—referring to content that is readily apparent—and *latent content*—referring to the "hidden" meaning of content that lies beneath the surface and is contextually based. There are two different data phases in conducting a qualitative content analysis. Phase 1 is Data Generation, whereby the content selected for study is coded so as to produce the data, and Phase 2 is Data Analysis, which involves the categorization and interpretation of the data. The emphasis on latent meanings and context, as well as the unobtrusive nature of primary content analysis, are key strengths of qualitative content analysis. From a Total Quality Framework (TQF) perspective, researchers face a number of challenges when conducting qualitative content analysis, including gaining access to the content they want to study, accounting for all relevant constructs, and training coders to consistently and accurately follow the coding scheme and not allow their own subjective preferences to affect the coded data they generate. Computer software programs can provide important assistance in the coding of manifest content, but these programs cannot handle the coding of complex latent content, for which the human brain is best suited.

6.1 INTRODUCTION

Content analysis is a research method conducted by both qualitative and quantitative researchers. The qualitative method and quantitative methods are quite different from each other in terms of the ways data are gathered and how researchers make sense from the findings, as well as in the purposes to which the researchers apply what they learn from the approach they deploy. Even with these differences, some researchers believe that the qualitative and quantitative approaches can (and should) be used to complement each other within the same larger research study in an attempt to achieve a "best of both worlds" perspective about what is being studied (Macnamara, 2005).

The use of content analysis appears to date back to the 18th century in Scandinavia when a process similar to content analysis was used to interpret the meanings of the symbols in the church hymns in *Songs of Zion* (Dovring, 1954). The quantitative approach to the content analysis method in the United States is most often traced back to mass media communications research, particularly the analysis of newspaper content in the early 20th century. Back then, content analysis was exclusively a quantitative method by which researchers investigated "yellow journalism" and wartime propaganda. Eventually, the application of quantitative content analysis evolved from a focus on newspapers to the inclusion of other emerging forms of communication such as radio and television. The goals and techniques of the quantitative content analysis method also evolved. What started as journalists' relatively simple calculation of newspaper space allocated to newsworthy, factually based articles in comparison to gossipy, small "news" items was embraced by behavioral and social scientists (e.g., sociologists Max Weber, Paul Lazarsfeld, and Harold Lasswell) who were interested in such matters as politically charged public opinion, social issues such as racism, and psychological constructs such as "fair and balanced" reporting, and who saw the method as a way to *quantitatively* track the "cultural temperature of society" (Hansen, Cottle, Negrine, & Newbold, 1998, as discussed in Macnamara, 2005, p. 1).

The *qualitative* approach to content analysis traces its roots to the mid-20th century when qualitative researchers began to modify the approaches that had been used by quantitative content analysis researchers. The purpose was to enrich what qualitatitve researchers believed was an overly sterile approach that focused preponderantly on *manifest* (surface) content and largely missed the richer *latent* content, consequently missing much of the meaning underlying the text or other form of content being studied. The "content" in qualitative content analysis often originates from other qualitative methods (e.g., transcripts from IDIs, group discussions, and ethnographic field notes). With this point in mind, qualitative content analysis researchers devised and advocated for a methodical process similar to quantitative content analysis but with a greater emphasis on subjective interpretations of the meaning in qualitative content so as to identify relevant themes and patterns (Zhang & Wildemuth, 2009; Hsieh & Shannon, 2005).

There is no shortage of definitions associated with the content analysis method. In fact, there appear to be no two definitions that are identical. At one extreme are qualitative researchers such as Kvale and Brinkmann (2009) who espouse a quantitative, narrowly defined view of content analysis, stating that it "is a technique for a systematic quantitative description of the manifest content of communication" (p. 203), whereas other researchers account for the importance of the latent aspects of communication that allow for more meaningful interpretations or inferences from the data. Two such researchers, Berg and Lune (2012), draw on several sources to define content analysis as "a careful, detailed, systematic examination and interpretation of a particular body of material in an effort to identify patterns, themes, biases, and meanings" (p. 349). Similarly, Krippendorff (2013) states that "content analysis is a research technique for making replicable and valid inferences from text (or other meaningful matter) to the contexts of their use" (p. 24). Information researchers Zhang and Wildemuth (2009) take the latent aspect one step further in their discussion of qualitative content analysis with the assertion that the aim is "to understand social reality in a subjective but scientific manner" (p. 308).

Regardless of the definition, there are six essential components to the content analysis method in qualitative research. Qualitative content analysis:

1. Encompasses all relevant qualitative data sources, including text, images, video, audio, graphics, and symbols.

2. Is a systematic, process-driven method.

3. Draws meaningful interpretations or inferences from the data based on both manifest and latent content.

4. Is contextual, that is, relies on the context within which the information is extracted to give meaning to the data.

5. Reduces a unit of qualitative data to a manageable level while maintaining the critical content.

6. Identifies patterns and themes in the data that support or refute existing hypotheses or reveal new hypotheses.

Looking at these elements of the content analysis method, we derive our own definition of **qualitative content analysis** as, namely, the systematic reduction or "condensation" (Graneheim & Lundman, 2004) of content, analyzed with special attention to the context in which it was created, to identify themes and extract meaningful interpretations of the data.

From a TQF perspective, our definition of content analysis carries with it the ingredients for credible and analyzable data—by way of the systematic process that guides the researcher to reliable and valid measurement, processing, and verification—that ultimately will lead to useful research outcomes by way of thematic development and extraction of meaningful implications.

Content Analysis as a Qualitative Method

The historical roots of content analysis as a quantitative method begs the question of its appropriateness in qualitative research design. Even our definition of content analysis speaks of the positivistic-sounding idea of the "systematic reduction" of data. But to assume that what we call qualitative content analysis is just a redressing of a quantitative approach would be badly mistaken. Content analysis may have grown to prominence because of its early use as a way to quantitatively calculate the extent of topical coverage in the mass media, but the adoption of the method by myriad researchers who understood the importance of the less obvious underlying meanings of the content brought content analysis to the realm of qualitative research. Krippendorff (2013) rightly states that "ultimately, all reading of texts is qualitative" (p. 22) in that it demands the reader's engagement to find meaning and that the perceived meanings will often vary from reader to reader.

The very nature of qualitative and quantitative research is what separates the two approaches to content analysis. Although the goal among both qualitative and quantitative researchers is to systematically reduce or condense the data without the loss of their essences, they tackle the meaningfulness of the data from different perspectives. Qualitative researchers *primarily* use an *inductive strategy*, by which new discoveries of meanings and interpretations are guided by the researcher's immersion in the data (i.e., the written text, images, video, audio, graphics, or symbols); that is, the core of their hypotheses development process is based on what they "see" in the data. Quantitative researchers, on the other hand, more typically begin with a *deductive strategy*—that is, with an a priori choice of a particular question or speculation—and then scour the data to find answers. Krippendorff (2013), a quantitative content analyst at heart, asserts that the quantitative approach is more efficient than, in his words, the "fishing expeditions" of qualitative content analysis because, by entering into the analysis with a specific research question, the researcher can "read texts for a purpose, not for what an author may lead them to think or what they say in the abstract" (p. 37). But from our perspective, this view simply reinforces the fundamental difference between the goals of qualitative and quantitative research. And it is those goals that ultimately determine whether a qualitative or quantitative approach to content analysis should be pursued.

The focus on a continual process of revising and developing meanings in the data based on new discoveries is another unique attribute of qualitative content analysis. Unlike quantitative content analyst researchers who set their coding scheme early in the research process—typically modifying it only slightly or not at all during data collection—qualitative researchers methodically and frequently revisit the content they are studying to better understand each relevant piece as well as its relationship to the entire context from which it was chosen (sampled), thereby modifying how and what they are coding throughout the data collection period. In this way, and as Krippendorff (2013) points out, qualitative content analysis puts the analyst in a *hermeneutic circle*[1] whereby interpretations are reformulated based on new insights related to, for example, a larger context. This more flexible, less rigid, approach to content analysis also embraces the notion of multiple meanings derived from multiple sources. A case in point is triangulation, which is used in qualitative analysis to verify the analyst's interpretations by considering alternative points of view or analyzing deviant cases. It is this more far-reaching consideration of the data—along with the added support of the research participants' verbatim comments that are typically included in the final research document—that is indicative of the unique qualities of the qualitative approach. Indeed, it is the inductive strategy in search of latent content, the use of context, the back-and-forth flexibility throughout the analytical process, and the continual questioning of preliminary interpretations that set qualitative content analysis apart from the quantitative method.

Basic Steps in the Qualitative Content Analysis Method

When researchers speak of qualitative content analysis, they are most likely referring to the analysis of written texts. As mentioned earlier, content analysis can be conducted utilizing a variety of data sources in addition to text—such as video, audio, and images—but the historical as well as the present-day use of content analysis typically centers on the written word. For this reason, our discussion of the basic steps involved in the process of qualitative content analysis focuses on textual content. A more detailed account of the uses of content analysis is provided later in this chapter.

The data sources that might be a focus in a qualitative content analysis include published (e.g., literature, newspaper articles) and unpublished (e.g., research interview transcripts, ethnographic field notes, corporate memoranda) documents; diaries and journals; Web blogs and other online site content; and letters, email messages, as well as other textual correspondence. Regardless of the type of written material, the researcher embarking on a content analysis has several important questions to consider prior to implementing the process:

- What are the key objectives of the research study? The objectives must be clearly defined and the researcher must thoroughly understand these objectives.

- What are the relevant constructs associated with the research objectives?

- What, if anything, is already known about these constructs in conjunction with the current research issue and objectives?

- Based on this information, is there any role for a **deductive approach** to the content analysis—for example, utilizing categories obtained in earlier research to identify relevant content and integrating new categories and themes as they emerge—or should the researcher commit entirely to an inductive approach throughout the process, allowing the method itself to reveal and define meaning in the data? Keep in mind, however, that it is not uncommon for researchers to use both deductive and inductive approaches in qualitative content analysis by "using a priori deductive codes as a way

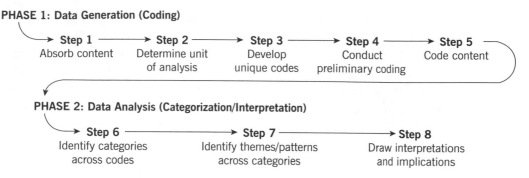

PHASE 1: Data Generation (Coding)

Step 1 → Step 2 → Step 3 → Step 4 → Step 5
Absorb content | Determine unit of analysis | Develop unique codes | Conduct preliminary coding | Code content

PHASE 2: Data Analysis (Categorization/Interpretation)

Step 6 → Step 7 → Step 8
Identify categories across codes | Identify themes/patterns across categories | Draw interpretations and implications

FIGURE 6.1. Phases and steps in qualitative content analysis.

to 'get into' the data and an inductive approach to identify new codes and to refine or even eliminate a priori codes" (Forman & Damschroder, 2008, p. 48).

The answers to these questions give the researcher the necessary tools to design a credible content analysis that accurately measures specific constructs as well as the overall research objectives.

Before a qualitative content analysis of textual content can be conducted, the researcher needs to prepare the material that will be analyzed to create findings and draw conclusions. This preparation might entail compiling (e.g., retrieving from an archive) relevant newspaper or document content, converting audio recordings of IDIs or group discussions into transcripts (including going back to the audio and/or video recordings, as necessary, to fine-tune the transcripts for accuracy), downloading Web posts, or otherwise collecting (amassing) the textual content of interest. At this point, there are eight basic steps in the qualitative content analysis method that are divided into two phases of the overall process: (1) coding the content, which generates the data that are analyzed in Phase 2, and (2) analyzing the data created in Phase 1 by identifying categories and themes and developing interpretations of the findings. These phases and steps are discussed in the following material and summarized in Figure 6.1.

Phase 1: Data Generation (Coding)

1. **Absorb the content.** The first critical step in a content analysis is to gain an understanding of the complete content: that is, the content from all data sources. In this step, the researcher is not making a conscious attempt to find meaning but rather to simply absorb what is there and get a sense of the "whole picture." This is accomplished by thoroughly reading and rereading the written material. The researcher may begin to hypothesize themes or connections in the content at this step and should record these musings in a reflexive journal or memo diary of some kind. The researcher's hypotheses may or may not hold up to scrutiny as he/she continues through the content analysis process.

2. **Determine the unit of analysis.** This unit might be particular to the text—such as the entire response to a particular question or each sentence in the content—or to the providers of the content—such as research participants of a certain age or clinical records by medical specialty. It should be emphasized, however, that the latter (i.e., using some aspect of the content providers as the unit of analysis) has the potential negative effect of obscuring important research findings due to ill-conceived assumptions. For example, a researcher who enters into a content analysis of interviews conducted with homeless women with the assumption that women of a certain age harbor unique attitudes may decide to use age segments as the unit of analysis. This close-minded approach to analyzing the content, however, neglects to look *across* age segments to identify an important psychological need common among women of all ages. Researchers more typically use some aspect of the text itself as a unit of analysis. Milne and Adler (1999), for example, believe that "sentences are far more reliable than any other unit of analysis" (p. 244) because sentences give contexts to words which otherwise would have little meaning. In contrast, Graneheim and Lundman (2004) state that "the most suitable unit of analysis is whole interviews or observational protocols" (p. 106) because this unit retains the whole entity yet is "small enough" to be analyzed as a context in the content analysis process. The reality is that the appropriate unit of analysis will vary from study to study. This issue is discussed in more depth in conjunction with the TQF in Section 6.3.

3. **Develop unique codes.** With a full appreciation of the content that is being studied (from Step 1) and a focused attention on the unit of analysis (from Step 2), the researcher is now prepared to systematically "comb" the content to develop a coding scheme. Codes are what enable the researcher to condense typically large amounts of textual content into a manageable—and analyzable—format. Code development involves carefully reading text from the perspective of the research objectives and associated constructs as well as the context in which particular words were spoken or ideas were conveyed. It is important, however, for the researcher to think about the research objectives in fairly broad terms so as to not miss unanticipated insights in the content. For instance, a researcher analyzing the content from a group discussion study conducted among cancer patients to determine the adequacy of communications during their recent enrollment in a clinical trial may fail to uncover an important research finding—such as that patients' concerns are more focused on other aspects of the process, such as excessive paperwork, than on communications—if code development is strictly focused on comments specific to communications.

Each code should be (a) clearly defined and (b) unique and independent (i.e., mutually exclusive) from the other codes. A clear definition of each code is also what establishes the uniqueness of the code. For this reason, codes defined by vague terms such as "quality" and "convenience" are inappropriate and need operational definitions that help the coder reliably and accurately identify the correct code and enable the analyst to later find meaning in the data. In a satisfaction study among patients at a local medical clinic, for example, a proper code for reasons why patients are satisfied with the clinic would not be "quality health care" (which is too broad and ambiguous to serve the researcher's needs) but rather "knowledgeable physicians" or "skilled nurses." Multiple unique codes can be assigned to any given text; for example, someone may have mentioned both the knowledge of the doctors as well as the nurses' skills in the same unit of text.

The coding scheme should be recorded in a codebook that, at the most basic level, details (a) the name or label of the code, (b) its definition, and (c) a verbatim example from the data. Because code development in qualitative content analysis is an iterative process—by which new codes are added and existing codes are revised as the researcher gains new insights in the course of coding—the codebook, at least initially, is a dynamic (i.e., not stagnant) document that is continually updated and improved and/or enhanced. The codebook is discussed more fully in Section 6.3 (see pp. 263–265).

4. **Conduct preliminary coding.** Once the initial codes have been developed, it is important to "test" their viability by coding a subset of the content; that is, doing a pilot test of the proposed coding scheme. Ideally, two or more coders will independently conduct this **preliminary coding** so that, when completed, coders (along with the researcher[2]) can meet to compare their code assignments and discuss, as well as resolve, any discrepancies. This check on intercoder consistency is critical to the credibility and analyzability of the final outcomes of all content analysis studies (i.e., not just qualitative ones). By talking through variations in how codes were interpreted and applied to the data by different coders, the researcher is likely to derive a new understanding of the codes as well as the content itself. Resolutions with the coding are made by consensus or, in the absence of consensus, by the principal researcher who has the final responsibility and the authority to make such decisions. The researcher also uses any issues that arise from the preliminary coding to update the codebook with revised or additional codes.

5. **Code the content.** At this step, the coders go about assigning codes to the entire set of contents that is being analyzed in a particular study. During this period, the principal researcher should meet regularly with the coders to learn about, discuss, and resolve any unanticipated issues in the coding of the content that do not appear to correspond with the existing coding scheme. The researcher can elect to further revise or add codes to the codebook, or more clearly instruct the coders in the use of an existing code.

It is essential to the content analysis method that coders are trained not only in the coding scheme but also in the importance of *capturing context*. Drawing meaning and inference by way of context in qualitative research is central to the qualitative content analysis method. Without a complete and accurate account of the context pertaining to a particular code assignment, the researcher may be led to inappropriate interpretations that ultimately weaken the usefulness of the research. Forman and Damschroder (2008) provide an example to illustrate the importance of context when coding. In their IDI study with kidney patients concerning visits to the nephrologist, the researchers created a "reassurance" code defined as the doctor providing the patient with "information to help relieve worry or fear." The text from an interview with one participant, who talks about her fear of the disease and how she felt "relieved" when the doctor told her not to worry about an unusual pain in her back, could certainly be coded as "reassurance." A problem arises, however, if the coder only codes the text pertaining to the patient's relief (at hearing that the pain is nothing to worry about) while failing to include the context in which this response was given, namely, the patient's fear of the disease. In this case, the code "reassurance" is not just about how the physician gave relief to the patient but why the patient needed relief in the first place—that is, the context in which the patient experienced relief from "worry or fear."

Phase 2: Data Analysis (Categorization/Interpretation)

6. **Identify categories across codes.** When the dataset is fully coded, the researcher can then look for meaningful categories across codes that will help illuminate possible connections and patterns. It is best to identify these categories after coding the dataset, rather than before, because the coding scheme will likely have shifted during the process. A category is any group of codes, along with the textual data to which they are assigned (on a manifest and latent contextual level, as discussed above), which share an underlying construct. For example, an analysis of diaries written by women at a county correctional facility might determine that the codes associated with on-site educational opportunities and on-site recreational sports activities are related to the feeling of empowerment. However, coded text can be associated with more than one category; so, for instance, educational opportunities might also be linked to another category, such as financial stability, and sports activities might be connected to the category "health care." Importantly, the further condensing of the data by way of categories should not obscure elements in the original content. The categories (like the coding process) are based on scrutiny at both the manifest and latent levels, which allows the categorization (like the coding) to be conducted without the loss of context and, to the contrary, enriching the meaning of the data.

7. **Identify themes or patterns across categories.** With the data coded and the pertinent categories established, the researcher is now prepared to look across the codes that define each category and across all the categories to discern themes or patterns in the data. To facilitate this identification process, researchers can simply use color marking pens (e.g., "highlighters") to signify the coded data based on particular categories/codes. It is typically more effective, however, to create some type of data display in the form of a worksheet or visual map. An extract of a data display for the earlier hypothetical study among female inmates is shown in Figure 6.2. As can be seen, a worksheet (which can be created in Excel or similar program) should have the categories running as "fields" or column headings across the top and each case that is being studied (e.g., each IDI participant, each diary submission, or each newspaper article included in the study)

Participant ID	Categories			
	On-site educational opportunities	**On-site recreational opportunities**	**Financial stability**	**Health care**
Mary S.	"Weekly access to online webinars is helping me keep up with my career."	"Daily workout sessions in the gym give me the feeling that I am not totally going to waste."	"I have no idea what's happening to my money. Hopefully I can keep up with my career enough to go right back into the job market when I get out of here."	"At least I feel like I am in good physical shape."
Rebecca G.	"I am reading more than ever before, which makes me feel like I have some control over my life."	"Physical activities in this place are a joke." "Without exercise, my body is getting fat and flabby."	No mention.	"I think I've gained about 50 pounds in here."
Kathy L.	"Twice a week there is an art class. Who would have thought I could draw?"	No mention.	"I wonder how much I could sell my art for."	"I have asked to see a doctor three times, but no one seems to care."

FIGURE 6.2. Example of a data display for a hypothetical qualitative content analysis study of diaries written by women confined to the county correctional facility. This data display was created in Excel.

running vertically representing a row. Within each cell of this grid, the researcher can record the input from each case pertaining to each category. Once completed, the data display can be color highlighted (or otherwise annotated) to reveal the extent (i.e., the number) of mentions of a particular concept or construct, as well as to provide a visual depiction of the conceptual patterns in the data.

Visual maps are also very effective in enabling the researcher to see the connections from which patterns can be more easily identified (e.g., compared to a worksheet). An example of this visual approach is the "concept map" Schilling (2006) created using PowerPoint software for his content analysis of IDI research among corporate managers concerning the subject of leadership (see Figure 6.3).

8. Draw interpretations and implications from the data. At this step in the content analysis process, the researcher should have already begun to frame his/her interpretations of the data and formed preliminary implications. As with all qualitative methods, it is important for the researcher to verify these interpretations and implications at this stage by way of triangulation (e.g., comparing the interpretations and implications drawn by multiple researchers on the same data and data display) and negative or deviant case analysis. With respect to the latter,

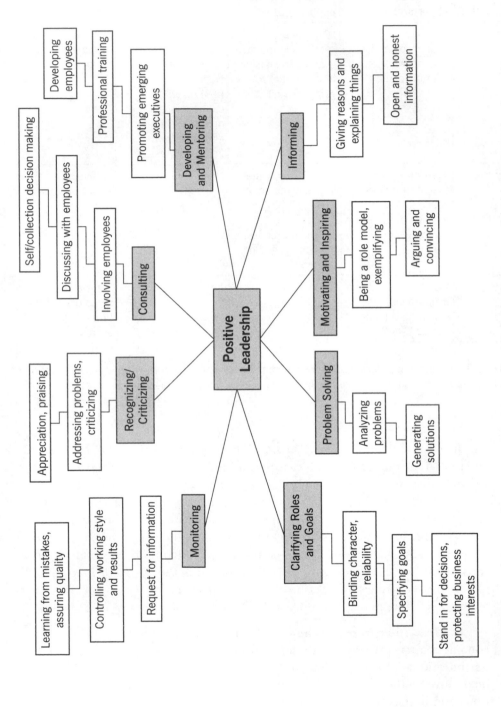

FIGURE 6.3. Example of a visual "concept map." From Schilling (2006). Reprinted with permission from *European Journal of Psychological Assessment,* 22(1), 35. Copyright 2006 Hogrefe & Huber Publishers.

the researcher should look at all early interpretations and implications with a skeptical eye, seeking instances or cases in the data that contradict his/her principal understanding of the outcomes.

For example, in the study mentioned earlier among female inmates at the county correctional facility, the researcher's initial finding from the data might be that there is a relationship between the ability to cope with prison life and physical activity (i.e., women who frequently participate in on-site recreational sports are coping better in prison than other women). The researcher will want to verify that finding, however, by examining data from women who seem to be coping well but who participate very little in physical activities at the prison, and by examining data from women who do a lot of physical activity but are not coping well. In this example, the actual interrelationship between coping and activity may be reversed, and it may be something else (i.e., not physical activity) that enables women to cope with prison life. This verification process may or may not alter the researcher's final analysis of the data, yet it adds completeness, accuracy, and ultimately Usefulness to the research.

Furthermore, all verification processes—as well as all other aspects of the study design and implementation—should be fully reported in the final document that is written about the study. These aspects relate to the Analyzability and Transparency components of the TQF (see Section 6.8).

Appropriate Uses of the Qualitative Content Analysis Method

As mentioned previously, the content analysis method in qualitative research is often used in combination with other qualitative methods; however, it is also used when content analysis itself is the primary or only method. In the first case, qualitative content analysis is focused on data generated by another qualitative method such as interviews, group discussions, or ethnographic observations—or by the open-ended responses to a quantitative survey—and plays a supportive analytical role with these methods (i.e., content analysis as the *secondary* method). Content analysis as a *primary* method is less common and is typically conducted when the source of content is an existing, naturally occurring repository of information such as newspapers. The distinction between these two approaches is summarized in Box 6.1.

Content Analysis as a Secondary Method

A systematic application of qualitative **content analysis as a secondary method** has been conducted across a variety of disciplines. Health care researchers have used content analysis to investigate a number of issues. For example, Söderberg and Lundman (2001) applied the content analysis method to analyze the results from 25 unstructured IDIs conducted with women inflicted with fibromyalgia, from which they isolated five areas in these women's lives impacted by the onset of this condition. In a similar approach, Berg and Hansson (2000) examined the "lived experiences" of 13 nurses working in dementia care at a psychogeriatric

---

**BOX 6.1. Qualitative Content Analysis Method:
Secondary versus Primary Approach**

Content analysis as a . . .	
Secondary method	Focuses on content generated by another qualitative method (i.e., IDIs, focus group discussions, observations in ethnography) and plays a supportive analytical role with these methods. Coding of this content generates the data that are used in the analysis stage of the study.
Primary method	Focuses on content generated by an existing, naturally occurring repository of information such as newspapers, consumer diaries, historical documents, television content, films, online blogs, and email communications. Coding of this content generates the data that are used in the content analysis study.

---

clinic who received clinical group supervision and supervised planned nursing care. These researchers conducted unstructured, "open-ended" IDIs with each nurse and used the data from their IDIs as the content on which they performed a content analysis that revealed two principal and five subordinate themes indicating supportive needs among nurses at the personal and professional level. In another example, Kyngäs (2004) studied the support network among 40 teenagers suffering from a chronic disease, such as asthma or epilepsy, by way of semi-structured IDIs. Content analysis in this instance showed six distinct social network categories for these adolescents, that is, parents, peers, health care providers, school, technology, and pets.

Other examples of using content analysis as a secondary method include the investigation of: (a) stress among elementary, middle, and high school teachers (Blase, 1986); (b) safety training needs among residential roofing contractors (Hung et al., 2013); (c) service needs among older people in the Iranian city of Bam following the 2003 earthquake (Ardalan et al., 2009); (d) marketing strategies related to imported facial herbal cosmetic products in Thailand (Thanisorn & Bunchapattanasakda, 2011); and (e) equipment dealers' expectations regarding the future of television "product enhancements" (Ptacek, 2009).

Content Analysis as a Primary Method

Qualitative **content analysis as a primary method** has also been used across a number of disciplines and draws on naturally occurring data sources (e.g., the media, consumer diaries, historical documents, and email communications; see Townsend, Amarsi, Backman, Cox, & Li, 2011) rather than data generated by another research method. These data sources are often textual in nature (i.e., written accounts of some kind; see below); however, this is not always the case. For instance, television content has been the focal point of public health researchers examining direct-to-consumer (DTC) prescription drug commercials (Kaphingst, DeJong, Rudd, & Daltroy, 2004) as well as sociologists such as David Altheide (1987), who utilized content analysis to study television news coverage of the Iranian hostage crisis. The analysis of patients' "scribbles" from art psychotherapy sessions (Egberg-Thyme, Wiberg, Lundman, & Graneheim, 2013) as well as racism and the depiction of interracial relationships in U.S.-made films (Beeman, 2007) are other examples of using qualitative content analysis as a primary method where the focus is on nontextual content.

Content analysis as a primary method to explore textual data has been used in (a) sociological research to investigate gender biases reflected in the Boy Scouts' and Girl Scouts' handbooks (Denny, 2011); (b) psychology to review the qualitative studies conducted with lesbian, gay, bisexual, transgender, and queer (LGBTQ) individuals that have been published in the past 10 years in counseling journals (Singh & Shelton, 2011); (c) mass communication to study the portrayal of female immigrants in the Israeli media (Lemish, 2000); (d) sports marketing to investigate the social outreach programs among the four major professional leagues via a content analysis of their respective community website pages (Pharr & Lough, 2012); and (e) corporate management, including studies that analyze the content of corporate mission statements to understand "the messages communicated to organizational stakeholders" (Morris, 1994, p. 908).

Using Qualitative Content Analysis to Study Online Social Media

The use of qualitative content analysis as a primary method to study online content goes beyond the examination of websites (e.g., Pharr & Lough, 2012) and reaches out to the numerous ways people interact with others on the Internet, collectively referred to as "social media." Online social media comprises blogs; social networking sites such as Facebook, Twitter, and LinkedIn; discussion boards, forums, and user groups (e.g., the eBay forum where members give advice and share information, and any one of the many Apple user groups for Mac users); and content-sharing sites such as YouTube. Work in adapting content analysis to the contexts of online social media is a slowly developing but burgeoning area. It is recognized that the capabilities and use of social media present researchers with new challenges. For instance, conventional textual analysis might be applied to blog posts, but potential complications arise when "interaction via comments, which are inherently relational," as well as the use of hyperlinks, are considered in the analysis along with the text (Herring, 2010, p. 242). Comments—made on blogs, networking sites, user groups, and content-sharing sites—and the use of hyperlinks are just two examples of how social media content is rarely isolated. To the contrary, social media content represents a highly integrated (or "social") form of communication for which finding themes or patterns within the multiplicity of interactions may present an extremely daunting task to the researcher. For this reason, information systems researchers such as Herring (2010) and Parker,

Saundage, and Lee (2011) advocate a different, nontraditional way of thinking about the content analysis method in terms of developing units of analyses, categories, and patterns based on the realities of the interactive, linked world of online social media. This new way of thinking includes analyses focused on specific aspects of Web content such as images, themes, features, and links, as well as studying multiple social media channels at the same time in order for "researchers to become highly immersed in the discourse across a wide range of social media" (Parker et al., 2011, p. 6).

Researchers in the health care industry have been particularly active using qualitative content analysis to study social and other Web-based phenomena. As an example, Nordfeldt, Ängarne-Lindberg, and Berterö (2012) used the content analysis method to examine essays written by 18 health care professionals who treat diabetes concerning their experiences using a Web portal designed for young patients with type 1 diabetes and their significant others. This purely text-based research led to implications for the future of online information centers, the role physicians can play in helping to build these online resources, and the ultimate benefits patients can realize from online information portals. Another example comes from Glenn, Champion, and Spence (2012), who used qualitative content analysis to investigate online news coverage (along with readers' comments) concerning weight loss surgery. This study was conducted via the Canadian Broadcasting Corporation's website and explored the messages (and "tone") conveyed in its news items on weight loss surgery and the potential for "weight-based stigmatization" in the news coverage. And López, Detz, Ratanawongsa, and Sarkar (2012) applied qualitative content analysis to study patients' online reviews of their primary care doctors, enabling them to identify global themes as well as specific factors that contribute to positive or negative levels of patients' satisfaction with their doctors.

Researcher Skills in Qualitative Content Analysis

The qualitative content analysis method requires that the researcher possess two essential skills; the ability to be (1) systematic and (2) sensitive and perceptive.

Systematic

The ability to adhere to a systematic approach to content analysis is important because each step of the process builds on the preceding steps and is only as accurate as the work that went before it. So, for instance, if the researcher elects to skip preliminary coding by which the developed codes are checked for "goodness of fit" (i.e., Step 4) and instead goes straight to coding the entire dataset (i.e., Step 5), the coding process (see pp. 235–238) may be slowed considerably due to coder errors and/or the necessity of making overly frequent revisions to the codebook. Not only must the researcher have the ability to follow the step-by-step sequence in content analysis, but equally important is the researcher's appreciation for the iterative process—that is, an appreciation of why each incremental step is necessary and why codes can be revised, as warranted, during coding.

Sensitive and Perceptive

The researcher conducting a content analysis needs to be particularly sensitive to the context in which relevant information is conveyed (either in the original verbal format or in written form). It takes a special ability, along with skills training, to (1) identify the textual data relating to the research objectives and (2) comprehend the meaning of these data within their contexts. This sensitivity to context and perceptive ability demand a researcher who knows how to look at the details and nuances within the data (e.g., the contradictions in journal entries, variations across contexts) and perceive the interactions apparent in the data display (created in Step 7), from which the researcher can "see" the patterns in the underlying constructs and derive meaningful interpretations.

Overall Strengths and Limitations of the Qualitative Content Analysis Method

Strengths

The most important strength of the qualitative content analysis method—whether it plays a primary or secondary role is its focus on context and extracting meaning from textual and nontextual data. Indeed, "the drawing of inferences [is] the centerpiece of this research technique" (Krippendorff, 2013, p. 31). Even quantitative leaning researchers (e.g., Krippendorff) can agree that it is the contextual meaning to be gained from the content analysis method that makes it so valuable. However, unlike quantitative content analysis, the qualitative method thrives on the complexity of the social world depicted in the content and embraces the notion that multiple themes or categories might apply to a single context. This willingness to immerse themselves in the content can reward qualitative content analysts with rich discoveries of the meanings associated with events, attitudes, and behavior, in addition to the inner workings of social, cultural, and organized groups. A related strength of the qualitative content analysis method is the manner in which it reveals inferences from the content—that is, by way of a systematic, step-by-step process. This incremental process facilitates the researcher's ability to find increasingly relevant meanings in the content, leading to credible and transparent outcomes.

Another advantage of the content analysis method is that it can be a reliable—as well as cost-effective—way to conduct retrospective or longitudinal research. To the extent that relevant data sources (e.g., newspapers, magazines, letters, diaries, corporate reports, research transcripts, films, television programs, and graphics) have been archived and are accessible, content analysis can be an effective method in tracking changes or monitoring trends. For instance, a content analysis study might be conducted to examine the cover stories of the top women's fashion magazines at one point in time and then conducted every 3 months for the next 10 years in order to identify shifts in the fashion industry and the underlying impetus or causes for these shifts. Or, health researchers working with people enrolled in a program for prediabetic screening and prevention might use the content analysis method to investigate nutritional and activity diaries across participants over time to investigate the impact of the program on participants' lifestyles and thereby help evaluate the effectiveness of the program. A longitudinal approach to content analysis can also be used in conjunction with other research methods—for example, to compare transcripts from two similarly constructed focus group studies conducted at different points in time.

An important strength of qualitative content analysis as a primary research method is that the content sources are naturally occurring (compared to second-tier sources such as IDI transcripts). As mentioned earlier, these naturally occurring sources might include television news coverage, Hollywood movies, the Boy and Girl Scouts' handbooks, a collection of paintings in a museum, corporate mission statements, or Web blogs. This method has the considerable advantage of being unobtrusive, meaning that the researcher using content analysis as a primary method can conduct this research without disrupting the very events, individuals, or groups being investigated. Without the mitigating variables that can result in sources of error from the data collection and transcription process in other research methods, the reality-based content that is studied when content analysis is conducted as a primary qualitative method enhances research quality by maximizing the credibility and analyzability—and ultimately the usefulness—of the outcomes.

Limitations

Just as the dynamic social interaction component of group discussions can present the researcher with both a benefit and a disadvantage to using the method (see p. 116), so too the ability to draw inferences and find meanings in the data represent key strengths as well as potential limitations to the content analysis method. The issue here revolves around the inherent constraints of extrapolating reliable and valid interpretations from textual and nontextual material, and the degree to which the qualitative researcher/analyst can derive sound inferences. For instance, content analysts can fall into the "trap" of (a) thinking there are causal relationships in the data when there are not, and/or (b) trying to mold their interpretations of the data to construct what they believe is a valid story, when it is not. As a result, a researcher's overly pressing need to tell a convincing story from the data may lead him/her to make inappropriate connections or ignore meaningful associations that do not support the story the researcher wants to tell. Even with careful attention to context, "causality cannot be established without high levels of subjectivity" (Stepchenkova, Kirilenko, & Morrison, 2009, p. 456), making any attempt to explain the cause of the relationships revealed in a content analysis speculative. The researcher can identify categories, patterns, and themes in the data with confidence, but not causality. Causal claims are particularly worrisome when using content analysis as a primary method (i.e., when analyzing naturally occurring documents or media), because the object of interest was created for some purpose other than research, and, in fact, the researcher may have little or no knowledge of what led up to the creation of a source material (e.g., decisions that were made to include or exclude certain content in a YouTube video) or relevant information pertaining to its creator (e.g., personal motivations or objectives). These traps related to causality and storytelling are fairly easy to fall into unless a systematic and conscientious approach is taken in the analysis and interpretation phases of the content analysis process.

There are three particularly interesting characteristics of textual and nontextual material used in content analysis as a primary method that may potentially limit the analyst's ability to draw meaningful interpretations from the data.

1. The first characteristic involves the original act of constructing the content material (e.g., the document, video, or photograph) and, specifically, the idea that this act, in and of itself, may alter the meaning of the subject matter. For example, in a study examining a series of newspaper articles regarding inner-city gang violence, the researcher may be unable to discern the realities of gang violence because, by the mere act of writing about gang violence, the reporter has (deliberately or not) reformulated its true nature and given the reader a biased account. Therefore, what the researcher may be studying in this example is the reporter's rendition of the violence, not the actual nature of the violence itself.

2. A second inherent characteristic that may affect interpretation is the instability or unpredictability of the content. Alexander George (2009), for example, talks about the "changes in the speaker's strategy," citing propagandists who routinely shift their communication depending on the situation or their particular objective at a given moment. George likens this research challenge to that encountered by a psychotherapist deciphering communication from a patient whose state of mind and intentions change frequently. In these cases, the creator of the content may have caused inconsistencies in the content that has little or nothing to do with the natural variation in the topics of the content but instead are due to the whims of the creator.

3. The third interesting characteristic of content used in qualitative content analysis as a primary method stems from the fact that it is often a product of a group of people rather than one individual. An example of this is "social bookkeeping," as discussed by Dibble (2009), whereby social systems such as corporations, government entities, etc., create certain documents that do not reflect the thinking of any one person (Dibble uses the example of the *Congressional Record*). Examples can be found in a variety of source material, especially in video or films and broadcast media where many people are typically involved in these productions. These multiauthored creations may obscure true intentions and thereby challenge the researcher's ability to infer meaningful connections in the content. Fields (1988), for example, conducted a "systematic" content analysis of television news, observing that the 1980 coverage of "right-wing Christian fundamentalists" usually showed reporters standing near churches, an American flag, or the White House, and came to this conclusion: "The juxtaposition of these symbols conveyed the message that fundamentalists were seeking political power" (p. 190). This interpretation might have been more credible if these newscasts were the creation of a single individual who made all the on-air decisions and whose position on the Christian fundamentalists was explicitly disclosed. But, as a product of many people in broadcast news with varying agendas, there is any number of alternative rationales that could be given to Fields's observation and the backdrop chosen for reporting (e.g., churches might be considered an appropriate setting to report on a Christian group, or the American flag might be deemed a suitable prop, given that Christian fundamentalists are an American phenomenon).

In addition to the issues pertaining to interpretations and the drawing of inferences, one other important limitation to the qualitative content analysis method is that it can be very labor intensive. This is an important limitation because it often discourages qualitative researchers from using content analysis either as a secondary method (i.e., to analyze the data collected from other qualitative methods) or as the primary method (i.e., where the focus of the study is on the analysis of naturally occurring textual and/or nontextual content sources). The systematic, step-by-step process of content analysis can require a substantial amount of dedicated time on the part of one or more coders/researchers, which can drive up the cost of the research as well as take researchers away from other important work for a considerable duration of time. Schilling (2006), for instance, discovered in his IDI research with top- and midlevel corporate managers that each interview required 24 hours just to get through the coding category process (i.e., Steps 1–6 in the process, outlined on pp. 235–238).

6.2   COMPUTER-ASSISTED QUALITATIVE CONTENT ANALYSIS

As discussed briefly in Chapter 3 (see p. 91), computer assistance in qualitative data analysis can play an important supportive role toward the goal of deriving useful interpretations of the research outcomes. Given the typical volume and complexity of the content, the qualitative content analysis method is especially conducive to the application of computer software solutions. Computer-assisted qualitative data analysis software (CAQDAS) programs continue to evolve and have become increasingly feature-rich for qualitative researchers across the social science and health care fields. Programs such as ATLAS.ti, NVivo, Hyper-RESEARCH, Ethnograph, MAXQDA, and Qualrus offer standard "code and retrieve" functions—allowing the researcher to search and organize content that has been coded—as well as a variety of additional capabilities. It is important to keep in mind, however, that CAQDAS programs deal only with manifest content on a very one-dimensional level (e.g., the coder can search for terms that the software can then "auto code"), relying heavily on the researcher to carry out various functions in order to identify the contextual and underlying (latent) meaning of the content. Silver (2010) outlines the tasks qualitative researchers can perform with CAQDAS programs as follows:

- Organize data.
  - Code.
  - Link.
  - Group.
- Explore data.
  - Annotate and memo.
  - Search.
- Integrate data.
  - Incorporate and reference.
  - Combine and convert.
- Interpret data.
  - Make connections.
  - Write.

Silver's model allows for the fact that CAQDAS enables the researcher to work back and forth among the four primary analysis components—organize, explore, integrate, and interpret—to retrieve, rethink, make comparisons, and find patterns or relationships in the data. By facilitating the researcher's ability to revise codes and rethink coding schemes and categories, CAQDAS addresses the critical need in qualitative content analysis to maintain flexibility.

A few specific features provided by a number of CAQDAS programs are particularly well suited to the content analysis method. For instance, the ability to hyperlink codes, portions of the text (e.g., quotations), and related material (e.g., photos, images, video) gives the researcher an efficient way to see how different aspects of the data support or contradict each other. Another tool, KWIC (or "key word in context"), is useful to the qualitative content analyst because it retrieves a word the researcher deems particularly relevant to the analysis within the context where it appears. Using the KWIC feature makes it fairly easy to understand how a word is used by individuals, and similar tools—such as a componential analysis in NVivo (Leech & Onwuegbuzie, 2011)—help the researcher find similarities and differences in word or concept comprehension across participants. An additional feature offered by some CAQDAS programs is the ability to create graphic visualizations or maps of the coded and linked data. This is particularly useful in being able to actually see multiple (and sometimes complex) connections across the dataset. Figure 6.4 shows a graphic representation of the data connections created in ATLAS.ti for a study concerning happiness.

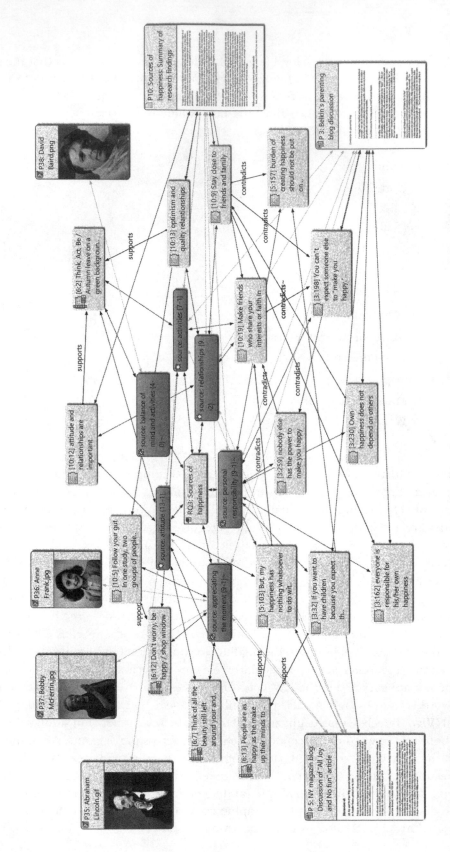

FIGURE 6.4. Example of a graphic visualization created by CAQDAS. From Friese (2013). Used with permission from the author Friese and ATLAS.ti.

Strengths of Computer-Assisted Content Analysis

An important strength of CAQDAS is its ability to manage a large volume of quali-tative data and to perform certain tasks in a quick and highly reliable (accurate) manner. As such, it allows researchers to tackle much more ambitious content analysis projects than they could possibly consider taking on without the use of computerized tools. This capacity is an overriding reason for utilizing CAQDAS programs: the vast amount of data—within, as well as across, types of content sources—that any one qualitative content analysis study can produce. For instance, a CAQDAS approach to analyzing the output from 10 focus group discussions (i.e., content analysis as a secondary method) will facilitate the process of link-ing manifest content to participants' sentiments and meanings, while allowing the researcher to identify themes and patterns across hundreds of pages of tran-scripts plus visual data (such as concept boards). Similarly, CAQDAS might be applied to the analysis of online bulletin board discussions (see Chapter 4, p. 121), which typically generate a massive quantity of written transcripts along with vari-ous images, documents, or videos uploaded by participants. Qualitative content analysis as a primary method can also involve large amounts of data, particularly when conducting a longitudinal study. A researcher, for example, exploring the amount and type of violence in Hollywood films in the last 5 years could benefit greatly from using CAQDAS to assist in organizing, coding, and categorizing the tremendous amount of textual manifest content from transcripts and annotations as well as actual video footage. Although CAQDAS does not fully relieve research-ers/coders of these functions, it would be a horrendous (and very expensive) bur-den to perform these tasks without CAQDAS assistance.

As noted above, in addition to providing a fast, efficient way to deal with a large volume of qualitative data, CAQDAS also has the potential for improv-ing the accuracy and reliability of the analysis compared to manual procedures (e.g., highlighting, sticky notes, color coding). The retrieval, organization, cat-egorization, and management of large sets of content (at the manifest level) can be a demanding and tiring process that opens the door for researcher fatigue and, potentially, human error. A computerized approach does not completely free the researcher from certain responsibilities in the content analysis method (e.g., coding and identifying latent meaning), but it does mechanize the accounting of words or phrases. This is important, for instance, when a researcher is conduct-ing a content analysis study concerning the information given about health side effects in print advertising for over-the-counter medication and needs an accurate account of the specific terminology that is used to discuss these side effects. The software provides this accountability function in a consistent manner, which adds to the reliability of the analysis process.

Three other strengths associated with the utilization of CAQDAS programs are (a) the accessibility of the data—"'live' contact to source data is always easy, which increases the researcher's closeness to data" (Lewins & Silver, 2009, p. 4); (b) the ability to conveniently store or archive a large amount of data (which is particularly important in longitudinal research when the researcher needs access to the data over a period of time); and (c) the availability of multiple file formats for saving and integrating the output (e.g., Excel, Word, PowerPoint).

Limitations of Computer-Assisted Content Analysis

For all of the strengths that support a computer-assisted approach to the qualitative content analysis method, there are also critical limitations. The most substantial limitation may be the sometimes seductive allure of the positive attributes associated with CAQDAS, as just discussed, especially those related to speed and efficiency, which may give the researcher the mistaken notion that computer software is all that is needed to conduct a credible and thorough analysis of the data. To the contrary, CAQDAS is simply a tool that may greatly assist the researcher in finding connections and patterns in the data, but it is only a tool and it is susceptible to misuse. As in all aspects of qualitative research, it is the researcher him/herself who is the instrumental component of the content analysis process and has the greatest impact on the outcomes. Therefore, it is the researcher, not CAQDAS, who is responsible for (a) developing the appropriate research question(s); (b) determining the rationale for exploring the data and defining codes; and, most importantly, (c) going beyond the manifest content to understand the contextual (latent) basis that gives meaning to the data. If the researcher does not take full charge of making the important conceptual decisions that are incorporated into the software, the CAQDAS will not provide valid or useful output. The possible misconception that the researcher can put away his/her discerning, analytical know-how and leave the analysis to the mechanical capabilities of CAQDAS programs poses a real threat to the integrity and ultimate usefulness of the research outcomes.

The reality is that a CAQDAS application is only as good as the particular features built into the software and the underlying assumptions on which the features are based. "The key, then, is not to get trapped by the assumptions of the program" (Weitzman, 1999, p. 1250), but rather to understand a program's strengths and limitations and maintain control of the quality of the research design, including the all-important functions of making meaning and interpretation. For instance, the researcher needs to keep in mind that a computer "solution" to qualitative content analysis will not be able to evaluate words and phrases in context. The software may offer elaborate Boolean search capabilities that return words or phrases of interest, but there is latent content associated with these words or phrases that the software is incapable of capturing. An example of this limitation is figures of speech such as irony and the use of metaphors (e.g., "It was raining cats and dogs"), where the validity of the researcher's search returns— and any subsequent connections made on the basis of these returns—is weak if left unchecked. Another example of how computer programs are unable to evaluate nuances in the data is the handling of phrases that are dual-coded. To illustrate, Schilling (2006) conducted a study on leadership in which "setting clear goals" and "setting realistic goals" were identified as two distinct categories of responses. However, a CAQDAS search for "clear goals" "and" "realistic goals" would miss the statement, "Leadership means setting clear, realistic goals." In this case, one of the inherent benefits of the content analysis method—that is, the ability to use multiple codes to fine-tune meaning in the data—would be weakened to the extent that the researcher relies on CAQDAS to do the "heavy lifting" in the qualitative analysis process.

Researchers are encouraged to evaluate each content analysis situation, decide on the appropriateness of a computer-assisted approach, and use CAQDAS only as a supplementary tool and with a full understanding of what it can and cannot do to assist in delivering meaningful and useful research outcomes.

6.3 APPLYING THE TOTAL QUALITY FRAMEWORK TO QUALITATIVE CONTENT ANALYSIS

As discussed in Section 6.1, qualitative content analysis can be conducted as (1) the primary research method whereby the researcher analyzes existing content such as newspapers, or (2) as a secondary method in combination with another research approach, such as IDIs or focus groups, that creates the content to be analyzed. In this section we talk about applying the TQF to studies where qualitative content analysis is utilized as either the primary or secondary method. The reader will notice that some elements of the TQF pertain more closely to content analysis as a primary rather than a secondary method, and vice versa. For instance, we begin with a discussion of defining the scope of a study—that is, coverage of the target population and sampling—which is a critical issue when designing research in which content analysis will be conducted as the primary method (i.e., to investigate naturally occurring sources of content). The particular relevance of quality design principles and recommendations to content analysis as a primary or secondary method are noted throughout this section.

Credibility

Qualitative content analysis is an extremely valuable research design because of its versatility and applicability to much of what qualitative researchers seek to accomplish in their quest for contextual meaning in the data. However, there are many potential threats to the credibility of the resulting data that researchers should proactively guard against to reduce or possibly eliminate their impact. These risks to credibility should be taken into account when researchers are interpreting their findings, advancing implications, and thereby addressing the usefulness of their qualitative content analysis study, tempering their conclusions as necessary.

The Credibility component of the TQF encompasses two broad areas of a content analysis research design: Scope and Data Gathering. *Scope* addresses the issue of coverage or, more specifically, how well the content that was analyzed represents the larger target population of content that is of interest. Data Gathering is concerned with the reliability and validity of the data to the extent that they have captured the essence of the constructs that the researcher purports to have addressed in the content being analyzed.

Scope

In qualitative content analysis, the nature of the target population differs from other types of qualitative research methods because it is not comprised of living beings but, rather, of textual or nontextual artifacts that are created when living beings communicate about something or interact with each other. Therefore, the target population in qualitative content analysis, when conducted as the primary method, is a preexisting body of content that the researcher wants to understand and draw conclusions about.

Coverage

In many cases, the set of content to be analyzed constitutes the entire target population. For example, a researcher whose objective is to conduct a content analysis of the entirety of letters written between two 18th-century lovers may have access to the entire set of letters as well as the time and resources to enable an analysis of the total population of letters. In such instances, the researcher is essentially conducting a census of the population of interest—that is, analyzing the entire population of interest—and, when this occurs, there is no chance of error in the representation (coverage) of that population. However, using the study of love letters as an example, there may be so many letters in the collection (population) that the researcher may instead choose to only analyze a subset of them. In this case, the lovers' entire set of letters is the target population from which the researcher will select a subset to serve as the content for this qualitative content analysis study.

The confidence by which this researcher can select a subset of letters from the population rests, in part, on his/her access to all the letters written by the lovers. Anything less than complete access to the entire population of letters may result in a selected subset that does not accurately represent the target population. For example, if the population of letters was known to have spanned a 15-year period but the researcher is unable to gain access to letters written in the first 3 years, the 12 years of letters in the researcher's possession would not represent the target population (i.e., the complete set of letters). The population as a whole, as well as any subset the researcher may draw from this population, may lead to errors in the analysis due to the possibility of materially different content and tone in the missing letters (i.e., letters from the first 3 years) compared to the letters in the years that are accessible. This **noncoverage** of the entire target population of letters between these two lovers could lead to serious bias in any of the conclusions reached by the researcher about the nature of the relationship between the lovers or other matters about which they were writing to each other.

The issue of noncoverage and inaccessibility of the total population of interest is particularly relevant when qualitative researchers choose to study a population of content that is extremely large in size (see the example below). In such instances, it is very important that the researcher determine with confidence, *prior to selecting a subset of content*, whether or not he/she has access to the entire target population. If not, the researcher's source of content is an incomplete representation of the target population and, if the content that is missing from the inaccessible portion of the target population is materially different from the content that is accessible, severe bias may result in the researcher's findings and conclusions, regardless of how much (what proportion) of the accessible content is analyzed.

For example, imagine that a researcher wants to use qualitative content analysis to study the conceptualization, role, and importance of female characters in the writings of J. R. R. Tolkien (cf. Skeparnides, 2002). Professor Tolkien began his body of fantasy writings in the 1910s and continued working on these creations for more than 50 years. In the process, he generated tens of thousands of pages of prose and poetry. Although his son, Christopher Tolkien, has selectively published a great deal of his father's unpublished works (including notes, letters, and unfinished manuscripts) during the four decades after his father's death, not all the original writings and scribbling of J. R. R. Tolkien are available. It would, therefore, be incumbent on the researcher in this example to investigate, think carefully about, and document/describe the extent and likely nature of the target population (all of Tolkien's original writings) that the researcher has no ability to access, and to try, as best as possible, to characterize the degree to which the part of Tolkien's writings the researcher is missing might contain conceptualizations of females that are materially different from those the researcher can select (sample) and use in a rigorous qualitative content analysis of Tolkien's writings. In the end, no matter how extensively the researcher studies the writings of Tolkien that are accessible, and no matter how many of these writings are subjected to the content analysis conducted by the researcher, the study is seriously weakened, in this example, due to the researcher's inability to select from the entire population of Tolkien's writings.

Although the researcher's ultimate goal is to have access to the entirety of the target population, the reality is that the qualitative researcher often faces the situation, like the Tolkien example, where complete access to the target population is just not possible or practical. Qualitative researchers frequently take on content analysis studies in which the research objective outdistances what the researcher can realistically expect in terms of a complete, unhindered access to the population of content, particularly when practical considerations (e.g., available research resources, time constraints) play a role. Beeman (2007), for example, conducted a content analysis concerning interracial relationships depicted in films made in the United States from 1980 to 2001. As her source for the population of films in this time period (from which she sampled 40), Beeman used a well-respected, "comprehensive" movie guide. Beeman acknowledges that "this guide does not include every film made in the United States from 1980-2001" (p. 696), but she supports her decision by emphasizing that the guide contains more than 20,000 movie reviews and mentions that the guide has been endorsed by *USA Today* and the *New York Times*.

Another example is the study conducted by Kaphingst et al. (2004) who examined the content of direct-to-consumer (DTC) prescription drug advertisements on television and "features of the ads that might interfere with consumers' comprehension of critical information" (p. 517). For this study, the researchers sampled 29 advertisements from a target population of DTC advertisements appearing on three major nationwide television networks—ABC, CBS, and NBC. The researchers admitted to the potential bias in the study due to limiting the target population to these three television networks (i.e., excluding other broadcast networks and cable channels) but defended their choice by stating that these networks reach "the largest cross section of the public" compared to "a narrower demographic group" reached by other networks and cable channels (p. 517).

These are just two examples of how qualitative researchers determine the scope of their target population based on the reality of research parameters. The crucial point to be made here is that qualitative researchers must reflect thoughtfully on how well the population of content that actually is sampled represents the target population of interest (e.g., all movies made between 1980 and 2001, all DTC advertisements on television) and judge the impact of a less-than-complete representation of the target population on the credibility of research outcomes. Like Beeman and Kaphingst et al. the responsible qualitative content analyst will fully disclose information about how the target population was defined; what, if anything, was missing from this population, given the intended research objective; and how an incomplete population of content may have biased the data as well as the interpretations of the findings.

Sample Design

Equally important to the credibility of a qualitative content analysis study is the method used for selecting the elements of content from the population of content (i.e., the sample design) that the study is investigating. Although some studies in which content analysis is the primary method will analyze all of the content in the population of interest, most will not do so because of the practical realities of research resources, such as the labor and time that are required. Instead, most of these types of qualitative content analysis studies will draw a subset of the population content for analysis. As with sampling for other qualitative methods, selecting a sample for content analysis research should ideally be done in a systematic and random manner. In this way the researcher will be generating data about a representative subset of the entirety of the content that is accessible.

If possible, the researcher should assemble a list of all the elements in the population of content that could possibly be selected for the sample and begin by looking carefully at the list to determine whether there is an underlying order that preexists (e.g., authorship, alphabetical, size, date), or if such a meaningful ordering could (and should) be created. It is important for the researcher to consider the orderliness of the list because it can have a direct effect on the representativeness of the sample that is drawn and, in turn, on the credibility of the study. Take, for example, the study of love letters mentioned earlier. If the collection contained several hundred such love letters (far more than the researcher had the time or need to analyze), the collection should (1) be ordered by which one of the lovers wrote the letters; (2) within each author, by the length of the letter (e.g., possibly categorizing them as short, medium, and long); and (3) within length by the date that the letter was written. In this way, once the researcher has determined how many letters to analyze for each author, a sample could be randomly and systematically drawn (e.g., every sixth letter after a random start[3]) across the entire ordered list so as to well represent each lover's set of letters (at least in terms of length and date).

Keep in mind that a content analysis of nontextual material may involve an "ordered list" of a different form. For example, Altheide (1987) conducted an "ethnographic content analysis" study to investigate television news coverage of the Iranian hostage crisis that began in 1979. In this case, the "ordered list" consisted of the 14-plus months of daily news coverage of the crisis on network television in the United States, from which Altheide systematically selected newscasts representing all 14-plus months as well as the weeks of each month.

Even if there is no inherent or meaningful ordering within the population of content, it is highly recommended that, when sampling is required (i.e., the researcher is not conducting a content analysis on the total population), the elements of content be selected across the entire content list. Likewise, the researcher is highly discouraged from selecting a sample by starting at the beginning of the content list and proceeding one consecutive element of content after the other (e.g., the first letter, the second letter, the third letter) until the desired number of elements of content have been analyzed. By selecting a sample of the content across the entire list of the population of content, the researcher is making it more likely that the quality of the final data will not be weakened by biases associated with the subset of content that was chosen for analysis.

After sampling is completed, there may be times when a researcher cannot locate all the items of content that were selected for the sample—content that the researcher had good reason to believe would be available but is not. This situation would be a form of "nonresponse" in content analysis. For example, if the researcher studying the series of love letters had gained permission to access these letters from the collection's owner, but upon working with the collection finds that some of the letters that had been selected for the sample are missing, the researcher will need to decide whether to replace these missing elements of content with other ones not previously selected for the sample. In these instances, and depending on the prevalence of missing letters, the researcher's decision will depend on whether there is reason to fear that the missing letters contained content that is substantially different from the content contained in the sampled letters that are not missing. If this is the case, it behooves the researcher to go back to the original list of content in the target population (e.g., the entire set of letters) and randomly select a replacement for each missing element. Regardless of what decisions a content analyst makes about the missing content, the researcher should fully disclose (a) the extent of missing content items in the sample, (b) whether the missing elements were known or suspected to differ from the available content in the sample, and (c) how the researcher decided to address the problem (e.g., whether and how missing content was replaced).

Data Gathering

Regardless of whether a qualitative content analysis is conducted as a primary or secondary method of investigation, the credibility of the outcomes rests greatly on the measuring processes. From a TQF perspective, the concerns regarding Data Gathering in qualitative content analysis differ from those that arise with other qualitative methods in that the researcher is working in the realm of the content itself, not the creation of the content. So, unlike IDIs, group discussions, or ethnography (Chapters 3–5), where the measurement issues revolve around potential sources of bias in the creation of data (e.g., interviewer bias, an interviewee's unwillingness to provide information), the measurement concerns in content analysis focus on how to effectively find meaning in content that already exists (i.e., content created by others). In this way, the primary data-gathering considerations in qualitative content analysis reside with the researcher/analyst rather than the content creators, with the center of attention on the coding and analysis process. The content analysis researcher deals with *what is*, and the manner in which acceptable coding procedures are followed to maximize the credibility of the research is the subject of data gathering.

In qualitative content analysis, we make the distinction between two broad phases of the analysis process—Phase 1: **Data Generation** (i.e., coding) and Phase 2: **Data Analysis** (i.e., categorization and interpretation) (see p. 235). The data for a content analysis are created by coding the content, involving all the preparatory steps to coding as well as the coding itself (see pp. 235–238 for a breakdown of the specific steps). The coded content then becomes the data that the researcher analyzes in the second phase of content analysis, when he/she makes sense of the data by way of categorizing and finding meaningful interpretations of the outcomes. The focus of the data-gathering section in this chapter is on how to optimize the quality of the data that are generated by the content coding (i.e., the first phase of the content analysis process), regardless of whether the content comes from content analysis conducted as a primary method (e.g., love letters, television newscasts) or as a secondary method (e.g., the analysis of IDI transcripts, observation field notes).

There are several important considerations pertaining to data collection that qualitative content analysis researchers need to take into account to maximize data quality and therefore the overall credibility of their content analysis study. These considerations are associated with the issues we raise on page 234 concerning the research objectives, related constructs, and the inductive approach; as well as the basic steps of the qualitative content analysis process outlined on pages 235–241. With this in mind, our discussion of data gathering addresses the following questions faced by a researcher conducting a qualitative content analysis study:

- What are the objectives of the study and what are the relevant constructs in the content?
- Will the researcher take a totally inductive approach to formulating the

coding system or will a deductive–inductive strategy be used, or some combinations of both approaches?

- What will be the unit of analysis that will form the basis for the development of codes?
- How will the codebook be organized and what will it contain?
- What will be the nature of the coding form?
- Who will code the content and what will coders need to be trained in?
- How will preliminary coding be conducted?
- How will coders be monitored to assure consistency and validity throughout the coding process?

Research Objectives and Relevant Constructs

From the perspective of gathering data, a researcher who wants to conduct a qualitative content analysis will first need to clearly define the principal research objective (and ancillary goals) of the study and determine which constructs will be measured from the content that is to be studied. By implication, content analysis studies do not try to measure all possible constructs in the content but rather try to link the constructs of interest to the study objectives. For example, Söderberg and Lundman (2001) conducted interviews with women afflicted with fibromyalgia with the specific objective of investigating what it means to "transition from being a healthy woman to being a woman living with [this disorder]" (p. 619). This objective clearly set the course for their content analysis of the IDI transcripts, which focused on the construct of transition and led them to identify various types of transitions experienced by these women (e.g., related to family life). In the previous example of a content analysis on the letters written by 18th-century lovers, the researcher may be interested in only a few very specific aspects of the communications between the two lovers—such as which lover had the most intense feelings toward the other, or whether the lovers were more happy or sad about their relationship, or which lover had the "most mature" feelings of love toward the other—which would guide the researcher's approach to the content analysis. The choice of constructs to study will differ depending on whether the researcher has made an a priori decision about the constructs of interest in the content or whether the researcher goes into the content with a completely open mind to see what important constructs are found, or something in between these two extremes. Such decisions are part and parcel of whether the researcher enters into a qualitative content analysis using a deductive and/or inductive approach (see p. 233).

In instances where the content genre has been studied before, the researcher may decide in advance on the constructs to investigate in light of uninvestigated hypotheses or important knowledge gaps that were identified in prior research. Denny (2011), for example, identified an "untapped dimension" in the research literature on gender messages—that is, the construct of "approach," or the expected attitudes of boys and girls as they approach certain activities—and addressed this gap in her study of the Boy Scout and Girl Scout handbooks by including a qualitative content analysis focused on how Scouts were encouraged to approach certain activities. Education researcher Blase (1986) used the general research literature on work-related stress to pinpoint "stress themes" (e.g., constructs such as "control") that he then applied to a qualitative content analysis concerning teacher stress and performance. In instances where a researcher has a research objective or population of content that has only briefly or never been studied, complete immersion in the content (i.e., an inductive approach) is necessary in order to develop the constructs that will be important to study in the content analysis project.

Ultimately, the credibility of data gathering in a qualitative content analysis study is associated with how well the researcher has identified and accounted for all relevant constructs (and all important aspects related to each construct). The extent to which the researcher will have reasonable knowledge of these constructs prior to the data generation (i.e., coding) phase of a content analysis will vary from study to study, and, indeed, the researcher may rely on the content analysis process itself to discover the pertinent constructs. Whatever the case, the researcher is obligated to explicitly identify these constructs at some point in time. Failure to do this will limit the quality of the information provided by a qualitative content analysis, as it will neither be complete nor robust in capturing information the researcher needs about each construct of interest to satisfy the objectives of the study.

A Deductive–Inductive or Totally Inductive Approach

Qualitative content analysis is generally considered to be an inductive process by which researchers identify meanings and connections in the data from the data itself, with little or no assumptions regarding coding schemes or the categories that encompass the underlying constructs. However, as discussed above, there are instances when a researcher will enter into a qualitative content analysis research project with a good sense of the topic area—because the researcher has conducted prior research on the topic and/or is aware of earlier research on the topic conducted by other researchers—and may be able to anticipate not only the relevant constructs but also one or more particular codes.

In these situations, the qualitative researcher will begin the data generation phase of the content analysis deductively (i.e., with predetermined codes) but continue the process by way of an inductive approach that continually modifies existing codes and creates new codes based on the researcher's immersion in the study data. An example of entering into the process deductively is the research on kidney disease discussed by Forman and Damschroder (2008), in which the code "clinical information" is predetermined, based on research in the literature connecting physician-provided information and patient trust.

A deductive–inductive approach is also highly appropriate when conducting longitudinal qualitative content analysis research (e.g., studying the nutritional/

activity diaries of patients with diabetes over a 5-year period) when many of the constructs as well as elements in the coding and categorization schemes developed in prior years may serve as the foundation from which new codes can be applied to the current study (e.g., the construct of "feeling trapped by circumstances" and patients' comments pertaining to the daily family routine and its impact on meal planning). A qualitative researcher might also use a deductive–inductive approach when a content analysis is being applied to the verbatim replies from survey respondents to open-ended questions that have been asked in prior surveys, which, over the years, have established a diverse and robust set of response constructs that are likely to emerge (in one form or another) in the current research. Importantly, however, the content analyst must always be mindful of the fact that it is ultimately the content of the current study—not the constructs, codes, or categories derived by other means—that primarily guides the qualitative content analysis process.

In contrast to a deductive–inductive approach, a qualitative content analysis researcher will often investigate a domain of content using a totally inductive strategy, whereby codes and categories (that represent a group of codes that share an underlying construct, e.g., codes that fit into the construct of "well-being") are developed without any predispositions or accumulated knowledge from an existing body of research. All approaches to qualitative content analysis require researchers to completely immerse themselves in the content and absorb the entirety of it, but the inductive method places a particular responsibility on the researcher to be sensitive, perceptive, attentive, as well as creative in order to identify and "grow" the codes and categories from the content under study. For this reason, it is especially important that the researcher seek a review from colleagues at the data generation stage concerning the credibility of the coding plan, because if the conclusions the researcher reaches at this point are not valid ones, then the data that are generated will be flawed and the credibility of the entire study likely will be undermined.

For example, consider a researcher who is studying the content from daily newspapers with large circulations to examine public opinion during the past century on the existence of paranormal activity. The researcher plans to take a purely inductive approach to this qualitative content analysis, given that little empirical research has been published on this subject matter. Once a representative set of content on this topic has been selected, the researcher absorbs the content by reading and thinking about the sampled articles on the topic. In this process, the researcher determines the most logical unit of analysis (see p. 236) and takes note of specific news items or newspaper content that addresses the objectives and constructs of interest as they are discovered. The researcher might note the nature of the "evidence" people cite to substantiate their assertions of having encountered paranormal phenomena, the range and intensity of the paranormal phenomena people report encountering, the range and intensity of the physical experiences people report having while in contact with a paranormal entity, and the role personal religiosity plays in the belief or disbelief of paranormal phenomena. As codes are identified and associated with the likely constructs (e.g., specific mentions of God might be coded depending on the exact reference to God, all of which would be categorized within the religiosity construct), the researcher consults with one or more colleagues and presents the coding and categorization schemes, along with the supporting content. The feedback received may or may not lead the researcher to revise these schemes; however, it is important for the qualitative researcher who is taking a totally inductive approach to spend the necessary time to engage in this methodical self-evaluative process in order to raise the likelihood that all important constructs have been identified and that the ultimate coding and categorization of the content will be credible.

The Unit of Analysis

As the researcher is absorbing the content and thinking about the range of constructs that should be studied in the content analysis, he/she is also considering what should be the unit of analysis. The "unit of analysis" refers to the portion of content that will be the basis for decisions made during the development of codes. For example, in textual content analyses, the unit of analysis may be at the level of a word, a sentence, a paragraph, an article or chapter, an entire edition or volume, a complete response to an interview question, entire diaries from research participants, or some other level of text. As mentioned earlier (see p. 236), the unit of analysis may not be defined by the content per se but rather by a characteristic of the content originator (e.g., person's age), or the unit of analysis might be at the individual level with, for example, each participant in an IDI study treated as a case. Whatever the unit of analysis, the researcher will make coding decisions based on various elements of the content, including length, complexity, manifest meanings, and latent meanings based on such nebulous variables as the person's tone or manner.

Deciding on the unit of analysis is a very important decision because it guides the development of codes as well as the coding process which creates the data for the second phase of qualitative content analysis, that is, the categorization/interpretation phase. If a weak unit of analysis is chosen, one of two damaging outcomes will result. First, if the unit chosen is too precise (i.e., at too much of a micro-level than what is actually needed), the researcher will set in motion a content analysis study that may miss important contextual information and may require more time and cost than if a broader unit of analysis had been chosen. An example of a too-precise unit of analysis might be small elements of content such as individual words. In turn, if the unit chosen is too imprecise (i.e., at a very high macro-level), important connections and contextual meanings in the content at smaller (individual) units may be missed, leading to erroneous categorization and interpretation of data in the subsequent phase of the content analysis process. An example of a too-imprecise unit of analysis might be the entire set of diaries written by 25 participants in an IDI research study, or all of the comments made by teenagers on an online support forum. Keep in mind, however, that what is deemed too precise or imprecise will vary across qualitative content analysis studies, making it difficult to prescribe the "right" solution for all situations.

Although there is no perfect prescription for every content analysis study, it is generally understood that content analysts should strive for a unit of analysis that retains the context necessary to derive meaning from the content. For this reason, and if all other things are equal, the qualitative content analysis researcher should probably err on the side of using a broader, *more contextually based* unit of analysis rather than a narrowly focused level of analysis (e.g., sentences). This does not mean that supra-macro-level units, such as the entire set of transcripts from an IDI study, are appropriate; and, to the contrary, these very imprecise units, which will obscure meanings and nuances at the individual level, should be avoided. It does mean, however, that complete paragraphs of a newspaper story or an entire television commercial or a complete record of a physician–patient consultation or the entirety of a research participant's response to the researcher's question are more likely to provide the content analysis researcher with contextual entities by which reasonable and reliable meanings can be obtained and analyzed across all sampled content. In the end, the researcher needs to consider the particular circumstances of the study and define the unit of analysis that is "as large as is meaningful . . . and as small as is feasible" (Krippendorff, 2013, p. 102).

Codebook and Coding Form

CODEBOOK. Code development and preliminary coding in a qualitative content analysis are accompanied by the development of a **codebook** that details what is to be coded and how the coding of the content will be conducted. The codebook begins as a fairly flexible document with new and revised codes incorporated as warranted (documenting when and what changes are made to the codes). Once the researcher is comfortable with the breadth and depth of codes that have been developed, the codebook may be finalized to use in coding the remainder of the content; however, it is not unusual for the codebook to be modified to some degree throughout the process. As shown in Figure 6.5, there are six essential components to the codebook:

- Unit of analysis and particular constructs of interest (if known).
- Name of the code.
- Description or definition of the code, along with a date when the code was last updated.
- How the code relates to other codes (e.g., in the example in Figure 6.5, the main EDUOPPTY [educational opportunity] code has several subcodes, including OLEDU [online education]).
- Any rules that may pertain to applying the code (e.g., "applies to any type of educational, career, or personal development opportunity provided by the facility").
- Examples of the code (taken from the study content).

Codebook

Unit of Analysis and Key Constructs	Code Name	Code Description and Date of Latest Update	Relationship to Other Codes	When to Apply	Examples
Unit of analysis: Each diary	EDUOPPTY	*Code description:* Specifically mentions educational opportunities that are provided by the facility (e.g., access to online webinars, art classes, workshops). *Last updated on:* December 5 at 10 A.M.	*This is a main code. Subcodes include:* OLEDU (online education) ARTCL (art class) CPUCL (computer skills class) FINCL (personal finances class) EECL (exercise equipment class)	Code applies to any mention of any type of educational, career, or personal development opportunity provided by the facility.	"Weekly access to online webinars is helping me keep up with my career." "Twice a week there is an art class. Who would have thought I could draw?"
Main construct: Well-being *Subordinate constructs:* Physical well-being Mental well-being Financial well-being			*Other related codes:* POSPHYWB (positive physical well-being) NEGPHYWB (negative physical well-being) POSMENWB (positive mental well-being) NEGMENWB (negative mental well-being) POSFINWB (positive financial well-being) NEGFINWB (negative financial well-being)		

Coding Form

Relevant Construct/ Issue	Relevant Code	Nature of Relevant Content	Example/Additional Feedback
Physical well-being	EDUOPPTY	I am seeing a lot of examples where the classes on how to use the exercise equipment are perceived as educational as well as giving women a workout and making them feel physically stronger.	"The weekly classes in the gym on how to use and operate the equipment (like the elliptical machine) have shaped me up, which makes me feel like my body is not totally going to waste."
Mental well-being	EDUOPPTY	There is a lot of overlap in the physical and mental well-being associated with the classes on how to use the exercise equipment in the gym. Mentally, it makes women feel like they are learning a new skill, keeping their minds sharp.	I see most of the comments pertaining to positive mental well-being from the exercise equipment classes coming from the women who have been at the facility for a long time (more than 5 years).
Financial well-being	EDUOPPTY	The educational opportunities at the facility seem to give many women confidence that they can do something productive when they are released from prison and provide themselves with an income.	"I wonder how much I could sell my art for if I continued drawing when I leave here." "I have learned so much about how to properly use the exercise equipment, I am thinking about applying for a job at the fitness center when I'm released."

FIGURE 6.5. Example of a codebook and coding form for a hypothetical content analysis study of diaries written by women confined to the county correctional facility. This example is used in Figure 6.2 (p. 239) showing a data display.

It is very important that the researcher provide considerable detail in the code descriptions and rules for applying the code as well as many examples of when and how the code should be applied. Doing so will make it more likely that coders are accurate and consistent in their coding.

As mentioned, the codebook for a qualitative content analysis project is a dynamic document. No matter how extensive and comprehensive it starts out, the codebook is likely to be supplemented and otherwise modified as the content coding progresses and new codes and coding rules are devised for unanticipated coding situations. Ultimately it is the responsibility of the researcher to create a codebook that is as comprehensive and unambiguous as reasonably possible and to also take responsibility for making certain it is modified and enhanced when that is called for. In this way—along with thorough coder training—the codebook will help the coders generate high-quality data on which the categorization/interpretation phase of content analysis and the credibility of the study overall depend.

CAQDAS in Codebook Development. CAQDAS programs can be useful in the development of a codebook. In addition to the features that aid in code and thematic development (see Section 6.2, starting on p. 248), these programs typically offer functions that facilitate setting up a codebook, with code names/labels, definitions, examples, and features that apply rules to the codes (e.g., the ability to specify "inclusion criteria" and "exclusion criteria" in NVivo). CAQDAS makes it relatively easy (compared to using only a manual approach) to make changes to the codebook as well as add memos or relevant notes pertaining to particular codes. These software programs also allow the researcher to evaluate intercoder reliability by way of comparing coders' work, which can be particularly useful when comparisons need to be made over numerous iterations of the codes. When using CAQDAS, the researcher should create written documentation for all the decisions that are made concerning how and why the software was used in a particular manner. This includes describing the researcher's objectives in using the software; the role the software played in developing, defining, and organizing the codes that appear in the codebook; and documenting any problems that were encountered.

As noted in Section 6.2, computer software for content analysis can be very good when used to create data about manifest content; in fact, in theory it is perfect for extracting data from content that represents counts and other such straightforward metrics. But it is usually a poor and inadequate substitute for what the human mind can accomplish when trying to apply complex logic to develop codes and generate data from latent meaning in the content. The shortcomings of the current content analysis software and the humans who creatively (or not) program that software should slowly decrease over time, but it seems unlikely that any cost-effective software for content analysis will be developed in the near future that mirrors the myriad decisions that the human brain can readily make about the meaning in content.

CODING FORM. From a TQF perspective, it is also important that coders utilize a **coding form** throughout the coding process. The coding form (see Figure 6.5) contains the key constructs (if known beforehand) and/or specific issues related to the research objective that may have surfaced in code development. The purpose of the coding form is to ensure that all coders are consistently mindful of these key constructs/issues and use the form to capture their feedback on how these constructs/issues are addressed in the content. For instance, a researcher conducting a qualitative content analysis study on corporate email communication—specifically, email messages sent from the human resources (HR) department to all employees—might have discovered during code development that certain aspects of these communications (e.g., the critical tone of the message, the employee's gender, the reading level, and the clarity of the message in terms of what it is asking the employee to do) are particularly relevant to the research objectives. As an adjunct to the coding of this content (per the codebook), the coders would also be asked to complete a coding form on which they can write (using paper or a computer device), for example, the evaluative nature of the message; the relevant code(s) associated with this message; whether it was positive, negative, or mixed; and an excerpt from the content to illustrate. The coding form would also ask coders to provide feedback on the other issues, such as gender (e.g., noting whether the email message was sent to a man or woman, and how, if at all, the communication reads differently depending on gender), reading level, and clarity of required action. The design of the coding form will vary from study to study, but it is important to keep the form short (preferably one or two pages printed, front and back) so as to not overburden coders and keep the research within reasonable time and cost parameters. The completed coding form should be attached to, and become a permanent component of, the coded content (an electronic attachment to the data file). Use of coding forms is meant to enhance the quality of data gathering in qualitative content analysis by adding validity and reliability—that is, credibility—to the research. Furthermore, the researcher can then use the coders' feedback from the coding form throughout the categorization/interpretation phase of data analysis as a supplement to understanding (adding meaning and context to) the data. For the sake of full transparency, the final research document should include examples of completed coding forms as well as examples of the data (i.e., coded content).

Coder Selection and Training

CODER SELECTION. It is a very important decision that researchers make in selecting those who will serve as coders, as the coding that eventually is done will be of no better quality than the ability and commitment of those who do the coding. Not unlike the two essential skills of the content analysis researcher—that is, the ability to be systematic and sensitive/perceptive (see Section 6.1, p. 244)—the chief characteristics that should be weighed in selecting content analysis coders are:

- Experienced in coding and demonstrated good coding skills.
- Meticulous work methods.
- Good intelligence.
- Knowledgeable about the subject area.
- Objective decision maker who does not let personal views of topics bias coding judgments.
- A disciplined decision maker who will closely follow the coding rules.
- Familiarity with, and success at, conducting the overall content analysis process.

Although it is true that the training coders receive is very important in determining the quality of coding they will do, the best training is not likely to compensate entirely for a deficiency of the desirable traits and abilities inherent to the coders themselves. Because of the importance of coders in the content analysis process, the qualitative researcher should identify the pool of individuals who will serve as coders well before the time the training is to begin, so as to make it more likely that good-caliber individuals will be available, without having to scramble at the last minute to find them.

CODER TRAINING. Once the coders are selected, the coding scheme has been devised, and a codebook created to guide the coding decisions that coders will make, a training curriculum for the coders needs to be created and implemented. The goal of the training is to imbue the coders with the specific knowledge, enthusiasm, and commitment they need to carry out high-quality and objective coding of the content. It is these coders who are creating the data that the researcher will categorize and interpret in the second phase of the content analysis, and it is in large part the quality of the training curriculum (and the quality of the codebook) that will signal to the coders the extent to which the researcher actually cares about the quality of the data the coders produce through their coding of the content.

The effectiveness of coder training depends, in part, on how much time coders are given to absorb the training materials. The researcher must decide whether it is more likely to help or harm the training process to provide the prospective coders with the training materials prior to the training. Whether or not materials are given beforehand, the decision should be based on the researcher's best judgment as to the approach that will most benefit the outcome of training. The point here is that there is no set rule that applies to each qualitative content analysis project. However, if the researcher decides it would be better to provide the training materials to the coders in advance of the training session, the coders must be told exactly what is expected of them in reviewing the material, including how long they should spend on their review prior to the training.

As noted, the credibility of a qualitative content analysis study relies greatly on proper coder training. From a TQF perspective, the training curriculum for coders on a qualitative content analysis project should include the following modules:

- **Introduction to the project.** An explanation is provided about the objectives of the project and the project's importance to the researcher and others with a vested interest in the findings. This is likely to take 15–60 minutes depending on what the researcher judges as best. This explanation should be as detailed as deemed informative to the coders, but it is important that the coders not be given information about anything that might compromise their objectivity. The researcher is responsible for thinking carefully about maintaining coders' objectivity and for deciding how to avoid the potential of unduly influencing coders during training. In particular, it is very important that the researcher not inform coders of any hypotheses the researcher may have or particular findings the researcher is "hoping for" in the outcomes. Since good coders generally want to do a good job for the sake of the researcher, telling them too much (or in some cases, anything) about the researcher's preferred expectations may bias their coding. Instead, coders should be made to understand that the researcher defines a "good job" as one in which the coders follow the coding procedures exactly as they have been devised and that coders not be concerned about the outcome of the findings that the researcher will discover when analyzing (categorizing and interpreting) the data the coders generate.

- **Detailed explanation of the codebook and use of the coding form.** Here the researcher methodically goes through the codebook, beginning with instruction on the unit of analysis and any constructs that have been identified, and explaining the definition and use of each code. At each point in the discussion, the researcher should entertain any questions coders may have and fully address their questions or comments before moving on. Once all aspects of the codebook have been discussed to the full satisfaction of the researcher and the coders, the coding form should be introduced. Coders should be told the purpose of the coding form, how they should use it, and an item-by-item explanation of what is contained on it, including reference to the corresponding code in the codebook (e.g., as in Figure 6.5, coders might be instructed to elaborate on the coding form how the EDUOPPTY code relates to the "physical well-being" construct). Once again, questions from the coders should be addressed immediately as they arise, because if the issues remain unresolved until later, they may interfere with the learning coders are trying to gain on subsequent topics. This portion of training is likely to take 1–2 hours depending on the complexity and length of the coding process.

- **Practice working with the codebook and coding form.** This practice may take up to 2 hours depending on the number of coders as well as the complexity and length of the coding process. At the start, coders should be given time to practice coding actual examples of the content the project is studying. Coders should not do this on their own but in the presence of the researcher and other coders so that questions can be asked and answered as they arise, and thereby all can benefit from this form of reactive training. Once the individual coding part of this practice is completed, the coders should break into dyads to compare their coding decisions with each other. The coders should then reassemble and the researcher should walk through all, or at least an extensive set, of the coding decisions to talk out how different decisions were made and which ones were the correct decisions for this project.

- **Use of a reflexive journal.** The coding form that coders complete during the coding process is one way that they can provide the researcher with their feedback and impressions of the content. A reflexive journal is another kind of note taking whereby coders can record their thoughts related to the content, the coding process, and/or the project. Unlike the coding form that coders complete as they code, the coders are asked to write in their reflexive journals once or twice a week (depending on the complexity and duration of the coding process). It should be emphasized that there are no rules to follow in completing the reflexive journal; to the contrary, coders should be encouraged to write whatever is on their minds that might be useful to the researcher in the second phase of the content analysis, that is, categorization and interpretation. An example of a reflexive journal format is shown in Chapter 2, Figure 2.2, page 42.

- **Timing and other project operational logistics.** The researcher should explain the timeline for the completion of coding, including any target dates that need to be met, as well as fundamental operational issues, such as the hours and location of the coding sessions and the terms of coders' employment.

Two additional steps should follow the training session. First, the coding that the individual coders completed during the practice should be scored or otherwise evaluated by the researcher to try to identify which of the coders, if any, will need additional training or possibly will need to be dropped entirely from the project. Second, the training session will most likely lead to insights about ways to improve the codebook. It is the researcher's responsibility to attend to this revision improvement process. Once the changes to the codebook have been finalized, a decision needs to be made about how to communicate these improvements to the coders. In some cases this can be done via a written memo (e.g., an email message) and in others the coders (as a group) may need to be given additional in-person training about the changes. In all cases, however, coders should be given the updated page(s) from the codebook showing the revised code description(s) and the date of the revision. Of note, if the codebook changes, the coding form also may need to be modified.

The detail provided in this section about the selection and training of coders in qualitative content analysis research (including the time required to carry out these training steps) may seem excessive to some readers. However, we do not believe that it is excessive at all. Rather, coders are central to the success of a qualitative content analysis study, and the prudent researcher will give great attention to these matters and commit considerable resources (time and money) to carry them out as well as possible.

Preliminary Coding

As with other research methods (such as the intercoder process in IDIs, see p. 91), it is highly advisable to conduct a preliminary test of the coding procedures that will be used in qualitative content analysis before the actual creation of the data in the coding process for the entirety of the content. The primary parts of qualitative content analysis that need to be scrutinized at this preliminary stage are the codebook, coding form, and how well coders do their job. During preliminary coding, the researcher strives to determine whether the coder(s) can create high-quality data from the selected content, utilizing the codebook and coding form that have been devised.

Preliminary coding entails the researcher's selection of one to three elements of content (e.g., love letters, television commercials, IDI participants) per coder and asking these trained coders to use the codebook and coding form to code the selected content. Ideally, the selected content should be a separate collection of content from the sample that is the focus of the study; however, in reality, this is often not possible in qualitative research. When this initial aspect of preliminary coding is completed, the researcher should meet with the coders and conduct a debriefing session in which the researcher reviews the coding and discusses each coding decision, including how coders made their decisions based on the codebook. The researcher should also review and discuss coders' comments and feedback on the coding forms. The debriefing provides the researcher with detailed information on the adequacy of the codebook and the coding form, from which the researcher will make all the revisions he/she deems necessary. Once those revisions have been made, it is advisable to do another round of preliminary coding. Even if the first debriefing session does not result in changes on the part of the researcher, it is advisable that coders be given another set of content to code to test the codebook and coding form an additional time. If nothing problematic arises after the second period of preliminary coding, the researcher will most likely begin the actual coding process for the entirety of the content under investigation.

As with the development of the codebook (see p. 265), CAQDAS programs typically integrate features that facilitate the coding process for coders and make comparing the coding across coders fairly easy. If the researcher has elected to use a CAQDAS program for the content analysis, this program can be useful in looking at coding results during the preliminary coding stage. For instance, these programs can show the researcher the extent of agreement across coders (e.g., as a percentage) as well as a statistical measurement of agreement, such as the kappa coefficient (see the discussion on "coding consistency," p. 272).

In a qualitative content analysis study where the researcher intends to do all the coding (i.e., without assistance from other coders), it is wise for him/her to engage someone else to independently conduct preliminary coding to test the codebook and coding form. The primary advantage to bringing in an outside party is that he/she can provide the researcher with an independent assessment of the credibility of the coding processes the researcher has created. Determining in this preliminary coding stage that the independent coder is unable to code the content to the researcher's satisfaction is very important information that merits the researcher's careful further thought. In particular, the researcher needs to reflect on, and later explain to anyone who will consume the research findings, (a) why independent preliminary coding did not match what the researcher would have deemed correct coding of the content, (b) the possible biases associated with the researcher's assumptions that may threaten the credibility of the study, and (c) any changes the researcher may have made to the coding process based on what was learned from this independent pretesting.

If, on the other hand, the independent preliminary coding yields data that conform closely to the researcher's own preliminary coding of the content, then that outcome is powerful evidence to support the credibility of the researcher's decision to code the content without the assistance of other coders.

It should be noted that this procedure of preliminary coding is similar regardless of whether the content is textual or nontextual in nature, or whether the content analysis is being done as a primary or secondary research method. Nontextual content—such as television broadcasts, graphic images, and Hollywood films—is treated in the same manner as written documents, with selected content shown to trained coders who utilize a codebook and coding form to code the content selection, are then debriefed, and finally asked to go through this process again until the researcher is satisfied with the codebook and coding form. For example, Beeman (2007), who investigated interracial relationships in films, tested her coding scheme on eight films (separate from her sample) to assess its effectiveness in coding various components of on-screen relationships prior to coding all 40 films in her content sample. In some instances, the researcher may want to convert visual material to text prior to preliminary coding—for example, when a researcher wants to conduct a qualitative content analysis on television newscasts analyzing only the spoken word (as opposed to the physical or behavioral characteristics of those reporting the news)—in which case, it is the researcher's responsibility to ensure that the process of creating transcripts adheres to the quality standards for transcriptions discussed in Chapters 3 and 4 (see pp. 90–91 in Chapter 3 and p. 154 in Chapter 4) to maximize the reliability of the coding effort.

Monitoring Coders

In order to ensure the credibility of data that are generated in qualitative content analysis during the coding process, the researcher must regularly monitor the consistency (reliability) and accuracy of the data that the coders are creating. Regardless of whether the researcher is doing all of the coding or working with trained coders, monitoring of the coding process should include regular reviews of the data generated, feedback on the coding forms, and each coder's reflexive journal. A discussion on monitoring the consistency and accuracy of coding follows.

CODING CONSISTENCY. Coding consistency boils down to documenting the extent to which the coding decision made by one coder would be made by another coder about the same element of content or by the first coder when coding the same content element on a second occasion—that is, the consistency of coding across coders (intercoder reliability) and by the same coder (intracoder reliability). There are many ways that the consistency of the coding done in qualitative content analysis research can be determined, including several statistical measures that can be calculated with the assistance of CAQDAS programs, such as Cohen's (1960) kappa coefficient and Krippendorff's (2013) alpha. Although the research literature generally suggests that a minimum consistency of 75–80% is needed to be considered "excellent agreement" (cf. Banerjee, Capozzoli, McSweeney, & Debajyoti, 1999; Krippendorff, 2004), the acceptable level of intercoder and intracoder agreement will be dictated by each qualitative content analysis situation, including the particular research objectives, the researcher's intended use of the outcomes, and available resources (i.e., the time and money available to spend on repeated measurements of consistency).

Whether or not statistical applications truly apply—or should ever constitute the only criterion—for measuring agreement in qualitative content analysis is debatable. In particular, the underlying assumptions in quantitative measures and statistical formulas based on discrete items are generally inappropriate with qualitative content analysis where the purpose is to discover the interrelatedness and nuanced meanings of the content. For this reason, statistical measures may result in an "over-simplification that compromises validity" in the data generated by a qualitative content analysis (Forman & Damschroder, 2008, p. 55). Other methods that take into consideration alternative perspectives of—or ways of looking at—the content, such as consensus building among coders, may be more suitable in qualitative content analysis.

Regardless of the method, when the researcher determines that intercoder agreement is fairly low or that coders have been too inconsistent (of course, one should never expect human coders to have perfect consistency in their coding decisions), the researcher needs to understand why the inconsistencies have resulted. There are two important issues here. First, decisions need to be made about the underlying cause of the inconsistencies—which is ascertained from the researcher reviewing the coding and comments made on the coding forms and reflexive journals, as well as from the researcher's discussions with the coders—and how to prevent these from occurring in the future, including the need to revise the codebook, possibly retrain the coders, and correct existing inconsistencies in all the elements of the content that have been coded to this point but not included in the sample of elements that were used to check coder consistency. Second, the researcher needs to make a one-by-one decision about the quality of coding being performed by each coder, and possibly retrain some or all of them on the entire coding process. As part of these individual evaluations, it may be deemed necessary to terminate coders who consistently underperform,[4] in which case, the remaining coders would need to recode all the content elements previously coded by the terminated coder(s).

Consistency When the Researcher Is the Sole Coder. Consistency is equally important when the researcher is the sole coder. Under these circumstances, the researcher should let some time pass (e.g., a few days) after initially coding some portion of the content before going back and coding those content elements again (without viewing the initial coding decisions). The researcher should then compare the congruence between his/her first and second coding decisions as they pertain to the same elements of content. In cases where there is a discrepancy between the two coding decisions, the researcher should consider possible reasons why different decisions were made about the same element of content. The researcher should then determine how to be consistent on these types of elements going forward and, if necessary, go back over all the previous coding to find and remedy other possible inconsistencies.

Once the researcher is satisfied with the consistency of the coding, he/she should ask one or two people to code a sample of the content elements the researcher already coded. This may require the researcher to train another person on the codebook and coding form. When the assigned coding has been completed, the researcher should compare his/her own coding to that of the other coder(s). By studying the elements where the researcher and the other coder(s) made different coding decisions, along with the researcher's notes in the coding form and reflexive journal, the researcher will seek explanations for the inconsistencies. Based on what the researcher concludes about the cause and importance of the inconsistencies (i.e., in some cases the inconsistencies may be negligible), the researcher may choose to dismiss the fact that inconsistencies exist or devise a plan to remedy the existing inconsistencies and avoid them from happening going forward. This process may need to be repeated one or more times during the study.

CODING ACCURACY. In addition to checking on the level of the consistency in the coding decisions, the researcher must also check on the **coding accuracy**; that is, the accuracy of the decisions that the coders are making during the coding process. This is important because a coder may be extremely consistent and yet be making incorrect coding decisions in the coding process. In this case, the coder's coding decisions are reliable (codes are being applied similarly across similar content) but weak on validity (the codes applied do not give a true account of the content coded). Periodic reviews of coders' coding decisions are critical to the credibility of the research outcomes. To this end, the researcher should schedule one-on-one meetings with coders to go over the coding, discuss any questionable coding decisions, and, in each instance, listen to the coder's understanding of the coded content and justification for the coding decision that was made. Ultimately the researcher is the final arbitrator for the study in terms of what is deemed an accurate coding decision. (Of course, those who eventually read the final research document, including journal reviewers and editors, could be considered the actual final arbitrators by deciding whether they believe that the study is credible.) It is possible that the researcher may find the coder's explanation plausible and judge that the code the coder applied to the particular content accurately represents the content element; this judgment, however, would require a revision of the codebook as well as a new training session to retrain coders on this adjustment. If, on the other hand, the researcher finds the coder's coding and logic for making that decision unconvincing, the researcher needs to thoroughly explain why the appropriate code matches the element of content and, as necessary, retrain the coder on the research topic and coding scheme.

Analyzability

As it applies to qualitative content analysis research, the Analyzability component of the TQF is concerned with the second broad phase of content analysis—that is, the categorization and interpretation of the data. Analyzability is where the researcher turns from generating the data by way of coding content in the first phase of the content analysis (see Credibility, pp. 253–274) to making sense of the data. The focus in the Analyzability component is on how to conduct complete and accurate analyses of the data that lead to reliable and meaningful interpretations of the content and achieve research objectives.

As noted previously, Analyzability embraces the two key elements of all qualitative analysis: Processing and Verification. In qualitative content analysis, Processing pertains to two of the three steps in the analysis phase (see the basic steps in qualitative content analysis, p. 235), that is, identifying categories (Step 6) and identifying themes (Step 7). Specifically, processing entails the organization and review of the data and ancillary references, such as coding forms and reflexive journals, in order to identify categories from which patterns or themes in the data emerge. The Verification element of the Analyzability component involves the all-important step of scrutinizing the researcher's interpretations of the research derived from the categories and themes identified in the data, and substantiating these findings by way of deviant cases, peer debriefings, and triangulation. By carefully considering their processing and verification procedures, researchers maximize the validity of their analyses and the ultimate usefulness of the outcomes.

It has been stated in earlier chapters that the burden of conducting qualitative analysis is relieved somewhat by the involvement of two or more skilled individuals who can collaborate and share in the process. This is no less true in qualitative content analysis where the volume of data, along with supporting material such as coding forms and reflexive journals, can be extensive. As with other methods, it is important that those involved in the analytical functions (including the lead researcher) work independently, only sharing their insights periodically. Identification of the same categories, themes, and similar implications in the data adds reliability and validity to the research findings.

Processing

The processing of data in qualitative content analysis is aimed at finding appropriate categories by which the researcher is able to locate meaningful patterns or themes that serve to explain the research outcomes. The categorization of data, like the coding of content, is conducted at both the manifest and latent levels in that the researcher is utilizing not just the data generated from codes but also the thoughts and interpretations recorded by coders and the researcher throughout the process. Like code development in the data-generating phase, the development of categories is a flexible, iterative procedure.

Category development should involve the following:

- Organizing of the data by code or groups of codes. For instance, a content analysis study concerning print advertisements for alcoholic beverages might have one code for "type of alcohol" but several codes for a construct such as "promoted benefits of alcohol use."

- Collecting and reviewing memos or notes recorded in the coders' coding forms and reflexive journals, as well as the researcher's own reflexive journal.

- Reorganizing the data (which has been organized by single codes or groups of codes) into meaningful clusters that convey a central construct or idea based, not only on the data itself, but also on anything else that has been learned about the data in the analysis of coding forms and reflexive journals.

- Finalizing and examining the derived clusters of data to define and label the categories.

When the relevant categories have been identified, the researcher can begin isolating patterns or themes in the data that address the research issues. As discussed on page 238, the researcher can look for patterns by using various colors of marking pens to highlight category content (e.g., coded content specific to the category); however, a more efficient method is to create a data display of some type. Figures 6.2 and 6.3 (on p. 239 and p. 240, respectively) are two examples of data display formats. CAQDAS can also be very useful in easily labeling, organizing, searching, sorting, and visually depicting the connections between categories. Whatever method is utilized, the fundamental purpose is the same: to provide the researcher with an informative visual representation of the categories in order to facilitate the discovery of appropriate patterns or themes in the data.

Following the identification and recording of appropriate themes, the researcher should step aside and then return to the data and categorization (possibly as soon as in a few days) to conduct another analysis of themes without reviewing the interpretations derived earlier. Waiting at least a few days before conducting a second (independent) analysis has two major advantages from a TQF standpoint. First, it allows the researcher to approach the data with a fresh mind a second time. And, as importantly, it allows the researcher's conscious and unconscious thought processes to informally consider the data in the time between the two analyses. Once the second (independent) analysis has been completed, the researcher should compare the findings from the two analyses to determine if any meaningful differences exist between them. If there are, the researcher must resolve these differences. The researcher also should document the differences and the rationale for the resolutions, so as to be able to include a summary of this step of the analysis process in the final research document.

We acknowledge that the processing approach described above may appear unduly burdensome to many qualitative content analysis researchers. But, it is highly consistent with what we believe should be every researcher's desire to embrace a rigorous approach to analyzing qualitative content analysis data. Not only will it make the findings more complete and accurate, it will also empower the researcher with more confidence in the value of the research findings.

Verification

The verification of the data concerns the last step of the qualitative content analysis process, which involves drawing interpretations and implications from the data. At this point in the process, the researcher has most likely—by way of the coding and processing procedures discussed earlier—begun to formulate ideas about the underlying meaning of the research outcomes. These preliminary interpretations are drawn from a wealth of information the researcher should have now gleaned from developing codes, working through the coding process, resolving issues in the organizing (and reorganizing) of the data, as well as the many meetings/debriefings and memos/notes recorded throughout the process with coders and other members of the research team.

From a TQF perspective, it is not good enough to settle on preliminary interpretations and implications of the outcomes as the final result of the research. Preliminary conclusions are fine as far as they go, but the prudent researcher will use these preliminary ideas only as a starting point to verification. A number of verification procedures have been discussed in earlier chapters as well as in Section 6.1 of this chapter. The three forms of verification most appropriate to qualitative content analysis are (a) deviant case analysis, (b) peer debriefings, and (c) triangulation.

Deviant or negative case analysis involves seeking out data and supporting content that contradict what appears to be a prevailing finding in the research. The researcher is looking for cases that refute an assumed interpretation to determine whether it adds doubt or actually helps to support the researcher's claim. An example highlighting how a deviant case analysis might add doubt to a researcher's finding is given on page 241.

Peer debriefings are also an important form of verifying preliminary interpretations from a qualitative content analysis study. Debriefings of some sort have taken place throughout the process, but peer debriefings at this final analytical stage are critical to understanding research outcomes. Because latent and contextual meaning play such a large role in qualitative content analysis, gaining the input from team members and knowledgeable colleagues is essential to appreciating different perspectives. Ideally (that is, to the degree there are sufficient time and resources), the researcher should provide the data, categories, themes, and ancillary materials (i.e., the coding forms, reflexive journals, and other recorded notations) to researchers who review and provide their own interpretations independently from the others. When all peer reviewers have completed and submitted their analyses, the researcher should meet individually and/or in a group with these individuals (in person, via telephone or Skype) to share interpretations in more depth. The outcome from these peer debriefings may or may not alter the final research findings; however, they will add valuable credibility and transparency to the research.

A third useful verification procedure in qualitative content analysis is triangulation. Triangulation allows the researcher to compare preliminary interpretations of the data with that obtained by other researchers (not unlike peer debriefings), by other sources (e.g., looking at data generated from a different sample of content from the target population), and by other methods. As far as method triangulation, the preliminary outcomes from a content analysis of racial bias in an organizational handbook, for example, might be compared to data from an IDI study with the organization's members concerning racial attitudes. Or, the researcher working on the content analysis study concerning female inmates at a county correctional facility (see p. 238) might compare preliminary findings from this research with those from an ethnographic study at the same facility where inmates' ability to cope and physical activities were carefully observed. These comparisons may or may not corroborate the researcher's findings that, for example, there is a direct relationship between coping and physical activity among female inmates, but it will assuredly provide important stability and credibility to whatever the researcher's final interpretations and implications of the data turn out to be.

Transparency

The Transparency component in the TQF supports the credibility and Analyzability components in that it requires the researcher to fully document and clearly present each aspect of the research. The researcher may have designed and executed a highly credible content analysis study and ensured that the outcomes were correctly processed and verified, but it is only by way of the complete disclosure of the research details that users of the research are able to draw their own insights. In particular, the goal of the Transparency component is to offer the reader of the final research document a thick description of the thinking and procedures involved in the study—including the strengths and limitations of the research—so that the reader will ideally arrive at a similar interpretation of the data (or, at least, will be able to derive his/her own interpretation of the data) and/or determine the applicability or transferability of the techniques or methods to other comparable contexts.

In creating the final version of the document for a qualitative content analysis study, the researcher will need to pay special attention to reporting the decisions that were made regarding the target population, the sampling of content, the first phase of analysis (i.e., coding, including Steps 1–5 of the eight basic steps to qualitative content analysis, see p. 235), the second phase of analysis (i.e., categorization/interpretation, consisting of Steps 6–8), and the techniques used to organize (and reorganize) the data into meaningful clusters. Although some aspects of this reporting coverage are needed for all qualitative methods, qualitative content analysis is unique in its objectives and its data sources, and may be relatively unfamiliar to the readers of the research document. To achieve transparency in a qualitative content analysis study, the researcher will need to create a final document that takes the reader through the research process, from beginning to end, and addresses such issues as:

THICK DESCRIPTION DETAILS FOR CONTENT ANALYSIS

■ The research objective, including the background, assumptions leading up to the determination of the key objective, and the a priori knowledge of relevant constructs.

■ The research method and why content analysis was considered the best approach.

■ The target population of content, including its breadth, depth, and the researcher's access to it.

■ The sampling of content from the target population, including the determination of sample size, procedures used to select the sample, and obstacles that needed to be overcome (e.g., access and possible biases or weaknesses in the data due to missing or inaccessible content). And, if all the content in the population was chosen, a rationale for that choice should be given.

■ The complications or decisions that were made in the coding and/or categorization and interpretation phases of the analysis process that led to redefining research objectives, sampling new content, or otherwise shifting the focus of the research design.

■ The selection and training of coders and other members of the research team who assisted throughout (e.g., in peer debriefings).

■ The procedures used to monitor coders and the outcome(s) of these efforts.

■ The development of codes, the codebook, and coding form (including samples of each).

■ The coders' reflexive journals, including examples of consistent problems they had in making decisions about certain data elements to be coded.

■ The techniques (and the rationale) that were used to organize and reorganize the data, as well as to collect and review coding forms and reflexive journals, to make sense of the data and identify categories and themes.

■ The use of CAQDAS, including the basis by which it was decided to use or not use CAQDAS, how it was used, and the benefits and drawbacks it posed in working with the research content and data.

■ The specific verification steps that were taken, how each verification procedure supported or refuted the researcher's preliminary interpretation of the data, and any action the researcher took as a result of the verification process.

Usefulness

The Usefulness component of the TQF represents the ultimate goal of all qualitative research design—that is, the ability to do something of value with the research outcomes. An ultimately useful qualitative content analysis study is one that (a) advances the state of existing knowledge with the discovery of new insights, (b) results in actionable next steps, and/or (c) generates new applications of the techniques or methods to similar contexts or research issues (i.e., transferability). In a qualitative content analysis study, the usefulness of the research hinges on (a) the representative sampling of content (as necessary), the correct determination of the unit of analysis, code development, and the coding process (Credibility); (b) the organization and review of the data as well as ancillary materials such as coding forms and reflexive journals, the identification of categories and themes, and the procedures used to verify preliminary findings (Analyzability); and (c) the complete disclosure in the final document of the details accounting for the processes and decision making throughout the course of the study (Transparency).

By achieving a useful research outcome, a TQF strategy has enabled qualitative content analysis researchers (a) to create a piece of research that will live on past its completion (by way of furthering next steps and/or motivating new applications of the design in related contexts), (b) to provide a strong base of confidence for the research findings among researchers and research sponsors, as well as (c) to raise the bar for quality standards in qualitative content analysis research design.

Case Study

A case study where content analysis was used as the primary method of investigation is presented starting on page 284. This research is an example of how many of the TQF concepts can and should be applied to qualitative content analysis, resulting in useful outcomes that advanced the knowledge of the depiction of women in print media and extended the discussion to include publications reaching large, diverse audiences.

6.4 CHAPTER SUMMARY

✓ Content analysis can be conducted as both a qualitative and a quantitative research method. This chapter focuses on the qualitative approach to content analysis.

✓ We define qualitative content analysis as the systematic reduction ("condensation") of content, which is analyzed with special attention to the context in which it was created, to identify themes and extract meaningful interpretations of the data.

✓ Qualitative content analysis includes the coding of, and extraction of meaning from, manifest content and latent content. Manifest content is information that is readily apparent and objectively determined (e.g., the number of times the word "quality" or the term "climate change" is used). Latent content is contextually based information that reveals the underlying meaning of the content.

✓ Researchers must decide whether they will use a deductive approach to creating their content codebook and/or an inductive approach. A deductive approach is one in which the researcher enters into the coding process with predetermined codes or constructs derived from earlier research. What is learned in the coding phase may cause the researcher to modify the codebook. When using the inductive approach, codes are developed without any predispositions or accumulated knowledge from an existing body of research.

✓ Qualitative content analysis involves eight steps that are distributed between two phases of the process. Phase 1 is Data Generation and comprises Steps 1–5, and Phase 2 is Data Analysis, encompassing Steps 6–8.

✓ In Phase 1, the researcher begins by "absorbing" (understanding) the content, determining the unit(s) of analysis, developing unique codes, creating a codebook that describes the coding scheme, doing preliminary coding to test the adequacy of the codebook and coding form, and then training a set of coders to code the content. In Phase 2, the researcher uses the coded content derived in Phase 1 to identify categories across codes, identify themes (patterns) across categories, and draw interpretations and implications.

✓ *Primary* content analysis is conducted when the source of content is an existing, naturally occurring repository of information such as material in textual archives (e.g., newspapers, written documents, books, letters, emails, blogs). *Secondary* content analysis is performed using content that was created by another qualitative research method, such as an in-depth interview, transcripts of focus groups, or ethnographic field notes. The content that is studied in content analysis can also be nontextual in nature such as videos, photographs, original paintings in a museum, etc.

✓ The emphasis on latent meanings and context, as well as the unobtrusive nature of primary content analysis (unobtrusive in that the data generation phase does not affect the preexisting content that is being coded), are key strengths of qualitative content analysis. The limitations revolve around the inherent constraints of extrapolating reliable and valid interpretations from textual and nontextual material.

✓ CAQDAS can be especially useful when handling a large volume of coded content, and it has the potential for improving the speed, accuracy, and reliability of the analysis compared to manual procedures. However, CAQDAS may give the researcher the mistaken notion that computer software is all that is needed to conduct a credible and thorough analysis of the data when, in fact, it is ill-equipped to tackle the contextual complexities that are important in qualitative content analysis. In this way, CAQDAS is simply a tool that can assist, but not replace, the researcher.

✓ From a Total Quality Framework (TQF) perspective, there are a number of important factors to consider when designing a qualitative content analysis study. One such factor is the researcher's access to the content being studied; specifically, whether or not the researcher has complete access and, if not, how the content that is accessible is the same or different from the content that is not accessible (i.e., noncoverage bias).

✓ A TQF approach also considers how the researcher samples the content, particularly the orderliness of the content and the many ways the ordered content can impact the selection of a sample.

✓ The Credibility component of the TQF outlines eight considerations that are important to the data-gathering process in order to maximize data quality. The researcher needs to consider (1) study objectives and relevant constructs, (2) deductive and/or inductive strategy, (3) unit(s) of analysis, (4) codebook, (5) coding form, (6) selection and training of coders, (7) preliminary coding, and (8) monitoring of coders throughout the process.

✓ When monitoring coders, the researcher should pay particular attention to coding consistency and accuracy.

✓ The processing of the data (an element of the Analyzability component of the TQF) involves the development of categories from which the researcher isolates patterns and themes that address the research issue.

✓ The three forms of verification most appropriate to qualitative content analysis are (a) deviant case analysis, (b) peer debriefings, and (c) triangulation.

6.5   EXERCISES AND DISCUSSION TOPICS

1. Assume that you have been asked to conduct a qualitative content analysis to investigate what has been written in the literature in the past 5 years concerning hospice services for cancer patients. Describe your research design in terms of the target population, sampling approach, inductive or deductive–inductive strategy, possible relevant constructs, and unit of analysis.

2. Conduct a qualitative content analysis on at least four videos on YouTube concerning a topic that interests you. Describe how you conducted this analysis following the eight steps in qualitative content analysis.

3. Select three articles (from the literature, online blog, newspaper, or magazine) of at least 700 words each on a related subject and develop a qualitative content analysis codebook based on common and contrasting ideas/comments in these articles.

4. Code the three articles (from Exercise 3) using your codebook and describe your process for monitoring consistency and accuracy in the coding.

5. Derive the categories and themes from the three articles (in Exercise 3). Explain how you identified these categories/themes, your preliminary interpretation of these data, and the steps you would take to verify your preliminary findings.

WEB RESOURCES

Note: In this book, we discourage qualitative researchers from overly relying on CAQDAS. There are, however, many online sources of information regarding CAQDAS for those who would like to learn more.

Friese, S. (2013). Proposing a new method for computer-assisted qualitative data analysis. In *IQM Master Class Webinar*. ATLAS.ti. Online access to the presentation available at *http://prezi.com/5notp28gegos/proposing-a-new-method-for-computer-assisted-qualitative-data-analysis*.

In this presentation, Friese makes the case for using CAQDAS, including many vivid examples that highlight the software's range of capabilities such as the visualization graphic presented in Chapter 6 (see Figure 6.4). Although Friese is a consultant for ATLAS.ti, a primary provider of CAQDAS, her presentation is unbiased, thorough, and well produced.

University of Surrey, CAQDAS Networking Project
www.surrey.ac.uk/sociology/research/researchcentres/caqdas

This website is a valuable resource that provides "practical support, training and information in the use of a range of software programs designed to assist qualitative data analysis." This site does not promote any one CAQDAS solution but rather provides a comprehensive package of information that helps the user choose and use CAQDAS. Included in this information is an up-to-date calendar of upcoming training sessions and conference events, as well as links to online articles, websites, and other resources. Christina Silver, a well-published authority on CAQDAS, is a research fellow working with the CAQDAS Networking Project whose background and publication information can be found on the website.

CAQDAS Websites

All of these sites offer free trial and/or demonstration versions.

ATLAS.ti
www.atlasti.com/index.html

Ethnograph
www.qualisresearch.com

HyperRESEARCH
www.researchware.com/products/hyperresearch.html

MAXQDA
www.maxqda.com

NVivo
www.qsrinternational.com/products_nvivo.aspx

Qualrus
www.qualrus.com

NOTES

1. Krippendorff (2013) uses the concept of the "hermeneutic circle" in content analysis to mean that "text is interpreted relative to an imagined context, and these interpretations in turn reconstruct the context for further examination of the same or subsequently available text" (p. 259).

2. In some instances, the "researcher" may also be the person who codes the content (i.e., the "coder"). This is typically the case when the study is being conducted by a small research firm or group where the principal researcher assumes many duties, including the coding function. In other instances, the researcher may be the person who is responsible for managing a number of people on a research team, including one or more coders who code the content.

3. Say, for example, there were 300 love letters (half written by one lover and half by the other lover) in the entire population, and the researcher decided to analyze 25 of the letters written by each of the lovers (i.e., a total of 50 letters, which is one-sixth of the total collection). Once the list of letters was ordered, the researcher would begin by randomly selecting a number from 1 to 6 and then would choose the first letter for the sample based on where it falls on the ordered list. If the random starting number was 2, then the researcher would select the 2nd, 8th, 14th, 20th, . . ., and 296th letters on the ordered list, and this would comprise the set of 50 love letters for the sample in this content analysis study.

4. When the second author was teaching a graduate class that required the class members to do an extensive content analysis project for a large circulation newspaper, it was determined that three of the students clearly did not follow the coding instructions in the codebook, for which they were trained, and essentially fabricated much of their data. These three students received a failing grade in the course and all of the content that they were assigned to code had to be recoded by the other students.

Qualitative Content Analysis Case Study

PURPOSE

The primary purpose of this content analysis study was to extend the existing literature on the portrayal of women's roles in print media by examining the imagery and
themes depicted of heterosexual college-educated women who leave the workforce
to devote themselves to being stay-at-home mothers (a phenomenon referred to as
"opting out") across a wide, diverse range of print publications. More specifically,
this research set out to investigate two areas of media coverage: the content (e.g., the
women who are portrayed in the media and how they are described) and the context
(e.g., the types of media and articles).

METHOD

A content analysis as the primary method for this study was the logical choice given
the textual nature of the content as well as the numerous prior studies that had been
conducted on the representation of women in print media that served as comparative
literature.

DESIGN

Credibility

Scope

This study examined a 16-year period from 1988 to 2003. This 16-year period was
chosen because 1988 was the earliest date on which the researchers had access to a
searchable database for sampling, and 2003 was the year that the term "opting out"
(referring to women leaving the workforce to become full-time mothers) became popular. A primary goal of the study was to examine imagery and themes in the coverage
of opting out across print media that reach large, diverse audiences; therefore, the target population from which articles for the analysis were drawn was a wide selection of
publications (purposively sampled from an obtained list) in terms of type (e.g., large
metro newspapers, national newsweeklies such as *Time*, women's magazines such as
Redbook, business publications such as *Business Week*, special-interest magazines such
as *Essence*) and circulation (i.e., targeting publications that reach national and large
metro audiences).

Sampling was conducted by keyword searches—most often, "stay-at-home mom"—
across three major databases. The researchers reviewed all search returns and
excluded articles that did not specifically address the topic of women opting out as
well as high-profile cases that received extraordinary media attention and therefore
would potentially bias the study sample. As a result of these search-and-review procedures, the researchers identified 51 articles from 30 publications that represented

Source: Kuperberg and Stone (2008).

a wide diversity of large-circulation print media. The researchers acknowledged that the sample "underrepresents articles appearing in small-town outlets."

The researchers provide an account of the publications and articles included in the sample, such as the average word count (950 words), the type of publication in which most articles were published (i.e., general interest newspapers and magazines), and the type of article (most were editorials or opinion/advice articles).

Data Gathering

In order to identify the units of analysis and aid in code development, the researchers conducted a pilot study with a subset of the sampled articles. From this, the researchers selected two units of analysis: the articles in their entirety and the women depicted in these articles. The pilot study also led to the development of specific codes (and codebooks) associated with each of the units of analysis. Researchers determined 10 code domains pertaining to the characteristics of the articles (e.g., type of publication) and six code domains associated with the characteristics of the women depicted (e.g., reasons for opting out, demographics). In order to have enough information to reliably characterize the women depicted in the articles, the women were only coded if the article described them in three or more sentences.

Coding was completed by three coders ("evaluators") who were trained on the codebook and were given clarification as needed. To maximize credibility, preliminary coding was conducted to check inconsistencies and measure intercoder agreement. Agreement among coders was more than 85%.

Analyzability

The content data obtained from coding revealed three primary patterns or themes in the depiction of women who opt out: "family first, child-centric"; "the mommy elite"; and "making choices." The researchers discuss these themes at some length and support their findings by way of research literature and other references. In some instances, they report that their findings were in contrast to the literature (which presented an opportunity for future research in this area). Their final interpretation of the data includes their overall assertion that print media depict "traditional images of heterosexual women."

Importantly, the researchers absorbed themselves in the sampled articles and, in doing so, identified inconsistencies in the research outcomes. For example, a careful reading of the articles revealed that many of the women depicted as stay-at-home mothers were actually employed in some form of paid work from home.

The researchers also enriched the discussion of their findings by giving the reader some context relevant to the publications and articles. For example, they revealed that 45 of the 51 articles were from general interest newspapers or magazines, a fact that supports their research objective of analyzing print media that reach large, diverse audiences.

And, the researchers performed a version of deviant case analysis, consisting of contrary evidence to the assertion made by many articles that there is a growing trend in the proportion of women opting out. Citing research studies from the literature as well as actual trend data, the researchers stated that the articles' claim that women were increasingly opting out had weak support.

Transparency

The researchers provide a clear understanding of (a) their research objectives, (b) the particular constructs of interest (the imagery and themes associated with the depiction of women who opt out of the workforce), (c) why this research is needed (it fills a gap in the literature and broadens the discussion), (d) their sample design, and (e) coding procedure. A limitation of their work was in the area of theme development, where details of that process would have better informed the reader as to the credibility of the Analyzability of the research as well as its transferability to a content analysis on similar issues.

Usefulness

Although the research literature concerning the depiction of women in the media is extensive, the research reported here contributes to the literature by focusing on a neglected topic—the imagery and themes conveyed in print media concerning women who opt out of the workforce to become stay-at-home mothers—as well as by extending the discussion by sampling print media aimed at a large, diverse audience.

CHAPTER SEVEN

Multiple Methods in Case-Centered Approaches

Case Study and Narrative Research

CHAPTER PREVIEW

A *multiple-method* (or multi-method) approach in qualitative research combines two or more qualitative methods to investigate a research question or phenomenon. It is distinctive from *mixed-methods* research in which researchers combine both qualitative and quantitative methods within one research project. In this chapter we use case-centered research—specifically, case study research and narrative research—to explore the multi-method approach. We define "case-centered research" as the utilization of multiple methods to investigate "complex" social units or entities while maintaining the cohesiveness of these entities throughout the research process. This chapter addresses many issues that case studies and narrative research share in common, and many other issues that are specific to only one of those methods. Case studies may involve the study of single or multiple cases, may be internally or externally focused, and often combine interrelated information from in-depth interveiws (IDIs), focus groups, and ethnography. The essence of narrative research is to learn "the story" underlying some phenomenon of interest by way of unstructured IDIs; however, the IDIs are generally supplemented with data from other qualitative methods to provide a thorough understanding of the narrative environment. Case-centered research is very challenging due to (a) the complexity of what is being studied and (b) the need to carefully interconnect and balance the different research methods that are deployed within the same larger study. This chapter discusses how to apply a Total Quality Framework (TQF) approach to case-centered research, addressing such issues as (a) defining the target population, (b) determining the methods and number of data collection events, and (c) the importance of researcher skills across methods. Special consideration is also given to the interviewer–narrator relationship in narrative research.

7.1 INTRODUCTION

This chapter is about qualitative research approaches that use multiple qualitative methods *within the same study* to create different (but complementary) types of data to address a particular research objective. We refer to these approaches as "multiple methods" research. In doing so, we explicitly differentiate multiple-method qualitative research from a **mixed-method approach**, where both *qualitative and quantitative* methods are used in the same study to collect and analyze data addressing a particular research question (cf. Creswell, 2009; Johnson, Onwuegbuzie, & Turner, 2007; Leech & Onwuegbuzie, 2007). A mixed-method research approach can enable the researcher to derive broader and deeper meaning in the data compared to a study conducted with only one method because the results from a qualitative study, for instance, can inform and add valuable meaning to the planning and/or the interpretation of the quantitative part of the study (Creswell, 2009; Hanson, Creswell, Clark, Petska, & Creswell, 2005; Johnson et al., 2007). For example, a mixed-method study might involve conducting focus group discussions with patients to discover the "subjective meanings" associated with their experience of living with a particular health condition in order to develop appropriate patient-centered intervention strategies that can then be tested in a highly structured quantitative clinical trial (cf. Hesse-Biber, 2012); or IDIs might be conducted with a sample of survey respondents after the gathering of survey data to enrich the understanding of their responses to the survey questionnaire.[1] However, like Creswell (2013), we believe that although it can be a valuable approach to research, mixed-method approaches are "a distinct methodology from qualitative inquiry" (p. 5), and therefore separate from the exclusive qualitative focus of this book. As such, mixed methods are not further addressed in this chapter.

In contrast to mixed methods, a **multi-method approach** in qualitative research is one in which the researcher *combines two or more qualitative methods* to investigate a research question or phenomenon. Although the terms "multi-method" and "multiple methods" are sometimes used to refer to qualitative–quantitative (or mixed-method) research (e.g., Brewer & Hunter, 2006; Snape & Spencer, 2003), we reserve this terminology for research strategies that incorporate more than one qualitative method and do not include any quantitative methods.

Multi-method research—due to the additional data collection and analysis considerations—has the potential disadvantage of consuming valuable resources such as time and available research funds. However, as discussed on page 293, this is not always the case and, under the appropriate conditions, multiple qualitative methods can prove very useful toward gaining a more fully developed complexity and meaning in the researcher's understanding of a subject matter compared to a single-method research design (cf. Denzin & Lincoln, 2011; Flick, 2007).

Ethnography (see Chapter 5, beginning on p. 168) is one such example. Observation is the principal method in an ethnographic study; however, it is often supplemented with other qualitative methods such as IDIs, group discussions, and/or documentary review in order to provide a more complete "picture" of the issue or phenomenon under investigation. Other applications of multi-method qualitative research are not uncommon. Lambert and Loiselle (2008), for instance, combined focus group discussions and IDIs in a study with cancer patients concerning their "information-seeking behavior." These researchers found that this multi-method approach enriched the study because one method helped inform the other—for example, group discussions identified relevant questions/issues that were then used in the IDIs—and contributed unique information—for example, the IDIs were effective in obtaining details of patients' information-seeking processes, but focus groups were more valuable in highlighting important contextual influences on these processes such as the physicians' preferences or recommendations. Lambert and Loiselle concluded that the multi-method research design "enhanced understanding of the structure and essential characteristics of the phenomenon within the context of cancer" (p. 235).

Previous chapters in this book have addressed the kinds of qualitative research methods, such as IDIs and focus groups, that are often combined into multiple-methods research studies. This chapter now concentrates on two special types of multiple-method qualitative research, case study and narrative research, each of which is a form of "case-centered" qualitative research.

Case-Centered Research

In this chapter we orient our discussion of the multi-method approach around a category of research in which multiple qualitative methods for data gathering collectively play complementary and supplementary roles. We refer to this type of research as "case centered," a term coined by Mishler (1996, 1999) and used by others (cf. Riessman, 2008) to denote a research approach that preserves the "unity and coherence" of research subjects throughout data collection and analysis. In addition to its multi-method strategy, we define **case-centered research** as consisting of two fundamental components that set it off from other qualitative research strategies: (1) focus on the investigation of "complex" social units or entities *in their entirety* (i.e., not just one aspect captured at one moment in time), and (2) emphasis on maintaining the cohesiveness of this entity throughout the research process rather than reducing the information to categorical data (cf. Riessman, 2008)—which, for example, happens in ethnography and content analysis (see Chapters 5 and 6).

In case-centered research each social unit or entity represents a "**case**." The case might be an individual (e.g., the life story of an imprisoned teenager), a group of people (e.g., the zoning committee on the town council), an organization (e.g., the regional operations of the Red Cross), an event (e.g., the response to a natural disaster), or a program or process (e.g., the implementation of a new physical education program in the county schools). Whatever the case under investigation may be, the case-centered researcher is obligated to think of, and analyze, each case *as a complete unit.* This means that the researcher is not looking for a way to overly condense the data into a few themes or categories but, instead, keeps the case intact by considering it in its entirety, as a complete whole. For example, the analysis of data gathered from a case-centered study concerning the life story of an imprisoned teenager (which might include the teenager's oral account of his or her life as well as stories and artifacts collected from the family) would consider the composite of information to understand, not just what was said or revealed in family documents, but also the sequence of events told, the temporal and geographical context of the information given, and the particular words used to convey the story. In this way, the researcher has not fragmented the participant's life story to develop concentrated categories but has kept it intact. Similarly, a case-centered research project to study the responses to a natural disaster would maintain a holistic picture of this case by retaining the people, organizations, and events within their respective contexts.

Case Study and Narrative Research

In order to provide a more nuanced understanding of case-centered research, we discuss its principles and concepts by way of two prominent case-centered approaches: **case study research** and **narrative research**. Both case study and narrative research share the core characteristics of case-centered research, which are (a) the use of multiple methods and (b) the treatment of the case as a complex unit or entity throughout data collection and analysis.

Although qualitative researchers conducting case study or narrative research are steadfast in their commitment to keeping the entirety of the case intact, they must remain flexible in the methods they choose to investigate the case. Indeed, such researchers employ a variety of methods depending on the particular needs of the research situation. For instance, a case study concerning a statewide drug prevention program might include IDIs with the program staff and volunteers, observations of program activities, group discussions with program participants, and a review of administrative documents. Similarly, in a narrative study to explore the teaching of eighth-grade science in a city's public schools, the researcher might incorporate a host of methods in order to adequately frame a complete picture (i.e., the **narrative environment**[2]), such as in-class teacher observations, teachers' **lived experiences**[3] captured by way of IDIs and/or autobiographical "essays," teachers' daily journal entries concerning classroom activities, and visual images of the classes in progress. Again, the focus of these multi-method, case-centered approaches is the totality of the case under investigation—that is, the state drug prevention program or the teaching of eighth-grade science in a city's schools.

A multi-method design serves an important function in case study and narrative research because it allows researchers to study the holistic nature of relatively complex entities or cases by tackling the research objective from all relevant methodological perspectives. Rather than limiting and possibly pigeonholing the research investigation into a series of IDIs, focus groups, or observations, the multi-method approach in case studies and narrative research leads the researcher to become totally immersed with the subject matter. A single-method study of the state drug prevention program, for instance, could provide insight from key stakeholders by way of conducting IDIs with staff or group discussions with program participants, but the study may fall short of providing the researcher (and therefore the study's funders) with an opportunity to gain a broader and deeper understanding of the program's strengths and weaknesses. Likewise, interviews with eighth-grade science teachers would contribute important personal perspectives related to their teaching role, but interviews alone may ultimately deliver too shallow an understanding compared to what the researcher could obtain from enriching teachers' stories by way of input from other contexts (e.g., in-class observation and daily journals).

As mentioned, the use of multiple methods and the treatment of the case as a complex unit are the two core characteristics of case study and narrative research. However, as summarized in Box 7.1 and discussed below, there are additional related aspects of these approaches that differentiate case study and narrative research from other qualitative strategies, some of which have been mentioned previously:

- The primary interest in case study and narrative research is on the case as a complete unit or entity—the subject of inquiry, such as the state's drug prevention program or the teaching of eighth-grade science.

- The "case" in case study and narrative research is more or less "bounded" in that it represents "a specific, a complex, functioning thing . . . [that] has a boundary and working parts" (Stake, 1995, p. 2). In case study research, this is typically a particular organization, a well-defined group of people, or a specific program. Most narratives are also bounded to the extent that they represent well-formed tales with a beginning, middle, and an end (although, as we discuss later in this chapter, narrative boundaries are not always so easily determined).

BOX 7.1. Case Study and Narrative Research: Differentiating Aspects Compared to Other Approaches

- Researchers deal with each case as a complete unit or entity.
- A case is a "bounded" entity in that it is composed of elements that define it.
- The methods used to gather data will likely vary within a study and from study to study.
- Multiple methods are used because each case, whether a single individual or multilayered organization, is studied as complex subject matter, encompassing multiple contexts and components.
- Analyses focus on the interconnectedness of the data elements and less so on reducing the data to just a few categories or themes.
- Chronology (sequence of events) plays a prominent role in analysis and interpretation.
- The final document needs to be written in a unique, engaging report format that conveys the plethora of interconnected details in a compelling and complete manner.

• The particular methods used to collect the data (e.g., IDIs, group discussions, observations) will most likely vary within a study and from study to study.

• The subject matter and research objectives of case studies and narrative research projects are typically very complex. Multiple methods are used because the focus of the research is multifaceted, involving various contexts, and deserving the inclusion of its many components in order to draw a unified interpretation of the case. A case study of a nonprofit organization with offices and programs in many locations, for instance, would have limited value as a case study if the qualitative researcher only explored one or two of the organization's programs in one geographic location, or explored just the opinions among members of the staff at the home office. The need for multiple methods comes into play even if the subject matter concerns a single individual (e.g., the earlier mentioned incarcerated teenager), because the researcher will draw on all facets of this individual's life to try to gain a complete and accurate understanding of the complex data that comprise any life story.

• By treating each case in a case study or narrative research project as a single entity, the researcher is not interested in reducing the data to the elements that represent a few highly specific categories or themes. It is the interconnectedness of all the elements associated with the case—that is, the "integrated system" (Stake, 1995, p. 2)—that is important. Case study research investigating employment practices at a large manufacturing company, for instance, would use various methods to investigate the connections among many factors, including staff training and job attitudes, outreach efforts, employment policies and benefits, union versus nonunion opportunities, plant versus office working conditions, and the job pool. Narrative research is also composed of related parts, consisting of the integrated pieces of the story itself as told by the narrator, as well as the broader connections (e.g., from different contexts, review of documents) that define and enrich the narrative environment.

• Chronology, or the sequence of events, can play a prominent role in the analysis and interpretation of case-centered research, including the case study and narrative approaches. For example, the chronology of events in case study research can lead to the investigation of variables in the events that have potentially caused certain effects (Yin, 2014); a case study researcher examining the effects of a community outreach program on local residents might link a noticeable shift in the receptivity of the program to managerial changes in the organization. Or, for example, in narrative research, an understanding of the chronology of lived moments (i.e., the experiences as lived by the narrator) would be important to the analysis of the biographical accounts of chronic illness.

• Case study and narrative research require a unique style of reporting in the final document. Because the focus is to maintain the case as a unit, without drastically reducing the data to recurring categories or themes, the researcher is faced with the challenge of communicating research outcomes—which may consist of a plethora of multifaceted, interconnected details—in a way that is compelling as well as accurate and complete. For this reason, case study and narrative research-ers are encouraged to abandon the more traditional research report format and develop a narrative or otherwise engaging reporting style that gains readers' attention and interest while also providing the rich details of the case(s) that allow readers to draw their own interpretations (Darke, Shanks, & Broadbent, 1998; Flyvbjerg, 2006; Stake, 1995; Yin, 2014).

Furthermore, case study and narrative research might be expected to cost much more than qualitative research that uses a single method for data collec-tion and also to take considerably more time to complete. Although this is true in many situations (e.g., when the study involves conducting face-to-face interviews at several locations, retrieving archival documents from obscure sources, and spend-ing many hours in the field to observe the progression of an event over time), it is not necessarily the case, particularly with the utilization of Internet-based solutions such as online webcam-enabled IDIs and various search (research) func-tions. However, even when additional resources (funding and time) are needed, case study and narrative research are important approaches when the research objective is to gain an unusually broad and/or in-depth understanding of a com-plex phenomenon.

The next two sections of this chapter provide a more thorough discussion of each of these case-centered approaches.

Case Study Research

There is a great deal written about case study research, and much of it revolves around two questions "What is a 'case'?" and "What *is* the research approach called 'case study'?" The fact that the literature across various disciplines is filled with theses and commentaries concerning these definitional issues points to a lingering interest as well as unsettledness among scholars on these questions.[4]

The first question, "What is a 'case'?", was considered earlier in this chap-ter (see p. 289), defining it as an entity such as an individual, group, organiza-tion, event, program, or process. With respect to the second question, "What *is* case study research?", VanWynsberghe and Khan (2007) concluded that research scholars have proposed more than 25 different definitions of case study research in the past 30 years. One point of contention is whether the case study approach should be considered a research "method." On one side of this debate are those who assert that case study is not a method because the researcher is unable to "collect data prescriptively" due to the absence of a specific set of procedures to "uncover the case" (VanWynsberghe & Khan, 2007), and, similarly, because there are varying ways to study a case, the researcher is not making "a methodologi-cal choice" but rather a choice of what or whom to study (Stake, 1994). Others, such as Yin (2014), argue that case study is a research method and, like other research methods, "is a way of investigating an empirical topic by following a set of desired procedures" (p. 23). It should be obvious from the multi-method focus of this chapter as well as our earlier discussion of the multifaceted aspects of case-centered research (see p. 292) that we do not consider case study research a single method but rather a research *approach* or *strategy* that utilizes multiple methods to address selected research objectives.

Even with an array of definitions associated with case study research, it is generally agreed that case studies are characterized by the in-depth exploration of social phenomena that are:

- Real versus conceptual, or "more concrete" versus "less concrete" (Yin, 2014), or specific versus general (Stake, 1995). This is the difference, for example, between studying a particular program at the YMCA versus something more nebulous such as the nature of the relationships between program staff and volunteers.

- Represented by one or more objects or entities (i.e., a single case or multiple cases).

- Complex or multifaceted, involving various interconnected elements (e.g., the elements in the case of a disabled participant in a YMCA program might include the physical capabilities of the participant, the participant's mental outlook, the participant's family members and friends, other program participants, the frequency and level of exertion in the program activities by the participant, the extent of conveniences provided by the YMCA for disabled people, the staff, the administrators, and the physical environment where the program is conducted).

- Contemporary (although they may be supported by historical data).

- Studied in their natural context.

- Studied by way of multiple methods.

Another question where different viewpoints abound revolves around theory; specifically, whether or not a primary function of case study research is to build on existing theory or develop new theory. Yin (2009) has been emphatic in his assertion that "theory development as part of the [case study] design phase is essential" (p. 35), although he more recently modified his rhetoric by stating that "*some* theory development as part of the design phase is *highly desired* (2014, p. 37, emphasis added). In contrast, other researchers such as Stake (1994, 1995) and Thomas (2010) eschew the prominence of the role of theorizing from case studies, believing that "damage occurs when the commitment to generalize or create theory runs so strong that the researcher's attention is drawn away from features important for understanding the case itself" (Stake, 1994, p. 238). As to our own thinking, we are of a mind similar to Eisenhardt and Graebner (2007) that case study research can effectively contribute to existing or new theory, but only when adequate quality-control measures are built into the research design (e.g., the selection of extreme cases to serve as exemplars of the research question, such as hospitals with the most severe outbreaks of staph infections to study hospital emergency preparedness policies).

TYPOLOGIES AND USES OF CASE STUDY RESEARCH. The typologies of Yin (2014) and Stake (1995) are "two key approaches" in case study research that "ensure that the topic of interest is well explored, and that the essence of the phenomenon is revealed" (Baxter & Jack, 2008, p. 545). As the reader will see from what is presented below, these frequently cited typologies do, in fact, present well-thought-out strategies in the conduct of case studies. The following discussion (and broad depiction in Table 7.1) provides brief synopses of Yin's and Stake's ways of approaching case study research.

Yin's Typology. Yin (2014) outlines four fundamental types of case studies on the basis of the number of cases and units of analysis in the study design. In his typology, Yin specifies two types of single-case designs—a study with one unit of analysis (Type 1) and a study with multiple units of analysis (Type 2)—and two types of multiple-case designs—once again, with a single unit of analysis (Type 3) and multiple units (Type 4). Because Yin believes that theory development is "highly desired" in case study design, it is not surprising that his explanations and examples for each of the four design types are fully couched around the premise of theory testing. For example, one of Yin's five reasons for selecting a single-case design (i.e., Type 1 and Type 2) instead of a multiple-case design (i.e., Type 3 and Type 4) is the study of "critical" cases that serve to "represent a significant contribution to knowledge and theory building by confirming, challenging, or extending the theory" (p. 51), such as the case study from Gallivan and Keil (2003) that challenged the idea that the success of a software product hinges on user–developer communication by studying a case where user involvement was high yet the software product failed. Another reason to opt for a single-case design, according to Yin, is when the goal is to investigate a "common" case, which then informs the situation in similar entities as it relates to "some theoretical interest." A study of a small business to investigate innovative processes is an example used by Yin of a common, single-case scenario. Yin's remaining three reasons to opt for a single-case design are in situations when the case is: (1) unique or extreme (e.g., a rare health condition); (2) "revelatory," giving the researcher access to something that has been inaccessible, such as a guarded military installation; and (3) longitudinal, that is, investigated over the course of some time period.

Multiple-case designs (i.e., Yin's [2014] Type 3 and Type 4) are particularly enveloped in a theoretical perspective: specifically, the notion of replication and

TABLE 7.1. Yin and Stake Case Study Typologies

	Yin	**Stake**
Single case	Type 1 and Type 2	Intrinsic Instrumental
Multiple cases	Type 3 and Type 4	Collective

its role in theory development. According to Yin, cases are selected for multiple-case designs that are expected to return results that support a proposition or theory ("literal replication") or, to the contrary, are expected to contradict or otherwise challenge the researcher's presupposed theoretical concept ("theoretical replication"). For example, in a case study to examine whether the use of a particular type of advanced X-ray equipment in area hospitals' emergency departments leads to more efficient (faster) patient care, the researcher might select nine cases: three hospitals utilizing the advanced X-ray equipment for all relevant emergency-room procedures (segment "A"); three hospitals that use this advanced equipment in some, but not all, of its X-ray procedures ("B"), and three hospitals that have this advanced X-ray equipment but use it very infrequently (i.e., they are primarily using older, dated machines ["C"]). In this scenario, the researcher would predict more efficient patient care in segment "A" hospitals (literal replication) and little or no improvements in patient care in segments "B" and "C" (theoretical replication).

Stake's Typology. Where Yin (2014) emphasizes theoretical development and the ability to say something beyond the specific cases studied, Stake (2006) asserts that "the power of case study is its attention to the local situation, not in how it represents other cases in general" (p. 8). To wit, Stake's typology of case study research is firmly grounded in either a narrowly or broadly defined aspect of the case itself. Stake (1994, 1995) divides case studies into three types: intrinsic, instrumental, and collective. The *intrinsic* case study is a single case that is uniquely important to the researcher. Unlike Yin's single-case designs that are geared to extend or otherwise develop theory, the purpose of Stake's intrinsic case study is solely aimed at learning about the case; in other words, it is the case—that is, the individual, group, organization, event, or other entity—and the very particular context of that specific case that is important in its own right, not if or how the case informs about other entities or situations. For example, the Kerr et al. (2006) case study of a community drug user organization in Vancouver and the Malenfant (2010) study of the scholarly communication system at the University of Minnesota are two illustrations of intrinsic case studies.

In contrast to an intrinsic case study, Stake's (1995) *instrumental* (single-case) and *collective* (multiple-case) studies are designed to "go beyond the case" to focus on understanding the particular but broader phenomenon of interest rather than the individual case per se. However, Stake is not linking instrumental and collective case studies to the idea of testing preconceived theories (á la Yin, 2014) but, rather, to the idea of using the peculiarities of any particular case to illuminate the phenomenon and magnify the understanding of the research topic (e.g., studying water safety training by way of one or more swimming instructors). In this respect, "the case is of secondary interest; it plays a supportive role, facilitating our understanding of something else" (Stake, 1994, p. 237) to cast a wider lens on a phenomenon, and to form only "tentative" generalizations rather than a "formal projection to cases that are not examined" (p. 90). Examples of instrumental case studies (i.e., where a single case was used to learn more broadly about a phenomenon) include Ricci (2006), who conducted a study with a sex offender to investigate the desensitization and reprocessing of traumatic memory as a complementary component to treatment; and Wasburn (2007), who used the case study of one university mentoring program to support the benefits of a "strategic collaboration" model for mentoring women faculty members. Examples of collective case studies (i.e., where multiple cases are used to learn about a phenomenon) include a study conducted by Crudden (2002), who examined a number of individuals to explore the factors important to job retention among employees after vision loss, learning (for example) about the importance of computer technology to job retention; and Bennett, Bishop, Delgarno, Waycott, and Kennedy (2012), who conducted an instrumental case study involving three universities to investigate the use of Web 2.0 technologies, and more broadly to identify the potential issues in instigating these technologies in higher education.

An Internal–External Classification. Both Yin (2014) and Stake (1994, 1995) offer useful typologies and perspectives on case study research: Yin, from the emphasis on theory (broadening the potential usefulness of case study research); and Stake, by way of his focus on the case as well as his recognition of the single intrinsic case that is important in its own right, not necessarily because of its potential predictive theoretical powers. An overarching differentiator in these typologies is the extent to which case study outcomes are intended to tell the researcher something that is solely about the case itself—that is, the outcomes are "internalized" to the particular case—or the outcomes are intended to tell the researcher something beyond the case, either by facilitating theory development and/or enlightening the researcher's understanding of a broader phenomenon—that is, the outcomes are "externalized" to situations outside the case.

In this internal–external classification (as shown in Table 7.2), an intrinsic case study as defined by Stake (1994, 1995) with its emphasis on what can be learned about the specific case itself, is an internal type of design because the research findings will only be used to inform that specific case—for example, a

TABLE 7.2. Internal–External Classification

	Focus of the research question in relationship to the case	
	Internal Corresponding to . . .	**External** Corresponding to . . .
Single case	Intrinsic (Stake)	Type 1 and Type 2 (Yin) Instrumental (Stake)
Multiple cases	**	Type 3 and Type 4 (Yin) Collective (Stake)

**Multiple-case-study research can only be externally focused because it is attempting to say something beyond each individual case.

case study to investigate a company's new customer referral program to inform their need for new social media solutions. Stake's instrumental and collective case types as well as Yin's case study designs (i.e., Types 1–4), with their emphasis on projecting case study results to something outside the case (i.e., a theory or phenomenon), are external types of designs because the researcher's primary focus is on extending the outcomes beyond the specific case(s); for example, a case study of one state government department to understand the impact of a new, more restrictive sick-leave policy on all state employees. Table 7.2 also shows that neither Yin nor Stake advocate a multiple-case approach with an internal focus because, in addition to the fact that Yin (2014) emphasizes the importance of building or creating theory in case study research (i.e., an external focus), an internal focus with multiple cases simply amounts to a series of internally focused single-case studies.

This internal or external distinction comes into play at the very outset of the case study research design and guides the researcher's assumptions and processes throughout the course of the study (as discussed in more detail in Section 7.2).

Narrative Research

The other major approach in qualitative research that we address in this chapter as an important exemplar of a case-centered strategy is narrative research. Although narrative research does not command a broad following within the larger qualitative research community, compared to the other methods covered in this book, we believe that narrative research has an important role to play as a case-centered strategy. From the ever-increasing literature on narrative research in journals such as *Narrative Inquiry* and *Qualitative Inquiry*, as well as the increasing use of narrative beyond academic circles—including the "major accomplishments in the domains of psychotherapy, organizational change, and conflict reduction" (Gergen & Gergen, 2006, pp. 112–113)—it would appear that "there is a narrative revolution going on" (Clandinin, 2012).

Narrative research investigates the stories of what narrative researchers call "lived experiences." These may be firsthand experiences of individuals, groups, organizations, and even governments. Regardless of the entity, it is the story that is the case or object of attention and the focal point of the research. Unlike the structured or semistructured IDI, discussed in Chapter 3, where the interviewer–interviewee relationship is directed in differing degrees by the researcher's question agenda that serves to extract information from the interviewee, the narrative researcher allows the narrator (i.e., the interviewee in narrative research) to be the guide, welcoming the narrator's stories wherever they may lead, by conducting a form of unstructured IDI whereby the researcher makes broad inquiries such as, "Tell me what happened when you joined the army," "Tell me about your professional life," "Tell me how you became a regular coffee drinker."

The belief in narrative research is that it is the narrated story—whether told orally, via some form of text or documents, and/or through the use of visual data (e.g., photographs, video, drawings)—that allows researchers to learn about individuals, society, and history, and that, indeed, "narrative inquiry [is] the study of experience as story" (Clandinin, Pushor, & Orr, 2007, p. 22).

Important to the conceptual framework of narrative research is what it means to "tell a story." The notion of a "story" in narrative research is unlike that associated with common, everyday uses of storytelling, such as news stories in the media, which often lack the specificity, organization, and connectedness that are imperative in the research narrative. Narrative research defines the "story" as a tale with sequence and consequence (Riessman & Quinney, 2005), wherein the events are "selected, organized, connected, and evaluated as meaningful for a particular audience" (Riessman, 2008, p. 3). In this way, the focus in narrative research is not only on the content of a story (which is obviously important) but also *how* the story is told and *why* it is told in a particular manner. Narrative researchers take a holistic approach by keeping together as a single case the sequential and consequential elements of the story; that is, the *what, how,* and *why,* in their analysis and by relinquishing the urge to reduce narrative data to contrived categories that may lose the all-important chronological structure and meaning in the narrative.

As a case-centered approach, narrative research represents a distinctly alternative strategy to case study research. Although the two methods share common attributes, such as the complexity of the entity or object (i.e., the case or narrative) being studied, the importance of context, and the use of a multi-method research design, there are important differences between the two strategies. In particular, and unlike the case study, narrative research conducted with individuals:

- Often relies on the narrator's knowledge from the past, what happened at some point earlier in time. We say "often" because there are exceptions, such as the use of a **photovoice** technique by which individuals' use still cameras and/or video to create diaries of their in-the-moment life events.

- Often, with the exception of techniques such as photovoice, does not accumulate data in the natural context as the "real" events were occurring.

- May rely entirely on the memory of the person telling the story and the choices that are made (be they conscious or unconscious) to tell the story in a particular way (e.g., the told events, the language used).

- Revolves around the narrator–researcher interaction and, in this sense, the resulting story is not so much the narrator's story as a story "co-constructed" by the narrator and the researcher.

- Often relies heavily on the researcher's interpretation of the narrative, which is a product of both the narrator's telling of the story and the researcher's understanding of its elements.

TYPOLOGIES AND USES OF NARRATIVE RESEARCH. Similar to other qualitative research methods—most notably, ethnography (see Chapter 5, p. 169)—there are varying ways in which researchers formulate their understanding of narrative research. For the most part, there are three (not mutually exclusive) ways to consider narrative inquiry by the type of:

- Narrative being studied: for example, life history, life story, biography, autobiography, or autoethnography.
- Analytical approach used by the researcher: for example, thematic, structural, dialogical/performance, or visual (Riessman, 2008).
- Scholarly discipline applied to the research: for example, psychology, sociology, or education.

The variations of narrative research across fields of study demonstrate that there is no one way to think about narrative inquiry and, indeed, the three delineated types—narrative, analytical, and discipline—are often comingled. For example, various factions of psychology have embraced the use of narrative: with heroin addicts to understand "how individuals phenomenologically wrestle with decisions at crucial transition points in their lives" (Singer, 2013, p. 46); in identity research, by which people's life stories can be analyzed from multiple perspectives, including the "small stories" within the "big stories" (Bamberg & Georgakopoulou, 2008), as well as the conditions that shape their stories and how the stories shape their life experiences (Esteban-Guitart, 2012); and to explore the connection between social stigma (e.g., not being accepted, being the target of discrimination) and intimacy in same-sex relationships (Frost, 2013). Sociologists such as Cederberg (2014) have considered the biographical narratives of migrants and how public discourse potentially molds these narratives of their lived experiences. And Luttrell (2003), also a sociologist, elicited visual and performance narratives from pregnant teenagers who were better able to express their life stories in these less structured approaches than in response to conventional narrative interviews, explaining that "the more I stayed out of their way, the more the girls would talk and free associate while doing these self-representations activities. For me, this meant giving up my more immediate desire to ask questions, make sense of, or put order into the girls' creative expression or their conversations" (p. 150).

Scholars from many other disciplines are also using narrative research. For example, educational researchers such as Clandinin and Connelly (1998) used "narrative histories" to study school reform by investigating the school as a "living place" where "teachers and the principal come to the landscape living and telling a complex set of interwoven stories of themselves as teachers, of children in this school, of the community" (p. 160). Austin and Carpenter (2008) used narrative research with mothers of children who are "disruptive" in the classroom (i.e., who have attention-deficit/hyperactivity disorder) to explore the "harsh and judgmental treatment" these mothers experience "from medical professionals, teachers, friends and family" (p. 379). Examples of the anthropological uses of narrative include such work as the analysis of the narrative elements in Eskimo folktales (Colby, 1973), and the use of historical narratives as "cultural tools" to examine the presentation of events in post-Soviet Russian textbooks (Wertsch, 2000). Communication and health care researchers have explored "illness narratives" by way of online conversations among people suffering from drug addiction in order to understand their life experiences and the effectiveness of online support (Jodlowski, Sharf, Nguyen, Haidet, & Woodard, 2007). Scholars in social work have demonstrated the challenges and benefits of conducting narrative research with marginalized segments of the population, such as teenage mothers (Harlow, 2009), young people from the child welfare system (Martin, 1998), and heterosexual serodiscordant couples (i.e., where one partner is HIV-positive and the other HIV-negative; Poindexter, 2003). And, social scientists engaged in performance studies, such as Madison (2003), have used the performing arts to communicate the stories of significant political moments in history; for example, utilizing the personal narratives of labor strike leaders and other service workers at the University of North Carolina to construct a performance of their story, staged in a crowded theatre, and, for the first time, acknowledging labor leaders' struggle for equality on campus.

Researcher Skills in Case-Centered Research

The reliance on multiple methods in case-centered research requires a unique set of researcher skills. Although many of these individual skills are germane to the research methods discussed in earlier chapters, it is the coming together of these particular skills that distinguishes the necessary abilities of the case-centered researcher from that of the researcher who is conducting single-method research such as an IDI, group discussion, or observation-only ethnographic study. The fact that case-centered research thrives on multiple methods is reason enough to suggest that special researcher skills are essential; however, the distinctive nature of case-centered research—that is, the focus on understanding an entity (whether it be a program, policy, organization, or an individual's narrative)—contributes greatly to the repertoire of talents required of the researcher.

Case study researchers such as Yin (2014) and Stake (1995) associate case studies with detective work, with the researcher acting as the investigator who is continually seeking "clues" in the evidence and following "leads" to try to draw accurate inferences (or, one might say, "crack the case"). In many ways, the same could be said about narrative research. Narrative researchers are also attending to the various facets of a story—not just the content but *how* the story is told (e.g., the use of language), *why* the story is told in a particular manner (e.g., the narrator's motivations), and the *context* in which the story is told. Like case study investigators, researchers exploring the narrative are intensely exploring these various facets for evidence that helps them understand the lived experience and narrative environment. Because the IDI method is often included in case study and, particularly, in narrative research, the effectiveness of evidence gathering frequently centers on the researcher's basic interviewing skills, as discussed in Chapter 3 (see pp. 55–56), pertaining to rapport building, active listening, and the like, as well as a set of distinctive abilities. As summarized in Box 7.2, these distinctive abilities include:

• Identifying the appropriate clues or asking the "right" questions that further an understanding of the case or give nondirectional encouragement to the telling of the narrator's story (e.g., "Please tell me what happened next").

• Relinquishing control and allowing the case to steer the direction of the investigation. In true detective style, case researchers follow the evidence or expose

> ## BOX 7.2. IDI Interviewer Skills
> ## Distinctive to Case-Centered Research
>
> Ability to:
>
> - Act like a detective by identifying clues and asking the "right" questions.
> - Relinquish control and allow the case to set the course of the investigation.
> - Adapt easily to changes in the research plan as deemed necessary in the course of investigation.
> - Pay attention to what is said and not said (e.g., motivation), written and not written.
> - Notice details and the sequence of events.
> - Think carefully about the physical and substantive context of the information obtained across all methods.
> - Accept all points of view with an open mind.
> - Take time and be patient with interviewees.
> - Act with "emotional maturity" in order to remain focused when the unexpected happens.

a story with the understanding that the balance of power—which, in other qualitative research, is most often tilted toward the side of the researcher who controls the course of the research process (e.g., the IDI, the group discussion, the observation)—resides not with the researcher, but with the case. It is the circumstances of the case that determine what methods to use, what avenues of inquiry to pursue, and when it may be necessary to deviate from the original research plan (e.g., a case study researcher investigating the use of technology in a state-funded farm program may determine a need to expand the research design to include unanticipated units of analysis, such as the farm operations participating in the program).

- Being flexible and adapting to unanticipated changes in the direction of the research, as necessary. The case researcher not only needs to relinquish control but also needs to adapt easily to modifications that may be necessary in the research plan. For example, it may be necessary to make multiple visits to an organization (in a case study) or to conduct repeated conversations with narrators (in narrative research) in order to acquire sufficient details and a complete understanding of the data.

- Listening—paying attention—to what is being said *and* to what is not said; that is, going beyond the detection of nonverbal cues such as facial gestures by also sensing the mood and motivations of the interviewee, as well as what is written and not written in documents. This might include, for example, a narrative researcher who asks the narrator to clarify or expound on a segment of the story when the narrator suddenly modifies his/her manner of speech, for example, by becoming especially slow and demure.

- Noticing the details and sequence of events (e.g., the chronology of events leading up to a company's reorganization of management, or the order of events in someone's life story).

- Paying attention to the physical and substantive context of the information being conveyed. Although attention to context is important in all qualitative research, context is particularly relevant in case-centered research where it becomes a basis by which various aspects of the case are analyzed. For instance, a series of IDIs conducted for a case study examining new school policies might reveal information from teachers that contradicts data provided by documents and other sources. In analyzing the case, the case researcher may strongly suspect that the fact that these IDIs were conducted in the offices of the school board (rather than each teacher's respective school) may have distorted (biased) teachers' feedback on school policies. Unfortunately, it may be impossible for the researcher to tease out this contextual effect, so it may be necessary for the researcher to reinterview these teachers multiple times to corroborate their comments, interview a new set of teachers (if possible) in a less intimidating environment than the school board offices, or ultimately abandon the study. Likewise, the context in which certain information is given (e.g., the point at which the interviewee mentions displeasure or brings up a controversial topic) is important in helping the case researcher link aspects of the case; for example, the teachers' complaints about a particular individual on the school board at a particular point in the interview may deepen the researcher's understanding of other data linking this school board member to certain aspects of the new policies.

- Open-mindedness, receptiveness, and nonjudgmental acceptance of all points of view and various life experiences.

- Patience, that is, allowing the interviewee the time needed to relate his/her account, or tell the story, without conveying any sense of hurriedness.

- Experience and "emotional maturity" (Chase, 2011) that enable the researcher to stay completely focused during the interview in order to evaluate the pertinence of the data being collected (in case study) or closely engage with the narrator (in narrative research). By "emotional maturity," Chase is referring to the interviewer's ability to remain focused and absorbed in the interview even when the interviewee becomes deeply emotional or relates very personal information that may be uncomfortable for the interviewer to hear. In this regard, Chase gives the example of asking her qualitative research students what they would do "if the interviewee cries" during the interview. Chase states, "Sometimes a student says that she or he will change the subject, a response that lets me know the student is not ready for narrative interviewing" (p. 424).

Although IDIs are often an important component to case-centered research, it is the emphasis on multiple methods or multiple sources of data that ultimately puts the researcher in the position to say something meaningful about the case. In addition to IDIs, case-centered researchers depend, in varying degrees, on passive and participant observation (discussed in Chapter 5, p. 174), document reviews, as well as visual imagery and performance (e.g., Liebenberg's [2009] study with low-income teenage mothers and Luttrell's [2003] study on teenage pregnancy mentioned earlier, p. 300). Stake (1995), for example, writes extensively about his case study at the Harper School that investigated school reform by way of numerous field trips with students, IDIs conducted at the school and the local police station, and classroom observation. And, in narrative research, Chase (2011) studied diversity issues at a university where her understanding of the narrative environment was informed by the use of IDIs; observations; and content analyses of college publications, the curriculum, and the school website. Therefore, in addition to IDI-related skills discussed earlier, the researcher needs the ability to integrate these other data sources, including the logistical know-how to coordinate these steps in the research process and the expertise to carry out these methods. To this end, the preferred case-centered researcher should be someone who has, or is in the process of developing:

- Experience and expertise in the ancillary methods that will be utilized in the particular study. A researcher, for example, may have an extensive background in conducting IDIs but have little experience in nonparticipant observation or document analysis.

- Organizational skills, such as the ability to plan and coordinate the order in which the various elements of the research design will be executed.

- Time management skills, such as a realistic understanding of what is involved in each step of the process and ability to allocate a reasonable timeframe to each step.

- The wherewithal (including professional stature and legitimacy) to obtain the necessary permissions to gain access to observation venues, participatory activities, documents, and the like.

Ethical Considerations in Case-Centered Research

Ethical considerations are important in all research endeavors that involve human subjects, but they take on heightened significance in qualitative research designs where researchers often work closely, and frequently face-to-face, with research participants, such as in case-centered research. In Chapter 5 we highlight the ethical issues pertaining to ethnography related to possible covert observation and the possible use of deception, which play a central role in many ethnographic research studies. Case-centered research is another example of a qualitative approach that presents the researcher with a unique set of ethical concerns. Of particular relevance is the highly detailed nature of case-centered research, which gathers a great deal of specific information on any one entity. For case studies, the ethical considerations are underscored by the contemporary focus of this research approach (i.e., case studies are typically conducted to investigate present-day programs, people, policies, events); and, the long, very personal stories derived from narrative research open up a variety of ethical dilemmas, not the least of which is the extent to which interpretations can (or should) be made when narratives are told outside their temporal and social contexts (Brinkmann & Kvale, 2008). In each instance—case study and narrative research—the dominant concern addresses the areas of confidentiality and privacy; specifically, that the researcher's subsequent detailed accounting of an existing phenomenon or individuals' stories will expose the identities of the participants (without their prior permission). The use of informed and voluntary consent as well as approval from institutional review boards (IRBs), when required, are essential. Similar to our discussion in Chapter 5, we emphasize here that case-centered researchers must not only disclose the various aspects of the research, emphasize the voluntary component, promise to keep participants safe, and pay particular attention to vulnerable population segments (e.g., children), but they must also effectively communicate the confidential nature of the research and take extra precautions to ensure participants' right to privacy. This can be particularly challenging when only one case is the focal point of the research (such as in single-case study designs). To address the issue of confidentiality, it is not unusual for case study and narrative researchers to preserve participants' anonymity in their final reports by changing participants' names as well as the names of the characters and places in their narratives. (A more detailed discussion of informed consent and IRBs can be found in Chapter 5.)

Two other areas of ethical concern are faced by narrative researchers. (1) how much to reveal to the participant at the consent stage; and (2) the interpersonal relationships between the researcher and the participants that are formed and are, indeed, often a hallmark of narrative research. With respect to the first concern, there is reluctance among researchers conducting a narrative study to divulge "too much" in the way of the study's research objectives. The thinking tends to be that too many details about the study's purpose will stifle or otherwise bias the participant's narrative and that "the 'scholarly good' of framing the study to the participant in a way that makes possible the kind of narration the researcher needs outweighs the 'moral' good of telling the participant the exact nature of the study" (Josselson, 2007, p. 540). But there may be exceptions to this general rule, and an ethical researcher will always put the well-being of the participant(s) ahead of the researcher's own agenda. Furthermore, when any deception is practiced, the narrative researcher has the obligation to debrief the participant(s) after the study has been conducted and try to undo any harm the deception may have caused (see Chapter 5 for a fuller discussion).

The close researcher–narrator relationships that naturally ensue in narrative research may also raise moral issues for the researcher. For example, on a more profound level than that of the IDI interviewer, the narrative investigator expends an enormous amount of energy establishing and maintaining rapport, trust, respect, and sincere empathy with the participant in order to gain access to an honest and complete telling of the narrator's lived experiences. This relationship, however, may be difficult to terminate—either because the participant is emotionally overcome from having revealed an anguishing story, and/or the participant has been emotionally rewarded by the encounter and wishes to continue the relationship with the researcher beyond the conclusion of the study (Jossel-son, 2007). Josselson likens the ending of the interview to the "termination process in psychotherapy, where it becomes important for both people to voice how they felt about the experience and to note its meaningfulness" (p. 544). For this reason, a debriefing session (or series of such sessions) with the participant—by which, among other things, the researcher asks for the participant's feedback on the narrative research interview experience and assures the participant of the value he/she has brought to the study's objectives—is a very important step before exiting from a narrative interview and possibly ending the relationship with the participant completely. The interviewer should be prepared at this final phase of the interview process to respond to the interviewee's concerns (if any) truthfully and as thoroughly as possible.

Overview of the Strengths and Limitations of Case-Centered Research

Strengths

A primary strength of both case study and narrative research is the focus on complex phenomena and the holistic strategy researchers employ to retain and give meaning to the many integrated components. These case-centered approaches tackle issues that go beyond the scope of other single-method qualitative research designs such as IDIs and group discussions. Case-centered research does not look at one point in time or one facet of a situation but rather considers the case in the depth of its entirety. This is made possible by the use of multiple methods, which is the cornerstone of case-centered research. For example, if the case concerns the use of technology at the university library, the case study design may surround the issue by going beyond onsite observations, IDIs, or group discussions with library users and staff, and incorporate a broader and more in-depth investigation, including (a) a complete review of the library's electronic databases; (b) the extent of users' access to Internet content (remotely and onsite); (c) the usability of its website across all digital devices, content, and amount of visitation; and (d) the use of and commitment to ongoing technological innovation. Likewise, narrative research to study the stigma of alcoholism would not be limited to a typical IDI with several alcoholics but also would embrace a full range of methods that attempt to look at the experience of living with alcoholism from different modes of communication, including orally via an unstructured IDI, in writing by way of a journal or diary exercise, and graphically in the form of a "self-identity drawing," asking the participant, "Could you try to draw who you think you are right now?" (Esteban-Guitart, 2012, p. 179). This approach in narrative research provides the researcher with a complex dimensionality to participants' stories while also bestowing on participants the freedom to express their stories in varying ways and allowing their stories to be heard.

There is also a "naturalness" associated with case studies and narrative research. For case studies, this comes chiefly from the context or, more specifically, the researcher's access to data taken from the subject's environment as it exists (e.g., the corporate environment to study the implementation of new employee training practices, a hospital's intensive care unit [ICU] facility to study organizational structure, a two-block urban neighborhood to study social contact). Narrative research derives its naturalness from the unstructured, open-ended questioning—by which the interviewer's interjections in the interview are mostly words of encouragement (e.g., "Please, go on," or "Tell me what made that event so memorable") or questions for clarification (e.g., "Was this the first time you encountered this situation?" "How far is it from your home to where you go for treatment?")—as well as the idea that "humans are storytelling organisms" (Connelly & Clandinin, 1990, p. 2) and that telling stories is a natural aspect of what it means to be a human being. This natural basis from which to gather data enables the researcher to witness, among other things, the sequence or order of situational or life events as well as the changes that have taken place within the life cycle bounded by the case.

Limitations

A limitation in case-centered research revolves around the possible negative effect of the researcher who may alter the study environment (e.g., biasing case study observations due to the observer's presence) or the narrative (e.g., bias resulting from the researcher–narrator verbal interactions or an excessive amount of co-construction of a story), thereby harming the quality of the research design, which should instead strive to maintain the natural elements associated with the case to every degree possible. As is true for other qualitative methods, a reflexive journal can help case study and narrative researchers monitor the naturalness of their study environments, particularly the potential impact they may be having in biasing the data. An example of a reflexive journal format is shown in Chapter 2, Figure 2.2, page 42.

Although case study and narrative research share common advantages that stem from their holistic focus on complex entities as well as the natural context in which the data are collected, there are, with the exception of potential researcher bias (discussed above), unique limitations to each of these approaches.

Potential Case Study Research Limitations

The potential limitations in case study research that have received the most attention, and contention, revolve around the area of analysis, specifically, the interpretation and subsequent use of the data. The controversy centers on "generalization"—a word many qualitative researchers are loath to use in association with qualitative research and a word we purposefully and actively have avoided in previous chapters—and the extent to which the data can explain phenomena or situations outside and beyond the specific scope of a particular study. On the one hand, there are researchers such as Yin (2014) who espouse "analytical generalization" whereby the researcher compares (or "generalizes") case study data to existing theory. From Yin's perspective, case study research is driven by the need to develop or test theory, giving single- as well as multiple-case study research explanatory powers—"Some of the best and most famous case studies have been explanatory case studies" (Yin, 2014, p. 7). On the other hand, there are researchers such as Stake (1995), who believes that the purpose of case study research is "particularization, not generalization" (p. 8), and Thomas (2010), who rejects the concept of theoretical generalizability in case study research, believing instead that "the goal of social scientific endeavor, particularly in the study of cases, should be exemplary knowledge . . . that can come from [the] case . . . rather than [from] its generalizability" (p. 576). Thomas goes further in asserting that simply attempting to generalize case study data will have the detrimental effect of dampening the researcher's "curiosity and interpretation" of the outcomes.

So, the prospective case study researcher is left with somewhat of a dilemma:

- Is my goal to generalize my case study to some greater theory?

- Is my goal to envelop myself in this particular case in order to find in-depth meaning and derive valid interpretations of the data for this case, and not to apply my results to a preconceived theory?

- Or do I want to strike some kind of balance and focus my analysis on "both the emergent theory that is the research objective and the rich empirical evidence that supports the theory" (Eisenhardt & Graebner, 2007, p. 29)?

This dilemma is considered in conjunction with the implementation process for case studies (Section 7.2, p. 313) and addressed more fully in Section 7.3 on applying the TQF to case study research.

Potential Narrative Research Limitations

The limitations associated with narrative research pertain to potential errors in data gathering (a central aspect of the TQF Credibility component), including various factors that can bias participants' narratives and thereby compromise the quality of the resulting data. The three key areas where such factors can negatively influence the outcome of the narrator's story are (1) the research context or environment in which the story is being told (e.g., the comfort or amenities at the physical location in a face-to-face interview); (2) the researcher (e.g., the appearance, mannerisms, and/or personality of the researcher and the intrusiveness or demanding nature of the questions, such as asking for a rationale to explain story events); and (3) the research participant (e.g., the accuracy/inaccuracy of recall, social desirability [i.e., how the narrator wants to be perceived; see Chapters 3 and 4], and an unwillingness to disclose the full story). This last factor can be a particular threat to the credibility of narrative data if the researcher is not on the lookout for the narrator's posturing or telling of the story in such a way to appear overly "heroic," "the victim," or other exaggerated portrayals that may be the image the narrator wishes to convey to the researcher as opposed to conveying a fully accurate image of what in fact happened.

7.2 PROCESS IN CASE-CENTERED RESEARCH

Quality outcomes from case-centered research are the result of a well-defined process that guides the researcher from start to finish. As for all qualitative research design, it is critical that a clear path be laid out by which case study and narrative research achieves credible and analyzable data. Although the specifics within the process will vary on a study-by-study basis, there exists an optimal flow or order to the implementation of case study and narrative research.

The first stage of the overall process, of course, is the determination and agreement among members of the research team that case-centered research is the appropriate approach for the particular research issue or objective. This determination is accomplished by a careful review of the distinctive aspects as well as suitable uses of case-centered research (discussed earlier in this chapter) along with the research scope and how the research will ultimately be used.

Once the appropriateness of case study or narrative research has been ascertained and the resources that will be needed to carry it out secured, there are six general steps in the process leading up to data collection, analysis, and reporting.

1. **Establishing priorities.** The success of the process as well as the final results of the research rest with establishing the priority of needs at the outset, based on a repeated and thorough examination of the research objective(s). At this initial phase, the research team defines the study around such questions as, Are we only interested in a specific case itself or is our intent to use the case to say something more broadly about a larger population of cases? Likewise, what is the role of theory development and the need for replication in conjunction with the research objective? What is the macro- or micro-level by which researchers need to collect and analyze data in order to meet the goals of the research?

2. **Determining the need for and conducting a literature review.** A review of the literature can serve a very important function when the research focus is external to (i.e., beyond) the case itself, with the purpose of the research to extend, confirm, or deny existing theory or hypotheses. In these instances, a literature review of similar work conducted by other researchers can advise the research team members on (a) how their study will overlap with or fill a gap in the existing body of empirical evidence, (b) refining the research question or general propositions, and (c) the specific factors or variables that are most associated with the research issue. A literature review, conducted from a TQF perspective (see Chapter 8), helps form the theoretical framework that will steer the design and implementation of the research. In contrast, a review of the literature is not as necessary when the study is internally focused, that is, when the researcher is only interested in learning about the case itself and not in comparing or theorizing outside the case; however, even in these instances, a literature review may help the researcher conceptualize the relevant constructs to measure.

3. **Selecting a single case or multiple cases.** The research objective, setting of priorities, and literature review (if conducted) should enable the research team

to define the case or cases that most appropriately satisfy the research goals. Going back to the internal–external classification discussed earlier (see p. 297), researchers might select a single case when the research outcomes will be used only to learn about the case itself, such as the physician–patient interaction at one city hospital or the lived experience of a victim of domestic violence. Multiple cases, on the other hand, will be selected when there is an external focus to extend a proposition or theory, such as the hypothetical X-ray equipment study discussed on page 296, or life stories from gifted students to learn about the factors that impact their and similar students' drive to succeed. The number of cases will depend on not only the literal or theoretical replication model (Yin, 2014, as discussed on p. 296), but also on the logistical or practical issues, such as the finite research funding, timeframe, and availability of sites/participants.

   4. **Determining the unit(s) and variable(s) of analysis.** The research team must decide on the specificity that is needed in the data collection process. There are two levels of specificity that need to be considered: (1) the unit(s) of analysis and (2) the **variable(s) of analysis**. The units of analysis represent the primary aspects of a case that will be the focus of investigation, whereas the variables of analysis are subcategories within the units of analysis that guide researchers in their examination of the units. For example, as seen in Figure 7.1, the units of analysis in a case study concerning the program operations of the local YMCA are the individual programs, and the variables to investigate within each unit (or program) include the activities/events, the participant profile, and the participant–staff ratio. In narrative research, researchers use different aspects of the narrative environment as their units and variables of analyses. In a study of gifted students, for example (shown in Figure 7.2), the units of analysis might be gifted students' life stories, biographical stories and documents from family members,

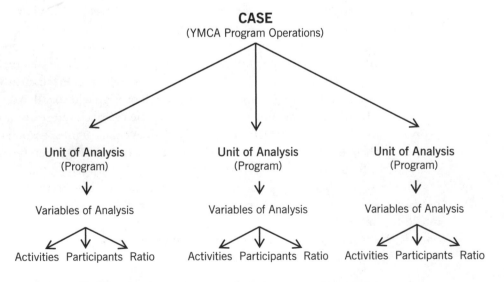

FIGURE 7.1. Unit(s) and variable(s) of analysis: Case study example.

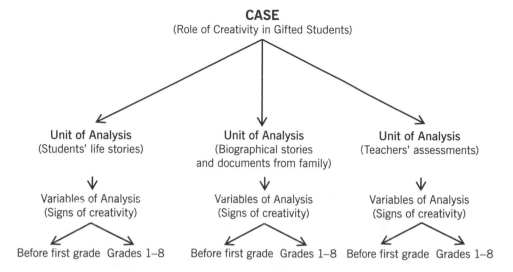

FIGURE 7.2. Unit(s) and variable(s) of analysis: Narrative example.

and teachers' assessments. The variables or factors within these units that are especially relevant to the research objectives—such as evidence in the stories/assessments that the student was particularly creative before the first grade and from the first to the eighth grade—would act as the variables of analysis.

5. **Identifying the appropriate methods.** Depending on the research objective and target entity (e.g., organization, program, group, or individual), the research team needs to select the appropriate methods to use to conduct the case study or narrative research. These are the methods that will be uniformly used across all cases (in multiple-case research) in the study. On-site passive or participant observation and IDIs are the methods often used in case studies, and the unstructured IDI (face-to-face or online) is frequently the primary method in narrative research. However, case study research may also employ group discussions and/or quantitative (survey) research, and both forms of case-centered research conduct document reviews (including archival records, possibly using content analytic techniques) and analyze physical and imagery artifacts (e.g., the written tests completed by students in water safety training class, the drawings completed by teenagers to express their self-identity narratives, or video diaries from employees who use wheelchairs).

In addition to considering the research objectives (including any theoretical notions) and the nature of the case, it is important for the researcher to keep two considerations in mind when selecting the appropriate methods: (1) Logistical or practical matters such as research funding, timeframe, and availability of sites/participants may dictate, to a large degree, the viability of certain methods; and (2) the emphasis of one method over another may shift once fieldwork begins—for example, scheduling conflicts may make it impossible for a case researcher to conduct IDIs, resulting in additional observations, or the narrative researcher may be denied access to personal documents that were intended to be used to better understand the narrators' life stories.

     6. Preparing for the field. In order to prepare for the fieldwork, the research team needs to do the following:

- Develop the appropriate tools such as an interview guide (even the narrative unstructured interviewer requires prompts to stimulate storytelling), observation grid (see Chapter 5, p. 206), and data recordkeeping file to store and keep track of notes, documents, recordings, and images by data source and case.

- Determine the role(s) each member of the research team will play[5] (e.g., interviewer, observer, recorder, document reviewer, and/or coordinator).

- Determine what, if any, problems exist in gaining access to the site(s) or individual(s), including schedules, availability, and issues with recruiting/cooperation.

- Obtain informed consent and, if necessary, IRB approval.

- Initiate preliminary interaction with research participants to identify any issues or problems and begin building rapport with those who will be involved in the study (e.g., visiting a selected site for a case study to go over the logistics, or informally meeting with a narrative participant to establish familiarity and a level of comfort with the researcher and the research process).

With the preliminary groundwork set, the research team is ready to embark on the all-essential data collection, analysis, and reporting phases of the research. Section 7.3 considers each of these phases in its application of the TQF to case-centered research.

7.3 THE TOTAL QUALITY FRAMEWORK APPROACH TO CASE-CENTERED RESEARCH

Both of the case-centered methods that are the primary focus of this chapter use multiple qualitative methods for gathering data. Several of these methods (IDIs, focus groups, ethnography, and content analysis) are discussed in detail in Chapters 3–6, and the discussions there include detailed attention to how the TQF should be applied to each of those methods. Therefore, in this section of the current chapter, we do not repeat what is in those previous chapters and instead focus on other unique TQF issues that affect case study and narrative research. In the case of the Credibility component of the TQF we have included separate sections for case study research and narrative research. For the other three components of the TQF, however, we have not broken out issues specific to these two forms of case-centered qualitative research because we believe the gist of what we say for Analyzability, Transferability, and Usefulness in case-centered research applies to both case study and narrative research.

Credibility

Case Study Research

Scope

For those case studies that are internally focused—that is, where the focus is entirely on understanding a single case without any intention or interest in advancing theory or otherwise looking beyond what is learned from the case study to apply or extend to something external to the case—the issue of defining the target population for the study is part and parcel of choosing the case that will be studied. In this way, the case chosen for the case study becomes the entire target population of interest for the study. However, for a case study that is externally focused—that is, where the objective is to develop or expand on theory or otherwise generate findings that can be applied beyond the case(s) studied in the particular project—defining the target population clearly and precisely is a crucial first step in planning the scope of the study. As part of this definition of the population—and unlike what is required for defining the target population in other forms of qualitative research—it may not be sufficient to merely define the target population in a descriptive sense (e.g., all women who have been treated for breast cancer in the past 5 years at the Yale University Hospital in New Haven, CT). This is particularly true when the goal of a case study is to expand on theory. An explication of the exact theoretical principles being investigated also needs to be written into the definition of the study's target population (e.g., stating that the study will examine the theory that focusing on treatment processes rather than on treatment outcomes helps bring about higher patient satisfaction with treatment and better outcomes in treating women with breast cancer). In this way, the researcher is specifying the particular aspect of the theory in relation to the target population (e.g., breast cancer patients) that the case study is trying to address.

A unique concern in case study research that the researcher employing a TQF strategy must consider next involves the number of data collection events that will be needed for each method in the case study. For example, if the case study is using IDIs, focus groups, and ethnographic observations to gather data, it is not enough for the researcher to make a priori decisions about how many interviews, discussions, and observations to complete. Instead, the researcher needs to simultaneously consider how data gathered by each of the different methods are likely to vary across methods and monitor this data variation throughout the field process (as opposed to thinking only about how data vary within a method). So, for example, it may be that what is learned by conducting IDIs will affect how many focus groups and observations should be carried out (and vice versa) as well as potentially lead to the inclusion of an additional method in the case study, such as document review. As a result, the decision about how much data to gather across all methods used in a case study is a much more dynamic (i.e., evolving) one than deciding about this issue when only one qualitative method is used for gathering data.

Another important consideration in the scope of a case study is participant cooperation. Cooperation is especially important in case study research because the whole point of using this approach is to collect as much data as possible on each unit and variable of analysis (as discussed on p. 310). Without a high level of cooperation, the case researcher will fail to capture the nuanced complexity of the case(s). The importance of gaining participants' cooperation to the credibility of qualitative data has been discussed throughout this book, and the reader can refer to these discussions for an understanding of the ways to achieve cooperation from a TQF perspective (in particular, see Chapters 3–5). In a multi-method case-centered approach such as case study, the researcher has an additional means of obtaining cooperation that is not possible in the single-method research designs discussed in earlier chapters: that is, the ability to leverage success in recruiting participants in one method so as to better gain cooperation in the other methods. For example, as the researcher is selecting and devising the recruiting strategies to use with the lists selected for the IDIs, focus groups, and observations that the case study will include, he/she should consider referencing the willingness of those who have already cooperated in the data collection for one method (e.g., the IDIs) to those being recruited to participate in the other methods (e.g., the focus groups and observations). In doing so, the researcher has instilled heightened legitimacy in the project among prospective participants and is very likely able to gain enhanced cooperation by progressively building on prior recruiting success.

Data Gathering

When using multiple methods for data collection in a case study, it is important that the researchers strive to achieve equal levels of excellence for each of the "tools" they devise to gather data across the different methods (e.g., IDI and group discussion guides, observation grids, and content analysis coding forms). The reason for this is that even one poorly designed, not well-thought-out measurement tool (e,g., an IDI guide) can undermine the quality of the entire case study. This may happen, for instance, when different members of the research team are assigned to planning and refining different methods, with one researcher designing the IDI guide, another developing the focus group guide, and yet another creating the observation grid. If just one of these data-gathering devices is faulty in some way (e.g., the IDI guide fails to address an important construct), the data collection effort for the entire study may yield biased data (and interpretations) as a result of conflicting and incomplete information from, for example, the IDI method. To avoid this, the researchers need to allocate ample time and resources to conduct inter-researcher checks on the measurement tools created, as well as to fully pilot-test the data collection tools and procedures for each method.

Nevertheless, even with considerable inter-researcher checks and pilot testing, it may be a challenge to complete a case study by the chosen methods. This may occur because there is a long time lag between data collection for the different methods, and what is learned from one method may no longer be comparable or relate to what was learned from a prior method because of non-negligible changes brought about by the passage of time in what is being studied. For example, a case study concerning a community's response to a devastating tornado might include IDIs with the local officials, a review of the governing body's disaster preparedness documents, and group discussions with community residents. However, if interviewing the local officials and analyzing documents take a priority, the group discussions with community residents may be conducted so long after the tornado event—when structures are being rebuilt and residents' recall of the event is less clear—that their input may be wildly different and inconsistent with data collected from the other methods.

For this and other reasons, it is important in case study research to remain flexible. The tornado disaster example illustrates a situation in which the researcher needs to be prepared to either conduct discussions with residents earlier in the process (e.g., by employing an additional moderator) or find an alternative approach to eliciting residents' input closer to the timing of the actual tornado event (e.g., on-site IDIs). The case study researcher should also retain the flexibility (and in fact has the responsibility) to change data collection approaches midstream as unanticipated insights are gained from the data as they are being gathered via a particular method. This flexibility can require a juggling act for the researchers, who must always strive to have the best data collection approaches in play, but at the same time keep the quality of the approaches across methods equally high. To those who are new to case study research, all of this may appear to be an impossible task, but in fact it is not, as many expert case study researchers routinely succeed in keeping the quality of their data gathering across methods in balance. Part of what is required for success is to be aware of this TQF imperative and to stay alert to its implications across all data collection methods throughout the time period in which data are being gathered for the case study.

An additional data-gathering issue in case study research that can threaten credibility is the potential problems in data quality that can result if the case study design is too ambitious and, as a result, attempts to take on more (e.g., in the way of methods and number of research events such as IDIs or observations) than is practicable given the research budget and/or the timeframe in which the research must be completed. If too much is asked of whomever is involved in gathering the data, such as asking one researcher to complete all IDIs, group discussions, and observations, then the quality of what he/she does is bound to suffer. Conducting high-quality case studies is often a difficult task because of the complexity of what is being studied, the various methods involved, and the need for a cadre of skilled, savvy, and experienced research staff. Because of these factors, it is prudent for anyone new to case study research to serve as an intern or apprentice before trying to play a lead role in data collection.

Narrative Research

Scope

As with case studies, if a narrative research project is meant to study only a particular person or group (i.e., internally focused research), and not meant to be used to advise on anything external to this focus, then the target population is only the person or group being studied. However, if the person or group being studied is meant to represent some larger group of persons/entities (i.e., the study is externally focused, such as studying the stories from selected cancer patients to inform medical practices for patients undergoing chemotherapy), then all the same concerns about defining the target population that apply to case study research also apply to narrative research.

Also similar to case study research, the narrative researcher must consider the methods as well as the number of research events in a multicase narrative study. Although the IDI is the primary method utilized in narrative research, it is the ability of the multi-method approach to examine various facets of the narrative environment that maximizes the ultimate usefulness of a narrative study. Our discussion in this section focuses on the IDI method; however, the reader is encouraged to refer to earlier chapters on how the TQF is applied to other methods, all of which the narrative researcher might use to investigate a narrative environment.

Since the researcher(s) in narrative research will need and want to develop a close and productive relationship with the person(s) that will be studied, it is critical that the researcher establish a strong first impression when making initial contact to seek the cooperation and compliance from the subject. The distinction that we make between cooperation and compliance is an important one in narrative research. Unlike IDIs and focus group research, where each participant typically provides data on only one occasion, narrative research may require many occasions for a narrator to sufficiently tell his/her story. Therefore, we reserve the word "cooperation" for the initial cooperation that is gained when a participant agrees to be involved in the research project. The word "compliance" is reserved for the ongoing cooperation the participant exhibits as the project moves ahead to its completion. Without cooperation *and* compliance the Credibility of a narrative study is seriously weakened. This is why the process of gaining cooperation in narrative research must not be rushed. Instead it should be viewed as a staged process in which success at a later stage is built upon the success of an earlier stage. From the TQF perspective, there is no fixed set or number of stages that is the "best" approach to gaining full cooperation and compliance, but it is advised that the researcher anticipate and think about at least seven stages:

1. Making initial contact.
2. Beginning to build rapport.
3. Solidifying rapport.
4. Gaining initial agreement from the subject to participate in the study.
5. Avoiding a backout.[6]
6. Gaining ongoing compliance.
7. Avoiding premature attrition.[7]

The chronology of this staging should not be interpreted to suggest that there needs to be seven discrete occasions (i.e., days and times) in which the narrative researcher interacts with a participant—such an approach would likely lead to a disastrous artificiality in the rapport-building process of narrative research.

Rather, the researcher should think of this sequence as a natural movement from one stage to the next, without having to go back to a previous stage to start over again from there. And, to be fully successful, this movement between stages needs to be tailored to the individual participant. So, for example, Stages 1 and 2 (i.e., initial contact and the beginning of rapport building) might be accomplished in the first meeting between the researcher and a potential participant, and Stages 5 and 6 (i.e., avoiding backout and gaining ongoing compliance) might be addressed by the researcher within the same subsequent contact with the participant. But exactly how the researcher achieves success at each stage is left to his/her skill and intellect in perceiving and responding to the individuality of the particular storyteller from whom narrative data will be gathered.

As a narrative researcher is gaining cooperation and maintaining compliance from a given storyteller, he/she must constantly attend to the equity (balance) in the relationship between the two of them. The benefits to the researcher in this relationship are obvious, but not necessarily as obvious for the storyteller participant. In other qualitative research methods where the researcher and participant have relatively brief contact, material (e.g., cash) incentives given to the participant may play an important role in achieving the equitable balance. But in narrative research it is highly unlikely that material incentives will provide enough benefit to the participant to be a primary motivation for him/her to continue with the study, and to do so in a manner consistent with the depth and quality of information input the researcher is seeking. Instead, intangible incentives that are linked to the participant's own motivation and gratification in telling his/her story are more likely to offset the inconvenience or stress experienced by the narrator's completing the project. Researchers whose whole demeanor sincerely (i.e., naturally, in an unforced manner) conveys a sense of interest, concern, and appreciation toward the storyteller will very likely succeed in rewarding the participant and thereby maintaining his/her engagement throughout the completion of the study.

Data Gathering

As previously mentioned, the IDI method most often used in narrative research takes the form of the unstructured interview where the interviewer is not so much equipped with a series of questions or topics as a reminder of the research objective and areas where clarification or words of encouragement may be particularly appropriate. In lieu of a formal interview guide, the interviewer may want to enlist certain aids. For instance, Elliott (2005) suggests using a "life history grid" (e.g., a spreadsheet with each row representing a specific year and the columns used to record life events) to facilitate biographical interviews when narrators may need some structure in which to place their life events, beyond an open-ended question such as "Tell me about your life." A TQF approach to narrative research fully supports the life history grid and other tools that may enable the narrative researcher to obtain more complete and accurate data that ultimately lead to more credible and useful outcomes.

Also as noted earlier in this chapter, because of the very close relationship that is likely to develop between the interviewer and storyteller in narrative research, the researcher must vigilantly guard against biasing some or all of the story that is told by the participant due to his/her behavior. This biasing can result from behaviors that are within the control of the interviewer (e.g., facial expressions that signal agreement or disagreement with what is being said, making evaluative comments about what is being said, paying closer attention to some parts of what is being said and less attention to other parts) and/or from characteristics that are part of the interviewer's own physical (e.g., hairstyle, body art, demographic characteristics) and behavioral (e.g., voice parameters, gesticulations) nature. Although it is true that the mere interaction of the interviewer with the narrator serves to shape the outcomes to some degree, researchers should be aware of, and consciously work to avoid, as much as is practicable, these potential biasing effects—that can lead to inaccuracies in the recording and interpretation of a narrator's story. As discussed throughout this book, it is strongly advised that the interviewer record his/her behavior or characteristics that possibly affected the data in a reflexive journal, which should be kept throughout the period of interaction the interviewer has with the storyteller.

Similarly, researchers in narrative research must guard against the narrator's telling of a story in ways that are wholly fictitious (untrue), embellished, and/or incomplete, including telling only part of the story and contextualizing some parts in a manner that leads to a misinterpretation of what actually took place. The storyteller may do this consciously (e.g., actively try to impress the interviewer) or unconsciously (e.g., succumb to the general tendency of humans to paint themselves in the best possible light by giving a socially desirable depiction of events or feelings). However, it is important to note that some unconscious factors may impact the narrator's story no matter what the interviewer does; for example, the limited ability of language to convey the complexities of experience and the limits of what the storyteller can remember or is made aware of upon reflection cannot be prevented (cf. Polkinghorne, 2007). Indeed, narratives represent what Gubrium and Holstein (2008) call a "complex stock of ingredients" that reflect an "interplay between experience, storying practices, descriptive resources, purposes at hand, audiences, and the environments that condition storytelling" (p. 250). And, although it is important for the researcher to be aware of these complexities, it is also important to acknowledge what the researcher can and cannot affect in terms of the ultimate quality of the outcomes.

For a narrator to be willing and able to tell his/her story in a way that the interviewer will gain a full and accurate understanding of the story, the narrator must believe and feel:

- Motivated to give a complete and honest account to the degree possible.
- That everything and anything the participant says is of interest to the interviewer.
- That the interviewer is supportive, conscientious, empathic, and wants nothing more (or less) from the participant than to understand the story being told.

Although, from a TQF perspective, we emphasize the importance of the interviewer–narrator relationship, the narrative researcher is cautioned that this relationship must not become too intimate (including emotionally), and that it is primarily the responsibility of the interviewer to keep this from happening. It is likely that few others, and possibly no one else, has ever listened to the storyteller in the way the interviewer should be listening, and this may cause at least some narrators to feel strong positive emotions toward the interviewer. Positive emotions can be a good thing to the extent that they motivate a rich telling of the narrative. However, there comes a nebulous point beyond which this close relationship may harm the validity of the research being conducted; for example, when the interviewer begins to lose objectivity and does not ask for clarification on key areas, or when the narrator cares so much about the interviewer's good will that some difficult or unpleasant past behaviors of the narrator are guardedly withheld. Narrative participants should not be expected to monitor the nature of the relationship they are developing with the interviewer. Instead, this is the responsibility of the interviewer and, as appropriate, the principal researcher overseeing the study.

As can be seen, the balance in the relationship between a storyteller and an interviewer in narrative research can be an extremely precarious one. Too much or too little closeness can seriously harm the credibility of the data being gathered, due to a loss of objectivity and/or the inability to capture complete data due to the absence of adequate rapport. This challenge is further complicated by the fact that this relationship is unlikely to be a static one in the course of the data collection period—meaning that it will likely change over time, with the two feeling closer at some times and less close at others. Regardless of what happens, it remains the responsibility of the researcher to be aware of such matters, to try to help the interviewer adjust the relationship dynamic with the narrator, as needed, during the period of interaction between the two, to document these relationship dynamics, and to take them into consideration as sense is being made of the data.

Analyzability

Most of the issues pertaining to the data-processing stage and data verification stage of case-centered research are covered in Chapters 3–6 in the ways they apply to how data from IDIs, group discussions, ethnography, and content analysis are processed and verified. The following discussion concentrates on those areas of Processing and Verification that are distinctive for the case-centered approach.

Processing

One of the unique aspects of case-centered research in terms of Analyzability is the need to make sense of, and to draw meaning from, several different sources of data about the same phenomenon of study. This reality ultimately boils down to the analytic challenge, for case study and narrative researchers, of "retaining the whole"—that is, retaining the interconnectedness of the data within and across the different sources in order to illuminate the entirety and complexity of the case. For a case-centered researcher to conduct this phase of the research well, the analysis must be multifaceted, with simultaneous attention paid to:

- Content (e.g., the information actually conveyed in an IDI or group discussion, or what was actually observed in an observation).

- Temporal sequence (e.g., in a documented organizational restructuring or the telling of the progression of a disease).

- Context (e.g., the juxtaposition of other events with the school board's decision to delay opening day at public schools, or the physical environment or characteristics of the interviewer that cause the narrator to tell a story in a particular manner).

- Linguistics (i.e., participants' use of words and language).

- Visual imagery (e.g., photographs provided in documents or the use of photos to tell a story).

From a TQF perspective, the case-centered researcher must not only be adept at each method utilized in a case or narrative study but must also understand how to link the various forms of data and draw meaning from the outcomes. This process can be facilitated by the use of grids or matrices similar to the observation grid discussed in Chapter 5 (see p. 206) and the life history grid mentioned earlier in this chapter. Given the array of data sources the case researcher may be dealing with, a matrix of some sort that accounts for the data *by data sources* is appropriate. This can be something as simple as a worksheet showing the methods (e.g., IDIs, group discussions, and observations) as rows along the left side and particular constructs or questions as column headings across the top.

To the extent that case-centered research involves the spoken word recorded in field notes and/or audio or video recordings, the researcher will be required to convert these to text that is suitable for analysis. Transcribing and the transcription process have been discussed elsewhere in this book (in particular, see Chapters 3 and 4) and are not repeated here. However, we note that the creation and use of transcriptions take on special meaning in narrative research, in which a primary goal is to maintain the narrative as a whole unit. To this end, the narrative researcher must decide how best to construct the transcripts so they retain the story as it was told, while also facilitating the researcher's ability to derive meaning from the data as it relates to the research objectives. This process might result in any number of transcription formats. For example, Riessman (2008) presents two transcriptions of a conversation she had with a Hindu woman in a study of infertility: One transcription was developed around the "coconstruction process" (i.e., the interviewer's role in the narrative as it was told), and another transcription excluded the interviewer and was structural in nature (e.g., the transcriber paid particular attention to how the narrative was spoken, such as pauses and intonations, from which "stanzas" or content groups could be formed). Another example is what Glesne (1997) called "poetic transcription" defined as "the creation of poem-like compositions from the words of interviewees" (p. 202).

What is important here, from a TQF perspective, is not so much the format or style of the transcriptions but rather the emphasis that is placed on upholding the entirety of the narrative and the researcher's ability to make credible interpretations of the data. Because the form of the transcription may impact the researcher's interpretations of the outcomes (e.g., a transcript that omits the interviewer might be interpreted differently compared to a transcript that includes every spoken word), it is incumbent upon the researcher to disclose the exact nature of the transcription process and the resulting transcript(s) in the final document.

As discussed elsewhere in this book (in particular, see Chapter 6), the use of computer-assisted qualitative data analysis software (CAQDAS) cannot replace the role the researcher (and other members of the research team) in coding and making sense of the data. This is especially true in case-centered research that deals with complex entities that are investigated by way of multiple methods that are not easily converted into a form compatible with CAQDAS. We agree with Yin (2014) when he states that "computerized tools cannot readily handle this more diverse array of evidence [from case study research]" (p. 135).

Verification

Two important verification techniques—triangulation and deviant or negative case analysis—are, to some degree, built right into the case-centered research approach. With its focus on multiple methods, case-centered research provides the researcher with a convenient basis by which to compare and contrast data derived from different methods and (in multiple-case research) multiple cases. In fact, these verification techniques should not only be considered during the analysis phase but also conducted throughout data collection in case-centered research. From a TQF perspective, the researcher should consistently review the data generated from the various methods, looking for information that supports or refutes data from one method compared to another, as well as possibly nuanced input that is totally unique (i.e., deviant) from all other data. In this way, the case-centered approach offers the researcher an important opportunity to continually assess the learning from the research and, as warranted, take the study design in a different direction (e.g., replacing one method for a different method, or adding a new variable of analysis, as defined on p. 310).

Verification is particularly important in narrative research when participants' life stories—especially those from marginalized groups such as victims of child abuse or welfare recipients—may be filled with violence, extreme poverty, or other circumstances outside the researcher's usual frame of reference. In these instances, researchers may take on "a mental state which prevents [them] from hearing and seeing the interviewees' point of view in its wholeness" (Krumer-Nevo, 2002, p. 315), requiring "the researcher to forget or temporarily to set aside the normative knowledge acquired from one's membership in a society, a family, or an educational system of values" (p. 316). This is where peer debriefings, multiple researchers working on the analyses and interpretations, deviant case analysis, and reflexive journals can play an important role in maintaining the quality of the analytical process. These verification procedures—as well as the steps taken in Processing—will also provide a level of rigor to narrative analysis that will enable the researcher to look critically at narratives as a "social phenomenon" (e.g., stories are told within social conventions or are co-created by the narrator and interviewer) and "not simply collect them as if they were untrammelled, unmediated representations of social realities" (Atkinson & Delamont, 2006, p. 170).

Transparency

Considerations about Transparency that are unique to case-centered research (i.e., those apart from Transparency considerations that apply to the individual qualitative methods used in case-centered research and that have been discussed in the Transparency sections of Chapters 3–6) include (1) the manner in which case study and narrative research reports are written, (2) the crucial attention to protecting confidentiality of the subjects that have been studied, and (3) making it easy for the research design to become the basis for others' work in future case study and narrative research (i.e., transferability).

Unlike the technical reports that are created for many other types of research studies, it is important that the documents that explain what was learned in a case study or in a narrative research project be written in an engaging manner that captures the sense and style of the "story" the researcher wants to convey about the case or the narrative. This style should be used to explain what was learned as well as the meaning and implications of those findings; however, it should also be used to convey information about how the study was carried out, including the various methods used and the data collection and analysis processes. In this way the substance of what was learned (i.e., the story of the case(s) that is derived from the details of the findings and their implications) and the form in which this information is conveyed (i.e., an engaging, story-like manner) are wholly compatible with each other.

As mentioned previously in this chapter, case studies and narrative research projects gather a great deal of in-depth and detailed data from multiple information sources. The amount of data that is gathered from any one source is typically much greater than the amount of data gathered from a source in other qualitative studies (e.g., IDIs or group discussions). Much of this information, especially in narrative research, may be extremely personal and private. Eliciting such information requires the researcher to gain the complete trust of each research participant. A good part of this trust can be gained via the participant's unquestioning belief that the researcher will do nothing with the information to harm him/her. The researcher can meet this obligation and protect the identity of research participants in the manner by which the documentation for a case-centered study is written, specifically by masking the names and any other possible identification of the actual source(s). Further, when a case study or narrative researcher drafts the research report, it is important that an impartial reviewer read and provide feedback on it, including an explicit statement as to whether the reviewer could deduce the identity of any of the individuals who participated in the research.

A final special TQF consideration for those creating documentation about a case study or a narrative research project is to actively strive toward conveying sufficient details about methods and analytic approaches to help future researchers in their use of case-centered methods. And from a self-serving standpoint, this approach should also help the researcher as he/she thinks ahead to future research that uses a case-centered approach. By using thick descriptions to describe and capture what was done in the case study or narrative research, the researcher is empowering all consumers of the research with knowledge about what worked well (and not so well) in the current project, and how to apply the findings of the current project to related issues and/or venues. In this way the researcher has added to the transferability of the research to other contexts.

Usefulness

Some may think that there is a direct relationship between the extensive effort that typically goes into case-centered research—in terms of the data collection and analytical requirements from executing multiple methods—and the usefulness of the findings and implications from the research. That is, the thinking may be that the inclusion of numerous data sources as well as the potential use of considerable resources (i.e., time and funding) should result in a proportionally greater value in terms of usefulness compared to a single-method research design. It is true that investigating a case from many perspectives (by way of multiple methods) provides a richer portrait of a case than any one method, but it is not true ipso facto. All of the methods, data sources, and resources in the world will not provide ultimately useful outcomes in case-centered research unless the TQF techniques and procedures we discuss in this and the other chapters have been carefully considered and, as appropriate, implemented in the research design. Even when the research is internally focused on just a single case, the ability to support new or existing theory, derive actionable next steps, and/or transfer the research design to other contexts—that is, achieve ultimate usefulness in the study—rests entirely on the soundness of the approach and the quality measures taken by the researcher to ensure valid results.

Case Study

A case-centered research study involving a 3-year investigation of working-class Latino parents of school children in urban Los Angeles is presented starting on page 329. This research project is an example of utilizing many TQF techniques—including disclosure of the sampling method, a discussion of potential researcher bias, and the use of various processing and verification procedures—that ultimately led to theoretical and practical implications, as well as to a logical next step.

7.4   CHAPTER SUMMARY

✓ A *multiple-method* approach in qualitative research combines two or more qualitative methods to investigate a research question or phenomenon. It is distinctive from *mixed-methods* research in which researchers combine both qualitative and quantitative methods within one research project.

✓ Multi-method research is discussed in the context of case-centered research, which, in addition to its use of multiple methods, we define as consisting of two fundamental components: (1) a focus on the investigation of "complex" social units or entities *in their entirety*, and (2) an emphasis on maintaining the cohesiveness of this entity throughout the research process rather than reducing the information to categorical data.

✓ Within case-centered research, the chapter focuses on case study and narrative research. Case studies are a qualitative research approach that typically combines IDIs, focus groups, and/or ethnography within the same investigation of some topic of interest. Narrative research primarily uses unstructured IDIs to gather data and then often supplements those data with data gathered by other qualitative methods to provide a thorough understanding of the narrative environment.

✓ Case study and narrative research may require greater resources (i.e., funding and time) than single-method research and are important approaches when the research objective is to gain an unusually broad and/or in-depth understanding of a complex phenomenon.

✓ Case studies can be conducted of a single case or of multiple cases. The focus of a case study can be classified as either "internal"—that is, the study's purpose is to learn about the case itself—or "external"—that is, the purpose of the study is to advance understanding of some theoretical topic or enlighten the researcher's understanding of situations outside the case.

✓ Narrative research investigates the lived experiences of those who are the subject of these studies. It is the narrator's story that is the case or object of attention and the focal point of the research.

✓ Researchers and interviewers doing case-centered research must have a wide array of skills, including (a) being detective-like in following clues; (b) being able to relinquish control; (c) adapting the direction of the research as needed; (d) being expert listeners; (e) paying attention to the context of the information being conveyed; (f) attending closely to details; and (g) remaining open-minded, patient, and emotionally mature.

✓ From an ethical perspective, the highly detailed nature of case-centered research requires special consideration because it gathers a great deal of specific information on any one entity. For case studies, the ethical considerations are underscored by the fact that this research approach often investigates present-day programs, people, policies, events, etc. In the case of narrative research, the long, very personal stories told by narrators may open up a variety of ethical dilemmas, including (a) the extent to which interpretations can be validly made when narratives are told outside their temporal and social contexts; and (b) how, at the conclusion of the study, to gracefully "end" the close researcher–narrator relationship that may have formed.

✓ There are six general steps in the process leading up to data collection, analysis, and reporting of case-centered research. As part of this process, there are two levels of specificity in data collection that need to be considered: (1) the unit(s) of analysis and (2) the variable(s) of analysis.

✓ From a TQF perspective, case-centered research shares all of the concerns that are associated with the individual research methods (e.g., IDIs, focus groups, ethnography) that are utilized.

✓ Beyond these concerns, case study researchers utilizing a TQF strategy need to carefully decide how much data to gather using any one method, basing these decisions in part on what has been learned about the topic under study from the other data collection methods. Also, the quality of the various tools (e.g., the interview and discussion guides) used to gather data in case study research needs to be uniformly high so that no one tool undermines the credibility of the entire study. For this reason, it is recommended that researchers pilot-test the tools and procedures associated with each method in a case study.

✓ A TQF approach to narrative research pays particular attention to the process of gaining initial cooperation from research participants as well as keeping these persons engaged throughout what can be a long process of telling their stories. The credibility of narrative research also hinges on the researcher/interviewer–narrator relationship. In particular, narrative researchers need to monitor the nature of their relationships with narrators and be alert to how well they are maintaining objectivity or exploring all relevant topics with their narrators. Similarly, narrative researchers should be attentive to the possibility that a narrator may be telling a biased story (e.g., distorted in a way that makes the narrator "look good").

✓ In terms of Analyzability, case-centered researchers need to simultaneously attend to (a) the content, (b) its temporal sequencing, (c) linguistics, and (d) visual imagery. The use of grids or matrices can be useful for linking the various forms of data and drawing meaning from the outcomes.

✓ Verification techniques of triangulation and deviant case analysis are built into the case-centered research approach by way of its use of multiple methods, which allow the researcher to compare and contrast data derived from the different methods.

✓ Narrative researchers need to attend closely to the verification stage, especially if a narrator has shared life experiences that are very different from those of the researcher. The researcher needs to guard against his/her own normative expectations, which would lead to biased conclusions about the meaning of what the narrator has said.

7.5 EXERCISES AND DISCUSSION TOPICS

1. Locate and define a case in your real-world environment (e.g., school, job, volunteer organization). Create a research question about this case with an internal or external focus (i.e., a question that is designed to illuminate an issue pertaining just to the case itself [internal] or to be applied to other cases or expand theory [external]). If you were to design a case-centered research approach around this case and research question, how would

you define the Scope in terms of the target populations (including the units and variables of analysis)?

2. Take the case study in the first exercise and describe the data collection methods you would use to investigate each target population (by way of the unit[s] and variable[s] of analysis) and support your choice of methods, including what each contributes to addressing the original research question.

3. What can you foresee as potential threats to the reliability and validity of the data gathered by way of these methods and what steps do you recommend to mitigate these threats?

4. Discuss the Processing and Verification procedures that you would specify for the analysis phase of this case study.

5. Suggest an alternative single-method approach to investigate the original research question and discuss the strengths and limitations of this approach, compared to the multi-method case research you designed, from the perspective of the four TQF components.

SUGGESTED FURTHER READING

Case Study

Vaughan, D. (1996). *The* Challenger *launch decision: Risky technology, culture, and deviance at NASA*. Chicago: University of Chicago Press.

Vaughan, D. (1997). The trickle-down effect: Policy decisions, risky work, and the *Challenger* tragedy. *California Management Review, 39*(2), 80–102.

Vaughan's research is a case study referenced by Yin (2014) as an example of a single-case research design that resulted in outcomes that provided broader implications (i.e., "generalized") to similar contexts outside the case. In both *The* Challenger *Launch Decision* (the 1996 book) and "The Trickle-Down Effect" (the 1997 article), Vaughan describes the findings and conclusions from her study of the circumstances that led to the *Challenger* disaster in 1986. By way of scrutinizing archival documents and conducting interviews, Vaughan "reconstructed the history of decision making" and ultimately discovered "an incremental descent into poor judgment" (1996, p. xiii). More broadly, Vaughan used this study to illustrate "how deviance in organizations is transformed into acceptable behavior," asserting, for example, that "administrators in offices removed from the hands-on risky work are easily beguiled by the myth of infallibility" (1997, p. 97).

Wright, P. M., White, K., & Gaebler-Spira, D. (2004). Exploring the relevance of the personal and social responsibility model in adapted physical activity: A collective case study. *Journal of Teaching in Physical Education, 23*(1), 71–87.

Based on Stake's (2000) collective case study approach, Wright et al. examined whether a physical activity program developed for underserved youth and adapted for a martial arts class could be "relevant and beneficial" for children with disabilities, specifically cerebral palsy. The study was designed around five students (i.e., cases), each of whom was participating in a physical activity class. The primary data-gathering methods included the instructor's lesson plans, observational field notes, and checklists pertaining to "responsible behavior" and "skill development"; participants' medical records; and interviews conducted with physicians, therapists, and parents. The results of this study found that the physical activity program had "the potential to promote an increased sense of ability, a positive learning experience, and positive social interactions" (p. 85).

Narrative Research

Frost, D. M. (2013). Stigma and intimacy in same-sex relationships: A narrative approach. *Qualitative Psychology, 1*(S), 49–61.

Harlow, E. (2009). Eliciting narratives of teenage pregnancy in the UK: Reflexively exploring some of the methodological challenges. *Qualitative Social Work, 8*(2), 211–228.

Both Frost and Harlow report on the use of narrative research with marginalized ("stigmatized") segments of society and the unique challenges that this type of research presents to the researcher. Frost's study focused on same-sex relationships and, specifically, how these relationships are affected by the psychological coexistence of stigma and feelings of intimacy. This study was conducted on the Internet with 99 participants. Frost provides an interesting account of the recruitment strategies, the rationale for the online mode, and other research design details. From this research, Frost identified six psychological strategies that participants' stories employed to convey the stigma of same-sex relationships and its association with intimacy. Frost concludes that "the findings portray a nuanced understanding of how couples experience stigma in their everyday lives [and] a narrative approach may be useful in studies of other marginalized relationships" (p. 59).

In her article, Harlow discusses the challenges involved in conducting narrative research with girls who became mothers when under 16 years of age. Specifically, Harlow discusses the difficulty of recruiting teenage mothers (even with assurances of confidentiality and payment of traveling expenses) as well as the apprehension among participants to tell their life stories—participants "did not want to prolong the experience and left at the earliest opportunity" (p. 220). These issues are explored by way of a reflexive analysis, that is, from the perspective of the young mothers and that of the interviewer.

WEB RESOURCE

Clandinin, D. J. (2012, September). A short video interview with Prof. Jean Clandinin. *BERA Conference.* Manchester, UK: YouTube. Retrieved July 8, 2013, from *www.youtube.com/watch?v=RnaTBqapMrE.*

This 10-minute video on YouTube is an interview conducted with Jean Clandinin—a well-published educational researcher cited often in Chapter 7—at the BERA (British Educational Research Association) conference in 2012. In the interview, Clandinin responds to four questions: (1) What is narrative inquiry? (2) What are the challenges in establishing narrative inquiry as a research approach? (3) Are there areas outside of the humanities where narrative inquiry can or should be utilized? and (4) What advice do you have for researchers who want to adopt a narrative approach?

NOTES

1. An example of mixed-methods research occurred in 1996, when a *New York Times* reporter, Michael Winerip, conducted qualitative IDIs with several residents of Canton, Ohio, as part of his year-long literary journalism research of the city's electorate. The residents first had been sampled and served as respondents in a quantitative survey conducted by the Ohio State University Center for Survey Research by two professors working with Winerip and the *Times.* That survey identified a representative sample of likely voters, who, despite identifying themselves as traditional Democrats, planned to vote for the Republican Presidential candidate Bob Dole (Kosicki & Lavrakas, 2000). By conducting his qualitative IDIs after

the gathering of quantitative survey data with a very particular subsample of the survey's respondents, Winerip was able to vastly enrich his understanding of their responses to the survey questionnaire.

2. "Narrative environment" refers to the broad context in which narratives are told or otherwise conveyed. Randall (2012) takes his definition of narrative environment from Bruner (1990), stating that a narrative environment is "that dimension of each setting that concerns how people talk and listen within it, how they recount and respond to one another's stories." An individual's family is the first to shape this environment, "instilling in us our basic sense of right and wrong, our beliefs about ourselves [and] our assumptions about the wider world" (p. 282). Narrative researchers are interested in gathering as much information as available on the narrative environment to better understand the contextual basis in which narratives have meaning.

3. "Lived experience" is a term used by narrative researchers to refer to the experience as told by the person who has lived through it. This term goes beyond the idea of a firsthand or direct experience of an event. Stories of lived experiences are rich in context and personal meaning for the narrator. For instance, a cancer patient's narrative about hope can be much more than an account of what it is to be a victim of cancer, but rather a much deeper story of the experience with specific embedded stories of when the patient lived through particularly high or low moments of hope.

4. Just a few examples in the literature that are devoted, in total or in large part, to the questions of "What is a 'case'?" and "What is the 'case study' research approach?" include Flyvbjerg, 2006; Gerring, 2004; Grünbaum, 2007; Herreid, 1997; Johansson, 2003; Platt, 1992; Qi, 2009; Ragin & Becker, 1992; Thomas, 2010; VanWynsberghe & Khan, 2007; Walker, 2005; Wilson & Gudmundsdottir, 1987.

5. In some instances, the "researcher" may also be the person who fills each of these roles. This is typically the case when the study is being conducted by a small research firm or group where the principal researcher assumes many duties, including the execution of all fieldwork. In other instances, the researcher may be the person who is responsible for managing a number of people on a research team, including one or more interviewers, moderators, and/or observers.

6. We use the term "backout" when someone who initially agrees to cooperate fails to even start that actual compliance.

7. We use the term "attrition" when someone who begins to comply with a narrative study fails to finish the entirety of what the researcher believes is needed to gain a full understanding of the person's lived experiences that are germane to the study. This could be due to various reasons, including prolonged serious illnesses or even death.

Case-Centered Research Case Study

PURPOSE

The purpose of this research was to explore the problems that Latino parents in urban Los Angeles face related to the schooling of their children and communication with educators. More specifically, this research utilized one particular college-access program for high school students to investigate the use of storytelling among a marginalized group of working-class Latino parents to examine whether "listening to the stories of parents of color may help urban educators and policy makers bridge the divide between students' home cultures and the culture of school" (p. 1370).

METHOD

A case-centered approach is a popular form of qualitative research among educational researchers. Stake (1995), Qi (2009), Bennett et al. (2012), Clandinin and Connelly (1998; Connelly & Clandinin, 1990), and Randall (2012) are just a few of the researchers who have applied either case study or narrative research to issues in education. The study presented here is another example of case-centered research in an educational setting. This was a fitting approach, given the researcher's access to and involvement with the "Futures Project"—a longitudinal study conducted in conjunction with an experimental college-access program for high school students—which fostered a case-centered study design relying on multiple methods within a narrative framework.

DESIGN

Credibility

Scope

The target population for this study was parents of high school students participating in the Futures Project. This project was conducted in partnership with UCLA to trace the trajectories of 30 students who participated in an experimental college-access program. The researcher used this population to draw a purposive sample consisting of 16 Latino or Black parents who were selected because of their diversity in race/ethnicity, educational attainment, English fluency, as well their students' grade point average (GPA) and gender. All 16 parents cooperated with the research. The researcher acknowledges that this sample was not representative of the target population but emphasizes that the goal was not to generalize but to build on critical race and sociocultural theory. Among the 16 parents who participated in this study, the researcher selected four Latino parents to further analyze; these parents are the focus of this paper. These four individuals were chosen because their stories stood out as "signature pieces" that expressed many of the concerns of other Futures parents, offering particular insight into family–school relations (which was a key research objective).

Source: Auerbach (2002).

The researcher admits that the four selected parents were not representative of the target population; indeed, they were better educated, more articulate, and more fluent in English compared to other parents. These parents did, however, represent a range in the "Latino immigration experience" and conveyed "struggles" similar to those expressed by others.

Data Gathering

This case-centered research involved a series of IDIs, conducted by the researcher in English and Spanish, over a 3-year period. In this same time period, the researcher also completed participant observations involving "family–school interactions" and program activities (e.g., conferences, fairs), as well as analyzed Futures program data such as school documents, transcripts from parent meetings, and student interviews.

The researcher acknowledges the potential for researcher bias in the study design. In particular, she points to the fact that she was a complete participant observer whose participation in events may have potentially biased the data (although she utilized a reflexive journal, peer debriefings, and member checks to remain mindful of this possibility). The researcher also concedes that her status as a White, middle-class woman potentially made her an outsider to the working-class Latino parents in this study, which may have hampered gaining candid input and/or her ability to truly understand these parents' concerns from their perspectives.

Analyzability

Processing

The researcher showed flexibility by embracing an iterative approach to data collection and analysis, with one informing the other simultaneously and throughout the fieldwork.

All IDIs conducted in the 3-year period were recorded and transcribed verbatim in English and Spanish. The researcher also used field notes; however, she does not state whether these notes were transcribed. Transcriptions of the parents meetings were also available.

The researcher used several aids to identify themes across individual cases while attempting to maintain the entirety of the single case, including case summaries and data displays. The researcher "scrutinized" the IDI transcripts along with the transcripts from the parents' meetings. The researcher used "narrative analysis"; however, it is not made explicit what this analysis entailed.

Parents' stories were analyzed from various perspectives: topically, theoretically, and in vivo codes (direct use of parents' words).

The researcher derived three "distinct narrative genres" from the data: (1) parents' life stories of their own struggles with school, (2) stories of being rebuffed by the school staff, and (3) counter-stories that challenged the status quo of the bureaucratic system.

Verification

The researcher used multiple verification techniques that included triangulation (i.e., comparing and contrasting data from the various methods), peer debriefings (i.e., discussions with research colleagues during the field period concerning her subjectivity), member checks (i.e., discussing her findings with parents), prolonged engagement in the field (i.e., 3 years), and reflexive memos.

Transparency

The researcher does not provide sufficient detail (e.g., the interview guide, the observation grid [if there was one], the documents reviewed, the data displays, or transcriptions) to enable another researcher to transfer the design to another context with a high degree of confidence. However, much of the research paper is devoted to the three genres of stories emerging from the research data, including commentary and interpretation of each story type as well as excerpts from parents' stories and relevant details in the analysis, which help to give the reader a real sense of the basis by which the researcher isolated these three classes of stories. Other researchers should find these details useful in investigating marginalized groups in similar school environments. Her coverage also provides an engaging report format. Although not included in this paper, the researcher strongly suggests that an audit trail of the research findings as well as a thick description were provided in her final document.

Usefulness

This research adds to the knowledge of family school relations among marginalized groups and of the impact narratives can have in improving the former and empowering the latter. The researcher discusses three specific ways that narratives can have a positive impact as well as the implication for policy makers and educators. As far as a next step, the researcher suggests that additional research be conducted to examine whether the three narrative genres are "common" among parents of color.

CHAPTER EIGHT

The Total Quality Framework Research Proposal and Other Practical Applications of the Total Quality Framework

CHAPTER PREVIEW

This chapter focuses on other ways that we believe the Total Quality Framework (TQF) can and should be applied, beyond its primary use in helping to design, implement, and interpret qualitative research studies. The main thrust of the chapter is to explain why and how the TQF should be applied to the organization and writing of any research proposal in order to make it more likely that the proposed research will be credible and useful. The chapter elaborates on eight recommended sections that should be included in qualitative research proposals. In addition, we explain how the TQF can serve anyone who is (a) evaluating a qualitative research proposal that someone else has written (including proposals for theses and dissertations), (b) conducting a literature review of past qualitative research studies, or (c) engaged in any form of evaluation of a qualitative research study (including those reviewing manuscripts submitted for publication consideration).

8.1 INTRODUCTION

A primary focus of this book has been on how to apply our TQF to enhance the credibility, analyzability, transparency, and ultimately the usefulness of qualitative research design as it relates to five major qualitative methods or approaches: in-depth interviews (IDIs) (Chapter 3), focus group discussions (Chapter 4), ethnography (Chapter 5), content analysis (Chapter 6), and multiple methods in case-centered approaches (case study and narrative research, Chapter 7). The purpose of this chapter is to go a step further and encourage readers to put their knowledge of the TQF to work in a very important applied arena: the crafting and evaluating of research proposals from a TQF perspective.

For example, we believe that a TQF approach to qualitative research deserves prominence in (a) the proposals written by graduate students working toward their theses and dissertations; (b) proposals written by researchers in the academic, government, not-for-profit, and commercial sectors responding to clients' requests for proposals (RFPs); and (c) proposals written for grants. In doing so, we hope to raise the bar on the critical thinking skills utilized by researchers in the preparation of qualitative research proposals, as well as the criteria by which thesis and dissertation proposal guidelines, RFPs, and grant application requests are formulated, and the processes by which these various types of proposals are evaluated by reviewers.

A TQF research proposal differs from other research proposal formats in one overarching way: Quality design issues (vis-à-vis the TQF) play a central role throughout the writing of the proposal and in the manner by which the proposal is evaluated. For instance, from the outset, the TQF proposal couches the introductory discussions concerning research objectives and the significance of the proposed research around the TQF Usefulness component with its emphasis on the new insights, next steps, and transferability about which the researchers, clients, and other users can be confident. Similarly, the literature review section of a TQF-oriented research proposal discusses, among other things, past research in the literature from the point of view of the four TQF components, highlighting how the proposed new research will improve on earlier work by incorporating a fundamental quality assessment of the reliability and accuracy of the previous studies being reviewed. The method section of the TQF research proposal elaborates on data collection with a discussion from the standpoint of the TQF Credibility component (i.e., Scope and Data Gathering) and data analysis in terms of the TQF Analyzability component (i.e., Processing and Verification). And unlike most research proposals, the TQF research proposal includes a section specific to Transparency, with an emphasis on the final deliverables, such as the importance of complete disclosure in the research report document and the inclusion of supporting materials, such as the reflexive journal, interview guide, and the like.

Section 8.2 describes the TQF research proposal by taking the reader through its key sections and discussing the relevant TQF concepts within each. For the purpose of this discussion, we utilize the following basic proposal section and content format. We recognize that formatting requirements for proposals vary across particular institutions and research sponsors; however, the application of TQF elements to this basic format structure can be readily adapted to other proposal configurations. We also acknowledge that the format outlined below may result in a lengthier proposal than is now typical, particularly when TQF principles are integrated explicitly into each proposal section, as discussed on pages 336–345, but we believe the result is a more complete and more compelling document that more fully informs the person reviewing the proposal. As importantly, such a document forces the researcher and the funder to think carefully about each aspect of the research from the standpoint of credibility, analyzability, transparency, and its ultimate usefulness. And, by extension what we describe below can be readily adapted to other proposals such as those for master's theses and doctoral dissertations.

As shown in Box 8.1 and discussed below, there are eight sections to the basic proposal format:

1. **Introduction.** A concise statement regarding the research topic, the research question, the significance of the proposed research, and the proposed approach.

2. **Background and Literature Review.** A full yet targeted discussion of the subject matter, including historical context related to the research topic, a review of other relevant research that has been conducted from a TQF perspective, and a discussion of how the proposed research advances knowledge by addressing gaps or issues identified and/or raised in earlier research.

3. **Research Questions or Hypotheses.** A discussion of the particular research questions or hypotheses the proposed research will investigate, including any preconceptions or assumptions (e.g., underlying theory or constructs, themes to explore) the researcher may have as an outgrowth of the TQF background and literature review discussion provided in the previous section.

4. **Research Design.** A detailed discussion from a TQF perspective of how the researcher plans to conduct the proposed research, including:

   - Method
   - Mode
   - Scope (e.g., target population, how the sample will be selected, sample size)

BOX 8.1. Sections of the Basic TQF Proposal Format

1. Introduction
2. Background and Literature Review
3. Research Questions or Hypotheses
4. Research Design
5. Research Team
6. Research Deliverables
7. Limitations of the Proposed Research
8. Research Schedule and Cost Estimate

- Data Gathering (e.g., research instrument, proposed content in terms of constructs and key areas to explore, potential bias in data collection)
- Analysis (plan for making sense of the data)
- Ethical considerations
- Dissemination of the findings

5. **Research Team.** An overview of who will work on the proposed research in each of the three main phases—data collection, analysis, and reporting—including how members of the research team have been or will be chosen, and the criteria for choosing team members as they relate to their professional abilities and their necessary experience with the research subject matter, and especially how that experience relates to the TQF components (e.g., which of the staff is experienced with Credibility issues, which with Analyzability issues, etc.).

6. **Research Deliverables.** A TQF-related discussion of Transparency in the proposed research by way of the level of detail in the final research report as well as the number and type of supporting, ancillary documents.

7. **Limitations of the Proposed Research.** Previous sections of the proposal will showcase the strengths of the proposed research from a TQF perspective. Despite those many strengths, every research study has limitations, in part due to the finite budget and finite time available to carry it out. In this section, the proposal will present a TQF critique of the proposed research design acknowledging its potential limitations, with special attention to threats to the study's Credibility (Scope and Data Gathering) that may be unavoidable with the proposed methods. In writing this subsection the proposal authors will engage in an important process of self-evaluation that will serve them in good stead as they conduct their study and later as they interpret it and disseminate its findings.

8. **Research Schedule and Cost Estimate.** An outline of a tentative timeframe within which the proposed research will be completed, a summary rundown of the researcher's responsibilities with respect to overseeing the proposed research (as they pertain to the research design and deliverables), and the estimated cost or cost structure to complete the study.

8.2 SECTION-BY-SECTION DISCUSSION OF THE TOTAL QUALITY FRAMEWORK RESEARCH PROPOSAL

The following discussion highlights how a qualitative researcher can and should incorporate elements of the TQF into each of the eight areas outlined above in order to produce a TQF research proposal. As the reader considers the important aspects of each section of a research proposal related to the TQF, it is equally important to be cognizant throughout the proposal-creation process of the prevailing goal: to communicate the quality standards that are expected to lead to credible, analyzable, transparent, and ultimately useful research results.

Introduction

The purpose of the introduction to the qualitative research proposal is to set the stage for what is to unfold in greater detail in subsequent sections. At this juncture, the researcher wants to clearly state (a) the research topic; (b) the particular question, problem, or issue the proposed research will address; (c) how addressing this issue will advance current knowledge or serve a particular need (i.e., why the proposed research is important); and (d) the basic methodological approach(es) that the proposed research will use to address this issue.

The TQF can and should be mentioned briefly within the introduction, with the researcher adding a preliminary explanation of the TQF in the text of the proposal (or in a footnote or appendix), if those who will be evaluating the proposal are not sufficiently familiar with it. For instance, a proposal for observational research pertaining to physician–patient consultations might follow statements concerning the research topic and issues being addressed with a short description of the TQF, including its components, terminology, and basic concepts (see Chapter 2), and why a TQF strategy is important to the integrity of the proposed research and why it is superior to a research study not structured around the TQF.

The introduction would then briefly discuss the ultimate usefulness of the proposed research, including why the research is needed in terms of the specific knowledge it will contribute to the research community (e.g., aspects of the physician–patient relationship that affect cancer patients' willingness to discuss sexual dysfunction with their physicians) and its value to a client (e.g., finding ways in which a particular hospital might modify the training their physicians receive about how to consult with cancer patients and patients' spouses/partners about sexual dysfunction).

The final part of the introduction is where the researcher addresses how the proposed research will fulfill the stated objectives by making brief mention of the basic method (e.g., ethnography) as well as how the researcher will deploy a TQF approach on the proposed research.

Background and Literature Review

This section of the research proposal gives the reader the necessary context in which to situate the relevance of the proposed study. Here, the proposal author provides background details about the particular target population (e.g., information regarding the participating oncologists and the medical facility where they practice and conduct patient consultations), past research efforts among this population (e.g., with similar types of physicians and/or their patients), and a discussion of pertinent research published in professional literature and presented at professional conferences.

In conducting the review of earlier research (either internal research with the same target population or others' research in the literature), the author of the proposal should pay particular attention to not only the compatibility of the subject matter but also the quality standards that were utilized in the design of each prior study. *Not all studies are equally reliable and valid; therefore, literature reviews conducted from a TQF perspective should not treat them as such.* In fact, if the review of a past study (even one published in a major journal) finds it lacking from a TQF perspective, it is possible the proposal author will not cite it at all or, if it is cited, its shortcomings should be duly noted. To the extent that earlier research is cited, the researcher should identify the ways in which these studies included appropriate steps to maximize Credibility (e.g., representative coverage as well as reliable and valid data gathering), Analyzability (e.g., accurate processing and verification of the data), and Transparency (e.g., full disclosure and thick description in the final document). In this regard, the proposal also should discuss the author's assessment of these earlier studies, emphasizing the strengths and limitations of that research from a TQF perspective.

Where there are key gaps in the literature—that is, areas within particular studies that are weak in one or more of the TQF components—the proposal author needs to explicitly discuss what is missing from a quality standpoint. For instance, the study from Forbat et al. (2012) discussed in Chapter 5 (see p. 178) concerning physician–patient consultation might be cited by the researcher for its relevance to the proposed research, with notice given to the purposive, rather than fully representative, sampling used in that study, which would inform the importance assigned to the findings from that study.

It is recommended that the researcher include a Literature Review Reference Summary Evaluation Table (see Table 8.1) in the proposal. This table allows the researcher to organize relevant past studies and to lay out the considerations of each as it relates to the TQF, giving proposal readers a conveniently encapsulated way to view compatible studies along with the researcher's comments on their strengths and weaknesses from a TQF perspective.

TABLE 8.1. Literature Review Reference Summary Evaluation Table

Reference	Study design considerations from a TQF perspective			
	Credibility	**Analyzability**	**Transparency**	**Usefulness**
Forbat, White, Marshall-Lucette, & Kelly (2012)	Purposive sampling to explore a range of patient types	Processing and verification procedures not documented	Provides details of the observations, including excerpts from field notes as well as site and patient information	Tackles a topic not widely found in the literature and identifies opportunities to enhance conversations about sexual function

Research Questions or Hypotheses

The background and literature review discussed in the previous section should provide the context for the research question(s) and/or hypotheses that the proposed research is designed to address. In this section, the proposal author must not only put forth the questions/hypotheses under study, but provide support as to why these are the ones that merit investigation. In doing this, the author should rely on the TQF to bolster the logical arguments that are advanced in support of these research questions/hypotheses.

The extent to which the research questions revolve around quality-design issues will depend, in part, on the results of the literature review and the nature of the research topic. For example, a proposal to study physician–patient consultations might state the primary research question as "What are the main factors that appear to contribute to the frequency and type of conversations concerning cancer patients' sexual functioning among a representative sample of the city clinic's oncology physicians?" The researcher may or may not harbor a hypothesis along with the research question. However, depending on the literature review, the researcher might enter into the research hypothesizing, for example, that the frequency and substance of physician–patient conversations concerning sexual function are associated with how closely the physician's demographic characteristics (e.g., age, gender, and race) match those of the patient. Or, a proposal on this topic may focus on methodological, rather than substantive, hypotheses such as noting TQF flaws in past research and hypothesizing that the author's proposed methods for the new study will avoid the problems of earlier research (which the researcher may believe led to biased findings and ill-advised recommendations) and thereby result in outcomes that are more credible and therefore more useful.

Research Design

With the proposed research put into context, the strengths and limitations of earlier studies discussed, and the research questions or hypotheses clearly stated and supported, the proposal author is now ready to explain the manner in which the proposed study will be conducted. Here is where the researcher will provide the details of each aspect pertaining to the execution of the proposed research (see pp. 334–335). Because each of these aspects has a role in the quality of the study's outcomes, elements of the TQF should be discussed explicitly throughout this section of the proposal.

Method and Mode

The proposal author should identify the method(s), and the mode(s) within the method(s), that will be used to contact study participants, gain their cooperation, and gather data for the proposed study. The proposal should go on to support the selection of the methods and modes by outlining the strengths—alone and in comparison to other approaches—with the acknowledgment of the limitations of the proposed design (which is discussed more fully later in the proposal; see p. 344). As an example, a researcher proposing a face-to-face and email IDI study of African American and Hispanic high school students in a particular school district would discuss the advantages of the IDI method in terms of the ability to establish rapport and develop a strong interviewer–interviewee relationship, thereby reducing the potential for bias (e.g., distortion in the interviewees' responses) and increasing the credibility of the data. This researcher would elaborate by linking the choice of method and modes to the research objectives. For instance, the researcher would explain that the goal of understanding the deep-seated factors that impact academic performance requires a research approach that is both personal in nature and creates a trusting environment wherein the interviewer can gather detailed, meaningful responses from the students to potentially sensitive questions, such as disruptive influences outside of school (e.g., family life). The researcher would then explain that no other qualitative method (or quantitative method) could effectively gain the depth of information sought by the proposed IDI study, but also acknowledges that the success of the study will hinge on well-thought-out techniques for sampling participants and gaining cooperation from the target population (examples of which should be included in the proposal). And, finally, the researcher would note that the face-to-face IDI method costs more and adds time to the study completion compared to other IDI modes, stating that this is one of the reasons that some of the IDIs will be conducted via email.

Scope and Data Gathering

A TQF research proposal clearly defines the target population for the proposed research, the target sample (if the researcher is interested in a particular subgroup of the target population, e.g., only African American and Hispanic high school seniors in the district who anticipate graduating in the coming spring), how participants will be selected for the study, what they will be asked to do (e.g., set aside school time for the IDI), and the general types of questions to which they will be asked to respond (i.e., the content of the interview). In discussing Scope, the researcher proposing an IDI study with African American and Hispanic high school students would identify the list that will be used to select participants (e.g., the district's roster of seniors who are expected to graduate); the advantages and drawbacks to using this list (e.g., not everyone on the roster may consider themselves to be African American or Hispanic); the systematic (preferably random) procedure that will be used to select the sample; and the number of students that will be selected as participants, including the rationale for that number and the steps that will be taken to gain cooperation from the students and thereby ideally ensure that everyone selected actually completes an interview (e.g., gaining permission from the school principal to allow students to take school time to participate in the IDI, and from parents/guardians for students under 18 years of age who cannot give informed consent on their own behalf).

The data-gathering portion of this section of the proposal highlights the constructs and issues that will be examined in the proposed research. This discussion should build on the previous two sections by providing details of the types of questions that will be asked, observations that will be recorded, or areas of interest that will be listened for in a participant's narrative. If possible, the researcher will include a draft of the research instrument (e.g., the interview or discussion guide, observation grid) in the proposal.

Importantly, the researcher needs to address the potential for biases in the data collection process, particularly potential researcher effects and participant bias. The proposal author should acknowledge the step(s) in the process most susceptible to bias from a TQF perspective, the potential source of the bias, and measures that will be taken to try to mitigate the threat of bias. In the IDI study of minority high school students, for example, the researcher might discuss the potential for inaccurate or incomplete responses from the minority students if African American and Hispanic interviewers are not used. This researcher should also discuss the steps that will be taken to maintain interviewer consistency across all interviews, specifically the interviewer training that will be conducted to ensure a consistent approach. The researcher should also acknowledge that interview participants may bias the data by withholding or fabricating information, and explain what techniques will be used to address this potentiality. So, for example, the proposal for the IDI study of African American and Hispanic students would likely emphasize the importance of building rapport in the early stages of the interviewer–interviewee interaction in order to later gain complete and truthful responses. Along with this, the proposal author should outline the rapport-building tactics that will be used in the research (e.g., preliminary communication with the students prior to the IDI and active listening skills that include exhibiting interest in the interviewee's comments and using words of encouragement throughout the interview). Throughout the Scope and Data Gathering subsections of the proposal, the elements of the TQF should be explicitly and implicitly woven into the text and used to organize the particulars about the data collection methods the researcher proposes to use.

Analysis

Quality measures to safeguard the credibility of the data are essential, but the final research outcome may be seriously jeopardized if the analysis phase is not thoughtfully carried out. For this reason, it is important for the research proposal to lay out how the researcher plans to handle the processing and verification of the data from a TQF perspective. For example, in methods where audio recordings need to be transcribed into text (such as face-to-face IDI and focus group methods), the researcher should be explicit in the proposal about the nature of the training the transcriptionist(s) will receive (e.g., concerning specific jargon or terminology) and who will be involved in creating and verifying the accuracy of the transcript(s). For a content analysis study, the researcher should discuss the process that will be taken to identify categories and themes in the data.

Equally important are the methods that will be used for the verification of the data, which, in a TQF research proposal, should be explicitly and clearly specified: Will the data be substantiated by way of deviant case analysis, peer debriefings, reflexive journal(s), and/or triangulation of some sort (e.g., data from other sources, methods, or investigators)? Only with an explicit and clear explanation of these analytical processing and verification methods will readers of the proposal have an informed basis to reach a confident judgment on whether the researcher will have the ability to draw credible, accurate interpretations from the research data.

Ethical Considerations

Every research proposal for studying human beings must carefully consider the ethical ramifications of engaging human subjects for research purposes, and this is particularly true in the relatively intimate, in-depth nature of qualitative research. As discussed in this book, it is incumbent on qualitative researchers to honestly assure participants who are aware they are to be the subjects of a research study of their confidentiality and right to privacy, safety from harm, and right to terminate their voluntary participation at any time with no untoward repercussions from doing so. The proposal should describe the procedures that will be taken to implement these assurances, including gaining informed consent, gaining approval from the relevant Institutional Review Board, and anonymizing participants' names, places mentioned, and other potentially identifying information. Special consideration should be given in the proposal to ethical matters when the proposed research (a) pertains to vulnerable populations such as children or the elderly; (b) concerns a marginalized segment of the population such as people with disabilities, same-sex couples, or the economically disadvantaged; (c) involves covert observation that will be conducted in association with an ethnographic study; or (d) is a narrative study in which the researcher may withhold the full true intent of the research in order not to stifle or bias participants' telling of their stories.

Dissemination of Findings

The author of the proposal should briefly explain the various ways in which the findings of the research are likely to be disseminated. In doing so, the means of dissemination noted should be matched to the "real-world" importance of the research study itself. For example, in some instances, the study may be disseminated only internally, but in other instances, the study outcomes may lead to a book being written, a series of news articles or blog posts, a made-for-television documentary, and/or a presentation at a professional conference.

Summary of the Research Design

At this juncture in the proposal, the researcher has made any number of references to the TQF and its guidance in designing the various aspects of the proposed research. To assist the proposal reader in keeping track of how the researcher has applied TQF principles, a summary of some kind is in order. A convenient device for organizing and displaying this summary is a schematic similar to Figure 8.1, where specific features in the proposed research are aligned with components of the TQF. For example, in summarizing Credibility-related issues, the researcher could mention the list that will be used to select a sample from the target population, the sampling approach, and steps that will be followed to minimize potential bias in the data collection.

Research Team

The principal researcher and the other people making up the research team (e.g., interviewers, moderators, observers, coders) that will be working on the proposed research are critical to the credibility of the data collected, the completeness and accuracy of the data analysis and interpretation, the transparency in the final documents, and ultimately the usefulness of the research. This is why a TQF research proposal includes a section that briefly: (a) identifies members of the team (either by name, if appropriate, or at least by job title and affiliation); (b) states the basis by which team members have been (or will be) chosen; (c) describes their knowledge of the subject matter or target population central to the proposed research; (d) identifies the particular philosophical or theoretical orientation of the principal researcher(s), as appropriate, and the effect this will have on how the study is conducted[1]; and (e) highlights the particular skills team members bring to the study.

For example, a researcher might propose a study for the state agency in charge of water resources involving face-to-face group discussions with environmental

TQF Component	Design Feature in Proposed Research
Credibility	
Scope	
Data Gathering	
Analyzability	
Processing	
Verification	
Transparency	
Usefulness	

FIGURE 8.1. Research design summary: Alignment of proposed design features with the TQF.

"activists" concerning environmental issues related to water use in the state. At the time of proposal writing, the researcher may not have determined the individuals who will be on the research team; however, the researcher might specify that there will be three members on the team, including the proposal author and two other researchers who (1) have 10 years' experience (each) conducting qualitative research, generally, and focus groups, specifically; (2) have worked with this particular state agency in the past and are familiar with the agency's operations; (3) have worked in the area of environmental issues for many years and, specifically, on issues related to water resources; and (4) bring unique skills to the proposed research (as discussed below).

The researcher might discuss team members' particular skills in terms of the roles they will play in conducting the study and the capabilities associated with those roles. Using the focus group study with environmental activists as an example, the person selected to moderate these group discussions could be described as someone who (a) is highly experienced in moderating focus groups and has particular experience moderating discussions with topic enthusiasts or activists; (b) understands the issues of primary importance to the state agency; (c) has been fully trained on how to minimize potential bias due to the moderator's behavior or inconsistency; and (d) possesses all the interpersonal skills of a good interviewer as well as the unique ability to manage group dynamics and effectively use enabling techniques in a group setting to gain deeper insights. Likewise, the individuals who will work on the proposed focus group analyses might be described as researchers who not only know the subject matter but are also experienced at (a) analyzing qualitative data on environmental issues, (b) identifying themes and patterns in the manifest and latent content of group discussions, (c) looking for outliers in the data that serve to support or refute preliminary interpretations, and (d) working closely with other researchers and the client to conduct debriefings that provide useful input in the analysis.

Research Deliverables

This section of the TQF research proposal should specify the documents as well as a sample of the details that will be included in the thick description provided in the principal final research document. For example, the types of details that might be listed in the final report for the aforementioned study with environmental activists might include (a) a description of the origins of the list used to recruit group participants and the TQF evaluation of the quality (representativeness) of this list; (b) the demographic composition of participants in each group and the rationale for electing to recruit, for example, homogeneous groups with respect to age; (c) the recruiting process and issues pertaining to participant cooperation; (d) the physical space in which the discussions were conducted and the individuals observing the discussions as they occurred; (e) the moderator's methods for managing the discussions, issues related to group dynamics, decisions made to modify the discussion guide, and the rationale for these changes; and (f) details about the transcription and coding processes as well as verification of the data.

In addition to the final research report that documents these details along with the researcher's interpretation and recommendations, the proposal should state that, in the interest of full disclosure, the researcher will also provide a copy of the screener used in recruitment, the moderator's guide, the moderator's reflexive journal, and any other supporting material.

Limitations of the Proposed Research

In this section, the proposal author will methodically apply the TQF to produce a critique of the proposed research design in ways that are consistent with what is previously stated in Section 4 (Research Design) of the proposal. That is, this section will contain subsections on Credibility (Scope and Data Gathering), Analyzability (Processing and Verification), Transparency, and Usefulness. In each of these subsections the researcher will acknowledge the likely limitations of the study design that is being proposed, and briefly opine on the likely implications of these limitations to the overall usefulness of the research. No qualitative (or quantitative) research study is perfect (with only strengths and no drawbacks). By readily (and unhesitatingly) acknowledging that there are limitations in the proposed design, the proposal writer takes the "high road" and thereby strengthens the case that the proposed design is the best one possible, given the funding (see next section), time, and other resources that are available to support the study. It also demonstrates that the researcher will be cognizant of these limitations in formulating conclusions and making recommendations based on the study's findings.

Research Schedule and Cost Estimate

When discussing the anticipated schedule and estimated costs for the proposed study, the researcher must be careful to allow for sufficient time and adequate costs associated with a TQF research approach. The following are examples of TQF parameters that must be accounted for in a TQF research proposal when calculating the research study's timeframe and costs:

- Obtaining a quality list representing the target population from which to sample.
- Ease or difficulty in gaining access to, and cooperation from, the sampled participants.
- Devising the data collection procedure(s).
- Pilot-testing the data collection procedure(s).
- Devising and implementing a data collection training curriculum to minimize biases and inconsistencies, including the use of a reflexive journal.
- Training and validation associated with data processing.
- Conducting one or more verification procedures.

- Writing a thick description of the research details.
- Compiling all the necessary documentation to submit along with the final report.

8.3 EVALUATING PROPOSALS USING THE TOTAL QUALITY FRAMEWORK

In addition to using the TQF to structure more rigorous and comprehensive research proposals, we believe that the TQF can and should be used by anyone who is evaluating a proposal for a research study that will use qualitative methods (e.g., members of a thesis or dissertation committee, funders at a granting agency or foundation, clients in the commercial sector). *It is our experience that too often those who evaluate research proposals are lax in holding the proposal author(s) accountable for doing research that is likely to be accurate and, in the end, useful.* We believe that one of the reasons for this is that the reviewers fail to use a comprehensive system to methodically think about the strengths and limitations of the proposed study design. In our view, the TQF is the very best system to apply when reviewing qualitative research proposals. It guides the reviewer through the many key issues that should be addressed satisfactorily by a qualitative research proposal and thereby helps the reviewer ascertain whether there are outstanding threats to the quality of the proposed research that have been ignored or remain unanticipated by the researcher(s).

In our view, proposal reviewers should set up a review system that allocates "points" to what they believe are the most important potential sources of bias and/or inconsistencies that could undermine the credibility of the data the study proposes to gather, or undermine the accuracy of the processing of the data or the sense-making analyses the researchers propose to conduct. Such a system should lead the reviewer to evaluate the proposal on all of the following TQF criteria:

Credibility

- How the target population has been defined.
- How the list representing the target population will be created.
- How the sample of participants will be chosen from the list(s) that will be used.
- How many participants the researcher proposes to gather data from or about and the justification that is provided for this number, including its adequacy for the purposes of the study; a discussion of how the researcher will monitor and judge the adequacy of this number while in the field should also be included.
- How the researcher will gain cooperation from, and access to, the sampled participants.

- How the researcher will determine if those in the sample from whom data was *not* gathered differ in critical ways on the topics being studied from those participants who did provide data.

- What the researcher will do to account for the potential bias that may exist because not everyone in the sample participated in the research (i.e., no data was gathered from some individuals).

- The extent to which the relevant concepts that will be studied have been identified.

- How the researcher has operationalized these concepts in order to effectively collect data on them in the research approach.

- How the researcher has articulated and supported the research hypotheses.

- How the data collection method(s) will be pilot-tested and revised as necessary.

- The precautions that will be taken to minimize (or at least better understand) the potential biases and inconsistencies that might be created in the data by those involved in data collection.

- The precautions that will be taken to assure high ethical standards throughout the entire study.

Analyzability

- How the researcher will process the gathered data for analysis.

- How the data analyses will be carried out to make sense and interpret the data.

- The particular verification procedures that will be used to assess the reliability and validity of the findings from the analyses.

Transparency

- How the researcher will make the methods and details of the research transparent and accessible to all who seek such information about the study.

Usefulness

- The extent to which the researcher has identified the value of the proposed study and built a compelling case that the findings will advance the state of knowledge on the topic, provide actionable next steps, and/or enable the research to be transferred to other comparable contexts.

Of course, the above list of criteria (or the reviewers' own adaptation of this list) should be shared with all those who will submit proposals for the reviewers' considerations. In doing so, these evaluation criteria will help guide the proposal authors, so they are certain to think carefully about each of these TQF issues and explicitly address each in their proposals.

8.4 RELATED USES OF THE TOTAL QUALITY FRAMEWORK IN REVIEWING RESEARCH REPORTS

Looking beyond the writing and evaluation of research proposals, we believe that the TQF can be readily applied to evaluating the accuracy and usefulness of all types of qualitative research reports and documents. Besides the final report of a qualitative research study, the TQF can be utilized to evaluate research-related conference papers and other presentations, journal manuscripts, as well as book chapters and the entirety of books themselves. And we believe this *should* be done routinely by reviewers and consumers of qualitative research.

For example, the TQF provides a logical, comprehensive, and interrelated set of criteria to apply when editors of research-related journals are establishing criteria by which their reviewers will judge the quality of the qualitative research being reported in a submitted manuscript. In this context, we believe the TQF should become the standard approach for evaluating whether a manuscript reports a study that is accurate and useful, and therefore worthy of publication. Moreover, these criteria provide a roadmap for researchers to use in writing their manuscripts, guiding them to report their methods and findings fully, in logical and transparent ways, so that other researchers are able to understand the details they need to make their own judgments concerning the value of the study's findings. This approach can and should be used with respect to conference papers/presentations, books, blog submissions, and the like.

8.5 CHAPTER SUMMARY

✓ The purpose of this chapter is to encourage readers to put their knowledge of the Total Quality Framework (TQF) to work in a very important applied arena—that is, the crafting and evaluating of research proposals from a TQF perspective.

✓ A TQF research proposal differs from other formats in that quality-design issues play a central role throughout the writing of the proposal and in the manner by which the proposal is evaluated. In essence, a TQF proposal forces the researcher and the evaluator to think carefully about each aspect of the research from the standpoint of credibility, analyzability, transparency, and its ultimate usefulness.

✓ There are eight sections to the basic proposal format: (1) Introduction, (2) Background and Literature Review, (3) Research Questions or Hypothesis, (4) Research Design, (5) Research Team, (6) Deliverables, (7) Limitations of the Proposed Research, and (8) Research Schedule and Cost Estimate. For each section, we present an explanation of the relevant TQF concepts and suggestions on how to apply the TQF.

✓ It is recommended that the proposal author include a Literature Review Reference Summary Evaluation Table that lists relevant studies from the literature along with their respective strengths and limitations from a TQF perspective.

✓ There are 18 specific TQF-related criteria that should be applied when evaluating any qualitative research proposal to identify the strengths and limitations of the proposal.

✓ Beyond the research proposal, the TQF can be used to evaluate all types of qualitative research documents, including conference papers and other presentations, journal manuscripts, as well as book chapters and the entirety of books themselves.

NOTE

1. For example, a feminist researcher proposing an IDI study with women may explain that her unstructured, versus semistructured, IDI style of interviewing is predicated on the belief that women represent a marginalized group whose lived experiences can only be told in an environment where the interviewer minimizes her control over the interview.

Glossary

Terms that are <u>underlined</u> are defined elsewhere in the glossary.

Acquiescence
A response pattern by which the <u>IDI</u> or <u>focus group</u> participant tends to agree or otherwise convey positive convictions regardless of the questions or topics discussed, resulting in biased data.

Active consent
In contrast to <u>passive consent</u>, a common type of <u>informed consent</u> by which research participants sign and return a written consent form agreeing to participate in the research study; or do so as a proxy for someone else, such as a parent signing to allow his or her child to participate in the study.

Active listening
An interviewing technique that encompasses a variety of interviewer skills that foster the interviewer–interviewee relationship by way of expressing the interviewer's interest in what is being said and encouraging the interviewee to communicate freely. Examples of these skills include paraphrasing (i.e., restating the interviewee's comment in the interviewer's own words) as well as nodding the head and interjecting words of encouragement (e.g., "Please, go on").

Analyzability
A component of the <u>Total Quality Framework</u> associated with the completeness and accuracy of the analysis of the data that have been gathered in a qualitative research study and the interpretations of the findings that result from the analyses. The two primary elements of Analyzability are <u>Processing</u> and <u>Verification</u>.

Asynchronous email messaging
An <u>in-depth interview</u> mode involving multiple email interviewer–interviewee exchanges that are conducted over a period of time (days or months) and not conducted in real time or via "chat." In this mode, the interviewee can respond at his or her convenience.

Asynchronous focus groups
<u>Focus groups</u> conducted online but not in real time (as are <u>synchronous focus groups</u>). The discussions typically extend over 2 or more days, with participants contributing to the discussions at their convenience within the allotted time period. Also referred to as "<u>bulletin boards</u>."

Bulletin boards	See <u>asynchronous focus groups</u>.
Case(s)	The social unit or entity in <u>case-centered research</u>. The case can be an individual, a group of people, an organization, an event, a program, or a process.
Case-centered research	A term coined by Mishler (1996, 1999) to denote a research approach that preserves the "unity and coherence" of research subjects throughout data collection and analysis. It consists of two fundamental and unique components: (a) a focus on the investigation of "complex" social units or entities (also known as "<u>case[s]</u>") in their entirety (i.e., not just one aspect captured at one moment in time), and (b) an emphasis on maintaining the cohesiveness of this entity throughout the research process. Two prominent case-centered approaches are <u>case study research</u> and <u>narrative research</u>.
Case study research	A <u>case-centered research</u> approach that depends on multiple methods to address research objectives and characterized by the in-depth exploration of social phenomena that are real versus conceptual; represented by one or more <u>cases</u>; complex or multifaceted, involving various interconnected elements; typically contemporary; and studied in their natural context.
Category	Any group of <u>codes</u>, along with the textual data to which they are assigned, that share an underlying construct. The identification of categories requires the researcher's sensitivity to the manifest and latent contexts of the content. Categories should be exhaustive and mutually exclusive.
Code(s)	A designation given to some portion (e.g., a phrase, a concept) of the qualitative data to define its meaning as it relates to the research topic. Each code should be explicit in its meaning and unique from the other codes. Also, "to code" or "coding" is the act of assigning codes to the <u>dataset</u>.
Codebook	A document created to account for each <u>code</u> developed for the <u>dataset</u>. The six essential elements of a codebook include (a) instructions on the aspect of the content that is to be coded, (b) the name of the code, (c) a description or definition of the code, (d) how the code relates to other (e.g., categorical) codes, (e) particular rules in applying the code, and (f) an example of the appropriate use of the code from the dataset.
Coding accuracy	In <u>qualitative content analysis</u>, one of two factors to consider when monitoring coders. In simple terms, coding accuracy refers to the validity of the coding decisions that are made by coders, and ultimately is determined by whether or not the principal researcher agrees with the coding decisions. Determining the extent of coding accuracy involves periodic reviews of the coders' coding decisions to check on their correctness. The other factor when monitoring coders is <u>coding consistency</u>.
Coding consistency	In <u>qualitative content analysis</u>, one of two factors to consider when monitoring coders. Determining the extent of coding consistency involves documenting the extent to which the coding decision made by one coder is made by another independent coder about the same element of content (intercoder reliability) or by the first coder when coding the same content element on a second occasion (intracoder reliability). The other factor when monitoring coders is <u>coding accuracy</u>.

Coding form	A document containing the key constructs (if known beforehand) and/or specific issues related to the research objective that may have surfaced in <u>code</u> development that is utilized by the coders to ensure that they are consistently mindful of these key constructs/issues and as a way to capture coders' feedback on how these constructs/issues are addressed in the content.
Complete participant observer	Along with <u>passive participant</u> and <u>participant–observer</u>, one of three types of <u>participant observation</u> wherein the observer willingly "goes native" by becoming a full-fledged member of the study group; for example, studying police procedures in an inner-city neighborhood by joining the police force and becoming involved in all the police-related activities on and off duty. When the group being studied is unaware of the research project (i.e., <u>covert observation</u>), a number of ethical issues must be considered.
Computer-assisted qualitative data analysis software (CAQDAS)	Computer programs that can facilitate <u>qualitative content analysis</u>, particularly when dealing with a large volume of complex data. Programs—such as ATLAS.ti, NVivo, and HyperRESEARCH—enable the researcher to search and organize data content that has been coded as well as facilitate development of the <u>codebook</u> and the analytic process by providing various ways to discover patterns in the data. CAQDAS may add speed and efficiency to the analysis of content data; however, CAQDAS is only as good as the particular features built into the software, and ultimately it is the researcher, not CAQDAS, who must possess the discerning, analytical know-how necessary to find meaning and interpret the data. For this reason, CAQDAS is considered a supplementary tool.
Constructivism-interpretivism	A research <u>paradigm</u> orientation that rejects the idea of one objective reality but rather embraces the notion that there are multiple realities that are socially constructed (and co-constructed with help from the researcher) in the research environment (Lincoln et al., 2011; Maxwell, 2013; Ponterotto, 2013; Schwandt et al., 2007).
Constructs	The topics that are being studied and thus measured in qualitative research. In some cases these are narrow and very precise and in others quite broad, multifaceted, and may even be ambiguous.
Content analysis as a primary method	<u>Qualitative content analysis</u> focused on content generated by an existing, naturally occurring repository of information such as newspapers, consumer diaries, historical documents, and email communications. Coding of this content generates the data that are used in the content analysis study. The primary method approach is in contrast to <u>content analysis</u> as a <u>secondary method</u>, which is the analysis of content generated by another research method.
Content analysis as a secondary method	<u>Qualitative content analysis</u> focused on content generated by another qualitative method (e.g., <u>in-depth interviews</u>, <u>focus group</u> discussions, or observations in <u>ethnography</u>) that plays a supportive analytical role with these methods. Coding of this content generates the data that are used in the analysis stage of the study. The secondary method approach is in contrast to <u>content analysis as a primary method</u>, which is the analysis of content generated by an existing, naturally occurring repository of information.

Contingent incentive A material incentive, such as cash, a gift card, or donation to charity, that is given to a research participant at the completion of a research event (e.g., an <u>IDI</u>). The incentive is offered when recruiting participants in order to motivate participation in the research.

Convenience sampling Selecting a study environment and/or research participants who are readily (and inexpensively) available and familiar to the researcher/observer. For example, a study to observe the staff–patient dynamic in a geriatric facility might be conveniently conducted at the facility where the researcher regularly visits his/her parents. Unlike <u>purposive sampling</u>, which may be necessary and/or beneficial to achieving the research objectives, convenience sampling may seriously threaten the <u>Credibility</u> and <u>Transferability</u> of a study.

Coverage bias A distortion in qualitative data that may result from sampling—or "covering"—only certain segments of the <u>target population</u>. If the part of the target population that is not covered differs on key measures of interest from the part of the target population that is covered, then the study's findings will be biased. For example, an ethnographic study concerning physical therapy procedures with recent amputees may lead to unrepresentative (biased) results if the researcher does not observe physical therapy sessions conducted with people in all age groups but interprets the findings as if they apply to all age groups.

Covert observation In contrast to <u>overt observation</u>, an unobtrusive observational technique used in <u>participant observation</u>, by which the observer assumes an undercover role with the study participants, who act without knowledge of the observer's true identity or purpose. Covert observation can pose several ethical issues that must be considered.

Credibility A component of the <u>Total Quality Framework</u> associated with the trustworthiness of the outcomes, and the confidence one can place in them, by way of minimizing researcher bias and uncertainty and providing results that are reasonably known to be an accurate account of reality within the particular parameters and limitations of the qualitative method(s) used in a study. The two primary elements of Credibility are <u>Scope</u> and <u>Data Gathering</u>.

Critical theory A research <u>paradigm</u> orientation that focuses on "the overarching goal to bring about social change by giving voice to and empowering the marginalized" (Fassinger, 2005, p. 157) and typically addresses the "systems of inequity such as classism, racism, sexism, and heterosexism" (Lather, 2004, p. 205).

Data Analysis phase Along with the <u>Data Generation phase</u> the second of two phases in the <u>qualitative content analysis</u> process. As Phase 2, Data Analysis involves the categorization/interpretation of the data (i.e., the coded content) created in Phase 1, by way of categorizing and finding meaningful interpretations of the outcomes.

Data Gathering	Along with <u>Scope</u>, an element of the <u>Credibility</u> component in the <u>Total Quality Framework</u> concerned with how well the data that are gathered actually measure what the researchers claim the study has measured. This domain is often referred to as "construct validity." It includes the effects on data quality that may cause uncertainty and/or bias related to the participants, the interviewers, and/or the tools used to gather that data.
Data Generation phase	Along with the <u>Data Analysis phase</u>, first of two phases in the <u>qualitative content analysis</u> process. As Phase 1, Data Generation involves the preparation and coding of the contents that become the data analyzed by the researcher in Phase 2.
Dataset	The amalgamation of the data gathered from sampled participants or documents.
Deductive approach	In contrast to an <u>inductive approach</u>, an analytical strategy in <u>qualitative content analysis</u> whereby the researcher enters into the analysis with a preconceived theory or hypothesis and scours the data to find evidence that supports or fails to support this premise. Similarly, a researcher might enter into the <u>Data Generation phase</u> of a content analysis with a predetermined coding scheme based on earlier research, which the researcher then modifies as necessary.
Delphi method	An approach, like the <u>nominal group method</u>, that is used as an attempt to find consensus on a particular problem or issue. The Delphi method involves a series of rounds (or a back-and-forth process) in which a selected panel of experts or knowledgeable people give their written opinions/agreement based on the outcome of each round. The panel never meets as a group, and the identities of panel members remain anonymous.
Deviant cases	An approach in <u>Verification</u>—termed "negative case analysis" by some—whereby the researcher actively seeks instances in the study data that contradict or otherwise conflict with the prevailing evidence in the data. The analysis of deviant cases compels the researcher to develop an understanding about *why* these cases exist, which should lead to a greater comprehension as to the strengths and limits of the research data and final interpretations.
Discussion guide	Similar to the <u>interviewer guide</u> used in <u>in-depth interviews</u>, the discussion guide is an outline of topics, issues, as well as suggested primary and follow-up questions that the <u>focus group</u> moderator uses to direct the course of the discussion. The organization of the topical areas (typically as a funnel, i.e., progressing from broad issues to a focus on the primary subject area) as well as the comprehensiveness of the topics to be covered, pertinence of the primary and follow-up questions to ask, and use of particular <u>enabling techniques</u> or <u>projective techniques</u>, play a significant role in determining the ultimate credibility and usefulness of the research outcomes.

Dual perspective	In ethnography, the ability to derive meaning from research participants' activities (as well as the study environment) by internalizing the viewpoint of the participants while maintaining an "outsider's" objectivity. A dual perspective demands that observers have the ability to actually put themselves into the "shoes" of unfamiliar cultures and social groups, sensing and recording events from the participants' vantage point, while also reflecting on the meanings as well as the observer's own values and possible biases.
Dyads	Focus group discussions consisting of two participants plus the moderator.
Enabling techniques	A type of facilitation technique that focus group moderators may use as an alternative approach to direct questioning. An enabling technique is one that modifies a direct question to make it easier for group participants to express their opinions. Word association and sentence completion are examples of enabling techniques.
Ethnography	A research approach based on primarily the observation method that is used to describe the beliefs, attitudes, processes, and behaviors of others by way of an in-context immersion or form of prolonged reality-based researcher–participant engagement.
Focus group(s)	A qualitative research data collection method that involves interviewing two or more people simultaneously, with the goal of fostering interaction among participants that results in an exchange of experiences and ideas. Also referred to in this book as "focus group discussions," "group discussions," "group interviewing," and "group interviews." A full-sized focus group typically consists of seven to 10, or more, participants and often lasts 90–120 minutes.
Gatekeepers	People who hold some type of authority or control over the access to one or more individuals and, in this way, have the power to provide or deny access to those members of the research population of interest. For example, a gatekeeper may be a receptionist or secretary in an office environment, a director at a primary care facility, a community leader, or a school principal.
Grounded theory	An approach developed by Glaser and Strauss in 1967 as "a general methodology for developing theory that is grounded in data systematically gathered and analyzed. Theory evolves during actual research, and it does this through continuous interplay between analysis and data collection" (Strauss & Corbin, 1994, p. 273).
Group dynamics	Used in this book to refer to the interactive environment in a focus group discussion, including the variety of personality types and contrary opinions that exists among group participants, which may lead to disruptive, domineering behavior or a "runaway" discussion that departs from the research objectives. A skillful moderator is able to manage the group dynamics while maintaining a supportive environment that encourages an interactive discussion addressing the research issues.

Hawthorne effect	In ethnography, the extent to which observed participants modify their behavior during an otherwise naturally occurring event due to the presence of the observer, leading to biased data that are no longer a credible (valid) representation of what actually would have occurred had the participants not been aware that they were being studied. For example, school teachers deviating from their usual teaching styles while being observed in order to conform more closely to school policies.
IDI(s)	See in-depth interviews.
In-depth interviews (IDIs)	A qualitative interviewing method, based on a prescribed research design that is used to gain a rich, nuanced understanding of the "thinking" (i.e., motivation) that drives behavior and attitude formation or otherwise leads to other consequences of research interest among members of a target population. The interviewer–interviewee relationship is the cornerstone of the research IDI, and the intense and individualistic nature of IDIs makes this one of the most personal of all qualitative research design methods. The interview format is often semistructured.
Inductive approach	In contrast to a deductive approach, an analytical strategy in qualitative content analysis whereby the researcher does not enter into the analysis with an a priori premise, but rather uses a hypotheses development process guided by a total immersion in the data, from which the researcher discovers new meanings and interpretations.
Informed consent	The ethical practice of providing research participants with complete information concerning the research—including the purpose, scope, process, confidentiality, dissemination, value, and voluntary nature of the research—prior to gaining their voluntary agreement to participate. In some instances, the researcher may be required to obtain a written and signed consent form.
Interview guide	Similar to the discussion guide used in focus groups, the interview guide is an outline of topics, issues, as well as suggested primary and follow-up questions that the IDI interviewer uses to direct the course of a semistructured in-depth interview. The topical areas are often highlighted in some way to designate the relative priority of each in relationship to the research objectives, with the topics organized as a funnel, that is, progressing from broad issues to a focus on the primary subject area.
Interviewer bias	The conscious or unconscious influence of an interviewer, as manifested via verbal and nonverbal behaviors and characteristics, within the context of an in-depth interview that may elicit false or inaccurate responses from the interviewee. This undue influence may be derived from the interviewer's demographic characteristics (e.g., age, race), physical appearance in the face-to-face mode (e.g., manner of dress), and/or personal values or presumptions. Along with interviewer inconsistency, interviewer bias is one of two factors in Data Gathering pertaining to interviewer effects that can impact the quality of interview data.

Interviewer effects	From the perspective of the Total Quality Framework, one of three aspects of Data Gathering in the in-depth interview method that must be considered in order to optimize the quality of the research outcomes. The two primary interviewer effects are interviewer bias and interviewer inconsistency.
Interviewer inconsistency	Along with interviewer bias, one of two factors in Data Gathering pertaining to interviewer effects that can harm the quality of interview data. Interviewer inconsistency concerns the degree to which interviewers deviate from the interview guide in a way that does not bias the overall findings (i.e., elicit inaccurate responses) but does lead to variation in the data across interviewees that does not truly exist. This false variation can lead the researcher to draw inaccurate conclusions from the study.
Key informants	People who are associated and engaged with the research participants, such as a nurse in the maternity ward or a member of the local Al-Anon support group, who facilitate the researcher's involvement with the study population. Key informants are invaluable in ethnography—particularly in covert observation or when targeting deviant groups—where they act as the ethnographer's advisors and supporters throughout the study. The ethnographer's relationship with key informants may extend over a lengthy period of time and culminate in true collaborative friendships. A key informant may or may not be a gatekeeper—that is, the person who provides the initial access to the participants.
Lived experience	A term used in narrative research to refer to how some portion of an individual's life has been experienced as told by the person who has lived through it. This term goes beyond the idea of a firsthand or direct experience of an event. Stories of lived experiences are rich in context and personal meaning for the narrator.
Member checking	An approach in Verification (also referred to as "member checks") whereby the researcher confirms the research findings and interpretations with the study participants. With the exception of question–answer validity, member checking is generally not endorsed from the perspective of the Total Quality Framework because it typically relies on participants' memory recall and places the reported outcomes in the hands of nonresearchers (i.e., participants), among other reasons.
Mini groups	Focus group discussions consisting of four to six participants plus the moderator.
Mixed-method approach	In contrast to a multi-method approach, a research design that combines qualitative *and* quantitative methods to collect and analyze data addressing a particular research question.
Moderator bias	Along with moderator inconsistency, one of two factors in Data Gathering pertaining to the focus group moderator that can harm (bias) the quality of the data by the manner in which the discussions are conducted. Moderator bias concerns the behavioral and other characteristics of the moderator that may alter participants' responses and make them inaccurate.

Moderator effects	From the perspective of the <u>Total Quality Framework</u>, one of three aspects of <u>Data Gathering</u> in the <u>focus group</u> method that must be considered in order to optimize the quality of the research outcomes. The two primary moderator effects are <u>moderator bias</u> and <u>moderator inconsistency</u>.
Moderator inconsistency	Along with <u>moderator bias</u>, one of two factors in <u>Data Gathering</u> pertaining to the <u>focus group</u> moderator that can harm the quality of the data by the manner in which the discussions are conducted. Moderator inconsistency involves unwarranted and unrepresentative variations in the data as the result of the moderator's inconsistent manner when conducting the group discussions.
Multi-method approach	In contrast to a <u>mixed-method approach</u>, a research design that combines two or more *qualitative* methods to investigate a research question or phenomenon; that is, a research strategy that incorporates more than one qualitative method and excludes quantitative methods.
Narrative environment	The broad context in which narratives in <u>narrative research</u> are told or otherwise conveyed. Narrative researchers are interested in gathering as much information as available on the narrative environment to better understand the contextual basis in which narratives have meaning.
Narrative research	A <u>case-centered research</u> approach that investigates the stories of <u>lived experiences</u> from individuals, groups, organizations, and even governments. It is the story that is the case or object of attention and the focal point of the research, with the narrative researcher allowing the narrators to be the guide, welcoming the narrators' stories wherever they may lead.
Nominal group method	A technique, like the <u>Delphi method</u>, typically used as an attempt to find consensus on a particular problem or issue. The nominal group method is a highly structured group format consisting of a panel of experts and a facilitator knowledgeable on the topic. This technique was developed as a modified approach to group discussions in order to circumvent group interaction effects, specifically the domination of one or two individuals.
Noncontingent incentive	A material incentive—such as cash, a gift card, or donation to charity—that is given to a research participant in advance of a research event (e.g., an <u>IDI</u>). The incentive is offered when recruiting participants in order to motivate participation in the research.
Noncoverage	Less than complete access to the <u>target population</u>, possibly resulting in an inaccurate representation of the population of interest. Individuals or contents that are inaccessible and materially different (in attitudes, behavior, or substance), compared to those that are accessible, can lead to serious bias in the research data and the study's findings.
Nonparticipant observation	One of two broad forms of observation (the other one being <u>participant observation</u>) in which the researcher's role is to strictly observe in a completely unobtrusive manner, without any interaction with the study participants, either remotely (i.e., <u>off-site nonparticipant observation</u>) or within the study environment (i.e., <u>on-site nonparticipant observation</u>).

Observation grid	Similar to an <u>observation guide</u> in that the grid reminds the observer of the events and issues of most import; however, the observation grid is specifically a spreadsheet or log that enables the observer to actually record and reflect on observable events in relationship to the research constructs of interest. The grid might show, for instance, the relevant constructs or research issues across the top (as the column headings) and specific areas of observation along the side (as the rows). See Figure 5.2 (p. 209) for an example of an observation grid.
Observation guide	Similar to the <u>interview guide</u> and <u>discussion guide</u>, an outline of the most pertinent observational components along with questions or issues related to each component. This guide (1) reminds the observer of the key points of observation as well as the topic of interest associated with each, and (2) acts as the impetus for an exercise in a <u>reflexive journal</u>, where the observer can reflect on his or her own relationship and contribution to the observed at any moment in time.
Observer bias	The behavioral and other characteristics (e.g., personal attitudes, values, and physical traits) of the observer in <u>ethnography</u> that may alter the observed event or otherwise bias the observations made by the observer. For example, an observer may knowingly (or not) impose subjective values on an observed event that he/she finds offensive; or an observer may exhibit personal characteristics (e.g., pertaining to age or racial identity) and/or inappropriate behavior (e.g., making personal comments during the observed event) that contributes undue influence to the data. Along with <u>observer inconsistency</u>, observer bias is one of two factors in <u>Data Gathering</u> pertaining to <u>observer effects</u> that can harm the quality of ethnographic data.
Observer effects	From the perspective of the <u>Total Quality Framework</u>, one of three aspects of <u>Data Gathering</u> in <u>ethnography</u> that must be considered in order to optimize the quality of the research outcomes. The two primary observer effects are <u>observer bias</u> and <u>observer inconsistency</u>.
Observer inconsistency	Along with <u>observer bias</u>, one of two factors in <u>Data Gathering</u> within the context of <u>ethnography</u> pertaining to the inconsistent manner in which the observer conducts the observations that creates unwarranted and unrepresentative variation in the data. Although the participants and activities will change from observation site to observation site, it is critical that the observer maintain consistent recording of the factors of interest. For example, an <u>on-site nonparticipant observer</u> conducting in-home observations of the use of media and technology would be introducing unwarranted variation in the data by observing and recording the use of television and gaming in some households, but not in others, where television and gaming activities took place.
Off-site nonparticipant observation	Along with <u>on-site nonparticipant observation</u>, one of two types of <u>nonparticipant observation</u> where the researcher observes study participants from a remote location. For example, observations of the teaching methods used in college medical training via remote monitors in an off-campus building.

Online community	A private, invitation-only website that may include from 300 to 500 or more members and exist for only a week or for several months. This approach is most frequently employed by marketing researchers who use online communities to observe consumers' interactions and "listen" as they discuss product and service-related issues. The researcher may intermittently ask community members questions or give them an activity to perform, but otherwise leaves them to get to know each other and form their own social dynamics.
On-site nonparticipant observation	Along with off-site nonparticipant observation, one of two types of nonparticipant observation where the observer is situated in the same "space" as the study participants but, like off-site observation, is devoid of observer–participant engagement. For example, observations of doctor–patient interactions by way of accompanying the doctor on his or her rounds.
Overt observation	In contrast to covert observation, an obtrusive observational technique used in participant observation by which the study participants are made aware of the research and the identity of the observer prior to the onset of fieldwork.
Paradigm	According to Guba and Lincoln (1994), "the basic belief system or world-view that guides the investigator, not only in choices of method but in onto-logically and epistemologically fundamental ways" (p. 105). This worldview "defines, for its holder, the nature of the 'world', the individual's place in it, and the range of possible relationships to that world and its parts, as, for example, cosmologies and theologies do" (p. 107).
Participant effects	From the perspective of the Total Quality Framework, one of three aspects of Data Gathering in ethnography that must be considered in order to opti-mize the quality of the research outcomes. The primary participant effect occurs when people alter their behavior as a result of being observed (i.e., the Hawthorne effect).
Participant observation	One of two broad forms of observation (the other one being nonparticipant observation) by which the observer is situated where the study participants are involved in the activities under investigation. In every case, participant observers are on site in the research context and engaged with the partici-pants at some level beyond pure observation. There are three variations of participant observation: passive participant, participant–observer, and complete participant.
Participant–observer	Along with passive participant and complete participant, one of three types of participant observation wherein the researcher becomes somewhat more (but not totally) engaged with the participants, even to the extent of par-ticipating in key areas under study and sparking friendships. For example, studying the cooperation of team members on the soccer field by going on the field with the team to hear firsthand what is discussed in the huddle. As a participant–observer, the researcher may employ overt observation or covert observation techniques.
Passive consent	In contrast to active consent, a less common type of informed consent by which research participants sign and return a written form by which they affirm that they do *not agree* (refuse) to participate in the research study.

359

Passive participant observer	Along with <u>participant-observer</u> and <u>complete participant</u>, one of three types of <u>participant observation</u> where the researcher plays a role that is primarily that of an observer but who also interacts with participants by way of asking questions or becoming involved in activities beyond or even unrelated to the critical areas of study. For example, helping out in the classroom in an observational study of course content. As a passive participant observer, the researcher may employ <u>overt observation</u> or <u>covert observation</u> techniques.
Peer debriefing	An approach in <u>Verification</u> to substantiate the researcher's findings and interpretations in a qualitative study that relies on the use of at least one impartial peer who has (a) expertise in the method and subject area, (b) objectivity, and (c) knowledge of the <u>Total Quality Framework</u>.
Persistent observation	A technique in <u>ethnography</u>, prescribed by Lincoln and Guba (1985) to "make it more likely that credible findings and interpretations will be produced" (p. 301), where the goal is "to identify those characteristics and elements in the situation that are most relevant to the problem or issue being pursued and focusing on them in detail" (p. 304).
Photovoice	Originally referred to as "photo novella," a technique devised by Wang and Burris (1997) as a form of participatory research, by which individuals are given cameras and asked to photograph life events/situations as they experience them. Wang and Burris developed this technique to allow people to record what was going on in their communities, promote dialogue within the communities, and ultimately reach policy makers who could make a difference in the communities. Photovoice has become a technique in <u>narrative research</u> as a way to enable individuals to tell stories of their <u>lived experiences</u> by way of taking still or video images. The <u>Total Quality Framework</u> approach does not endorse photovoice as a stand-alone technique due to the potential for <u>selection bias</u>.
Postpositivism	A research <u>paradigm</u> that typically focuses on utilizing traditional scientific methods where the emphasis is on maintaining objectivity and controlling variables in order to approximate one "reality" (Lincoln et al., 2011; Ponterotto, 2013).
Preliminary coding	In <u>qualitative content analysis</u>, a pilot test of the proposed coding scheme with a subset of the content. Ideally, two or more coders independently conduct preliminary coding so the data they generate can be compared. The researcher may then engage the coders in a discussion of the coding discrepancies.
Preliminary data	The data as they exist at the completion of the fieldwork phase, before they have been processed and verified. For example, the interviewer's notes and recordings immediately after a series of <u>in-depth interviews</u>.
Processing	Along with <u>Verification</u>, an element of the <u>Analyzability</u> component in the <u>Total Quality Framework</u> concerned with transforming or correcting the <u>preliminary data</u> prior to conducting the analyses. For example, the preliminary data may need to be converted from audio to text, or online participants' responses may have been incorrectly tagged and need to be adjusted for the transcripts.

Projective techniques	A type of facilitation technique that <u>focus group</u> moderators may use as an alternative approach to direct questioning. A projective technique delves into participants' less conscious, less rational, less socially acceptable feelings by way of indirect exercises. Picture sorts and guided imagery are two examples of projective techniques.
Prolonged engagement	A technique in <u>ethnography</u>, prescribed by Lincoln and Guba (1985) to "make it more likely that credible findings and interpretations will be produced," whereby the researcher allocates the necessary time in the field for "learning the 'culture', testing for misinformation introduced by distortions either of the self or of the respondents, and building trust" (p. 301).
Purposive sampling	The deliberate selection of particular individuals or groups of people for interviewing or observation because of their relationship to the research problem. Purposive sampling is used when (a) the research objectives are aimed at a very specific type of individual or group; (b) only certain people have the sought-after knowledge or expertise; and/or (c) the population of interest is very small in size.
Qualitative content analysis	The systematic reduction of content, analyzed with special attention on the context in which the content was created, to identify <u>themes</u> and extract meaningful interpretations of the data. There are eight basic steps divided into two phases of the overall process—<u>Data Generation</u> and <u>Data Analysis</u>. Qualitative researchers *primarily* use an <u>inductive</u> approach rather than a <u>deductive approach</u> to content analysis.
Question–answer validity	A form of <u>member checking</u> by which the <u>IDI</u> interviewer or <u>focus group</u> moderator paraphrases interviewees'/participants' comments to confirm or clarify the intended meaning. This technique also enables the interviewer to ascertain whether a participant has interpreted the interviewer's question as it was intended.
Referential adequacy	A concept endorsed by Lincoln and Guba (1985) to "make it more likely that credible findings and interpretations will be produced" (p. 301), whereby the qualitative researcher sets aside "a portion of the data to be archived—not included in whatever data analysis may be planned—and then recalled when tentative findings have been reached" (p. 313). For example, the archived data might be used by other researchers to question the interpretations derived by the study investigator.
Reflexive journal	A written document that is kept by the researcher (and possibly by others involved in conducting the research, e.g., interviewers, coders, observers) during the field and analysis processes to account for process details (e.g., decision making) as well as provide personal thoughts and insights on what happened during the study (e.g., possible <u>interviewer bias</u>). The reflexive journal is an invaluable resource that the researcher can use in the <u>Verification</u> process to review and judge the quality of data collection as well as the soundness of his/her interpretations during the analysis phase.

Satisficing	A response pattern by which the <u>IDI</u> or <u>focus group</u> participant expends minimal cognitive effort to think upon the answers to the interviewer's/ moderator's questions and instead opts for the easiest, most accessible response, such as "I don't know," or provides a quick guess at the number of times he/she has engaged in certain behavior without any serious thought and conveying an inaccurate account of the true frequency of his/ her behavior.
Saturation	A fundamental concept in <u>grounded theory</u> by which the researcher continues to collect data until no new insights or topics of interest emerge.
Scope	Along with <u>Data Gathering</u>, an element of the <u>Credibility</u> component in the <u>Total Quality Framework</u> concerned with how well a qualitative research study ends up representing the population of humans and/or documents the study is investigating. It includes possible biases and uncertainties caused by any weaknesses in the initial sample's representation of the study's <u>target population</u>.
Selection bias	A potential form of bias in qualitative research data generated from participant-driven methods (e.g., mobile <u>IDIs</u> and the <u>photovoice</u> technique in <u>narrative research</u>) that give remote, unobserved participants near-complete control of what is and is not shared with the researcher. As a result, the researcher cannot be certain whether he/she is collecting thorough and accurate data. For example, mothers who are asked to photograph and record the home environment as they go about the daily care of their infants may or may not capture the entirety of the home setting that is relevant to the research objectives. In this manner, selection bias negatively impacts the <u>Credibility</u> of a qualitative study.
Semistructured in-depth interview (IDI)	An <u>in-depth interview</u> format that is highly conversational in nature, with the interviewer referring to an <u>interview guide</u> to ensure that the relevant issues are covered, but modifying the questions for each interview as warranted by the particular responses or circumstances of the interviewee.
Social desirability bias	Inaccuracy in the research data resulting from responses to the interviewer's or moderator's questions by a participant who, intentionally or unintentionally, overreports positive aspects about him/herself and/or underreports negative aspects (e.g., a father who exaggerates the amount of time he spends with his children).
Structured in-depth interview (IDI)	An <u>in-depth interview</u> format that is relatively formal and rigid, with the interviewer asking an explicit set of questions, as written and in the prescribed order.
Synchronous focus groups	<u>Focus groups</u> conducted online when all the participants and the moderator are present at the same time. This approach comes closest to the real-time discussions of the face-to-face and telephone modes, and can be conducted in a text chat or audio–video format. Synchronous discussions can be difficult to manage and require moderators who are specifically skilled in effectively handling the fast pace of simultaneous engagement online.

Systematic sampling	An orderly approach for choosing members of the <u>target population</u> (taken in a random fashion from a list that has been assembled to represent that population) that essentially ensures that the selected sample is representative of the population under investigation.
Target population	The entire group of individuals, documents, or other entities the researcher is interested in investigating and for which the researcher's findings are meant to apply.
Themes	Patterns in the coded data that emerge under scrutiny, revealing the essence of the outcomes. This identification process is made easier by way of visual displays such as Excel worksheets or visual maps.
Thick description	A complete account in the final research document of the phenomena under investigation as well as rich details of the data collection and analysis processes and interpretations of the findings. For example, in <u>ethnography</u> a detailed portrait of the cultural or social "scene" that the observer took away from an observation site—and the research processes employed to derive the final outcomes (including the <u>Scope</u>, <u>Data Gathering</u>, <u>Processing</u>, and <u>Verification</u> procedures)—allowing a consumer of the study to better determine the applicability (i.e., <u>transferability</u>) of the study's methods, findings, and recommendations to other research contexts. A thick description creates an audit trail by including all relevant materials, such as <u>reflexive journal</u>(s), transcripts, field notes, and the <u>codebook</u>.
Total Quality Framework (TQF)	A comprehensive perspective for creating (conceptualizing), managing, and interpreting quality research designs and evaluating the likelihood that a qualitative study provides information that is valid and useful for the purposes for which the study is intended. It comprises four major interrelated components: <u>Credibility</u>, <u>Analyzability</u>, <u>Transparency</u>, and <u>Usefulness</u>.
Transcription	The process of converting field notes and audio recordings (or audio from video recordings) to (typically) electronic text format. In most cases, this process results in a verbatim transcript or document for each <u>in-depth interview</u>, <u>focus group</u>, or observation undertaken in a qualitative study.
Transferability	The extent to which other researchers or users of the research can determine the applicability of the research design and/or the study findings to other research contexts (e.g., other participants, places, and times). This is primarily determined by way of <u>thick description</u>.
Transparency	A component of the <u>Total Quality Framework</u> associated with the complete disclosure of the research design, fieldwork, and analytic processes in the final document, including the specific aspects of these processes that impacted the outcomes and interpretations of the data. This is done primarily by way of the rich (i.e., abundant and thorough) details of <u>thick description</u> that enable a consumer of the study to better determine the applicability (i.e., <u>transferability</u>) of the study's methods, findings, and recommendations to other contexts.
Triads	<u>Focus group</u> discussions consisting of three participants plus the moderator.

Triangulation
An approach in <u>Verification</u> that uses multiple sources to contrast and compare study data to establish supporting and/or contradictory information to ultimately give the researcher and users of the research a more balanced and deeper understanding of the outcomes than relying on the study data alone. The most common forms of triangulation discussed in this book are those that compare study data with data obtained from another data source ("data triangulation"), a different method ("method triangulation"), and another researcher ("investigator triangulation").

Unit of analysis
In <u>qualitative content analysis</u>, the basis by which <u>codes</u> are developed for a particular qualitative <u>dataset</u>. These codes are then assigned to the data, by which meaningful <u>categories</u> and <u>themes</u> can be identified. The unit of analysis might be a specific subject area discussed in an <u>in-depth interview</u> or <u>focus group</u>, or an activity observed within a certain timeframe, or a complete narrative or document (e.g., a letter). In <u>case-centered research</u>, the unit of analysis represents the primary aspect(s) of a <u>case</u> that will be the focus of investigation.

Unstructured in-depth interview (IDI)
An <u>in-depth interview</u> format that places the control of the interview with the research participant, enabling this individual to tell his/her personal story concerning the subject matter without substantial "interference" from the interviewer.

Usefulness
A component of the <u>Total Quality Framework</u> associated with the ability to do something of value with the research outcomes, including the extent to which the data collection methods, the findings, interpretations, and recommendations of a qualitative research study are of value to researchers and their sponsors as well as students and other users of the research. The Usefulness component is a function of the other three TQF components—<u>Credibility</u>, <u>Analyzability</u>, and <u>Transparency</u>—and is the definitive goal of the research.

Variable of analysis
In <u>case-centered research</u>, a subcategory within the <u>unit of analysis</u> that guides researchers in their examination of the unit. For example, the activities or events (as the variable of analysis) within each YMCA program (the unit of analysis).

Verification
Along with <u>Processing</u>, an element of the <u>Analyzability</u> component in the <u>Total Quality Framework</u> whereby the researcher is seeking evidence that supports or refutes early explanations of the findings, using both supportive and contradictory input to provide a rich, meaningful analysis. The primary means advocated by the TQF to verify qualitative data are (a) <u>peer debriefings</u>, (b) <u>reflexive journals</u>, (c) <u>triangulation</u>, (d) <u>deviant cases</u>, and, to a lesser degree, (e) <u>member checking</u>.

References

Adler, P. (1990). Ethnographic research on hidden populations: Penetrating the drug world. *National Institute on Drug Abuse Research Monograph, 98,* 96–112.

Agar, M. (2006). An ethnography by any other name. . . . *Forum Qualitative Sozialforschung/ Forum: Qualitative Social Research, 7*(4), 1–24.

Akkerman, S., Admiraal, W., Brekelmans, M., & Oost, H. (2006). Auditing quality of research in social sciences. *Quality and Quantity, 42*(2), 257–274.

Allen, C. (1997). Spies like us: When sociologists deceive their subjects. *Lingua Franca, 7,* 31–33.

Alquati Bisol, C., Sperb, T. M., & Moreno-Black, G. (2008). Focus groups with deaf and hearing youths in Brazil: Improving a questionnaire on sexual behavior and HIV/AIDS. *Qualitative Health Research, 18*(4), 565–578.

Altheide, D. L. (1987). Ethnographic content analysis. *Qualitative Sociology, 10*(1), 65–77.

American Anthropological Association. (2004). *Statement on ethnography and institutional review boards.* Arlington, VA: Author.

American Anthropological Association. (2012). *Statement on ethics: Principles of professional responsibility.* Arlington, VA: Author.

American Association of University Professors. (2000). *Institutional review boards and social science research.* Washington, DC: Author.

American Psychological Association. (2010). *Ethical principles of psychologists and code of conduct* (Vol. 57). Washington, DC: Author.

American Sociological Association. (1999). *Code of ethics and policies and procedures of the ASA Committee on Professional Ethics* (Vol. 119). Washington, DC: Author.

Andriotis, K. (2010). Heterotopic erotic oases. *Annals of Tourism Research, 37*(4), 1076–1096.

Angrosino, M., & Rosenberg, J. (2011). Observations on observation. In N. K. Denzin & Y., S. Lincoln (Eds.), *The Sage handbook of qualitative research* (4th ed., pp. 467–478). Thousand Oaks, CA: Sage.

Appleton, S., Fry, A., Rees, G., Rush, R., & Cull, A. (2000). Psychosocial effects of living with an increased risk of breast cancer: An exploratory study using telephone focus groups. *Psycho-Oncology, 9*(6), 511–521.

Arcury, T. A., & Quandt, S. A. (1999). Participant recruitment for qualitative research: A site-based approach to community research in complex societies. *Human Organization, 58*(2), 128–133.

Ardalan, A., Mazaheri, M., Naieni, K. H., Rezaie, M., Teimoori, F., & Pourmalek, F. (2009). Older people's needs following major disasters: A qualitative study of Iranian elders' experiences of the Bam earthquake. *Ageing and Society, 30*(1), 11–23.

Atkinson, P., & Delamont, S. (2006). Rescuing narrative from qualitative research. *Narrative Inquiry, 16*(1), 164–172.

Aubert, A., Melgar, P., & Valls, R. (2011). Communicative daily life stories and focus groups: Proposals for overcoming gender violence among teenagers. *Qualitative Inquiry, 17*(3), 295–303.

Auerbach, S. (2002). "Why do they give the good classes to some and not to others?": Latino parent narratives of struggle in a college access program. *Teachers College Record, 104*(7), 1369–1392.

Austin, H., & Carpenter, L. (2008). Troubled, troublesome, troubling mothers: The dilemma of difference in women's personal motherhood narratives. *Narrative Inquiry, 18*(2), 378–392.

Bailey, D. C. (2012). Women and *Wasta*: The use of focus groups for understanding social capital and Middle Eastern women. *The Qualitative Report.* Retrieved February 4, 2013, from *www.nova.edu/ssss/QR/QR17/bailey.pdf.*

Baker, L. (2006). Observation: A complex research method. *Library Trends, 55*(1), 171–189.

Baker, R., Miller, C., Kachii, D., Lange, K., Wilding-Brown, L., & Tucker, J. (2014). Validating respondent identity in online samples: The impact of efforts to eliminate fraudulent respondents. In M. Callegaro, R. Baker, J. Bethlehem, A. Göritz, J. Krosnick, & P. J. Lavrakas (Eds.), *Online panel research: A data quality perspective* (pp. 441–456). London: Wiley.

Baker, S. E., & Edwards, R. (2012). How many qualitative interviews is enough?: Expert voices and early career reflections on sampling and cases in qualitative research. *NCRM Review Paper.* Retrieved September 3, 2012, from *http://eprints.ncrm.ac.uk/2273/4/how_many_interviews.pdf.*

Bamberg, M., & Georgakopoulou, A. (2008). Small stories as a new perspective in narrative and identity analysis. *Text & Talk, 28*(3), 377–396.

Banerjee, M., Capozzoli, M., McSweeney, L., & Debajyoti, S. (1999). Beyond kappa: A review of interrater agreement measures. *Canadian Journal of Statistics, 27*(1), 3–23.

Barbour, R. S. (2001). Checklists for improving rigour in qualitative research: A case of the tail wagging the dog? *British Medical Journal, 322*(7294), 1115–1117.

Baxter, J., & Eyles, J. (1999). The utility of in-depth interviews for studying the meaning of environmental risk. *Professional Geographer, 51*(2), 307–320.

Baxter, P., & Jack, S. (2008). Qualitative case study methodology: Study design and implementation for novice researchers. *The Qualitative Report, 13*(4), 544–559.

Beck, C. T. (2005). Benefits of participating in Internet interviews: Women helping women. *Qualitative Health Research, 15*(3), 411–422.

Beeman, A. K. (2007). Emotional segregation: A content analysis of institutional racism in US films, 1980–2001. *Ethnic and Racial Studies, 30*(5), 687–712.

Belzile, J. A., & Öberg, G. (2012). Where to begin?: Grappling with how to use participant interaction in focus group design. *Qualitative Research, 12*(4), 459–472.

Bennett, S., Bishop, A., Dalgarno, B., Waycott, J., & Kennedy, G. (2012). Implementing Web 2.0 technologies in higher education: A collective case study. *Computers & Education, 59*(2), 524–534.

Berends, L., & Johnston, J. (2005). Using multiple coders to enhance qualitative analysis?: The case of interviews with consumers of drug treatment. *Addiction Research and Theory, 13*(4), 373–381.

Berg, A., & Hansson, U. W. (2000). Dementia care nurses' experiences of systematic clinical group supervision and supervised planned nursing care. *Journal of Nursing Management, 8*(6), 357–368.

Berg, B. L., & Lune, H. (2012). *Qualitative research methods for the social sciences* (8th ed.). Boston: Pearson.

Bergman, M. M., & Coxon, A. P. M. (2005). The quality in qualitative methods. *Forum Qualitative Sozialforschung/Forum: Qualitative Social Research, 6*(2, Art. 34).

Bernard, H. R. (2011). *Research methods in anthropology: Qualitative and quantitative approaches* (5th ed.). Lanham, MD: AltaMira Press.

Blase, J. J. (1986). A qualitative analysis of sources of teacher stress: Consequences for performance. *American Educational Research Journal, 23*(1), 13–40.

Blumberg, S. J., & Luke, J. V. (2013). *Wireless substitution: Early release of estimates from the*

National Health Interview Survey, January–June 2013. U.S. Department of Health and Human Services, Centers for Disease Control and Prevention, National Center for Health Statistics. Available from *www.cdc.gov/nchs/nhis.htm*.

Bogardus, E. S. (1926). The group interview. *Journal of Applied Sociology, 10*(4), 372–382.

Bowker, N., & Tuffin, K. (2004). Using the online medium for discursive research about people with disabilities. *Social Science Computer Review, 22*(2), 228–241.

Bradbury-Jones, C. (2007). Enhancing rigour in qualitative health research: Exploring subjectivity through Peshkin's I's. *Journal of Advanced Nursing, 59*(3), 290–298.

Brewer, J., & Hunter, A. (2006). *Foundations of multimethod research: Synthesizing styles.* Thousand Oaks, CA: Sage.

Briggs, C. L. (1986). *Learning how to ask: A sociolinguistic appraisal of the role of the interview in social science research.* Cambridge, UK: Cambridge University Press.

Brinkmann, S., & Kvale, S. (2008). Ethics in qualitative psychological research. In C. Willig & W. Stainton Rogers (Eds.), *The Sage handbook of qualitative psychology* (pp. 263–279). London: Sage.

Brinkmann, S., & Kvale, S. (2015). *Interviews: Learning the craft of qualitative research interviewing* (3rd ed.). Thousand Oaks, CA: Sage.

Brown, R. N., Kilgore, M. A., Blinn, C. R., & Coggins, J. S. (2012). Barriers to effective state timber sale program administration: A qualitative assessment. *Journal of Forestry, 110*(5), 249–256.

Brüggen, E., & Willems, P. (2009). A critical comparison of offline focus groups, online focus groups and e-Delphi. *International Journal of Market Research, 51*(3), 363–381.

Bruner, J. S. (1990). *Acts of meaning.* Cambridge, MA: Harvard University Press.

Carson, D., Gilmore, A., Perry, C., & Gronhaug, K. (2001). *Qualitative marketing research.* London: Sage.

Catterall, M., & Ibbotson, P. (2000). Using projective techniques in education. *British Education Research Journal, 26*(2), 245–256.

Cederberg, M. (2014). Public discourses and migrant stories of integration and inequality: Language and power in biographical narratives. *Sociology, 48*(1), 133–149.

Charmaz, K. (2008). Views from the margins: Voices, silences, and suffering. *Qualitative Research in Psychology, 5*(1), 7–18.

Chase, S. E. (2011). Narrative inquiry: Still a field in the making. In N. K. Denzin & Y. S. Lincoln (Eds.), *The Sage handbook of qualitative research* (4th ed., pp. 421–434). Thousand Oaks, CA: Sage.

Christensen, P., Mikkelsen, M. R., Nielsen, T. A. S., & Harder, H. (2011). Children, mobility, and space: Using GPS and mobile phone technologies in ethnographic research. *Journal of Mixed Methods Research, 5*(3), 227–246.

Civicom. (2011). *Ups and downs.* Retrieved February 21, 2013, from *www.civi.com/marketingresearch/mobile_qual_globally.html*.

Clandinin, D. J. (2012, September). A short video interview with Prof. Jean Clandinin. *BERA Conference*, Manchester, UK. Retrieved July 8, 2013, from *www.youtube.com/watch?v=RnaTBqapMrE*.

Clandinin, D. J., & Connelly, F. M. (1998). Stories to live by: Narrative understandings of school reform. *Curriculum Inquiry, 28*(2), 149–164.

Clandinin, D. J., Pushor, D., & Orr, A. M. (2007). Navigating sites for narrative inquiry. *Journal of Teacher Education, 58*(1), 21–35.

Clifford, S. (2012, July 30). Social media are giving a voice to taste buds. *The New York Times*, p. A1.

Cohen, J. (1960). A coefficient of agreement for nominal scales. *Educational and Psychological Measurement, 20*(1), 37–46.

Colby, B. N. (1973). A partial grammar of Eskimo folktales. *American Anthropologist, 75*(3), 645–662.

Communispace. (2011). *Worth a standing ovation: Forrester groundswell submissions from our partners 2007–2011.* Retrieved April 17, 2013, from *www.communispace.com/clients/forrestergroundswell.aspx*.

Conn, L. G., Oandasan, I. F., Creede, C., Jakubovicz, D., & Wilson, L. (2010). Creating sustainable change in the interprofessional academic primary care setting: An appreciative inquiry approach. *Journal of Research in Interprofessional Practice and Education, 1*(3), 284–300.

Connelly, F. M., & Clandinin, D. J. (1990). Stories of experience and narrative inquiry. *Educational Researcher, 19*(5), 2–14.

Cook, K., & Nunkoosing, K. (2008). Maintaining dignity and managing stigma in the interview encounter: The challenge of paid-for participation. *Qualitative Health Research, 18*(3), 418–427.

Cotton, D. R. E. (2006). Implementing curriculum guidance on environmental education: The importance of teachers' beliefs. *Journal of Curriculum Studies, 38*(1), 67–83.

Cotton, D. R. E., Stokes, A., & Cotton, P. A. (2010). Using observational methods to research the student experience. *Journal of Geography in Higher Education, 34*(3), 463–473.

Cramer, H., Shaw, A., Wye, L., & Weiss, M. (2010). Over-the-counter advice seeking about complementary and alternative medicines (CAM) in community pharmacies and health shops: An ethnographic study. *Health and Social Care in the Community, 18*(1), 41–50.

Creswell, J. W. (2009). *Research design: Qualitative, quantitative, and mixed methods approaches.* Thousand Oaks, CA: Sage.

Creswell, J. W. (2013). *Qualitative inquiry & research design* (3rd ed.). Thousand Oaks, CA: Sage.

Crudden, A. (2002). Employment after vision loss: Results of a collective case study. *Journal of Visual Impairment & Blindness, 96*(9), 615–621.

Culley, L., Hudson, N., & Rapport, F. (2007). Using focus groups with minority ethnic communities: Researching infertility in British South Asian communities. *Qualitative Health Research, 17*(1), 102–112.

Curasi, C. F. (2001). A critical exploration of face-to-face interviewing vs. computer-mediated interviewing. *International Journal of Market Research, 43*(4), 361–375.

Darke, P., Shanks, G., & Broadbent, M. (1998). Successfully completing case study research: Combining rigour, relevance and pragmatism. *Information Systems Journal, 8*(4), 273–289.

Denny, K. E. (2011). Gender in context, content, and approach: Comparing gender messages in Girl Scout and Boy Scout handbooks. *Gender & Society, 25*(1), 27–47.

Denzin, N. K. (2001). The reflexive interview and a performative social science. *Qualitative Research, 1*(1), 23–46.

Denzin, N. K., & Lincoln, Y. S. (2011). The discipline and practice of qualitative research. In N. K. Denzin & Y. S. Lincoln (Eds.), *The Sage handbook of qualitative research* (4th ed., pp. 1–20). Thousand Oaks, CA: Sage.

Dibble, V. K. (2009). Four types of inference from documents to events. In K. Krippendorff & M. A. Bock (Eds.), *The content analysis reader* (pp. 121–131). Thousand Oaks, CA: Sage.

Dicks, B., Soyinka, B., & Coffey, A. (2006). Multimodal ethnography. *Qualitative Research, 6*(1), 77–96.

Dovring, K. (1954). Quantitative semantics in 18th century Sweden. *Public Opinion Quarterly, 18*(4), 389–394.

Duggan, M., & Brenner, J. (2013). *The demographics of social media users-2012.* Washington, DC: Pew Research Center. Retrieved April 13, 2013, from *www.pewinternet. org/2013/02/14/the-demographics-of-social-media-users-2012.*

Duggleby, W. (2005). What about focus group interaction data? *Qualitative Health Research, 15*(6), 832–840.

Egan, J., Chenoweth, L., & McAuliffe, D. (2006). Email-facilitated qualitative interviews with traumatic brain injury survivors: A new and accessible method. *Brain Injury, 20*(12), 1283–1294.

Egberg-Thyme, K., Wiberg, B., Lundman, B., & Graneheim, U. H. (2013). Qualitative content analysis in art psychotherapy research: Concepts, procedures, and measures to reveal the latent meaning in pictures and the words attached to the pictures. *Arts in Psychotherapy, 40*(1), 101–107.

Eisenhardt, K. M., & Graebner, M. E. (2007). Theory building from cases: Opportunities and challenges. *Academy of Management Journal, 50*(1), 25–32.

ElBoghdady, D. (2002, February 24). Naked truth meets market research. *The Washington Post,* p. H1.

Elliott, J. (2005). *Using narrative in social research: Qualitative and quantitative approaches.* London: Sage.

Ellis, C. S. (1986). *Fisher folk: Two communities on Chesapeake Bay.* Lexington: University Press of Kentucky.

Esteban-Guitart, M. (2012). Towards a multi-methodological approach to identification of funds of identity, small stories and master narratives. *Narrative Inquiry, 22*(1), 173–180.

Fassinger, R. E. (2005). Paradigms, praxis, problems, and promise: Grounded theory in counseling psychology research. *Journal of Counseling Psychology, 52*(2), 156–166.

Ferrell, B. R., Grant, M. M., Funk, B., Otis-Green, S., & Garcia, N. (1997a). Quality of life in breast cancer survivors as identified by focus groups. *Psycho-Oncology, 6*(1), 13–23.

Ferrell, B. R., Grant, M., Funk, B., Otis-Green, S., & Garcia, N. (1997b). Quality of life in breast cancer: Part I. Physical and social well-being. *Cancer Nursing, 20*(6), 398–408.

Fields, E. E. (1988). Qualitative content analysis of television news: Systematic techniques. *Qualitative Sociology, 11*(3), 183–193.

Fine, M., & Sirin, S. R. (2007). Theorizing hyphenated selves: Researching youth development in and across contentious political contexts. *Social and Personality Psychology Compass, 1*(1), 16–38.

Flick, U. (2007). *Designing qualitative research*. London: Sage.

Flyvbjerg, B. (2006). Five misunderstandings about case-study research. *Qualitative Inquiry, 12*(2), 219–245.

Forbat, L., White, I., Marshall-Lucette, S., & Kelly, D. (2012). Discussing the sexual consequences of treatment in radiotherapy and urology consultations with couples affected by prostate cancer. *BJU International, 109*(1), 98–103.

Forman, J., & Damschroder, L. (2008). Qualitative content analysis. In L. Jacoby & L. A. Siminoff (Eds.), *Empirical methods for bioethics: A primer* (pp. 39–62). Oxford, UK: Elsevier.

Frazier, L. M., Miller, V. A., Horbelt, D. V., Delmore, J. E., Miller, B. E., & Paschal, A. M. (2010). Comparison of focus groups on cancer and employment conducted face to face or by telephone. *Qualitative Health Research, 20*(5), 617–627.

Freidenberg, J. (2011). Researching global spaces ethnographically: Queries on methods for the study of virtual populations. *Human Organization, 70*(3), 265–278.

Friese, S. (2013). Proposing a new method for computer-assisted qualitative data analysis. In *IQM Master Class Webinar*. ATLAS. ti. Available from *prezi.com/5notp28gegos/ proposing-a-new-method-for-computer-assisted-qualitative-data-analysis*.

Frost, D. M. (2013). Stigma and intimacy in same-sex relationships: A narrative approach. *Qualitative Psychology, 1*(1), 49–61.

Funk, L. M., & Stajduhar, K. I. (2009). Interviewing family caregivers: Implications of the caregiving context for the research interview. *Qualitative Health Research, 19*(6), 859–867.

Gallivan, M. J., & Keil, M. (2003). The user-developer communication process: A critical case study. *Information Systems Journal, 13*(1), 37–68.

Garcia, A. C., Standlee, A. I., Bechkoff, J., & Cui, Y. (2009). Ethnographic approaches to the Internet and computer-mediated communication. *Journal of Contemporary Ethnography, 38*(1), 52–84.

Gatson, S. N., & Zweerink, A. (2004). Ethnography online: "Natives" practising and inscribing community. *Qualitative Research, 4*(2), 179–200.

Geertz, C. (2003). Thick description: Toward an interpretive theory of culture. In Y. S. Lincoln & N. K. Denzin (Eds.), *Turning points in qualitative research: Tying knots in a handkerchief* (Vol. 3, pp. 143–168). Walnut Creek, CA: AltaMira Press.

George, A. (2009). Quantitative and qualitative approaches to content analysis. In K. Krippendorff & M. A. Bock (Eds.), *The content analysis reader* (pp. 144–155). Thousand Oaks, CA: Sage.

Gerber, E. (2007). Seeing isn't believing: Blindness, race, and cultural literacy. *Senses & Society, 2*(1), 27–40.

Gergen, M. M., & Gergen, K. J. (2006). Narratives in action. *Narrative Inquiry, 16*(1), 112–121.

Gerring, J. (2004). What is a case study and what is it good for? *American Political Science Review, 98*(2), 341–354.

Gibson, L. (2010, June). *Using email interviews* (No. 9, pp. 1–7). Manchester, UK: National Centre for Research Methods. Retreived October 7, 2012, from *http://eprints.ncrm. ac.uk/1303/1/09-toolkit-email-interviews.pdf*.

Glenn, N. M., Champion, C. C., & Spence, J. C. (2012). Qualitative content analysis of online news media coverage of weight loss surgery and related reader comments. *Clinical Obesity, 2*(5–6), 125–131.

Glesne, C. (1997). That rare feeling: Representing research through poetic transcription. *Qualitative Inquiry, 3*(2), 202–221.

Gong, F., Castaneda, D., Zhang, X., Stock, L., Ayala, L., & Baron, S. (2012). Using the associative imagery technique in qualitative health research: The experiences of home-care workers and consumers. *Qualitative Health Research, 22*(10), 1414–1424.

Graneheim, U. H., & Lundman, B. (2004). Qualitative content analysis in nursing research: Concepts, procedures and measures to achieve trustworthiness. *Nurse Education Today, 24*(2), 105–112.

Greene, J. C. (1994). Qualitative program evaluation: Practice and promise. In N. K. Denzin & Y. S. Lincoln (Eds.), *Handbook of qualitative research* (pp. 530–544). Thousand Oaks, CA: Sage.

Griffiths, M. D. (2011). A typology of UK slot machine gamblers: A longitudinal observational and interview study. *International Journal of Mental Health and Addiction, 9*(6), 606–626.

Grønkjær, M., Curtis, T., de Crespigny, C., & Delmar, C. (2011). Analysing group interaction in focus group research: Impact on content and the role of the moderator. *Qualitative Studies, 2*(1), 16–30.

Grünbaum, N. N. (2007). Identification of ambiguity in the case study research typology: What is a unit of analysis? *Qualitative Market Research: An International Journal, 10*(1), 78–97.

Guba, E. G. (1981). Criteria for assessing the trustworthiness of naturalistic inquiries. *Educational Communication and Technology Journal, 29*(2), 75–91.

Guba, E. G., & Lincoln, Y. S. (1994). Competing paradigms in qualitative research. In N. K. Denzin & Y. S. Lincoln (Eds.), *Handbook of qualitative research* (pp. 105–117). Thousand Oaks, CA: Sage.

Gubrium, J. F., & Holstein, J. A. (2008). Narrative ethnography. In S. Hesse-Biber & P. Leavy (Eds.), *Handbook of emergent methods* (pp. 241–264). New York: Guilford Press.

Haenfler, R. (2004). Rethinking subcultural resistance: Core values of the straight edge movement. *Journal of Contemporary Ethnography, 33*(4), 406–436.

Halcomb, E. J., Gholizadeh, L., DiGiacomo, M., Phillips, J., & Davidson, P. M. (2007). Literature review: Considerations in undertaking focus group research with culturally and linguistically diverse groups. *Journal of Clinical Nursing, 16*(6), 1000–1011.

Hammersley, M., & Atkinson, P. (1995). *Ethnography: Principles in practice* (2nd ed.). London: Routledge.

Hancock, K. (2012, October). Redefining the message. *Quirk's Marketing Research Review, 26*(10), 30–32.

Hansen, A., Cottle, S., Negrine, R., & Newbold, C. (1998). *Mass communication research methods*. London: Macmillan.

Hanson, W. E., Creswell, J. W., Clark, V. L. P., Petska, K. S., & Creswell, J. D. (2005). Mixed methods research designs in counseling psychology. *Journal of Counseling Psychology, 52*(2), 224–235.

Harlow, E. (2009). Eliciting narratives of teenage pregnancy in the UK: Reflexively exploring some of the methodological challenges. *Qualitative Social Work, 8*(2), 211–228.

Harper, S. R., Davis, R. J., Jones, D. E., McGowan, B. L., Ingram, T. N., & Platt, C. S. (2011). Race and racism in the experiences of Black male resident assistants at predominantly White universities. *Journal of College Student Development, 52*(2), 180–200.

Herreid, C. F. (1997). What is a case? *Journal of College Science Teaching, 27*(2), 92–94.

Herring, S. C. (2010). Web content analysis: Expanding the paradigm. In J. Hunsinger, L. Klastrup, & M. Allen (Eds.), *International handbook of Internet research* (pp. 233–249). Dordrecht, The Netherlands: Springer.

Herzog, H. (2005). On home turf: Interview location and its social meaning. *Qualitative Sociology, 28*(1), 25–47.

Hesse-Biber, S. (2012). Weaving a multimethodology and mixed methods praxis into randomized control trials to enhance credibility. *Qualitative Inquiry, 18*(10), 876–889.

Hesse-Biber, S. (2014). Feminist approaches to in-depth interviewing. In S. Hesse-Biber (Ed.), *Feminist research practice: A primer* (pp. 182–232). Thousand Oaks, CA: Sage.

Hill, C. E., Knox, S., Thompson, B. J., Williams, E. N., Hess, S. A., & Ladany, N. (2005). Consensual qualitative research: An update. *Journal of Counseling Psychology, 52*(2), 196–205.

Hofstede, A., van Hoof, J., Walenberg, N., & de Jong, M. (2007). Projective techniques for brand image research: Two personification-based methods explored. *Qualitative Market Research: An International Journal, 10*(3), 300–309.

Hsieh, H.-F., & Shannon, S. E. (2005). Three approaches to qualitative content analysis. *Qualitative Health Research, 15*(9), 1277–1288.

Hughes, A. (2010). The challenge of contributing to policy making in primary care: The gendered experiences and strategies of nurses. *Sociology of Health & Illness, 32*(7), 977–992.

Hughey, M. W. (2008). Virtual (br)others and (re)sisters: Authentic black fraternity and sorority identity on the Internet. *Journal of Contemporary Ethnography, 37*(5), 528–560.

Humphreys, L. (1970). *Tearoom trade: Impersonal sex in public places.* Chicago: Aldine.

Humphreys, L. (1975). *Tearoom trade: Impersonal sex in public places* (enlarged edition). New York: Aldine.

Hung, Y.-H., Winchester, W. W., Smith-Jackson, T. L., Kleiner, B. M., Babski-Reeves, K. L., & Mills, T. H. (2013). Identifying fall-protection training needs for residential roofing subcontractors. *Applied Ergonomics, 44*(3), 372–380.

Irvine, A. (2011). Duration, dominance and depth in telephone and face-to-face interviews: A comparative exploration. *International Journal of Qualitative Methods, 10*(3), 202–220.

Isabella, S. (2007). Ethnography of online role-playing games: The role of virtual and real contest in the construction of the field. *Forum Qualitative Sozialforschung/Forum: Qualitative Social Research, 8*(3), Art. 36. Available at *www.qualitative-research.net/index.php/fqs/article/view/280/616.*

James, N., & Busher, H. (2009). *Online interviewing.* London: Sage.

Jason, L. A., Pokorny, S., & Katz, R. (2001). Passive versus active consent: A case study in school settings. *Journal of Community Psychology, 29*(1), 53–68.

Jendrek, M. P. (1994). Grandparents who parent their grandchildren: Circumstances and decisions. *The Gerontologist, 34*(2), 206–216.

Jodlowski, D., Sharf, B. F., Nguyen, L. C., Haidet, P., & Woodard, L. D. (2007). "Screwed for life": Examining identification and division in addiction narratives. *Communication & Medicine, 4*(1), 15–26.

Johansson, K., Holmström, H., Nilsson, I., Ingvar, C., Albertsson, M., & Ekdahl, C. (2003). Breast cancer patients' experiences of lymphoedema. *Scandinavian Journal of Caring Sciences, 17*(1), 35–42.

Johansson, R. (2003). *Case study methodology.* Keynote address presented at the International Conference on Methodologies in Housing Research, Stockholm, Sweden, Royal Institute of Technology.

Johnson, R. B., Onwuegbuzie, A. J., & Turner, L. A. (2007). Toward a definition of mixed methods research. *Journal of Mixed Methods Research, 1*(2), 112–133.

Jordan, B., & Lambert, M. (2009). Working in corporate jungles: Reflections on ethnographic praxis in industry. In M. Cefkin (Ed.), *Ethnography and the corporate encounter* (pp. 95–133). New York: Berghahn Books.

Josselson, R. (2007). The ethical attitude in narrative research: Principles and practicalities. In D. J. Clandinin (Ed.), *Handbook of narrative inquiry* (pp. 537–566). Thousand Oaks, CA: Sage.

Jurgens, F. J., Clissett, P., Gladman, J. R. F., & Harwood, R. H. (2012). Why are family carers of people with dementia dissatisfied with general hospital care?: A qualitative study. *BMC Geriatrics, 12*(1), 57.

Kaphingst, K. A., DeJong, W., Rudd, R. E., & Daltroy, L. H. (2004). A content analysis of direct-to-consumer television prescription drug advertisements. *Journal of Health Communication, 9*(6), 515–528.

Karchmer, R. A. (2001). The journey ahead: Thirteen teachers report how the Internet influences literacy and literacy instruction in their K–12 classrooms. *Reading Research Quarterly, 36*(4), 442–466.

Karp, D. A., & Tanarugsachock, V. (2000). Mental illness, caregiving, and emotion management. *Qualitative Health Research, 10*(1), 6–25.

Kavanaugh, K., & Ayres, L. (1998). "Not as bad as it could have been": Assessing and mitigating harm during research interviews on sensitive topics. *Research in Nursing & Health, 21*, 91–97.

Kenyon, A. J. (2004). Exploring phenomenological research: Pre-testing focus group techniques with young people. *International Journal of Market Research, 46*(4), 427–442.

Kerr, T., Small, W., Peeace, W., Douglas, D., Pierre, A., & Wood, E. (2006). Harm reduction by a "user-run" organization: A case study of the Vancouver Area Network of Drug Users (VANDU). *International Journal of Drug Policy, 17*(2), 61–69.

Kim, Y. (2010). The pilot study in qualitative inquiry: Identifying issues and learning lessons for culturally competent research. *Qualitative Social Work, 10*(2), 190–206.

Kitzinger, J. (1994). The methodology of focus groups: The importance of interaction between participants. *Sociology of Health & Illness, 16*(1), 103–121.

Kivits, J. (2005). Online interviewing and the research relationship. In C. Hine (Ed.), *Virtual methods: Issues in social research on the Internet* (pp. 35–50). Oxford, UK: Berg.

Koenig, S., & Neuman, W. (2012, August). There's the beef. *Quirk's Marketing Research Review, 26*(8), 26–28.

Koro-Ljungberg, M. (2010). Validity, responsibility, and aporia. *Qualitative Inquiry, 16*(8), 603–610.

Kosicki, G., & Lavrakas, P. J. (2000). Mixing literary journalism and precision journalism in the coverage of the 1996 presidential election. In P. J. Lavrakas & M. W. Traugott (Eds.), *Election polls, the news media, and democracy* (pp. 142–161). New York: Chatham House/CQ Press.

Kreuter, F., Presser, S., & Tourangeau, R. (2008). Social desirability bias in CATI, IVR, and Web surveys: The effects of mode and question sensitivity. *Public Opinion Quarterly, 72*(5), 847–865.

Krippendorff, K. (2004). Reliability in content analysis: Some common misconceptions and recommendations. *Human Communication Research, 30*(3), 411–433.

Krippendorff, K. (2013). *Content analysis* (3rd ed.). Thousand Oaks, CA: Sage.

Kroll, T., Barbour, R., & Harris, J. (2007). Using focus groups in disability research. *Qualitative Health Research, 17*(5), 690–698.

Krueger, R. A., & Casey, M. A. (2009). *Focus groups* (4th ed.). Thousand Oaks, CA: Sage.

Krumer-Nevo, M. (2002). The arena of othering: A life-story study with women living in poverty and social marginality. *Qualitative Social Work, 1*(3), 303–318.

Kuperberg, A., & Stone, P. (2008). The media depiction of women who opt out. *Gender & Society, 22*(4), 497–517.

Kusenbach, M. (2003). Street phenomenology: The go-along as ethnographic tool. *Ethnography, 4*(3), 455–485.

Kvale, S. (2006). Dominance through interviews and dialogues. *Qualitative Inquiry, 12*(3), 480–500.

Kvale, S., & Brinkmann, S. (2009). *Interviews: Learning the craft of qualitative research interviewing* (2nd ed.). Thousand Oaks, CA: Sage.

Kyngäs, H. (2004). Support network of adolescents with chronic disease: Adolescents' perspective. *Nursing and Health Sciences, 6*(4), 287–293.

Lambert, S. D., & Loiselle, C. G. (2008). Combining individual interviews and focus groups to enhance data richness. *Journal of Advanced Nursing, 62*(2), 228–237.

Lather, P. (2004). Critical inquiry in qualitative research: Feminist and poststructural perspectives: Science "after truth." In K. DeMarrais & S. D. Lapan (Eds.), *Foundations for research: Methods of inquiry in education and the social sciences* (pp. 203–215). Mahwah, NJ: Erlbaum.

Lavrakas, P. J. (2010). Telephone surveys. In P. V. Marsden & J. D. Wright (Eds.), *Handbook of survey research* (pp. 471–498). Bingley, UK: Emerald Group.

Lavrakas, P. J., Blumberg, S., Battaglia, M., Boyle, J., Brick, J. M., Buskirk, T. D., et al. (2010). *New considerations for survey researchers when planning and conducting RDD telephone surveys in the U.S. with respondents reached via cell phone numbers.* Deerfield, IL: American Association for Public Opinion Research Cell Phone Task Force.

LeCompte, M. D., & Goetz, J. P. (1982). Ethnographic data collection in evaluation research. *Educational Evaluation and Policy Analysis, 4*(3), 387–400.

Leech, N. L., & Onwuegbuzie, A. J. (2007). A typology of mixed methods research designs. *Quality & Quantity, 43*(2), 265–275.

Leech, N. L., & Onwuegbuzie, A. J. (2011). Beyond constant comparison qualitative data analysis: Using NVivo. *School Psychology Quarterly, 26*(1), 70–84.

Lehoux, P., Poland, B., & Daudelin, G. (2006). Focus group research and "the patient's view." *Social Science & Medicine, 63*(8), 2091–2104.

Lemish, D. (2000). The whore and the other:

Israeli images of female immigrants from the former USSR. *Gender & Society, 14*(2), 333–349.

Lenhart, A. (2012, March). *Teens, smartphones & texting*. Washington, DC: Pew Research Center. Retrieved February 13, 2013, from *www.pewinternet.org/files/old-media//Files/Reports/2012/PIP_Teens_Smartphones_and_Texting.pdf.*

Leo, R. A. (1995). Trials and tribulations: Courts, ethnography, and the need for an evidentiary privilege for academic researchers. *American Sociologist, 26*(1), 113–134.

Lewins, A., & Silver, C. (2009). *Choosing a CAQDAS package* (6th ed.). Working paper. CAQDAS Networking Project and Qualitative Innovations in CAQDAS Project (QUIC).

Leydon, G. M., Boulton, M., Moynihan, C., Jones, A., Mossman, J., Boudioni, M., et al. (2000). Cancer patients' information needs and information seeking behaviour: In-depth interview study. *British Medical Journal, 320*(7239), 909–913.

Liebenberg, L. (2009). The visual image as discussion point: Increasing validity in boundary crossing research. *Qualitative Research, 9*(4), 441–467.

Lincoln, Y. S. (1995). Emerging criteria for quality in qualitative and interpretive research. *Qualitative Inquiry, 1*(3), 275–289.

Lincoln, Y. S., & Guba, E. G. (1985). *Naturalistic inquiry*. Beverly Hills, CA: Sage.

Lincoln, Y. S., & Guba, E. G. (1986). But is it rigorous?: Trustworthiness and authenticity in naturalistic evaluation. *New Directions for Program Evaluation, 30*(1), 73–84.

Lincoln, Y. S., Lynham, S. A., & Guba, E. G. (2011). Paradigmatic controversies, contradictions, and emerging confluences, revisited. In N. K. Denzin & Y. S. Lincoln (Eds.), *The Sage handbook of qualitative research* (pp. 97–128). Thousand Oaks, CA: Sage.

Line, T. (2008). *The attitudes of young people towards transport in the context of climate change*. Unpublished thesis, University of the West of England, Bristol, UK.

López, A., Detz, A., Ratanawongsa, N., & Sarkar, U. (2012). What patients say about their doctors online: A qualitative content analysis. *Journal of General Internal Medicine, 27*(6), 685–692.

Luttrell, W. (2003). *Pregnant bodies, fertile minds: Gender, race and the schooling of pregnant teens.* New York: Routledge.

Lyall, M., & Bartlett, A. (2010). Decision making in medium security: Can he have leave? *Journal of Forensic Psychiatry & Psychology, 21*(6), 887–901.

Mabweazara, H. M. (2010). Researching the use of new technologies (ICTs) in Zimbabwean newsrooms: An ethnographic approach. *Qualitative Research, 10*(6), 659–677.

MacLean, L. M., Meyer, M., & Estable, A. (2004). Improving accuracy of transcripts in qualitative research. *Qualitative Health Research, 14*(1), 113–123.

Macnamara, J. (2005). Media content analysis: Its uses, benefits and best practice methodology. *Asia Pacific Public Relations Journal, 6*(1), 1–34.

Madison, D. S. (2003). Performance, personal narratives, and the politics of possibility. In Y. S. Lincoln & N. K. Denzin (Eds.), *Turning points in qualitative research: Tying knots in a handkerchief* (Vol. 3, pp. 469–486). Walnut Creek, CA: AltaMira Press.

Magolda, P. M. (2000). Accessing, waiting, plunging in, wondering, and writing: Retrospective sense-making of fieldwork. *Field Methods, 12*(3), 209–234.

Malenfant, K. J. (2010). Leading change in the system of scholarly communication: A case study of engaging liaison librarians for outreach to faculty. *College and Research Libraries, 71*(1), 63–76.

Maliski, S. L., Rivera, S., Connor, S., Lopez, G., & Litwin, M. S. (2008). Renegotiating masculine identity after prostate cancer treatment. *Qualitative Health Research, 18*(12), 1609–1620.

Mancini, J., Baumstarck-Barrau, K., Simeoni, M.-C., Grob, J.-J., Michel, G., Tarpin, C., et al. (2011). Quality of life in a heterogeneous sample of caregivers of cancer patients: An in-depth interview study. *European Journal of Cancer Care, 20*(4), 483–492.

Marcus, G. E. (1995). Ethnography in/of the world system: The emergence of multi-sited ethnography. *Annual Review of Anthropology, 24*(1), 95–117.

Marecek, J. (2003). Dancing through mindfields: Toward a qualitative stance in psychology. In P. M. Camic, J. E. Rhodes, & L. Yardley (Eds.), *Qualitative research in psychology:*

Expanding perspectives in methodology and design (pp. 49–69). Washington, DC: American Psychiatric Association.

Mariampolski, H. (2006). *Ethnography for marketers: A guide to consumer immersion*. Thousand Oaks, CA: Sage.

Markham, A. M. (2004). The Internet as research context. In C. Seale, G. Gobo, J. Gubrium, & D. Silverman (Eds.), *Qualitative research practice* (pp. 328–344). London: Sage.

Marshall, C., & Rossman, G. B. (2011). *Designing qualitative reserach*. Thousand Oaks, CA: Sage.

Martin, F. E. (1998). Tales of transition: Self-narrative and direct scribing in exploring care-leaving. *Child & Family Social Work, 3*(1), 1–12.

Matthews, J., & Cramer, E. P. (2008). Using technology to enhance qualitative research with hidden populations. *The Qualitative Report*. Retrieved October 7, 2012, from *www.nova.edu/ssss/QR/QR13-2/matthews.pdf*.

Maxwell, J. A. (2013). *Qualitative research design: An interactive approach* (3rd ed.). Thousand Oaks, CA: Sage.

May, F. (2011). Methods for studying the use of public spaces in libraries/Les méthodes tion des espaces publics dans ies bibliothéques. *Canadian Journal of Information & Library Sciences, 35*(4), 354–366.

McCoyd, J. L. M., & Kerson, T. S. (2006). Conducting intensive interviews using email: A serendipitous comparative opportunity. *Qualitative Social Work, 5*(3), 389–406.

McGough, M., Frank, L. L., Tipton, S., Tinker, T. L., & Vaughan, E. (2005). Communicating the risks of bioterrorism and other emergencies in a diverse society: A case study of special populations in North Dakota. *Biosecurity and Bioterrorism: Biodefense Strategy, Practice, and Science, 3*(3), 235–245.

McLafferty, I. (2004). Focus group interviews as a data collecting strategy. *Journal of Advanced Nursing, 48*(2), 187–194.

Merriam, S. B. (2009). *Qualitative research: A guide to design and implementation*. San Francisco: Jossey-Bass.

Merton, R. K. (1987). The focussed interview and focus groups: Continuities and discontinuities. *Public Opinion Quarterly, 51*(4), 550–566.

Merton, R. K., & Kendall, P. L. (1946). The focused interview. *American Journal of Sociology, 51*(6), 541–557.

Miles, M. B., & Huberman, A. M. (1984). Drawing valid meaning from qualitative data: Toward a shared craft. *Educational Researcher, 13*(5), 20–30.

Miles, M. B., Huberman, A. M., & Saldaña, J. (2014). *Qualitative data analysis: A methods sourcebook*. Thousand Oaks, CA: Sage.

Mills, D., & Ratcliffe, R. (2012). After method?: Ethnography in the knowledge economy. *Qualitative Research, 12*(2), 147–164.

Milne, M. J., & Adler, R. W. (1999). Exploring the reliability of social and environmental disclosures content analysis. *Accounting, Auditing & Accountability Journal, 12*(2), 237–256.

Mishler, E. G. (1986). *Research interviewing: Context and narrative*. Cambridge, MA: Harvard University Press.

Mishler, E. G. (1996). Missing persons: Recovering developmental stories/histories. In R. Jessor, A. Colby, & R. A. Shweder (Eds.), *Ethnography and human development: Context and meaning in social inquiry* (pp. 73–100). Chicago: University of Chicago Press.

Mishler, E. G. (1999). *Storylines: Craftartists' narratives of identity*. Cambridge, MA: Harvard University Press.

Moen, J., Antonov, K., Nilsson, J. L. G., & Ring, L. (2010). Interaction between participants in focus groups with older patients and general practitioners. *Qualitative Health Research, 20*(5), 607–616.

Mollen, C. J., Barg, F. K., Hayes, K. L., Gotcsik, M., Blades, N. M., & Schwarz, D. F. (2008). Assessing attitudes about emergency contraception among urban, minority adolescent girls: An in-depth interview study. *Pediatrics, 122*(2), e395–e401.

Morgan, D. L. (1996). Focus groups. *Annual Review of Sociology, 22*, 129–152.

Morris, R. (1994). Computerized content analysis in management research: A demonstration of advantages & limitations. *Journal of Management, 20*(4), 903–931.

Morrison-Beedy, D., Côté-Arsenault, D., & Feinstein, N. F. (2001). Maximizing results with focus groups: Moderator and analysis issues. *Applied Nursing Research, 14*(1), 48–53.

Morrow, S. L. (2005). Quality and trustworthiness in qualitative research in counseling psychology. *Journal of Counseling Psychology*, 52(2), 250–260.

Morse, J. M., Barrett, M., Mayan, M., Olson, K., & Spiers, J. (2002). Verification strategies for establishing reliability and validity in qualitative research. *International Journal of Qualitative Methods, 1*(2), 13–22.

Murray, S. A., Boyd, K., Kendall, M., Worth, A., Benton, T. F., & Clausen, H. (2002). Dying of lung cancer or cardiac failure: Prospective qualitative interview study of patients and their carers in the community. *British Medical Journal, 325*(7370), 929.

Murthy, D. (2008). Digital ethnography: An examination of the use of new technologies for social research. *Sociology, 42*(5), 837–855.

National Research Council. (2003). *Protecting participants and facilitating social and behavioral sciences research*. Washington, DC: National Academies Press.

Nicholas, D. B., Lach, L., King, G., Scott, M., Boydell, K., Sawatzky, B., et al. (2010). Contrasting Internet and face-to-face focus groups for children with chronic health conditions: Outcomes and participant experiences. *International Journal of Qualitative Methods, 9*(1), 105–122.

Nordfeldt, S., Ängarne-Lindberg, T., & Berterö, C. (2012). To use or not to use: Practitioners' perceptions of an open Web portal for young patients with diabetes. *Journal of Medical Internet Research, 14*(6), e154.

O'Donnell, A. B., Lutfey, K. E., Marceau, L. D., & McKinlay, J. B. (2007). Using focus groups to improve the validity of cross-national survey research: A study of physician decision making. *Qualitative Health Research, 17*(7), 971–981.

O'Reilly, M., & Parker, N. (2013). "Unsatisfactory saturation": A critical exploration of the notion of saturated sample sizes in qualitative research. *Qualitative Research, 13*(2), 190–197.

Orgad, S. (2006). *The cultural dimensions of online communication: A study of breast cancer patients' Internet spaces*. London: LSE Research online. Available at *http://eprints.lse.ac.uk/2517*.

Osse, B. H. P., Vernooij-Dassen, M. J. F. J., Schadé, E., de Vree, B., van den Muijsenbergh, M. E. T. C., & Grol, R. P. T. M. (2002). Problems to discuss with cancer patients in palliative care: A comprehensive approach. *Patient Education and Counseling, 47*(3), 195–204.

Paechter, C. (2013). Researching sensitive issues online: Implications of a hybrid insider/outsider position in a retrospective ethnographic study. *Qualitative Research, 13*(1), 71–86.

Parker, C., Saundage, D., & Lee, C. Y. (2011). Can qualitative content analysis be adapted for use by social informaticians to study social media discourse?: A position paper. In *ACIS 2011: Proceedings of the 22nd Australasian conference on information systems* (pp 1–7). Sydney, Australia.

Partridge, H., Menzies, V., Lee, J., & Munro, C. (2010). The contemporary librarian: Skills, knowledge and attributes required in a world of emerging technologies. *Library & Information Science Research, 32*(4), 265–271.

Patton, M. Q. (1978). *Utilization-focused evaluation*. Beverly Hills, CA: Sage.

Patton, M. Q. (1999). Enhancing the quality and credibility of qualitative analysis. *Health Services Research, 34*(5, Pt. 2), 1189–1208.

Patton, M. Q. (2002). *Qualitative research and evaluation methods* (3rd ed.). Thousand Oaks, CA: Sage.

Peek, L., & Fothergill, A. (2009). Using focus groups: Lessons from studying daycare centers, 9/11, and Hurricane Katrina *Qualitative Research, 9*(1), 31–59.

Pharr, J. R., & Lough, N. L. (2012). Differentiation of social marketing and cause-related marketing in US professional sport. *Sport Marketing Quarterly, 21*(2), 91–103.

Platt, J. (1992). "Case study" in American methodological thought. *Current Sociology, 40*(1), 17–48.

Poindexter, C. C. (2003). Sex, drugs, and love among the middle aged: A case study of a serodiscordant heterosexual couple coping with HIV. *Journal of Social Work Practice in the Addictions, 3*(2), 57–83.

Poland, B. D. (1995). Transcription quality as an aspect of rigor in qualitative research. *Qualitative Inquiry, 1*(3), 290–310.

Polkinghorne, D. E. (2007). Validity issues in narrative research. *Qualitative Inquiry, 13*(4), 471–486.

Ponterotto, J. G. (2006). Brief note on the origins, evolution, and meaning of the qualitative research concept "thick description." *The Qualitative Report, 11*(3), 538–549.

Ponterotto, J. G. (2013). Qualitative research in multicultural psychology: Philosophical underpinnings, popular approaches, and ethical considerations. *Qualitative Psychology, 1*(S), 19–32.

Pope, C., Ziebland, S., & Mays, N. (2000). Qualitative research in health care: Analysing qualitative data. *British Medical Journal, 320*(7227), 114–116.

Provoost, V., Pennings, G., De Sutter, P., Gerris, J., Van de Velde, A., & Dhont, M. (2010). Patients' conceptualization of cryopreserved embryos used in their fertility treatment. *Human Reproduction, 25*(3), 705–713.

Ptacek, C. H. (2009). Using morphological content analysis to mine insights from qualitative interviews. *Quirk's Marketing Research Review, 23*(3), 34–39.

Purvis Cooper, C., Merritt, T. L., Ross, L. E., John, L. V., & Jorgensen, C. M. (2004). To screen or not to screen, when clinical guidelines disagree: Primary care physicians' use of the PSA test. *Preventive Medicine, 38*(2), 182–191.

Qi, S. (2009). Case study in contemporary educational research: Conceptualization and critique. *Cross-Cultural Communication, 5*(4), 21–31.

Rabiee, F. (2007). Focus-group interview and data analysis. *Proceedings of the Nutrition Society, 63*(04), 655–660.

Ragin, C. C., & Becker, H. S. (Eds.). (1992). *What is a case?: Exploring the foundations of social inquiry.* Cambridge, UK: Cambridge University Press.

Rainie, L., & Poushter, J. (2014). Emerging nations catching up to U.S. on technology adoption, especially mobile and social media use. *Fact Tank: News in the Numbers.* Retrieved March 17, 2014, from *www.pewresearch. org/fact-tank/2014/02/13/emerging-nations-catching-up-to-u-s-on-technology-adoption-especially-mobile-and-social-media-use.*

Randall, W. (2012). Composing a good strong story: The advantages of a liberal arts environment for experiencing and exploring the narrative complexity of human life. *Journal of General Education, 61*(3), 277–293.

Reilly, J. R., Gallagher-Lepak, S., & Killion, C. (2012). "Me and my computer": Emotional factors in online learning. *Nursing Education Perspectives, 33*(2), 100–105.

Reynolds, J., Kizito, J., Ezumah, N., Mangesho, P., Allen, E., & Chandler, C. (2011). Quality assurance of qualitative research: A review of the discourse. *Health Research Policy and Systems, 9*(1), 43.

Ricci, R. J. (2006). Trauma resolution using eye movement desensitization and reprocessing with an incestuous sex offender: An instrumental case study. *Clinical Case Studies, 5*(3), 248–265.

Riessman, C. K. (2008). *Narrative methods for the human sciences.* Thousand Oaks, CA: Sage.

Riessman, C. K., & Quinney, L. (2005). Narrative in social work: A critical review. *Qualitative Social Work, 4*(4), 391–412.

Robinson, S. (2011). Convergence crises: News work and news space in the digitally transforming newsroom. *Journal of Communication, 61*(6), 1122–1141.

Robson, C. (2011). *Real world research* (3rd ed.). West Sussex, UK: Wiley.

Rogers, W. A., Gilbert, D. K., & Cabrera, E. F. (1997). An analysis of automatic teller machine usage by older adults: A structured interview approach. *Applied Ergonomics, 28*(3), 173–180.

Rolfe, G. (2006). Validity, trustworthiness and rigour: Quality and the idea of qualitative research. *Journal of Advanced Nursing, 53*(3), 304–310.

Rosenhan, D. L. (1973). On being sane in insane places. *Science, 179*(19), 250–258.

Rowe, S., & Wolch, J. (1990). Social networks in time and space: Homeless women in Skid Row, Los Angeles. *Annals of the Association of American Geographers, 80*(2), 184–204.

Rubin, H. J., & Rubin, I. S. (2012). *Qualitative interviewing: The art of hearing data* (3rd ed.). Thousand Oaks, CA: Sage.

Russell, G., Advocat, J., Geneau, R., Farrell, B., Thille, P., Ward, N., et al. (2012). Examining organizational change in primary care practices: Experiences from using ethnographic methods. *Family Practice, 29*(4), 455–461.

Sands, R. G., & Krumer-Nevo, M. (2006). Interview shocks and shockwaves. *Qualitative Inquiry, 12*(5), 950–971.

Sauer, A., & August, S. (2012, July). *Small leaps, big purchase decisions: Using digital qual to capture product transitions.* Presented at the MRMW North America Conference, Cincinnati, OH.

Schilling, J. (2006). On the pragmatics of qualitative assessment. *European Journal of Psychological Assessment, 22*(1), 28–37.

Schouten, J. W., & McAlexander, J. H. (1995). Subcultures of consumption: An ethnography of the new bikers. *Journal of Consumer Research, 22*, 43–61.

Schrooten, M. (2012). Moving ethnography online: Researching Brazilian migrants' online togetherness. *Ethnic and Racial Studies, 35*(10), 1794–1809.

Schwandt, T. A., Lincoln, Y. S., & Guba, E. G. (2007). Judging interpretations: But is it rigorous?: Trustworthiness and authenticity in naturalistic evaluation. *New Directions for Evaluation, 114*, 11–25.

Seale, C., & Silverman, D. (1997). Ensuring rigour in qualitative research. *European Journal of Public Health, 7*(4), 379–384.

Silver, C. (2010, April). *CAQDAS tools for visual analysis*. Presented at the Mixed Methods seminar "Using software tools in visual analyses," Surrey, UK.

Silverman, D. (2013). What counts as qualitative research?: Some cautionary comments. *Qualitative Sociology Review, IX*(2), 48–55.

Sim, J. (1998). Collecting and analysing qualitative data: Issues raised by the focus group. *Journal of Advanced Nursing, 28*(2), 345–352.

Singer, J. A. (2013). Living in the amber cloud: A life story analysis of a heroin addict. *Qualitative Psychology, 1*(S), 33–48.

Singh, A. A., & Shelton, K. (2011). A content analysis of LGBTQ qualitative research in counseling: A ten-year review. *Journal of Counseling & Development, 89*(2), 217–226.

Skeparnides, M. (2002). A reflection of Tolkien's world: Gender, race, and interpretive political, economic, social and cultural allegories. *Grey Havens*. Retrieved August 2, 2013, from *http://tolkien.cro.net/tolkien/mskeparn.html*.

Small, W., Kerr, T., Charette, J., Schechter, M. T., & Spittal, P. M. (2006). Impacts of intensified police activity on injection drug users: Evidence from an ethnographic investigation. *International Journal of Drug Policy, 17*(2), 85–95.

Smith, A. (2013). *Smartphone ownership: 2013 update*. Washington, DC: Pew Research Center. Retrieved August 18, 2014, from *www.pewinternet.org/files/old-media//Files/Reports/2013/PIP_Smartphone_adoption_2013_PDF.pdf*.

Smith, J. M., Sullivan, S. J., & Baxter, G. D. (2009). Massage therapy services for healthcare: A telephone focus group study of drivers for clients' continued use of services. *Complementary Therapies in Medicine, 17*(5), 281–291.

Snape, D., & Spencer, L. (2003). The foundations of qualitative research. In J. Ritchie & J. Lewis (Eds.), *Qualitative research practice* (pp. 1–23). London: Sage.

Snow, D. A. (1980). The disengagement process: A neglected problem in participant observation research. *Qualitative Sociology, 3*(2), 100–123.

Söderberg, S., & Lundman, B. (2001). Transitions experienced by women with fibromyalgia. *Health Care for Women International, 22*(7), 617–631.

Spradley, J. P. (1972). Down and out on skid row. In S. Feldman & G. W. Thielbar (Eds.), *Life styles: Diversity in American society* (pp. 340–350). Boston: Little, Brown.

Spradley, J. P. (1980). *Participant observation*. New York: Holt, Rinehart & Winston.

Stacey, K., & Vincent, J. (2011). Evaluation of an electronic interview with multimedia stimulus materials for gaining in-depth responses from professionals. *Qualitative Research, 11*(5), 605–624.

Stacey, M., & Eckert, C. (1999, August). An ethnographic methodology for design process analysis. Presented at the 12th International Conference on Engineering Design, Munich, Germany.

Stake, R. E. (1994). Case studies. In N. K. Denzin & Y. S. Lincoln (Eds.), *Handbook of qualitative research* (pp. 236–247). Thousand Oaks, CA: Sage.

Stake, R. E. (1995). *The art of case study research*. Thousand Oaks, CA: Sage.

Stake, R. E. (2000). Case studies. In N. K. Denzin & Y. S. Lincoln (Eds.), *Handbook of qualitative research* (2nd ed., pp. 435–454). Thousand Oaks, CA: Sage.

Stake, R. E. (2006). *Multiple case study analysis*. New York: Guilford Press.

Stake, R. E., & Schwandt, T. A. (2006). On discerning quality in evaluation. In I. Shaw, J. Greene, & M. Mark (Eds.), *The Sage handbook of evaluation* (pp. 404–418). London: Sage.

Stepchenkova, S., Kirilenko, A. P., & Morrison, A. M. (2009). Facilitating content analysis in tourism research. *Journal of Travel Research, 47*(4), 454–469.

Stevens, P. E. (1996). Focus groups: Collecting aggregate-level data to understand community health phenomena. *Public Health Nursing, 13*(3), 170–176.

Strauss, A., & Corbin, J. (1994). Grounded theory methodology: An overview. In N. K. Denzin & Y. S. Lincoln (Eds.), *Handbook of qualitative research* (pp. 273–285). Thousand Oaks, CA: Sage.

Sturges, J. E., & Hanrahan, K. J. (2004). Comparing telephone and face-to-face qualitative interviewing: A research note. *Qualitative Research, 4*(1), 107–118.

Sugiura, L., Pope, C., & Webber, C. (2012, June). Buying unlicensed slimming drugs from the Web: A virtual ethnography. Presented at the 3rd annual ACM Web Science conference, Evanston, IL.

Tates, K., Zwaanswijk, M., Otten, R., van Dulmen, S., Hoogerbrugge, P. M., Kamps, W. A., et al. (2009). Online focus groups as a tool to collect data in hard-to-include populations: Examples from paediatric oncology. *BMC Medical Research Methodology, 9*(1), 15.

Tewksbury, R. (2002). Bathhouse intercourse: Structural and behavioral aspects of an erotic oasis. *Deviant Behavior: An Interdisciplinary Journal, 23*(1), 75–112.

Thanisorn, R., & Bunchapattanasakda, C. (2011). Marketing strategies of imported herbal cosmetic products in Thailand. *Information Management and Business Review, 3*(4), 217–221.

Thomas, E., & Magilvy, J. K. (2011). Qualitative rigor or research validity in qualitative research. *Journal for Specialists in Pediatric Nursing, 16*(2), 151–155.

Thomas, G. (2010). Doing case study: Abduction not induction, phronesis not theory. *Qualitative Inquiry, 16*(7), 575–582.

Thomson, S. B. (2011). Sample size and grounded theory. *Journal of Administration & Governance, 5*(1), 45–52.

Thornberg, R. (2008). Values education as the daily fostering of school rules. *Research in Education, 80*(1), 52–63.

Tobin, G. A., & Begley, C. M. (2004). Methodological rigour within a qualitative framework. *Journal of Advanced Nursing, 48*(4), 388–396.

Todd, N. R. (2012). Religious networking organizations and social justice: An ethnographic case study. *American Journal of Community Psychology, 50*(1–2), 229–245.

Tolhurst, H., & Dean, S. (2004). Using teleconferencing to enable general practitioner participation in focus groups. *Primary Health Care Research and Development, 5*(1), 1–4.

Toner, J. (2009). Small is not too small: Reflections concerning the validity of very small focus groups (VSFGs). *Qualitative Social Work, 8*(2), 179–192.

Tongco, D. C. (2007). Purposive sampling as a tool for informant selection. *Ethnobotany Research and Applications, 5,* 147–158.

Townsend, A., Amarsi, Z., Backman, C. L., Cox, S. M., & Li, L. C. (2011). Communications between volunteers and health researchers during recruitment and informed consent: Qualitative content analysis of email interactions. *Journal of Medical Internet Research, 13*(4), e84.

Traulsen, J. M., Almarsdóttir, A. B., & Björnsdóttir, I. (2004). Interviewing the moderator: An ancillary method to focus groups. *Qualitative Health Research, 14*(5), 714–725.

U.S. Bureau of the Census. (1994). *We asked . . . you told us: Telephone and vehicle availability.* Washington, DC: U.S. Department of Commerce. Retrieved September 22, 2012, from *www.census.gov/prod/cen1990/cqc/cqc26.pdf.*

Vandebosch, H., & Van Cleemput, K. (2008). Defining cyberbullying: A qualitative research into the perceptions of youngsters. *CyberPsychology & Behavior, 11*(4), 499–503.

VanWynsberghe, R., & Khan, S. (2007). Redefining case study. *International Journal of Qualitative Methods, 6*(2), 80–94.

Veseth, M., Binder, P.-E., Borg, M., & Davidson, L. (2012). Toward caring for oneself in a life of intense ups and downs: A reflexive–collaborative exploration of recovery in bipolar disorder. *Qualitative Health Research, 22*(1), 119–133.

Vogt, D. S., King, D. W., & King, L. A. (2004). Focus groups in psychological assessment: Enhancing content validity by consulting members of the target population. *Psychological Assessment, 16*(3), 231–243.

Wahl, A. K., Gjengedal, E., & Hanestad, B. R.

(2002). The bodily suffering of living with severe psoriasis: In-depth interviews with 22 hospitalized patients with psoriasis. *Qualitative Health Research, 12*(2), 250–261.

Walker, R. (2005, March). *What is a case study?: The use of case studies in research and evaluation.* Presented at the NCRM case study workshop, University of Southampton, Southampton, UK.

Wang, C., & Burris, M. A. (1997). Photovoice: Concept, methodology, and use for participatory needs assessment. *Health Education & Behavior, 24*(3), 369–387.

Wasburn, M. (2007). Mentoring women faculty: An instrumental case study of strategic collaboration. *Mentoring and Tutoring, 15*(1), 57–72.

Waxman, L. (2006). The coffee shop: Social and physical factors influencing place attachment. *Journal of Interior Design, 31*(3), 35–53.

Weitzman, E. A. (1999). Analyzing qualitative data with computer software. *Health Services Research, 34*(5, Pt. 2), 1241–1263.

Wertsch, J. V. (2000). Narratives as cultural tools in sociocultural analysis: Official history in Soviet and post-Soviet Russia. *Ethos, 28*(4), 511–533.

Wertz, F. J. (2014). Qualitative inquiry in the history of psychology. *Qualitative Psychology, 1*(1), 4–16.

West, R. (2012, July). *Lather, rinse, repeat: Getting into the shower and other private places with mobile qualitative.* Presented at the MRMW North America Conference, Cincinnati, OH.

Whittemore, R., Chase, S. K., & Mandle, C. L. (2001). Validity in qualitative research. *Qualitative Health Research, 11*(4), 522–537.

Wilkinson, S. (1999). Focus groups: A feminist method. *Psychology of Women Quarterly, 23*(2), 221–244.

Williams, J. P. (2006). Authentic identities: Straightedge subculture, music, and the Internet. *Journal of Contemporary Ethnography, 35*(2), 173–200.

Williams, M. (2007). Avatar watching: Participant observation in graphical online environments. *Qualitative Research, 7*(1), 5–24.

Williamson, S., Twelvetree, T., Thompson, J., & Beaver, K. (2012). An ethnographic study exploring the role of ward-based advanced nurse practitioners in an acute medical setting. *Journal of Advanced Nursing, 68*(7), 1579–1588.

Wilson, B. (2006). Ethnography, the Internet, and youth culture: Strategies for examining social resistance and "online–offline" relationships. *Canadian Journal of Education, 29*(1), 307–328.

Wilson, S. M., & Gudmundsdottir, S. (1987). What is this a case of?: Exploring some conceptual issues in case study research. *Education and Urban Society, 20*(1), 42–54.

Winslow, W. W., Honein, G., & Elzubeir, M. A. (2002). Seeking Emirati women's voices: The use of focus groups with an Arab population. *Qualitative Health Research, 12*(4), 566–575.

Wolcott, H. F. (2008). *Ethnography: A way of seeing* (2nd ed.). Lanham, MD: AltaMira Press.

World telecommunication/ICT indicators database. (2014). International Telecommunication Union. Retrieved August 18, 2014, from *www.itu.int/en/ITU-D/Statistics/Pages/stat/default.aspx.*

Yin, R. K. (2009). *Case study research: Design and methods* (4th ed.). Thousand Oaks, CA: Sage.

Yin, R. K. (2011). *Qualitative research from start to finish.* New York: Guilford Press.

Yin, R. K. (2014). *Case study research: Design and methods* (5th ed.). Thousand Oaks, CA: Sage.

Zemke, D. M. V., & Shoemaker, S. (2007). Scent across a crowded room: Exploring the effect of ambient scent on social interactions. *International Journal of Hospitality Management, 26*(4), 927–940.

Zhang, Y., & Wildemuth, B. M. (2009). Qualitative analysis of content. In B. M. Wildemuth (Ed.), *Applications of social research methods to questions in information and library science* (pp. 308–319). Westport, CT: Libraries Unlimited.

Zickuhr, K. (2013). *Who's not online and why.* Washington, DC: Pew Research Center. Retrieved August 18, 2014, from *www.pewinternet.org/files/old-media//Files/Reports/2013/PIP_Offline%20adults_092513_PDF.pdf.*

Author Index

Subject Index

An *f* following a page number indicates a figure; an *n* following a page number indicates a note; a *t* following a page number indicates a table. Page numbers in bold refer to entries in the Glossary.

About the Authors

Margaret R. Roller, MA, has been a research professional for 40 years. She is currently in private practice, where she works with some of the largest U.S. and global commercial and nonprofit organizations on multifaceted qualitative research studies. Before establishing her consulting firm, she served as research manager for AT&T, the *Los Angeles Times*, and Prentice Hall. Ms. Roller has designed and conducted thousands of qualitative studies involving a wide assortment of qualitative research methods, has presented and published numerous papers and articles on qualitative research design, and has been the author of the widely read blog *www.researchdesignreview.com*, which addresses qualitative research design issues. Ms. Roller has worked with firms in Eastern Europe and the Caucasus region to develop their research capabilities, and with the Qualitative Research Consultants Association to develop a college qualitative research course. She currently serves on the exam development committee for the Marketing Research Association's Professional Researcher Certification.

Paul J. Lavrakas, PhD, a research psychologist, serves as a senior methodological research consultant for several public and private sector organizations. He is also a Senior Fellow at the independent research organization NORC at the University of Chicago and a Visiting Scholar at Northern Arizona University. Dr. Lavrakas has used quantitative and qualitative research methods extensively throughout his more than 40 years as an active research practitioner. His many publications include, most recently, the coedited volume *Online Panel Research: A Data Quality Perspective.* Past president of the American Association for Public Opinion Research, he served as vice president and chief methodologist for Nielsen Media Research and was on the faculties of Northwestern University and The Ohio State University.